1957

НЯН

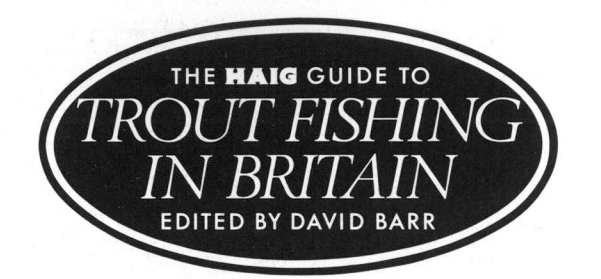

THE **HAIG** GUIDE TO
TROUT FISHING
IN BRITAIN
EDITED BY DAVID BARR

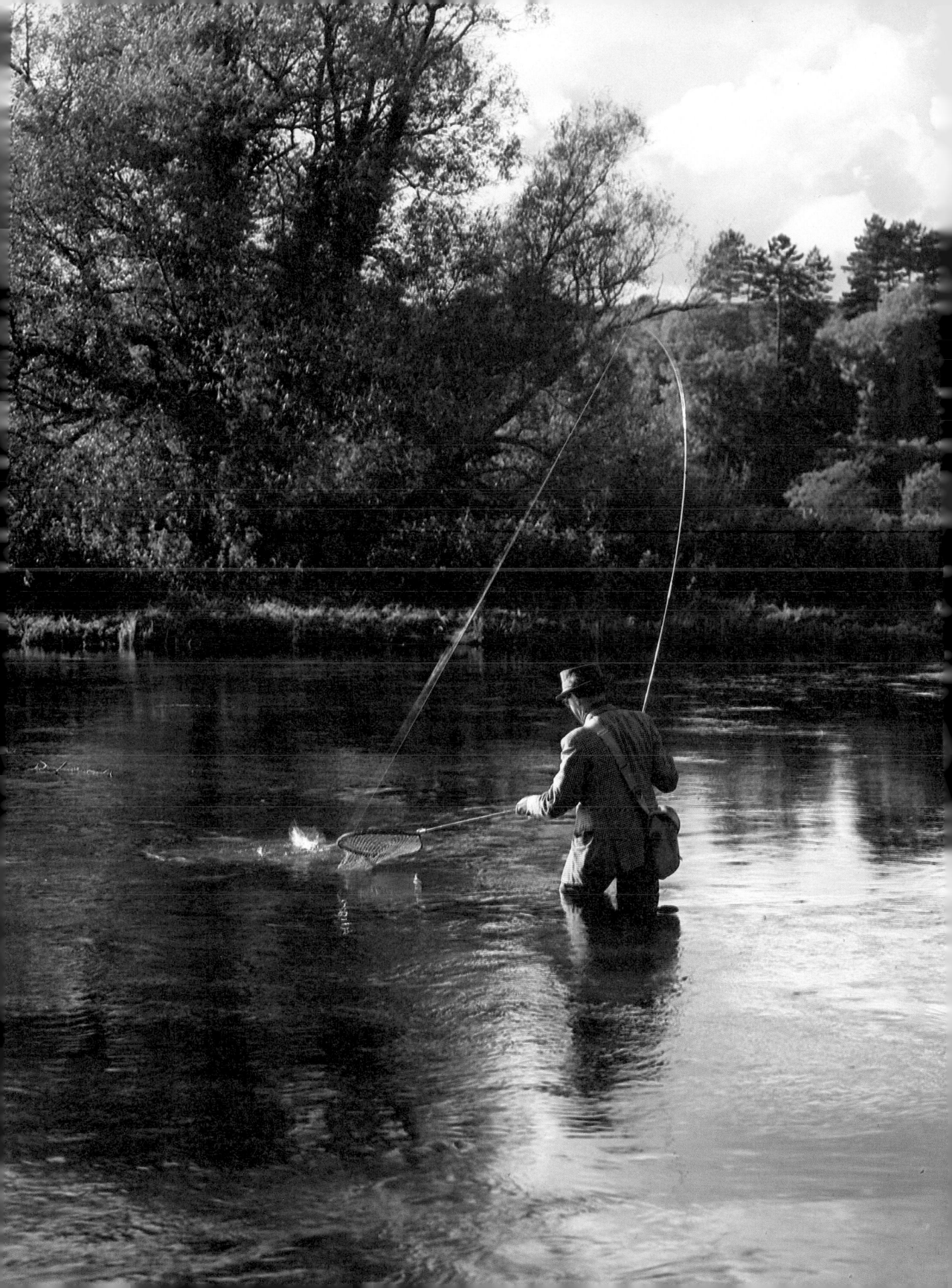

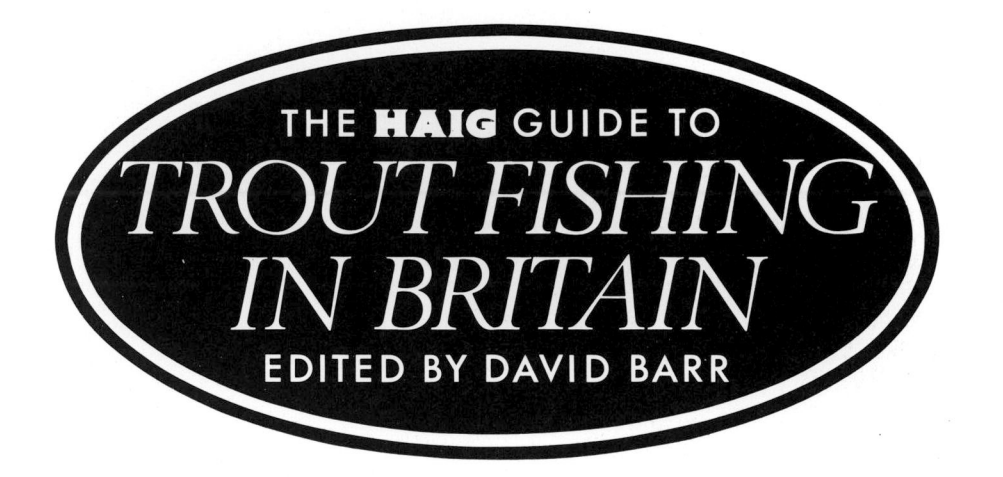

THE **HAIG** GUIDE TO
*TROUT FISHING
IN BRITAIN*
EDITED BY DAVID BARR

WILLOW BOOKS
COLLINS, LONDON

Frontispiece: Reflections on the Test

CONTENTS

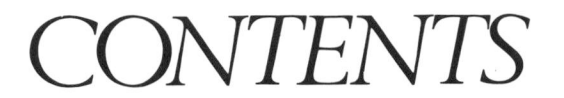

Authors' contributions as follows:

David Barr Norfolk rivers, Derwent, Dove, Wye
Terry Cousin Eden system, Eden, Eamont,
Lowther, Irthing, Petteril, Caldew
Malcolm Hall Lune and tributaries, Ribble
Eric and Ian Hay Hampshire rivers, Test, Itchen,
Meon, Beaulieu
Drew Jamieson Tweed, Clyde, Tay, Spey,
Scottish lochs and lakes
Gordon Mackie Kennet, Lambourn, Windrush,
Coln, Wessex rivers
Moc Morgan Welsh waters
Harry Munro Don
Tiny Neish Deveron
Arthur Oglesby Wharfe, Ure, Nidd, Yorkshire
streams
Ken Roberts Tyne, Bowmont, Coquet
Mike Weaver The South West rivers
John Wilshaw Still waters in England

The contributors, the editor and the producers
of this book would like to thank a multitude of
helpful people. In particular they single out for
particular mention Susan Abbott, Dr Marjorie
Barr, Jean Blower, Fred Burton, Faith L Butler,
Jemima Cookson, Alastair Drew, Roy Eaton,
Kirsty Ennever, G M Gillson, J Gregory, Lesley
Harrison, J D Kelsall, John Norman, Linda
Powell, Anne and Conrad Voss-Bark, John
Webster, G J Young, the South West Water
Authority, Witherby & Co Ltd

Produced by Robert Dudley and John Stidolph
Maps by Robert Burns
Index by Geraldine Christy
Designed by Peter Bridgewater
© Antler Books Ltd 1983
First published in 1983 by Willow Books,
Collins, 8 Grafton Street, London W1

British Library Cataloguing in Publication Data
The Haig guide to trout fishing in Britain.
  1. Trout fishing Great Britain
  I. Barr, David
  799.1'755   SH687
  ISBN 0 00 218030 8

Typesetting by Input Typesetting Ltd London
Colour separations and printing by New Interlitho Milan

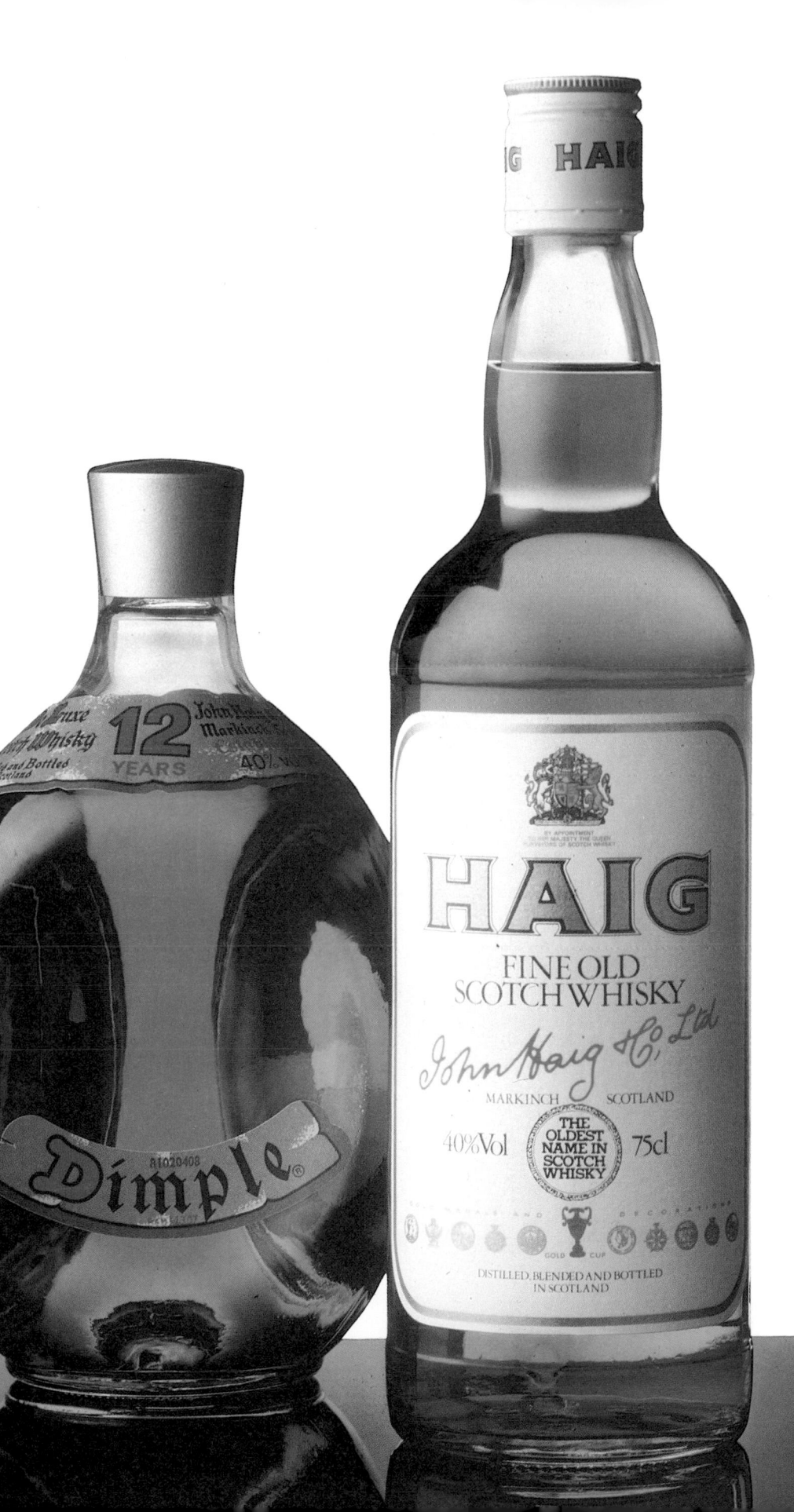

INTRODUCTION

To my mind there are two great British traditions – one is Haig whisky, the other is trout fishing.

So what could be more appropriate than a book about one great British tradition sponsored by the inventors of another?

There is after all, a great common bond between the two – both rely on rivers and streams for their existence. And I can think of no greater pleasure in life than a peaceful day spent on the banks of some quiet river, with a hip flask of my favourite scotch in my pocket to keep me company.

This book is a celebration of one of my great passions in life – trout fishing. I would like to share with you some of the experiences of forty five years of trout fishing on rivers and streams all over Britain: the excitement of first viewing that 'spotted monster', the thrill of the catch as well as the moments of disappointment at the ones that get away.

Trout fishing has always been a great challenge to the angler. The trout is a worthy and elusive quarry, the pursuit of which requires expertise and skill. I hope that this book will introduce some newcomers to the joys of trout fishing as well as pleasing the old heads, and that at the end of it there will be many on to whom my enthusiasm has brushed.

James Wolfe Murray
Managing Director, John Haig & Co Ltd

THE CONTRIBUTORS

David Barr, the editor of this book, has written articles on fishing for many of the leading magazines in England, USA, and (suitably translated) France. He edited the widely acclaimed companion volume, *Salmon Fishing in Scotland*, and is the author of the (non fishing) *A Family Way*. A Cambridgeshire solicitor and an adviser to the British Tourist Authority he spends all his spare time fishing.

Charlotte Blower took a holiday job at a trout farm between getting her BSc and starting teaching at a comprehensive school in Peterborough.

Terry Cousin is a freelance writer who is also a keen and skilled fly fisherman, intimately connected with the administration of fishing.

Malcolm Hall, another dedicated trout fisherman, works as a PE lecturer in Cumbria.

Colonel Eric Hay and his son **Ian** share an unrivalled knowledge of the rivers of Hampshire. As proprietors of The Rod Box in Winchester they have their fingers on the local tackle industry and have a highly organised agency for the letting of fishing.

Drew Jamieson, whose contribution to *Salmon Fishing in Scotland* aroused such admiration, is a fisheries manager, an angler and freelance journalist of distinction living in Edinburgh.

Gordon Mackie is the author of *How to Start Trout Fishing*. He reserves a hundred days a year for fishing and contributes regularly to *Trout and Salmon* and other fishing journals.

Moc Morgan is a retired headmaster whose written accounts of fishing in Wales are beginning to qualify for the title 'legendary'.

Harry Munro is a highly skilled trout fisherman and a regular contributor to the *Aberdeen Press and Journal*.

Tiny Neish is Water Bailiff to the Huntly Angling Association and a very well known Deveron character.

Arthur Oglesby is internationally known as a fishing writer, photographer and organiser of fly fishing courses.

Ken Roberts is an expert on the Greenwell's Glory and on trout fishing in Northumbria. He contributes to various journals including *Northern Life*.

Wilson Stephens is still bewitching readers of *The Field* (of which he was Editor for twenty six years) with his contributions under the pseudonym 'Dabchick'.

Mike Weaver is Marketing Manager of the West Country Tourist Board. He has a rare knowledge of trout fishing in the South West and is the Devon correspondent for *Trout and Salmon* and fishing correspondent for *Devon Life*.

John Wilshaw is a former feature writer for *Angling Times* who has been the highly successful Editor of *Trout Fisherman* since its inception. He still manages to find plenty of fishing time.

A NOTE FROM THE EDITOR

There are such great numbers of streams and rivers in England, Scotland and Wales in which, or in parts of which, brown trout are to be found, that it would have been impossible to give space or mention to every one. Excellent books of the 'Where to Fish' category successfully achieve this kind of cover. In a guide such as this, which is a celebration of the brown trout, of brown trout fishing and of some of the more interesting waters in which brown trout are to be found, there have been some difficult and reluctant decisions as to what should or should not be included. Though reliance has been placed on the knowledge of the contributors (nearly all of whom are able to claim particular areas as their own domains) it would be unfair to blame them for omissions that may irritate some readers – sufficient to say, there is a limit to what this particular pint pot can contain.

The same applies to the still waters, a term which includes everything from a put-and-take pond of quarter of an acre to the mighty reservoirs like Kielder and Rutland. Still waters proliferate by the day and we have purposely avoided the purely commercial fisheries (if fishery is a term that can sensibly be applied to some of them) but it is hoped and believed that the ones that have been selected are a good cross-section.

To our apologies for any genuine oversights, may our thanks be added to all who have helped with the compilation of this book.

David Barr

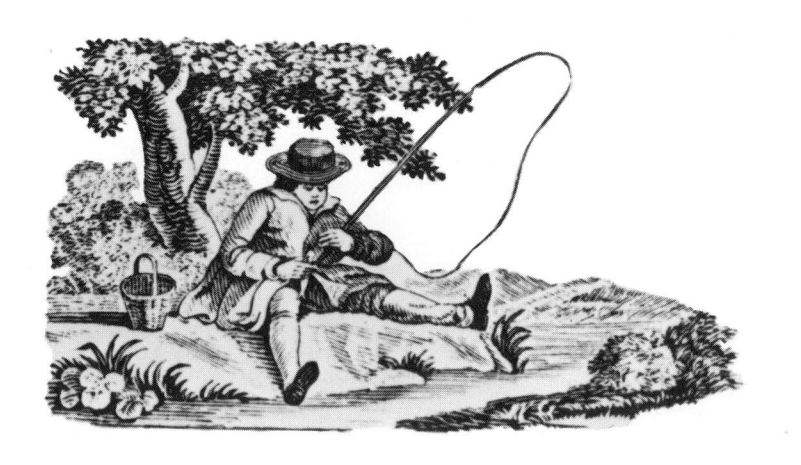

A PERSONAL INTRODUCTION TO TROUT FISHING

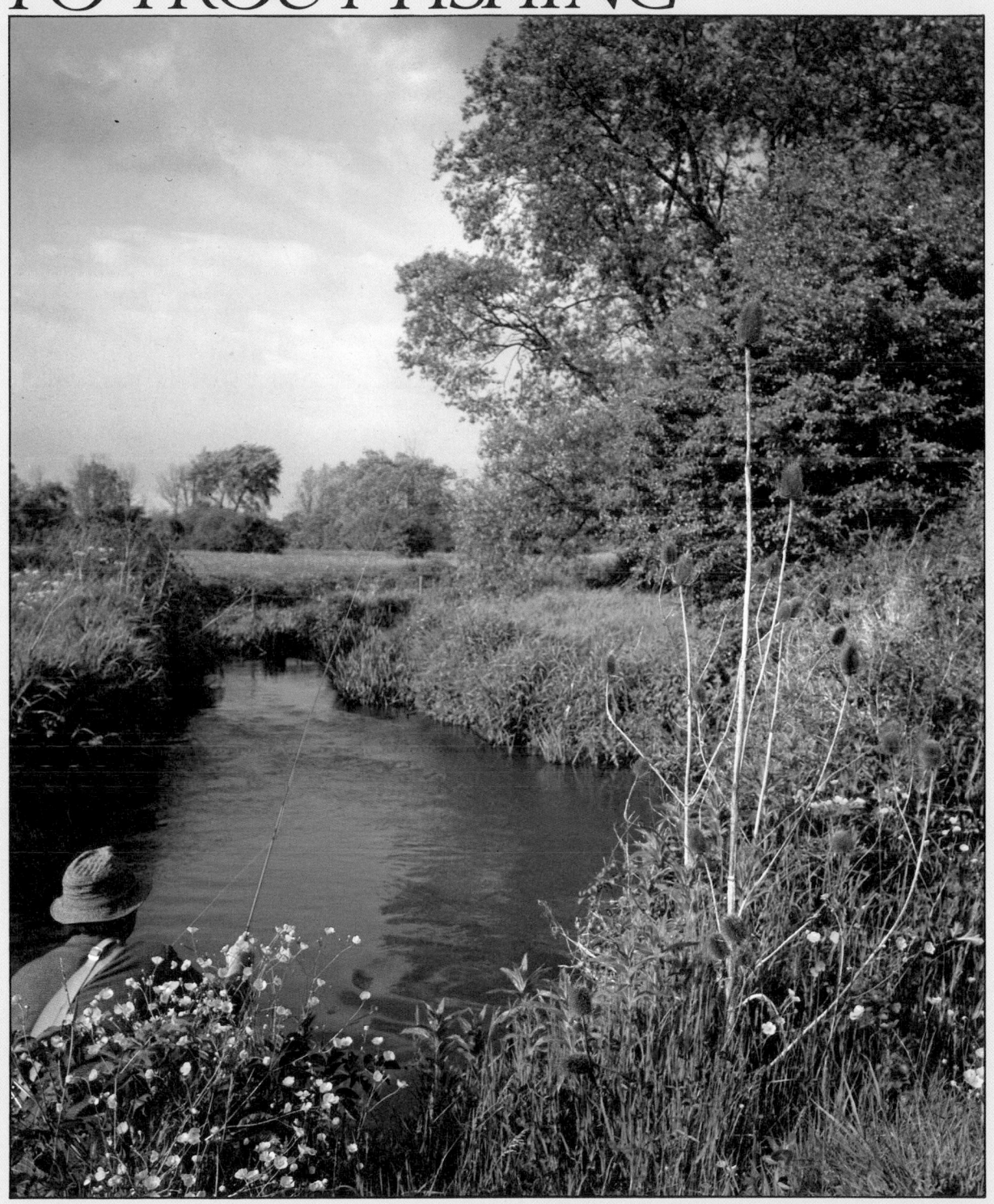

T HE excitement of the trout was paralysing. I dreamed of them each night. Brought up on a fishing diet of tiny roach, barely able to pull the float under the surface, there had suddenly come into my life these magnificent fish, poised, spotted, lightning swift and unbelievably powerful.

The little roach stream in which I had been fishing had developed a few trout as one might develop swollen glands or chicken pox. One day there were none – the next, there they were, a foot long or even more, motionless in their chosen positions except for their rhythmically moving gills, hanging (as if from a string) in the gentle chalk stream current. A sudden or unguarded move produced a puff of mud and the fish had vanished – rather like a trick evolved by Maskelyne or Devant, who at the time were bewildering children with their sleight of hand. Occasionally I succeeded in floating my pea sized piece of paste past their noses. With contempt they watched it go by, not even bothering to vanish. Even when I became more sophisticated and managed to cast a worm so that it tumbled by them, there were only two occasions when there was action, when there was a surge and a boil in the water before my line and gut came back to me, hookless. Their ferocity and uncatchability made me tremble. Sadly the skills acquired in the passing years have deprived me of the same apprehension; even so my admiration still grows.

A year or two later, in a Thames flood at Goring, I floated three little pink worms down the coloured water in search of perch. The rod was nearly wrenched from my hands. For a second my gut (or was it Japanese gut substitute?) held – and I saw, just for that second, this enormous, golden, spotted creature, framed in the floodwater, before, with a shake of its head, it took off for mid river. No wonder I could never think of these fierce and lovely fish except as uncatachable monsters.

I finally found catchable trout at Maresfield, in a tiny Sussex brook that flowed – and still does – below the road that leads to Uckfield. A school friend had invited me there to play cricket, but in the brook, which flowed round his garden, I spotted excitements that no cricket could match – the quick grey brown shapes of fish that were unmistakeably trout. I returned the next day (two hours in a No 408 bus) with my small rod and a tin filled with brandlings. By dint of looking like the invisible man, I managed to fool three trout – each of which must have weighed quite six ounces – into being caught. It was the most exciting fishing day of my life – yet this was the day that lost me a little of the cutting edge, when I learned that trout were, given the right tackle and conditions, catchable. It is one of the deep beauties of trout fishing that as soon as one hurdle is cleared, another one looms ahead, which is why every year the coming of spring presents to all trout fishermen new and vivid promises.

Trout will live and thrive in nearly any kind of clean water, moving or still – but they will only breed if the water is running. The tiniest moorland streamlets will display little corner pools four inches deep perhaps and three feet long, where a tiny,

11

scurrying black form will demonstrate the existence of a troutlet. Quite muddy rivers can provide trout with conditions that suit them, at least in their headwaters. Too often, further downstream, such waters will also contain pike –each one an expert at making very short work of small trout. During those adolescent years in Sussex I discovered a dozen tiny streams which eventually flowed into the Cuckmere or the Ouse or the Rother, which contained a head of small wild brown trout. Not always so small, either. I took a leviathan near Hellingly that weighed two pounds ten ounces, and was, bar an aged and toothless pike, the greatest fish I had ever landed.

Fishing my way down one of these brooks, in the early thirties, edging towards Burwash, I allowed myself the unpermitted luxury of some casts into the Bateman's water, from which a plump creature of three quarters of a pound was extracted. Suddenly, my heart ceased to beat as a high-pitched voice, from a very old man that I immediately recognised as a very distinguished old man, barked "Any fish left?" before turning on his distinguished heel and stumping off. It is not everyone who has been made to feel foolish and ashamed by Rudyard Kipling.

From such humble places it is but a short and enjoyable step to those magic rivers where trout thrive in huge numbers and grow to great sizes, where indeed, my leviathan might be in danger of being put back as undersized – these are the Tests, Itchens, Driffields and Kennets of this world. The sternly pure water, spring fed, relying on neither storm nor tempest, produces food in such abundance that the growth rate is three or four times greater than in less exalted streams.

Trout are fished for according to the type of rivers in which they live. I never dreamed of using anything but a worm in my tiny Sussex streams; no other lure would have been possible among lines of trees and bushes overhanging water that was nowhere more than four feet wide. With age, my prejudices have developed. I cannot think of many circumstances (other than hunger) in which I would fish with anything but a fly. One of these would be upstream clearwater worming on certain rivers at times when fly fishing is ineffective. I know I would not be good at it.

My introduction to fast moving trout water and to fly fishing was effected at Dulverton, on the River Barle, under the careful eye of Fred Tout. He was an inspired teacher and had me throwing flies across the Barle within a morning. At half a crown an hour it was unrivalled value. More important, he taught me the tricks of the craft, the names of flies, the places where the huge trout that I knew must be there, might lie. He had, I learned later, a sense of country humour in his classification of trout by size. I never did understand at the time the hush that followed my announcement to a room full of grown ups that I had caught a trout big enough to be described as a John Thomas.

Many years later I returned to the Barle and with a day ticket fished the water on which I had had my first lessons. I had a lovely day fishing upstream with Fred Tout's

The Lambourn. Before the evening rise

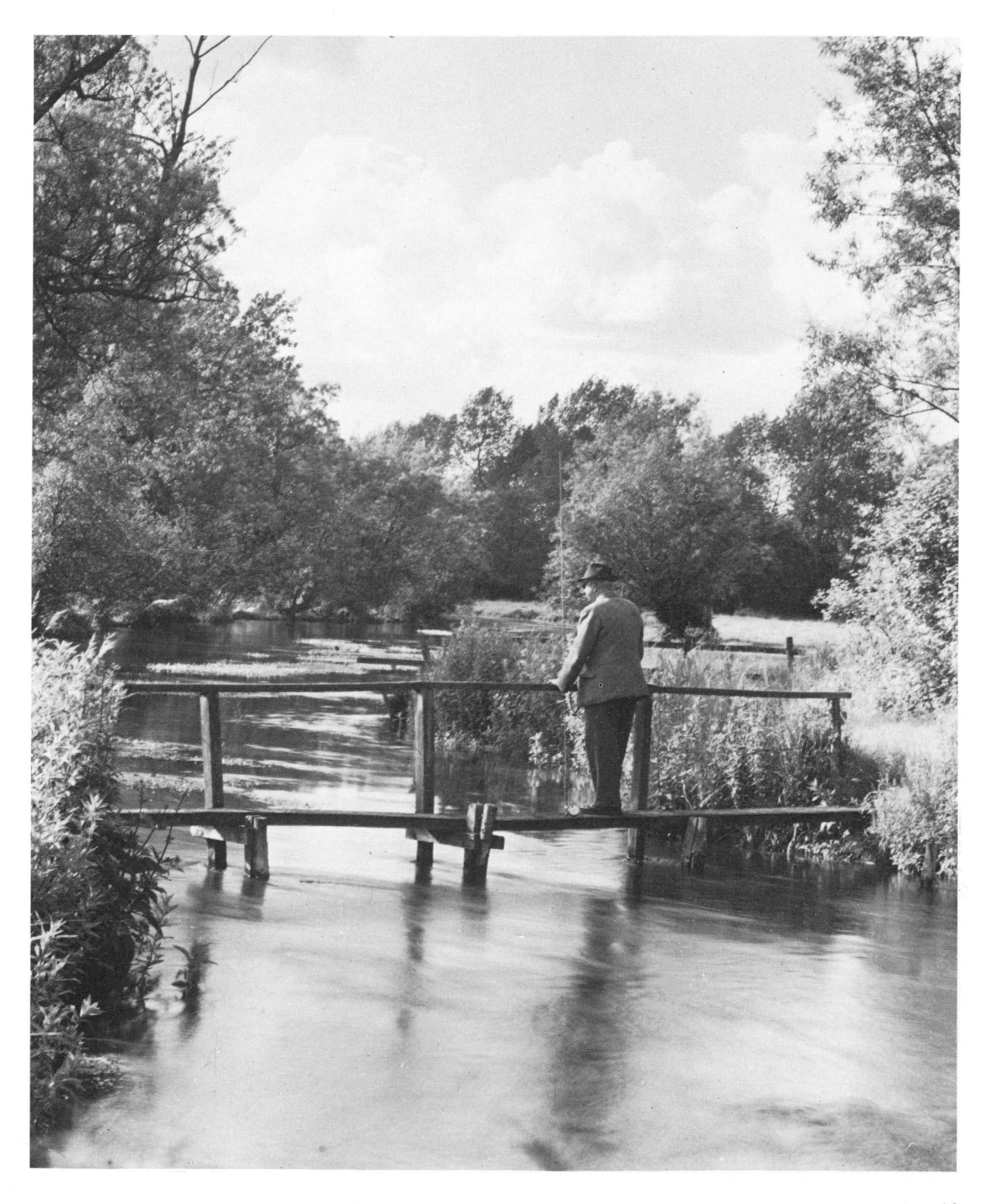

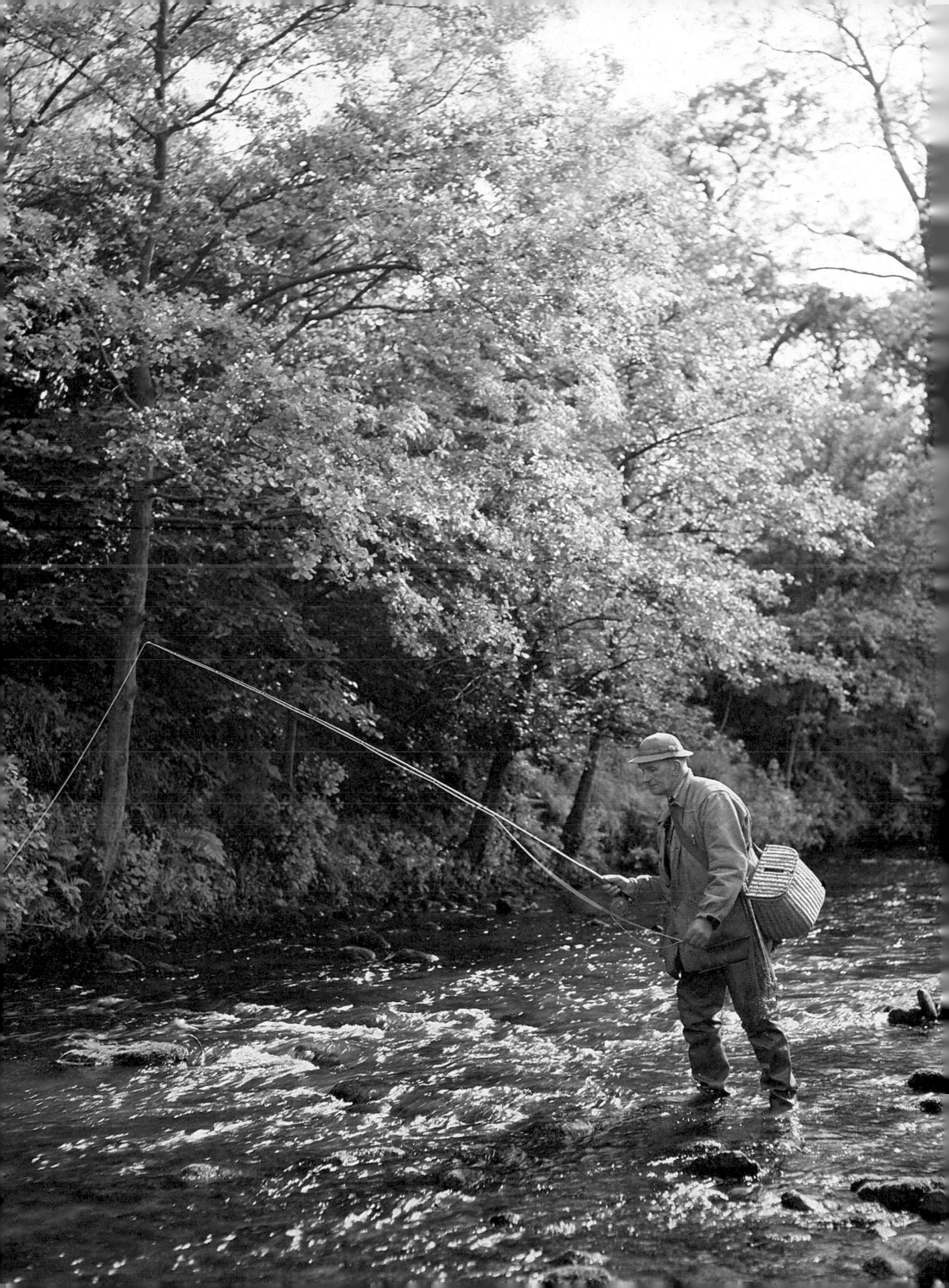

White water on the Yorkshire Derwent

special Barle fly, the Beige, and catching a number of half pound John Thomases. The only change was that the Barle had shrunk considerably – there was no great skill needed to cast across it.

So far my focus has been on the brown trout which live and breed in running waters. There are also the still waters, the lakes and the reservoirs, where stocked brown trout give enormous excitement and pleasure to tens of thousands of anglers. A trout stream is like a garden; it needs careful tending; its stocks can be diminished by over fishing and its resident population has to be fished for with restriction. Some of the river gardens have already been tended (with an eye on nature's inadequacy) in a way that will keep rich visiting fishermen happy. Even on rivers like the Test concentrated stocking with large fish had been going on for many years before the popularity and development of the reservoirs. It was done in a most gentlemanly fashion. From adjacent carriers, enough large fish were introduced into the beat, daily, to keep the fishermen successful. By and large they were not difficult to catch but the system gave much – if very expensive – pleasure. It was certainly not called 'put-and-take' fishing – the name given today, without much affection, to the same game in its most commercialised form.

The reservoirs were always, because of their size, very different. No matter how many trout were injected weekly, they soon dispersed far and wide – and did not take long to learn to become wary of most artificial lures. The challenge of the reservoirs produced the generation of fishermen (including vast numbers of recruits from coarse fishing) for which there was no room on the rivers, a generation that did not mind fishing side by side and which, with ingenuity and skill, produced all kinds of new fishing techniques, and created a demand for a new and different range of tackle.

The brown trout has a famous brother, a fish with a rainbow stripe that runs from gill to tail. In good condition it is a lovely fish, rivalling in colour the red and black spots and golden colours of the brown trout. When of migratory stock and when it escapes to the sea (it never happens here, sadly) it returns to the rivers (to spawn) as the most beautiful fish of all, the huge, swift and almost invincible steelhead. It is only during the past thirty years that the rainbow trout has made an important impact on fishing and fishermen in the United Kingdom. Previously it was mainly a fish with which a few rich men stocked their lakes and which for some unexplained reason, only thrived and bred in the Derbyshire Wye. In North America it is indigenous and exists naturally in as large a quantity as the browns.

Rainbow trout are exciting to catch, and are usually more obliging than brown trout. One of the fishing magazines gave its readers stickers for their cars which carried the slogan 'I'm forever chasing Rainbows'. It was extraordinary how often, wherever one was, the stickers could be seen.

15

On the Norfolk stream on which I have done the bulk of my trout fishing during the past years, we have twice in a decade stocked a lake through which the stream flows with small numbers of rainbow. A few were caught, slightly but not dramatically enlarged, during the season that followed, but after that there was nothing, or almost nothing. The other fish, true to the rainbow tradition when it is stocked into non enclosed waters, vanished. In the three years that followed our last and final stocking, only three have been caught, all in deep pools (where one might also expect to find the biggest brown trout) and all of a size that for our particular stream, was exceptionally large. We thought three big fish a very poor return out of a hundred. Perhaps the downstream beats thrived.

The mixture of brown and rainbow trout, even if the rainbows could be persuaded to breed, is never likely to succeed in this country. The brown trout spawn earlier and the later spawning rainbows, seeking the same marriage beds, would inevitably disturb the brown trout. The result would probably be the loss of the native brown trout. The Derbyshire Wye is the most important river in which the rainbow trout has established itself as a breeding species.

In this book it is assumed that the fly is the accepted method of trout fishing. No space will be given to catching them on bait, live or dead, but this might even so be the moment to tell the apochryphal story of my own biggest trout.

I was recovering from World War II and living in the Winchester area. I had already begged myself several days on the Itchen and the Test. Those were the times when people were nice to the returning warriors, assuming (wrongly in my case, but who was I to disillusion them?) that they were all heroes. I only had one 'No' from the fishery owners on the Test – when I called at an enormous mansion surrounded by the lovely river, pressed the bell, heard distant footsteps, then the sound of bolts being withdrawn and came face to face with a large lady in a tiara and a very long dress. I gave her my spiel and there was a pause as our eyes met in a long stare. "We only" she said "permit our friends to be our guests". The closing door shut out any further conversation followed by the quick replacement of bolts.

My reception at The Old Grange, Warmington was very different. My map had shown me three lakes; my eyes had revealed nymphing trout in the top one. The Palladian front of this huge house was far more imposing than that of the tiaraed lady. I was greeted, in not very good English, by Mr Wallach, who had come, not all that long ago, from Poland. He was a very nice man indeed and lonely enough in that vast establishment, to enjoy conversation with a stranger. His permission to fish was cordial and only qualified in two respects – kill any coarse fish – and dry fly only.

It took me no more than an hour's fishing to realise that trout were few and far between – and most unlikely to be caught on dry fly. They had an almost inexhaustible

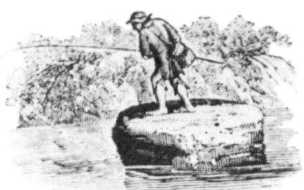

supply of roach fry on hand. For two days I turned my hand to roach fishing and discovered the finest, without any doubt, at that moment in Great Britain. In one morning alone I caught thirty five over a pound and a half, and up to, but not more than, two pounds. The paste also lured a two pound trout. That was in the middle lake.

When I walked down to the lower lake, in the evening, I went in search of even more staggering roach, but what I glimpsed cruising slowly around a wooden structure five yards from the bank, was the biggest trout I had ever seen. Dutifully I placed a few Lunn's Particulars in front of his nose, but it was like offering a bull a blade of grass. I doubt whether he even noticed. At that moment all my good principles and high intentions left me. I dug out of my fly box my biggest fly – a large furry Coachman – turned over a log, found myself by great good luck a fat lobworm which I impaled on the Coachman, waited for the trout to patrol on my side of the wooden structure and gently cast the worm towards him. He never hesitated – but it took me ten minutes to land him on my fine dry fly, tapered gut. As I slid the fish up onto the bank, trembling with excitement and guilt, a voice behind me said "That is very good indeed." It was Mr Wallach and he gently removed the fly from the monstrous jaws. A fortnight afterwards there appeared in the late lamented *Sporting and Dramatic* the story of the catching of a brown trout weighing four pounds eight ounces, on a Coachman at The Grange, Warmington, Winchester. This must be the ideal illustration that crime can sometimes pay – and make both robber and robbed happy.

Apart from aberrations like this one, I have spent the latter years disciplined to fishing for trout with fly only and, because of the kind of streams that have been available to me, nearly always using dry fly and nymph, as being the most effective means of filling the plastic bag that I now carry around with me.

Trout fishing seasons vary according to the water authority in which the river, lake or reservoir is situated. On the west side of the country the season tends to open earlier – early or mid March; on the east, sometimes as late as mid April. By 30 September most of the brown trout fishing is coming to an end (as it certainly should as most of the ladies are very pregnant by then). Trout fishing is allowed on Sundays, even in Scotland where it is forbidden to fish for salmon and sea-trout that day. The Tay on a Sunday is an impressive sight, with hundreds of trout fishermen in position where the day previously the salmon fishermen stood. It is not true, as a scurrilous Scot told me, that they use larger trout flies on the Tay on Sundays than on any other river in the United Kingdom. There are no water authorities in Scotland but the statutory close season for brown trout runs from 7 October to 14 March. Individual fishing organisers usually extend this from 30 September to 31 March. There is no statutory close season in Scotland for rainbow trout but winter makes a good substitute.

A SALUTE TO THE TROUT

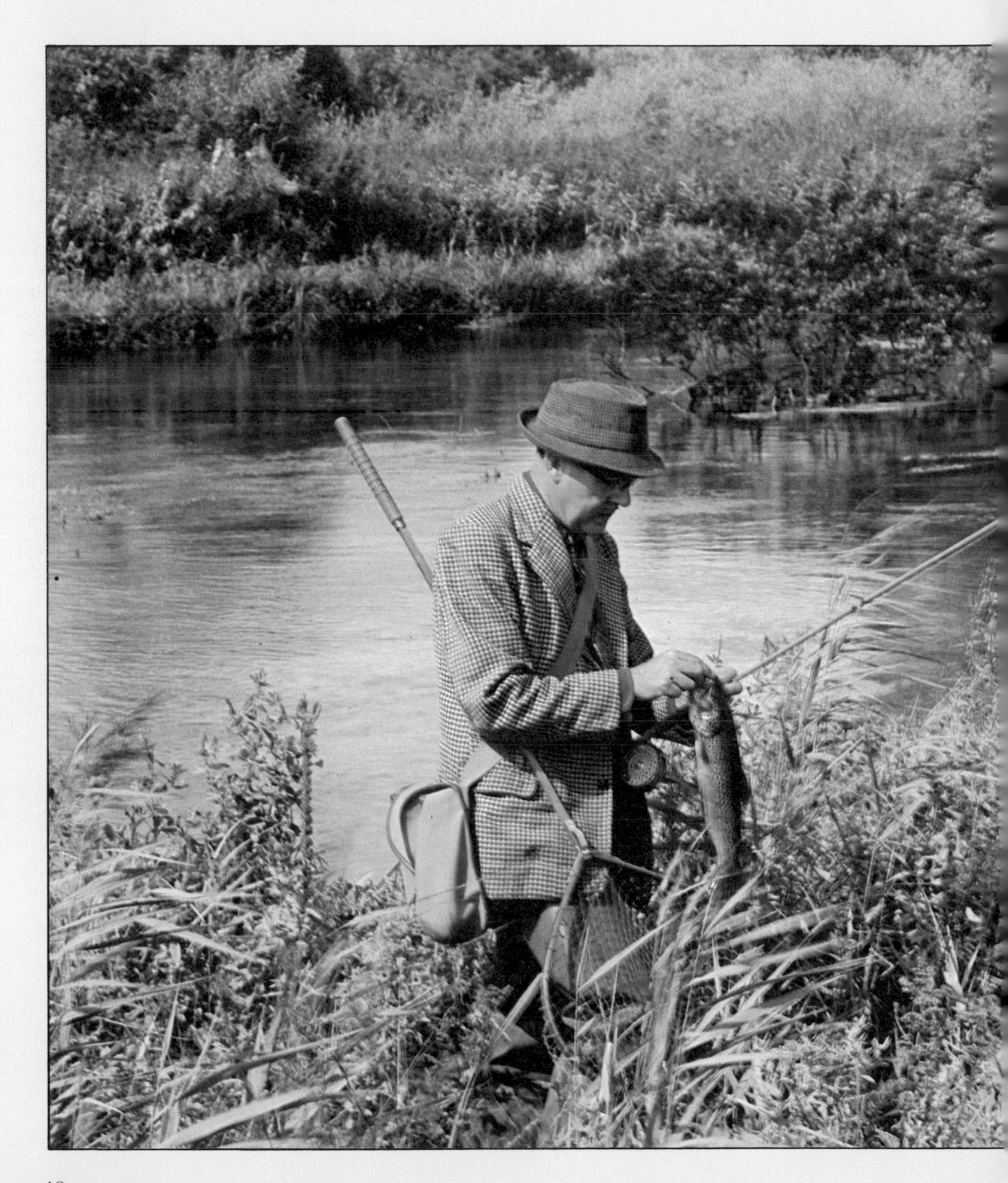

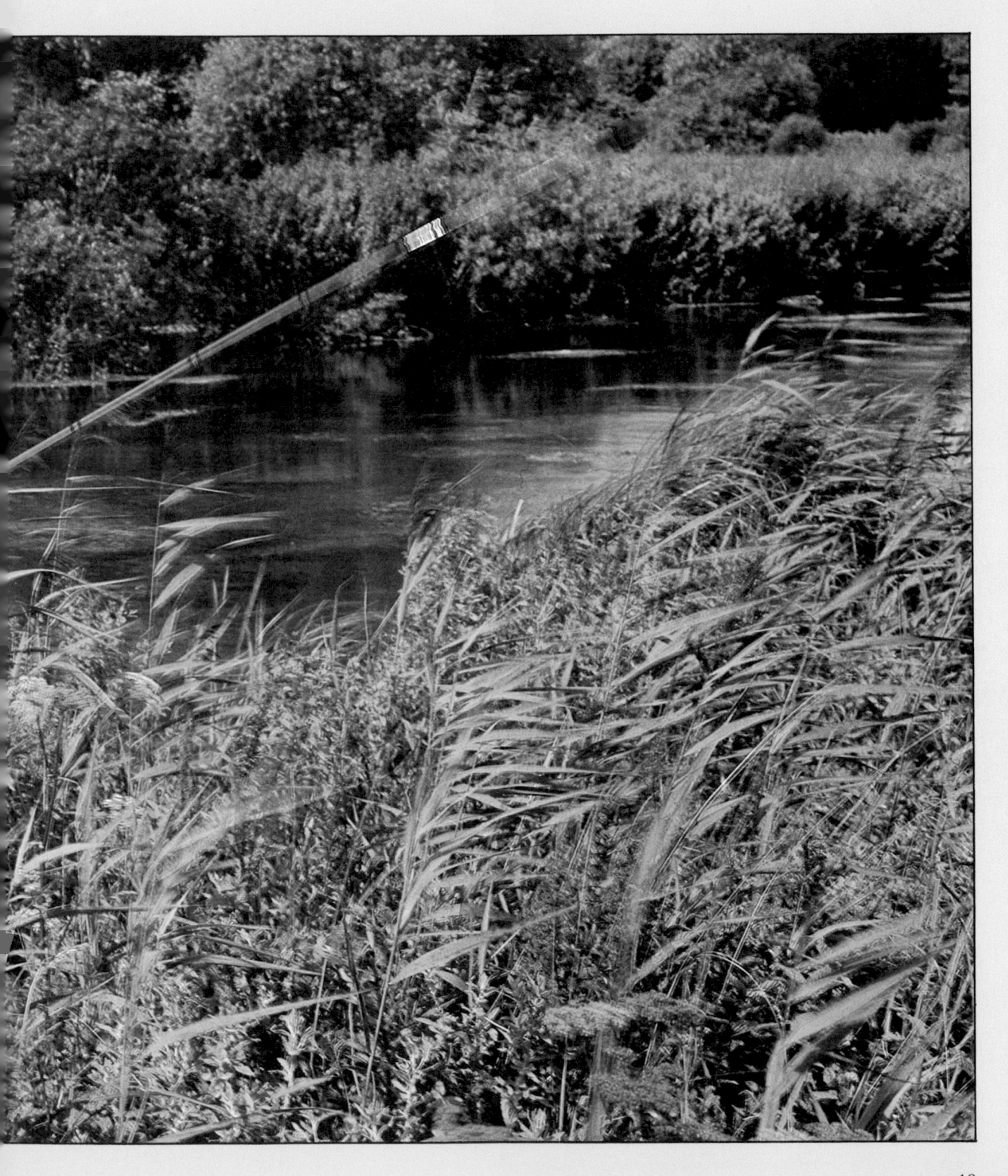

OF all the unifiers in outdoor sport, none excels the trout. On this single species of fish a far flung community of human enthusiasts, many millions strong, vector their hearts and minds. From trout comes the whole code of discipline and attitudes which constitute fly fishing. Because of trout, a rich pattern of scenes and pleasures has emerged. Devotees from many contrasting nations have elevated fly fishing into something near a way of life. United in their regard for trout, this global community share the same commitment in the same way, full of rivalry but devoid of enmity. Only golf can equal the international spell of fly fishing. Football disqualifies itself by rancours. Cricket's appeal is limited in comparison; athletics a transient phase in human lifetimes; and it is no skin off the fox's nose that his disciples number fewer than one per cent of those of the trout. Without trout, fly fishing itself would be a minor tactic instead of a major sporting philosophy.

The salmon is hailed by a minority of fly fishers as their major quarry. But only fifty per cent of salmon fishing is fly fishing, and much of that is in name only. Of that fifty per cent, eighty per cent is undeniable lure fishing, far removed from the basic ethics which make true fly fishing distinct from other angling skills. The questions and the answers in trout fishing are the same the world over.

> *The trout that haunts the Beaverkill*
> *Will wave the same sarcastic tail,*
> *When falsely struck, as him my skill*
> *Would vainly lure from Tweed or Kale. . .*

So wrote John Buchan (the first Lord Tweedsmuir, novelist, soldier, politician and pro-consul and a great angler on Scottish Border waters) in greeting to the fly fishers of North America. His theme has a wider application. It holds good wherever trout swim, the slim rod arches, and flies fall lightly; wherever men foregather in the dusk to tell of the day that has passed, and to warm the cockles of their hearts; and wherever the same men, deprived by worldly affairs for long months of the pursuit of trout, dream dreams and see visions of what awaits them when next they tread the banks.

Their waters may be classic streams in southern England, famed in sport's most graceful literature; small brooks between windy uplands; streams rampaging out of Wales with all the fervour of Cymric invaders; lochs lying like silver crescents amid purple Scottish heather; winding streams flanked by fuchsia in Ireland's golden west; rock filled torrents in Scandinavia; resounding Balkan gorges; wide Canadian rivers where pine tops reach for the sky like the tips of green flames; great lakes in Argentina with the Andes snow in the background, where the Spanish speaking gillies answer to Welsh names; waters in far Kashmir, even the haunted Shalimar itself, on which boats shaped like water lilies take fishermen serenely to the best lies; waters in New Zealand

The peaceful Itchen below Winchester

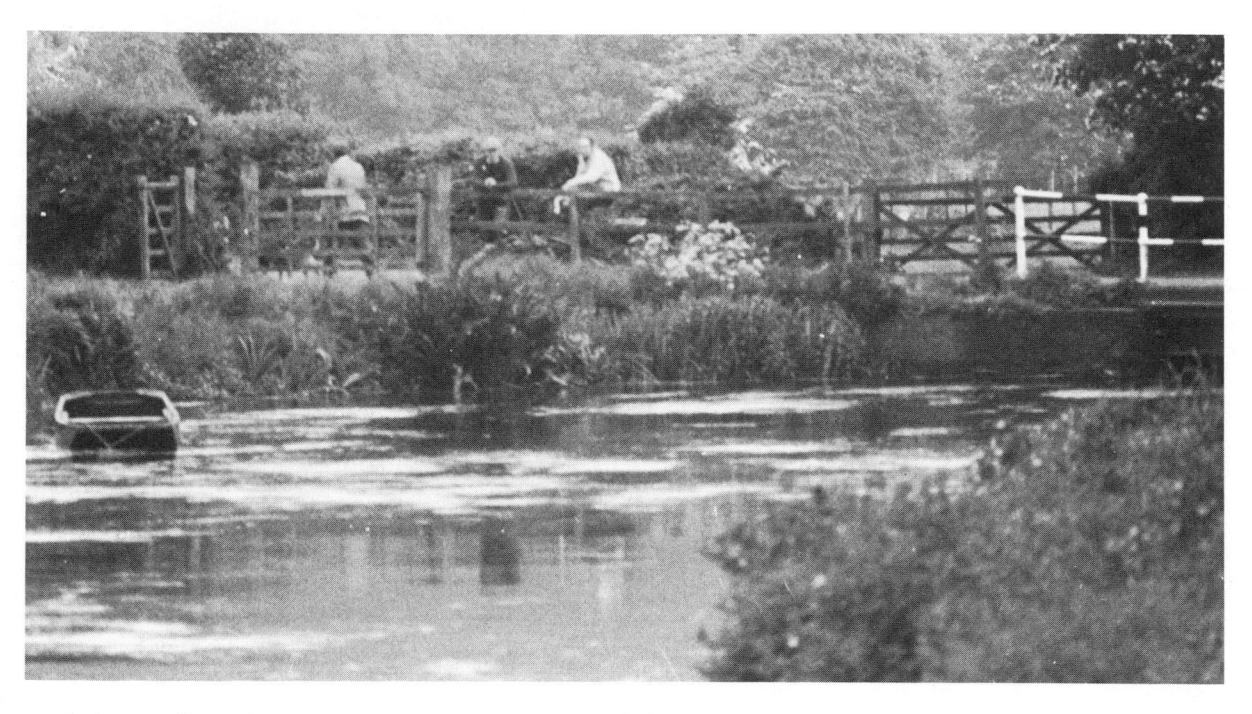

and Australia where men contemptuous of other subtleties deploy wrists of steel and hands like silk. Here, there, and everywhere else that trout inhabited or have been made to colonise, they have exerted their magnetism on the human race.

The unity of the trout fishing community derives from the separateness of the trout itself. To go out for roach and, finding they are not 'on', to catch bream instead is commonplace. But the trout is not an alternative, nor are there alternatives to it. The trout is an end in itself, an alpha and an omega, all or nothing. It is possible to catch trout inadvertently when trying for other fish, but difficult to catch something else other than grayling when out for trout. Trout fishing, a serious but not dull matter, does not admit of compromises, of laughing things off when failures occur. That there are better fish in the water than have come out of it, as is airily said by more carefree though not happier fishermen, is no balm to a trout fisher's spirits. If there are better fish in the water, then they ought to have come out of it; the fact that they did not is the measure of his own inadequacy. It is a question of him or them; in fly fishing there are neither alibis nor surrounding distractions.

The effects which trout have on their human contacts are reflections of the character of trout themselves, their mystique, their powerful attractions, their prestige as sporting trophies, their paramount importance to those who fall under their spell. To say that a man is a trout fisherman creates an instant image seldom belied, give or take a few physical details. He and his kind are quizzical, argumentative fellows, conspicuous for their private jargon, intermittent absences, convivial nature, wind tanned faces and

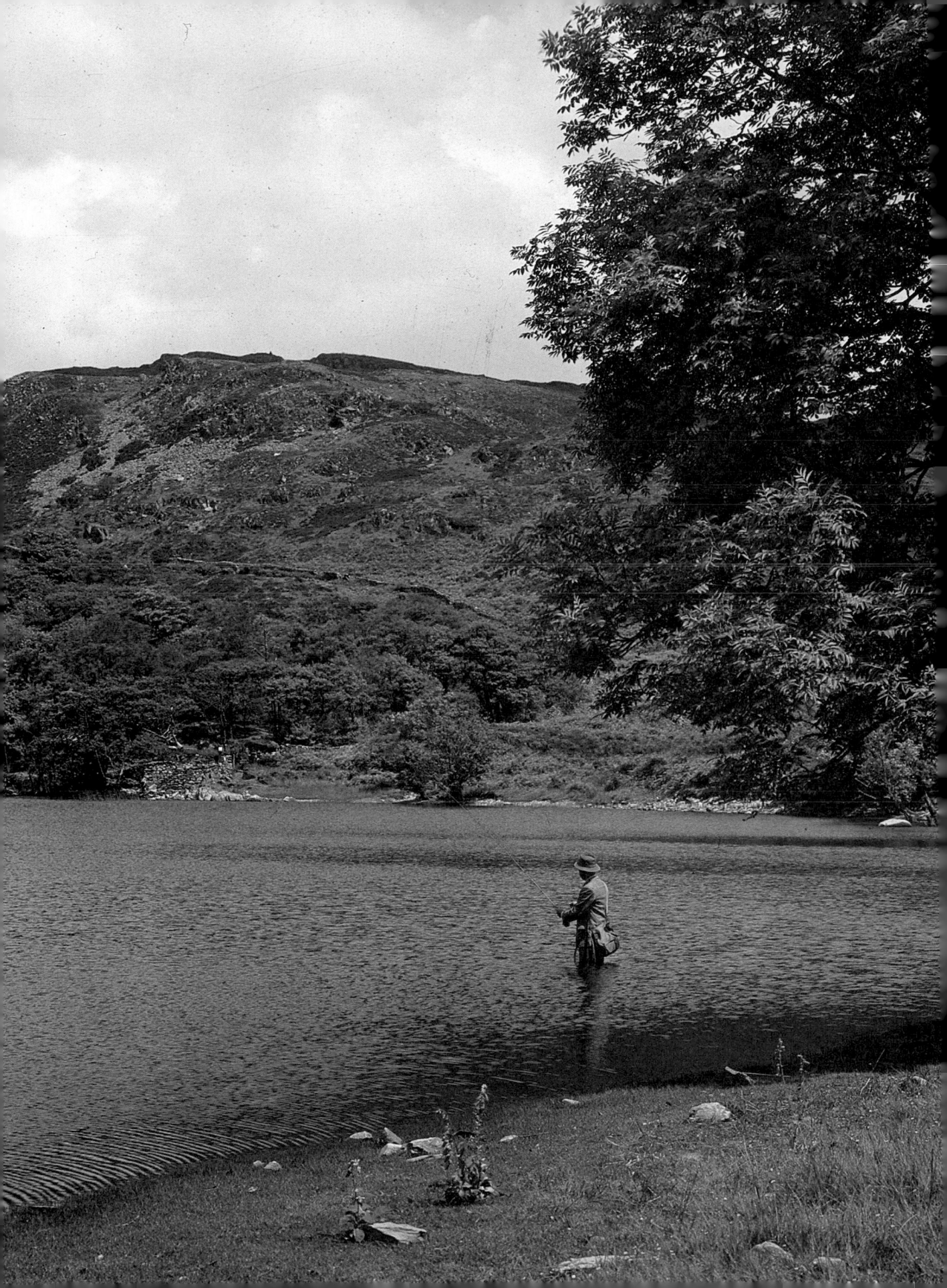

Lake Fishing. Nannau, North Wales

formidable powers of narration. Since the word 'fellow' still retains some remaining implications of masculinity, it must be added that not all trout fishers are male. The Diana element in the sport is now so well established as to be no longer remarkable, except that it should have emerged so recently. No sport gives greater scope to the feminine qualities of attention to detail, neatness of hand, observation, and persistence. Nor is any action in sport more fittingly performed by a lady than the elegant and rhythmic casting of a fly line. Theirs has become a welcome and a decorative presence.

The question arises, 'What is a trout that it should captivate so distinctive a segment of humanity?' To that there are many answers. Some transcend the factual. That the trout is a freshwater spawning fish of the *Salmonidae* family, varying in adult weight between four ounces and twenty odd pounds, some sub-varieties of which have taken to an andronymous way of life and become known as sea-trout, is ascertainable from any dictionary. What dictionaries cannot tell is the infinite variety of trout, their magic, mystique and mythology.

Unlike most natural species, so identical that all their members are as alike to each other as the theoretical citizens of a communist state, trout are as diverse as mankind. Streamlined, golden backed, red spotted, strong of tail and shoulder, they hang regally below man made lashers in chalk streams. As dark and darting shadows they flick across the rock pools of moorland becks, black backed and rusty marked in the landing net. Pink flanked and huge, they leap in the evening light from the mirror surfaces of the great new stillwaters, revealing their rainbow title and American origin. Dark and orange bellied, recalling among old timers the traditional Loch Leven strain, they live tenaciously in the acid waters of the peat counties from Cape Wrath to Co Kerry. And so Nature changes their image round the globe.

The fact that of all the trout caught in a modern British season, more will have been hatched and reared in stews, then turned in to lakes and rivers near the season's start, than are bred naturally, has mingled and increased the different strains and types of trout, and made them independent of locality as fish farms have multiplied and spread their products round the country. The same process occurs in continental Europe and America. Whether this is for good or ill, or some of each and in what proportion, is not to be argued here. For most trout fishers one trout characteristic matters above all else. How big?

The trout we catch and the trout we dream about coincide only rarely. We live, and fish, in the hope of something special, of a monster so excelling the norm that it will dominate our diaries, our memories, and our conversation; that it will spread our fame far and wide, enabling us to face the world as giants. But monster trout are no different from other trout, and indeed vary in weight between four ounces and about twenty pounds, their distinguishing characteristic being size only in terms of the place and circumstances of their capture.

The quarry. Brown trout in clear water

My own modest contributions to the monster range have been six pounds twelve ounces from the Test, and four pounds fourteen ounces from the Otter in Devon. There is no doubt in my mind which was the better monster (or, as the Americans have it, 'lunker'). There are men whose contributions are far from modest, and who pay much gold to fish in particular places where trout of between eighteen and twenty pounds are 'guaranteed' to be catchable, having been pelleted up to that weight in captivity, and are indeed caught. They have my best wishes in continuing their efforts

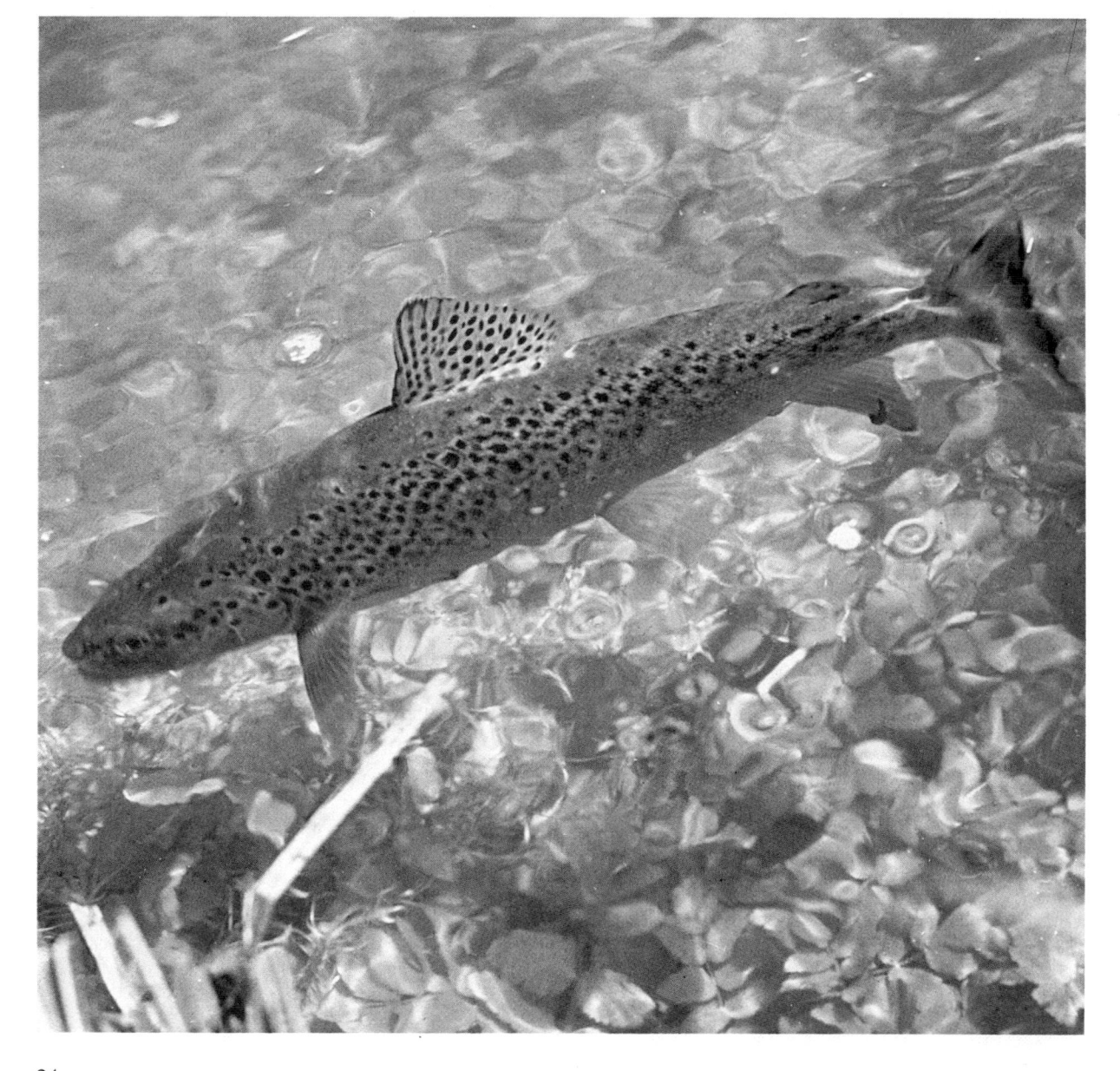

in these doubtless hallowed spots. In contrast, my teenage daughter has caught in a Scottish burn a monster of distinctly more than one pound (it was not even necessary to blow on the scales). She would not change it for either of mine named, which she suspects were flukes anyway. Monsterhood in a trout is not a matter of mensuration and gravitational pull, but exists in the mind of the captor.

There are, indeed, other calibrations. In the camera's eye, for instance, in the headlines or, most enviably, on the platter on which a monster lies in state in the hotel foyer with its neat little card naming the triumphant rod. Not that he really needs naming, for it is customary on these occasions for the hero of the day to loiter within a yard or two of his trophy, preferably between it and the bar hatch whence he can call up doubles for acquaintances with souls so dead that they threaten to pass the mighty corpse without buying one for him.

A little vainglory is a joyous thing. But it is not the whole truth, or a great part of it. The truth is the complex texture of weather, waterflow, wind and sunshine, fly, weed, drag, trees, bird voices, our own skills and nerves, all woven round the spotted marvels that lie in the inscrutable waters before our very eyes, though we may not see them. Some we come to know as old friends through months, perhaps years, of common interest until in that primeval amalgam of love and conquest, we play them to the net and knock them on the head. Then the savour seems to leave the season unexpectedly early. The scene seems bleaker, the river duller until fate and one's own fancy combine to provide a successor.

When we look back on the trout we have known we realize that there always is a successor, always other trout to become so important to us that in their presence we find ourselves 'the world forgetting, by the world forgot' once we learn their inner secret. Monsters or tiddlers, leopard spotted or swarthy, there they are; and there are we. The lore of the trout is in a simple equation. We have our hopes and our ambitions. They have the wisdom of serpents, and the spirits of gods and devils in our not unequal contest.

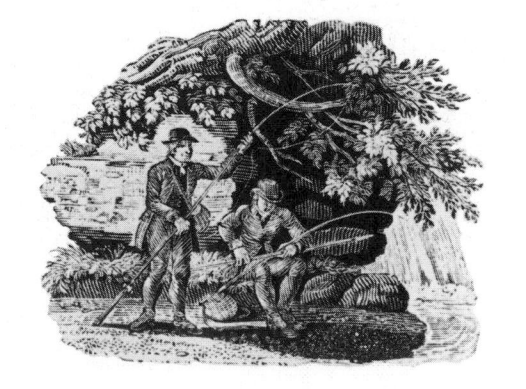

TACKLE FOR THE TROUT FISHERMAN

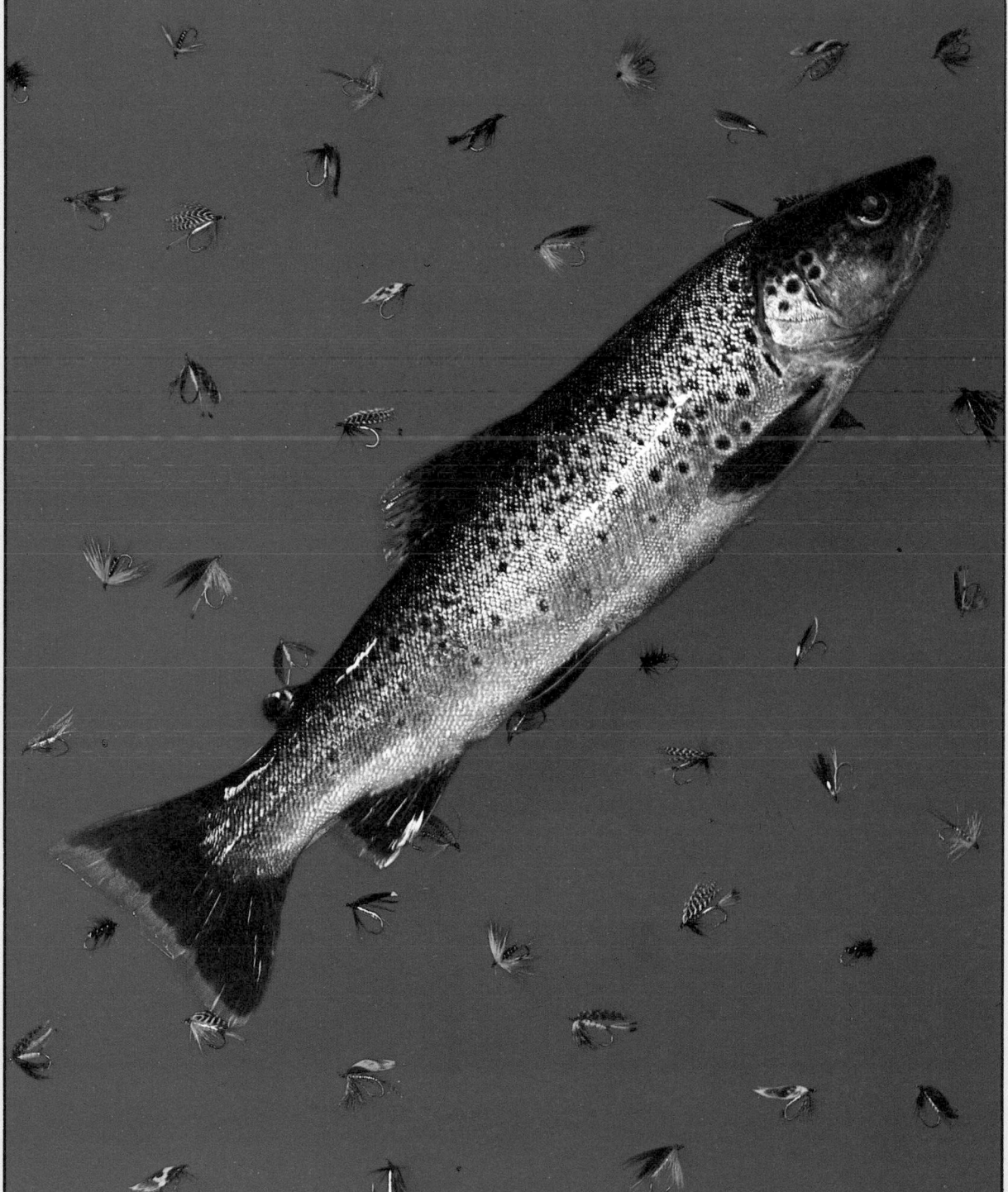

THE peak of every trout fisherman's ambition forty and more years ago was to own a split cane rod. The tackle makers competed with one another at prices that seem trivial now (but didn't then, in those days of cheap labour and money shortage) to produce those beautiful rods. They were marketed, bound and gleaming – almost too lovely to touch – in neat cases, complete with spare joint and frequently tucked lovingly into aluminium tubes (with cup tops that pulled off with a low 'poong'). Their snowy cork handles seemed too good to grip with wet or grubby hands; at the tops gleamed agate rings; their steel ferrules fitted so snugly that unless one had first been very careful with the right kind of lubricant, taking them apart became a mammoth and hair raising task that involved the application of heat – or even desperate measures with pliers. These rods came in all sizes (each with the distinguishing marks of its manufacturers) from seven to nine foot, and in all strengths. There were whippy creatures for downstream fishing through to the stately ones for the long accurate casts needed on the broad and exalted waters of the Test. Those fine split cane rods (particularly those created by the tackle super stars, Hardy Brothers) have become collectors items. Rods sixty and seventy years old are still straight, true and completely serviceable. In the late forties the manufacturing process was eased by the advent of the new glues and adhesives. Instead of the whipped and re-whipped split cane there appeared built cane, equally efficient and equally gracious to use, but less labour intensive.

The split and built cane rods were the predecessors of further advances in plastics – the glass fibre/fibreglass rods that arrived on the market in time for the fishing explosion – and probably helped it on its way. They were cheap, and in accordance with the tackle industry's tradition, well made and well finished tools that would cast as far or further than the cane rods and with the same, or very nearly the same delicacy. Here for thousands of newcomers to the sport was the good car, minus the smoothness and comfort of the Rolls Royce, but one which would carry its owner in comfort to his destination.

Finally – the carbon-fibre rods, the lightest (and most powerful) of the lot; they are also the most delicate and of course the most expensive – though their price is now dropping month by month. Even semi-competent people can now buy kits and convert them into fine rods. Among the leaders in carbon-fibre rodmanship is the Huntingdonshire firm of Bruce and Walker who, though their name was made by the excellence of their salmon rods, produce trout rods that are as good. Carbon-fibre has almost become a status symbol on the banks of river and reservoir, but I will confess that for trout fishing I rely on my Sharpes built cane 88 – or perhaps I should say my 88 and my 84. One of the top joints lost an argument with a car door – and its top four inches. They make a pair of rods that fish well in any ordinary circumstances – including the rigours of the big reservoirs.

Lines have progressed in similar manner. Older fishermen will still have happy memories of the Kingfisher dressed silk lines, shiny and sweet smelling, objects that deserved the drying and annointing that they demanded. Labour intensive to manufacture, they too have become casualties of plasti-culture. They have been succeeded by floating, slow sinking, semi-floating, quick sinking and numerous other varieties of plastic lines that market demand has produced by the million. They have certainly added a new ease to casting; they take no looking after; they last long enough to make each year's use not too costly – and my only complaint is their classification by decimal codes that makes my hands move towards my pockets in search of a calculator. Those who hesitated to move from gut to nylon showed no such indecision with the new lines.

In the old days fishermen had to put up with gut casts, tapered to 3, 4 or 5^x according to strength or lack of it, and needing ten minutes soaking before use. Along came, to everyone's relief, the nylon casts – leaders – traces – call them what you will. Dyed in the wool people like myself continued to use gut long after doing so made any sense, but when we finally capitulated and learnt the appropriate knots we realised how foolish we had been. Nylon can be bought tapered, or it can be turned into a tapered cast by joining together lengths of diminishing strength and thickness – it is all very simple, very cheap and almost foolproof. Moreover the backroom boys have really progressed in this particular sphere. 'New and improved' means just what they say. The diameters have diminished without loss of strength; the texture has made the nylon increasingly invisible.

That brings me to the end product, the flies, fished one, two, three and even four at a time. In the reservoirs and in fast streams where the fishermen sometimes fish downstream and across, teams of flies are used. For the upstream fisherman the single fly, floating or sunk, is what is needed.

The entomologist kind of fisherman will examine the insects that come floating by him and decide not only what their names are, but what stage of development they have reached. He will then put on an imitation. Though this may be effective, I find it difficult to forget how absurdly different is the tiny transparent insect from even the best of human imitations. Almost, if not quite as effective as knowledge of entomology, is a knowledge of what trout are likely to take at various times of the year – whether in the shape of a nymph, a floating fly, or something tied to be eye catching that is fished fast downstream. We trout fishermen agree with a sad smile that we could very easily get by for a normal season with a dozen carefully chosen flies – but it would spoil a lot of our fun if we were discouraged from accumulating our collections of flies in the infinite variety of sizes and colours in which they are made. One of the great adages of fly fishing is that it is always sensible to use locally tied flies – and this folly alone adds dozens to the contents of the fly boxes of fishermen who like variety in their sport. Pandering to this very attractive and human foible, we have furnished in

For reservoir use. Trout flies tied by Richard Walker

this book, wherever possible, the names of flies that have special virtues on the streams and rivers we have described.

Everything else a trout fisherman needs, from landing net, waders and rain wear to funny hat is clearly a matter of choice and personality.

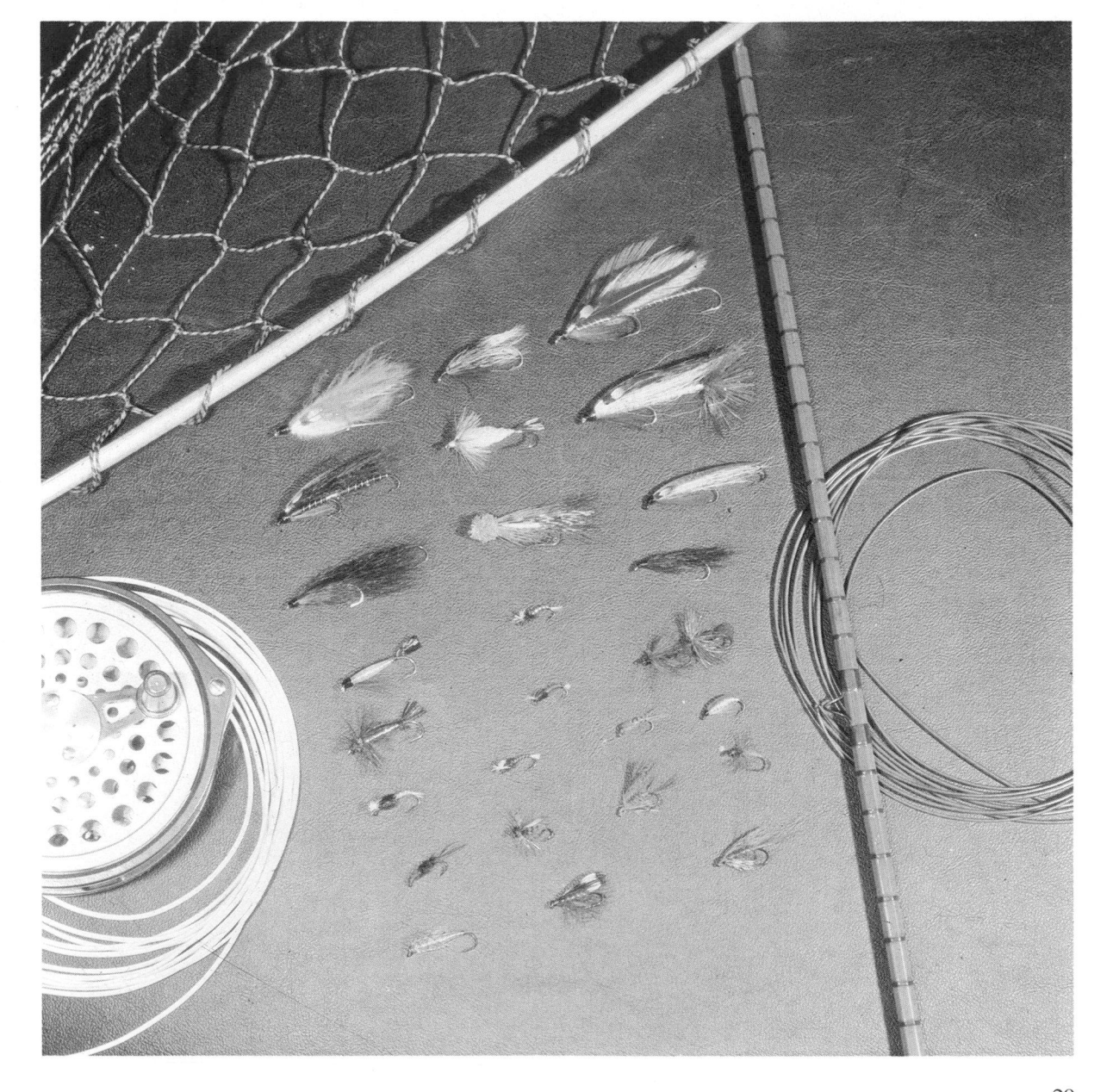

TROUT FARMING

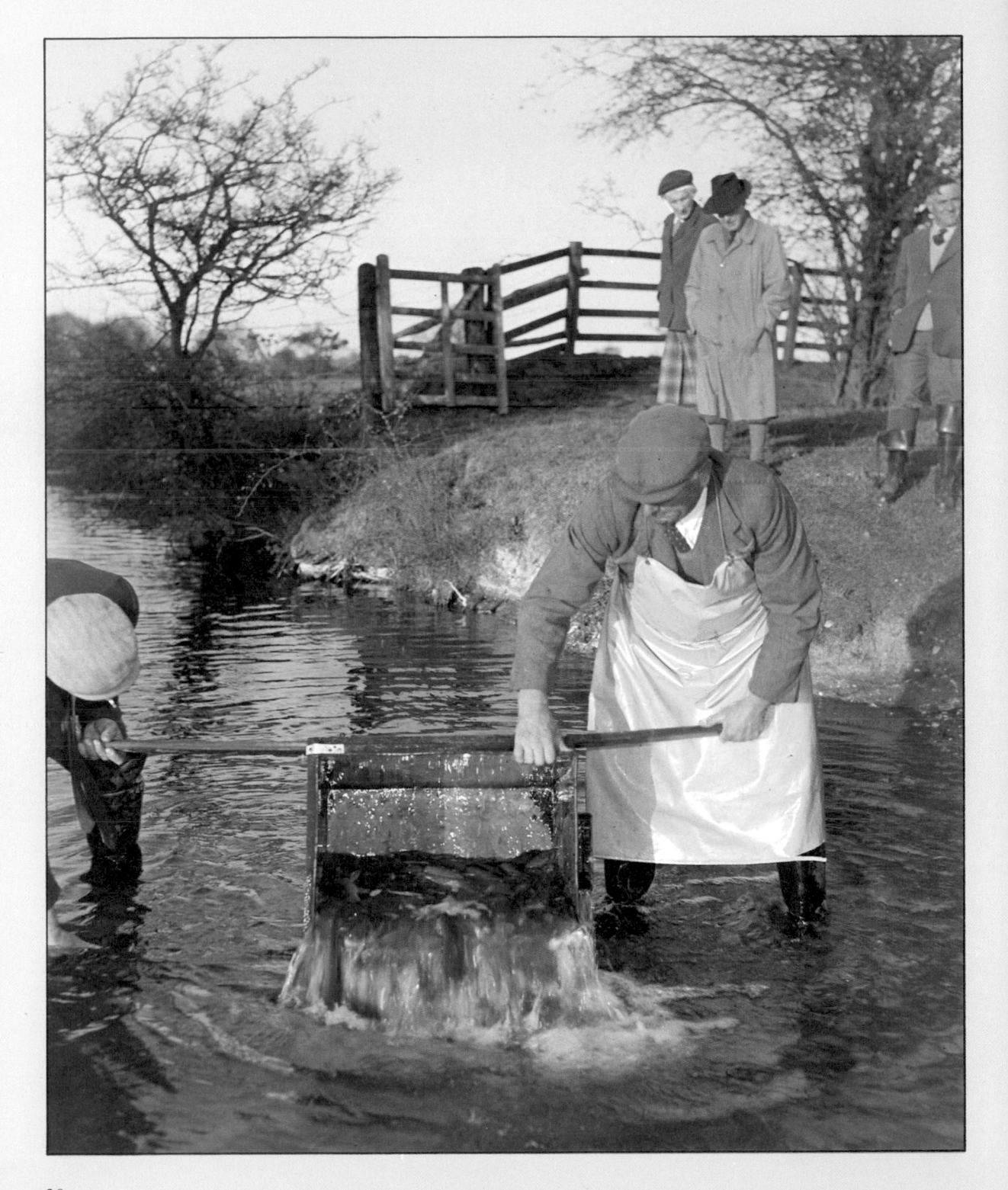

MY trout farm has been in existence for four years. It is situated on the banks of the River Eamont, which flows from Ullswater to the Eden. The site was previously a small mixed farming unit, and before that a flour mill on the Lowther Estates. The site has thus long used its water supply to create revenue.

The farm uses a series of circular and rectangular concrete tanks which contain, at the time of writing, 200,000 rainbow trout. There would be on average 80,000 to 100,000 fry weighing about five grams each and about 40,000 fingerlings weighing about thirty grams each and the rest of varying sizes up to as big as three pounds. Rainbow trout are farmed in preference to brown trout for several reasons; the main one is economic, for a brown trout takes roughly twice as long as a rainbow to reach a given size. Most farms provide for the table as well as for stocking rivers, and indeed, higher stocking densities can be employed if the fish are being bred for the table.

It is possible to rear trout from eggs, but that is a highly specialised and technical activity. The farm I worked at, as a matter of policy, bought eggs from hatcheries. A stocking pattern was practised, purchasing fry twice a year in May and August. The May fingerlings, given the right conditions, will be ready for the market (eight ounces plus) from November onwards; the August ones are usually ready the following spring. The cost of buying fish varies from £25–£35 for 1,000 at site, and these fingerlings average a hundred fish to the pound weight.

For any trout farm, a consistent and reliable water supply is essential. It is an advantage to have a large body of water upstream to regulate diurnal and seasonal temperature changes. Since my farm has Ullswater upstream from it, it means that there are higher and therefore more beneficial water temperatures later on in the year than would otherwise be the case. However, by contrast, in the spring the water takes longer to reach the optimum growth temperature.

The rate of growth of the fish is heavily dependent on the water temperature. The optimum growth temperature on average is 18°C. Extremes of temperature cause problems. If the water is cold (below 4°C) feeding, and therefore growth, is minimal. Conversely if the water is too warm (22°C or more) the level of dissolved oxygen in the water gets too low to allow feeding. This is because the digestion of food requires a substantial amount of oxygen, and within five minutes of feeding the oxygen demand is at its maximum. Even if food is withheld at this temperature the fish are not out of danger, as at temperatures above 24°C they start to die due to heat stress. Altogether unusually warm weather creates hair raising hazards.

Autumn is a particularly worrying time for fish farmers whose business is based on rivers, as blocking of filters will occur on a predictably frequent basis during both day and night. This alters the level and flow pattern in the tanks drastically and in a very short space of time. If the water flow in a tank is stopped, fish death due to asphyxiation can occur on a large scale within a matter of minutes.

Selection at the Bibury trout farm

The particular site described here was also prone to heavy flooding, which necessitated the building up of the tank sides above flood level. Flooding can cause a lot of damage to the site as a whole, reducing its operational life.

As far as disease is concerned, the most crucial factor lies in attaining a workable balance between stocking levels and the amount of water available. High stocking levels in combination with low water flow would probably lead to some disease problem, as these two factors will produce ideal circumstances for outbreak and transmission of the common diseases to which fish are prone. The reason for this is that many of the agents of commoner fish diseases are present in every normal water course. In most cases it is not possible to escape the dilemma, as an understocked farm is financially not viable. As with other types of farming there are various notifiable diseases, which in many cases are treated in the same way as those which occur in other farm animals (slaughter, transportation controls etc).

A fish farm requires the presence of somebody with knowledge of the farm, twenty four hours a day, every day. Day to day running of the farm involves manual feeding four times daily with a pelleted diet, specially formulated for trout and graded in sizes according to the size of fish being fed. The fish are sampled at regular intervals to monitor growth patterns. The amount of food being fed is adjusted according to the size of fish, to the total weight of fish in the tank and to the water temperature.

When the fish reach a manageable size (about three ounces) they are graded by hand using a grading table, and separated for growing-on and finishing. This means that every trout on the farm will have been counted, graded and transported at least three times before leaving the site, which indicates how labour intensive fish farming is.

The rainbow trout (the battery hen of the fish world) is bred and produced in countless thousands in fish farms up and down the land. There are few fisheries left (still waters or otherwise) which operate without artificial stocking and the type of fish that is bought depends on the various stocking policies. Some managers stock yearly with thousands of fry, having calculated on their probable survival rate; most, however, take on the expense of stocking with sizeable fish. One syndicate at least allows half a dozen 'lollipops' (fish of three pounds or more) to be planted in difficult and unlikely places to keep the members fishing those rather than the obvious pools.

Although fish farming is one of the most precarious of occupations (so much so that insurance companies very often will not take on the risk) it can be financially rewarding, and fish farmers have that inner warmth which comes of providing satisfaction to both anglers and diners.

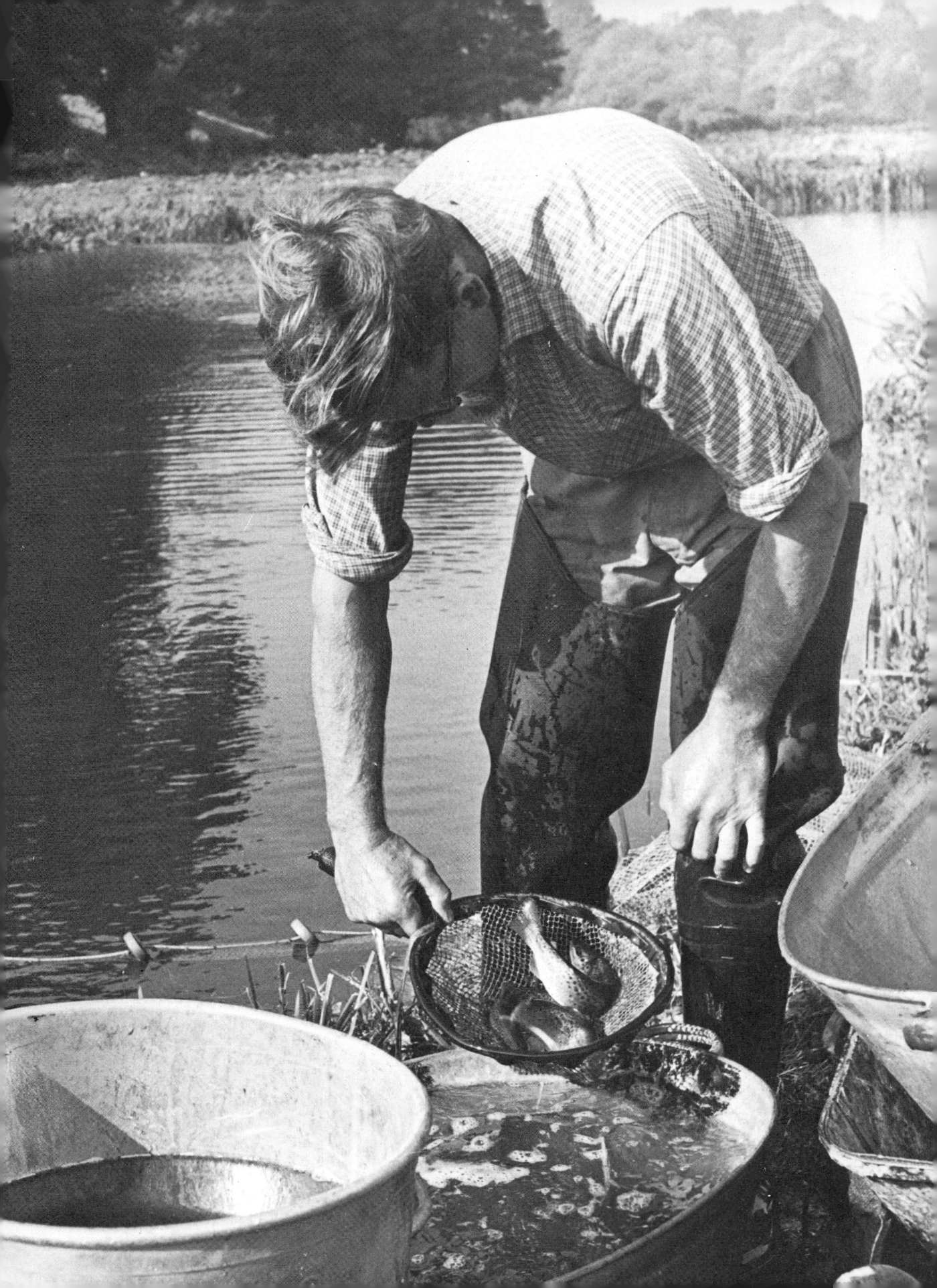

CHALK STREAM MECHANICS

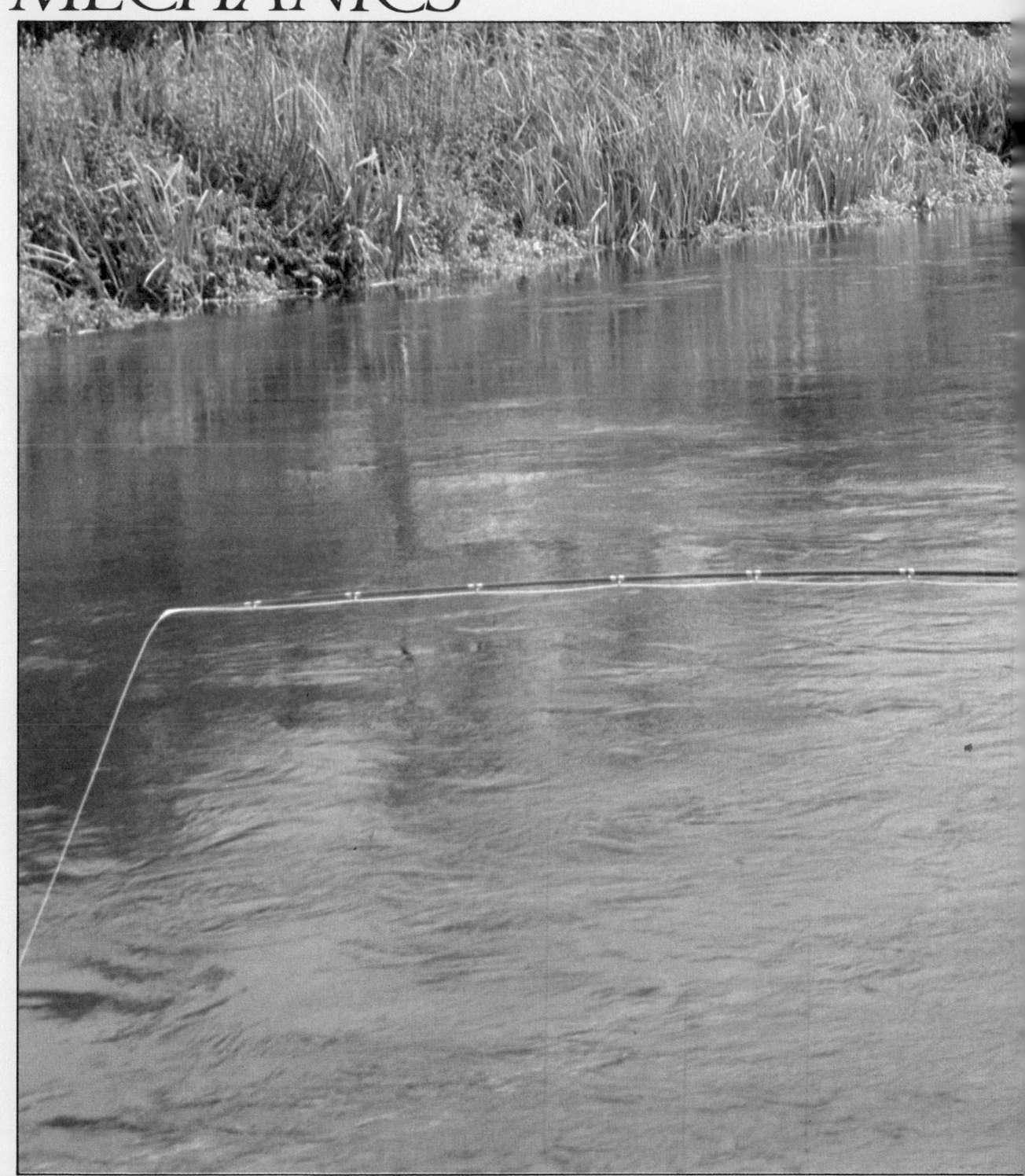

Gordon Mackie dry fly fishing on the Itchen

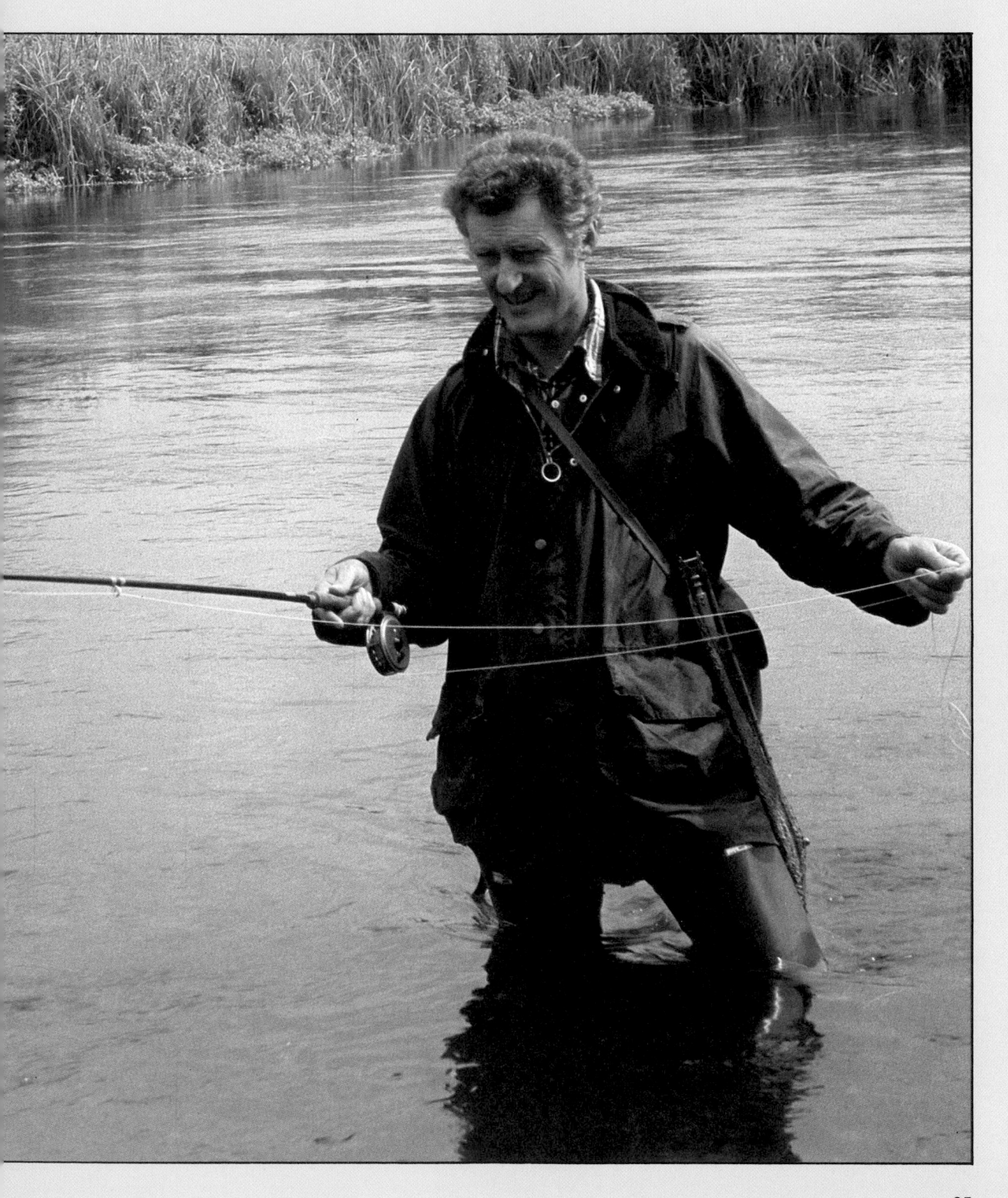

Beauty on a chalk stream

BENEATH the chalk downlands of central southern England an area of water exists which may be likened to a vast underground reservoir. This is the Aquifer. Chalk is porous by nature, so that the hills act like giant sponges, absorbing rain water rather than allowing the surface run-off and evaporation, which occurs in areas of different geological make up. Here, rain water soaks into the dense chalk deposit, whose surface lies beneath a very shallow layer of earth. As it filters gradually through the chalk, the water is cleansed of all impurities, taking on a crystal clear quality.

The surface of this reservoir is called the water table. It is not flat, as the surface of a lake would be, but is dome shaped, following roughly the contour of the hill in which it lies. The overall level of the water table varies according to the rain water totals.

Early each year the springs 'break', beginning to flow from the Aquifer into the stream in February or March. The quantity of water which issues from the springs during the trout season will depend upon the height of the water table, so that after a long period of dry weather, such as that in 1975 and 1976, flows of spring water are reduced, or may cease altogether.

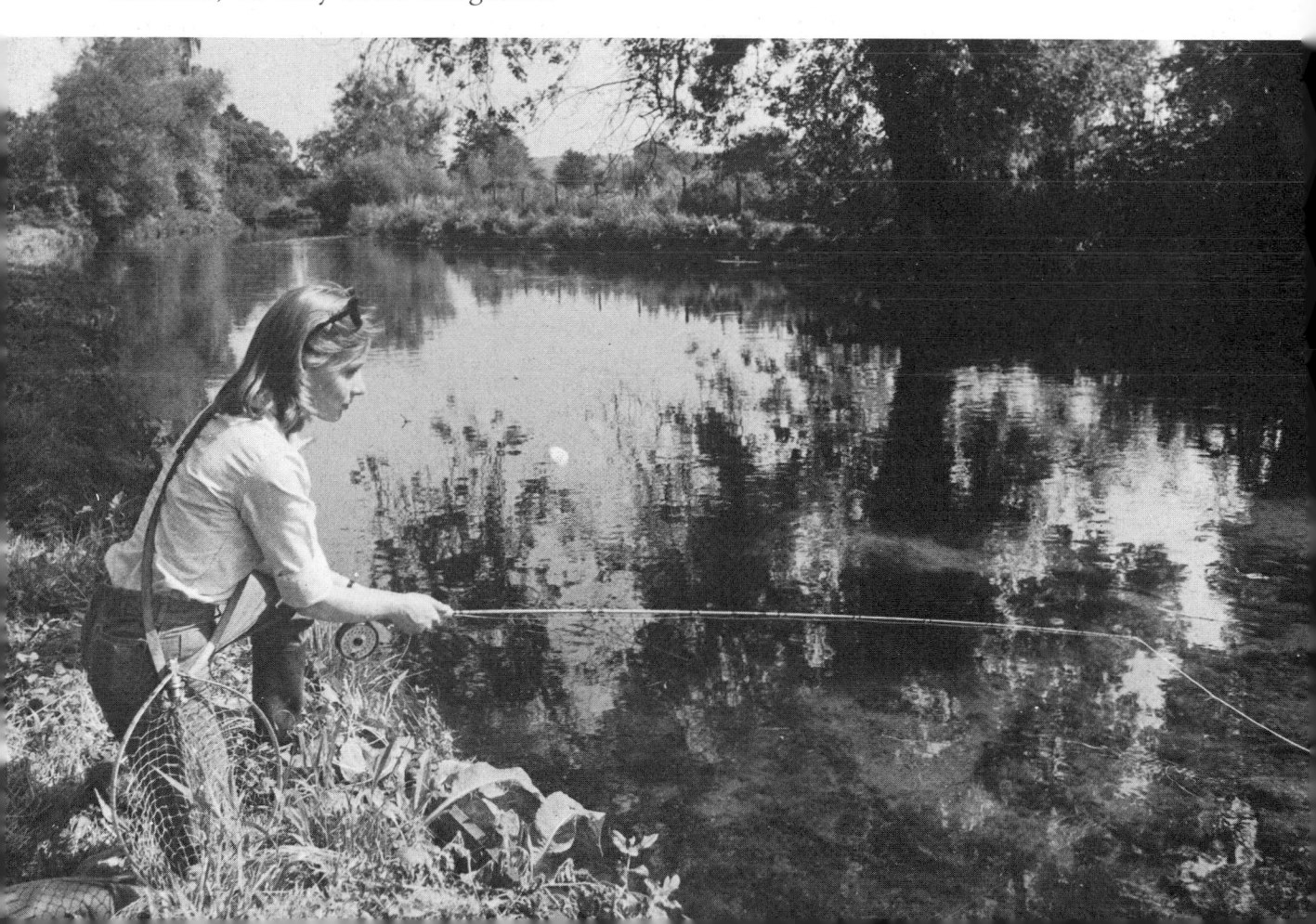

Upper Itchen. The surge of water

As the water table is lowered, the upper reaches of chalk streams, and particularly the winterbournes, small tributary streams whose source is up on the downland itself, are the first to become affected. Since they then lie above the water table, at least in part, these areas become dry in summer. If the water table is especially low, either because of lack of rainfall, or because the downland for any reason absorbs a lesser quantity of moisture (there is some evidence to suggest that modern ploughing methods, or possibly some 'collapse' of the land's crust, may allow less absorbtion and cause more surface run-off), or if water abstraction is creating an artificially low water table, the middle reaches, even the lower reaches, can also become dry.

It might be imagined that where heavy bore hole abstraction occurs, the whole water table would fall and result in reduced river flows. This is apparently not the case. It is 'dented' as it were, but only in the immediate area of the bore hole. Water authority engineers call this dent the 'cone of depression' and elsewhere the water table will remain at its natural level. It is therefore clearly vital that each bore hole should be sited with the utmost care, for chalk streams in this area are becoming noticeably shallower and slower flowing, and head waters appear to be drying up more and more. These treasured rivers must not be allowed to die.

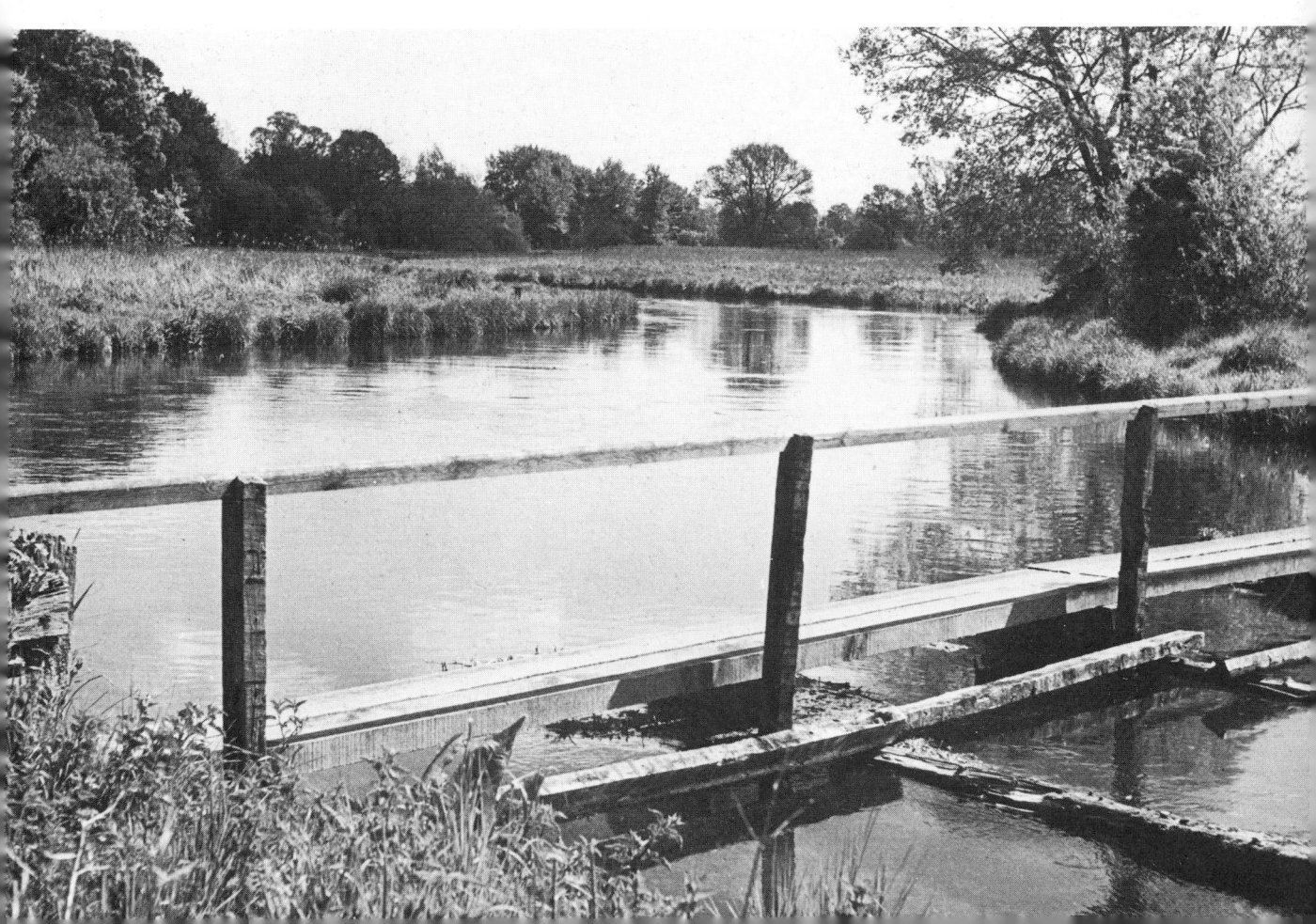

KEEPERING AND RIVER MAINTENANCE

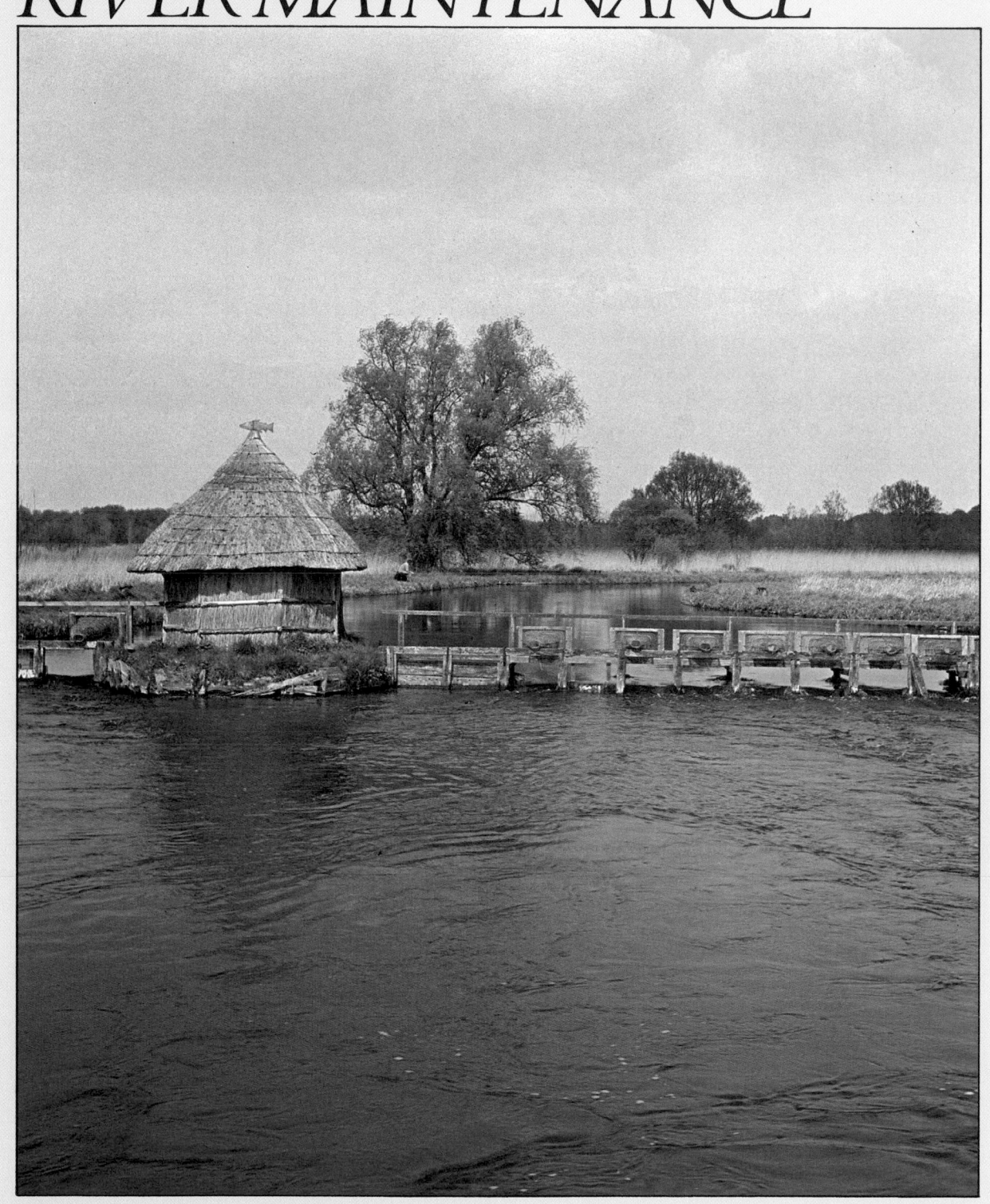

A chalk stream in prime condition has a gin clear flow of water which runs over the chalk and gravel river beds and is filtered constantly through the luxurious growth of weed. The clarity however must be assisted by man. There will be areas in which mud will accumulate naturally; that is due to certain types of weed growth and a locally decreased or insufficient rate of flow. The art of weed cutting cannot be overstressed and must be worked at selectively. Weed is indispensable because it provides food and shelter for the fish and helps to maintain, as necessary, a satisfactory depth of water.

There are, however, good and bad weeds. The former such as ranunculus and water celery, enjoy rooting in shallow gravel or chalk beds whilst bad weeds, like starwort and marestail, collect around them banks and mounds of mud which, if not attacked, will systematically build up. Mud completely alters the flow and course of a river – it is undesirable and also a difficult enemy to be rid of completely.

The art of cutting weed, therefore, lies in the trimming of the good weed and the selective removal of the bad mud holding weed, thereby allowing the water to flow freely and keep the river clear, unrestricted and in fine condition. The water will do the work itself if given help.

Certain weeds are better than others for holding food and all forms of subaqua life upon which the fish may feed. Even mud is not wholly without its advantages. It too does hold food such as the mayfly larvae.

The flow rate of the main Hampshire rivers is controlled throughout the entire length of each water by a series of hatches which may be raised or lowered as necessary, and also by weed cutting. In addition there are at certain places flood hatches for use in case of emergency.

During the normal heavy rains of winter and early spring, care must be taken to avoid flooding; however, no serious damage occurs in these valleys since, owing to the location of the flood hatches, floods rarely spread to dwellings. A bad side effect of flooding is that artificial manure from farmland is washed into the river, and this can nourish the weed growth, often to great and unwelcome effect.

During the fishing season (normally 3 April – 31 October) after rain, the waters may rise and become coloured. This condition normally clears within a matter of hours depending, of course, on the severity of the storms. One of the great attributes of a chalk stream is that it does not come into real spate due to the sponge effect of the ground; there is a very limited volume of 'run-off' water.

The Test and Itchen Fishing Association Ltd and the Hampshire River Keepers Association lay down specific weed cutting dates for the rivers Test and Itchen. It is only during these dates that the weed may be cut. Fishermen, therefore, know well in advance of the season what to expect. It may be of interest to note that many fishermen can enjoy a day during weed cutting, despite the 'rafts' of cut weed from upstream

Top man at work. Mick Lunn on the Itchen

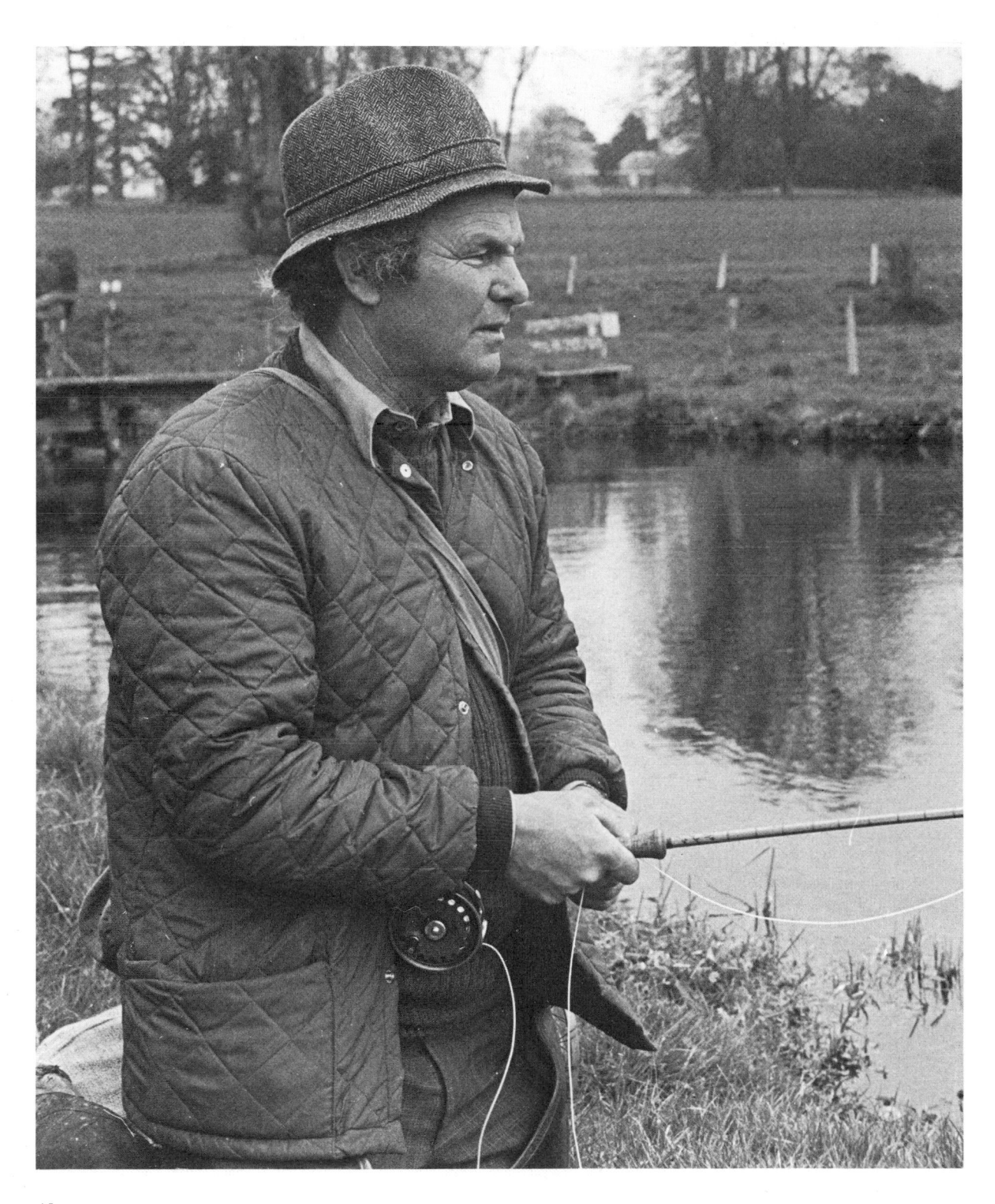

which make casting extremely difficult. As they float downstream they carry with them on the underside a 'running buffet' of especially good food which the fish follow keenly. A fisherman's dry fly will add to this menu, if cast to land alongside a raft of caught-up weed, and often a fish will dart out from underneath for a positive take. The difficulty, of course, when fishing in such conditions, lies in the danger of being 'weeded' when the fish in its fight will head straight into the weed either to become stuck there, with the enmeshed cast, or even exert such strain that the cast will break.

The banks of all rivers require particular attention in order to ensure that water voles and the water itself do not damage the structure. Flooding of banks is highly detrimental and can weaken them quickly. A systematic maintenance scheme is, therefore, a prerequisite on all waters, as is the control of watercress, weeds and overhanging vegetation.

Each river varies regarding the amount of maintenance required, but in general a good flow of fresh, clear water, over a gravel and/or chalk bed, adequately covered with a controlled, selected weed growth capable of providing cover for the fish, with a wholesome food supply, and secured on either side by well maintained banks with a fringe of natural vegetation to a height of two to three feet, provides a specification for the perfect chalk stream.

Many of the beats on the Itchen and Test with their tributaries fall within such high standards. It is, however, only fair to say that Nature also has her way which man cannot always, and sometimes never will, adjust or alter. That is what makes the work and responsibilities of the chalk stream river keeper so arduous and demanding – particularly when, in addition, he is likely to have to run a hatchery for the stocking of his water.

Without disrespect to the salmon gillies (who normally have a built in dislike of bank maintenance) the trout stream keepers have a far harder, more continuous and more responsible job.

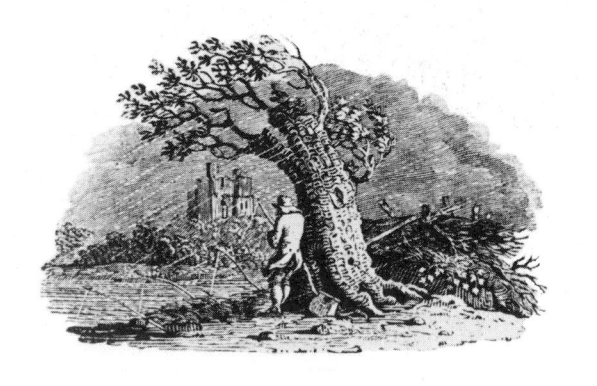

A SHORT GUIDE FOR
THE CHALK STREAM TYRO

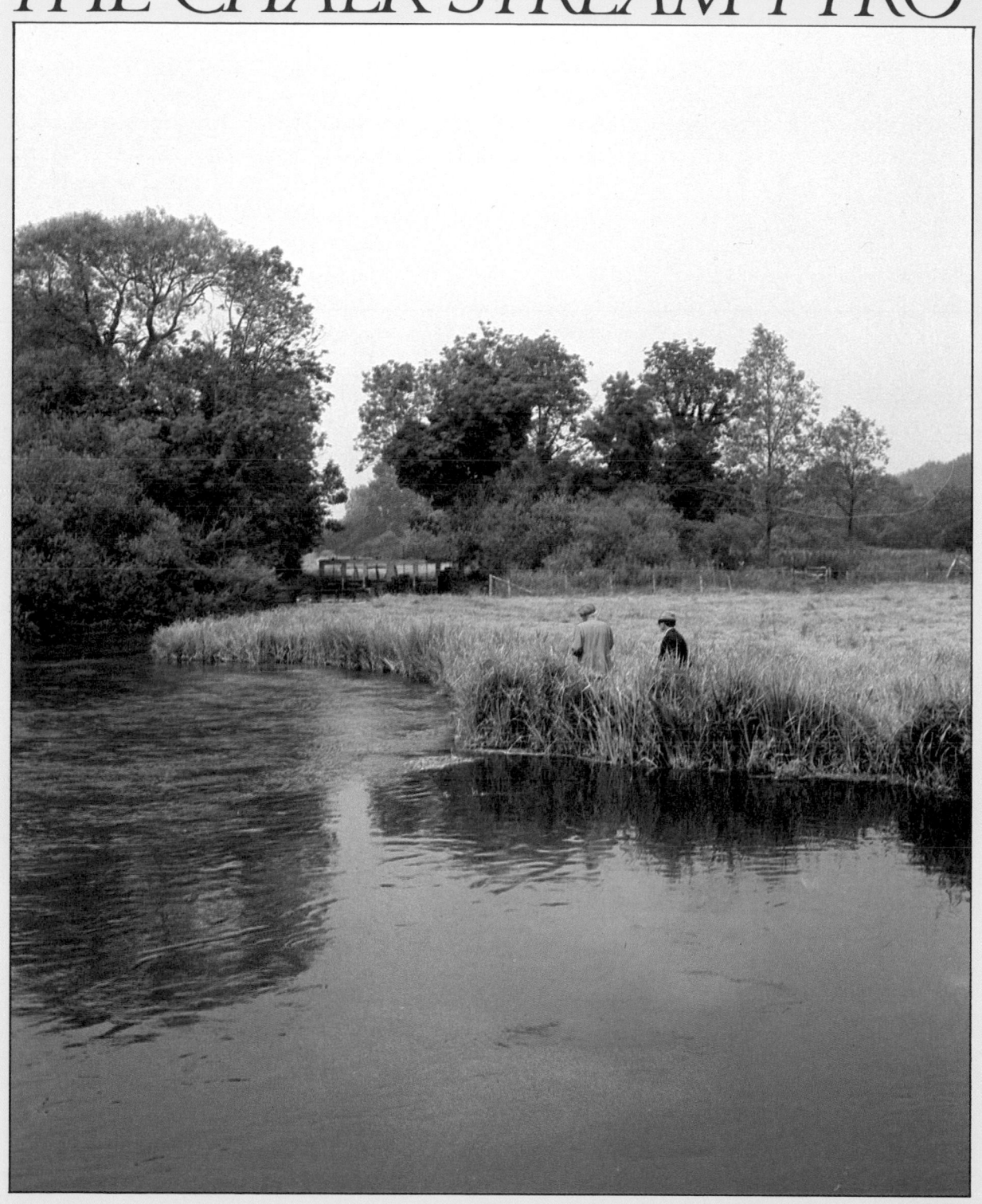

GILLIES are unusual in Hampshire and so a majority of fishermen have to stalk the fish for themselves; this stalking is the key to success. The dry fly chalk stream technique is totally different from any other kind of fly fishing and a strict code of etiquette is observed.

Let us take a typical fishing day. The fisherman, or rod, arrives on the water in, shall we say, mid July; the keeper greets him and shows him his beat for the day's fishing. The keeper will usually point out one or two fish to whet the appetite and may advise the rod on the flies that have been hatching on the previous day. He then departs to carry out his own day's duties. From now on the rod is on his own.

Golden rule number one is to walk downstream to the bottom of the beat, making sure that he keeps as far away from the river as possible so as not to disturb the fish. With the clear water, the need for care cannot be over emphasised. The fly should be starting to hatch off from roughly 11 o'clock onwards and from then on the fish should start to rise. This is where the great stalk begins and therefore spotting the quarry is essential; a good pair of polaroid spectacles is a great help. The rod walks up the bank as invisibly as possible, making use of all natural cover and finally spots a fish rising upstream of him in front of a large bed of ranunculus weed; the fish is rising to flies on the surface, and is positioned halfway across the river. The approach should be quiet and slow, and the rod should find a suitable position from which to cast, at least ten yards below the fish.

The fisherman now has to use his skill in selecting the correct fly from his box, matching, if possible, the hatch of natural fly. The appropriate amount of line is stripped from the reel whilst making false casts and the fly should be presented two feet upstream of the fish, landing, it is hoped, like thistledown. The fly must drift down naturally without any drag otherwise the fish will not accept it; even then he often may totally disregard it. The fisherman must cast again and again, giving the fish a series of opportunities to feed.

Golden rule number two: don't give up before changing to another fly. Keep showing the fly to the fish, providing of course you have not put the fish off the feed – in fishing terms 'put it down'. Let us be optimistic and say that after changing the fly twice the fish rises to it. He will gently lift his nose out of the water, simultaneously opening his mouth, and suck the fly down. A magic moment.

Golden rule number three: on no account strike too quickly; try to suppress your excitement and let the fish be on his downward movement before setting the hook. Nor must you give a sharp strike lest you break the fine cast and leave the fly in the fish; just raise the rod firmly and positively thus setting the hook. Play the fish with the rod as upright as possible and let the fish take line in the initial stages of the fight; because of the luxurious growth of weed and other obstacles, you will have to take control of the fight as soon as possible and bring the fish to the net.

One always hopes that all continues as easily for our fisherman, but many factors can hinder success; the day wears on and the daytime rise will generally be over by 2 pm at that time of year. The wise fisherman will take his lunch and allow himself a rest before the evening rise starts. If however the bag by this time of day is empty, the fisherman can still use his skill with a nymph fished in exactly the same manner except that he will have to spot the fish in his lie and cast the nymph well upstream of the fish; he must then watch, like a hawk, either the fish for any aggressive movement or the tip of the line for any tell tale signs showing that the fish has taken the nymph.

The evening rise in July usually starts in earnest around 7.30 – 8 pm and it is at this time that the fisherman must remember where (during his wanderings) he has seen good fish during the day and marked them, because he will be casting to rising fish only and part of the skill in evening fishing is to decide which are the larger fish. At this time of year, the Sherry Spinner is the most widely used fly, as the blue winged olive is hatching off in profusion; even so one must remember that blue winged olive duns may also hatch off in the evening, so that the fish get the option of duns and spinners at virtually the same time.

Final words about evening fishing. Towards the end of the spinnerfall, sedges will be on the water so fishing can continue well into darkness or as long as the fish are feeding. The fisherman may be weary by now, but the keeper probably will have visited the rod to make sure all is well with a word or two of encouragement.

All fish killed must be entered in the register with a description of flies and conditions. The end of the day is peaceful, and the fisherman should leave the river bank to the barn owls hunting for their supper, with a feeling of satisfaction and contentment.

FLIES ESSENTIAL TO EVERY DRY FLY MAN'S BOX			
DUNS		SPINNERS	
APRIL	JULY	APRIL	JULY
Gold Ribbed Hare's Ear	Pheasant Tail	Lunn's Particular	Yellow Boy
Large Dark Olive	Tups	Houghton Ruby	Sherry Spinner
Greenwell	BWO		
Iron Blue	Sedges		
MAY	AUGUST	MAY	AUGUST
Large Dark Olive	BWO	Lunns Particular	Sherry Spinner
Iron Blue	Caperer	Houghton Ruby	
Blue Upright	Sedges	Spent May	
Mayfly	Black Gnat		
JUNE	SEPTEMBER	JUNE	SEPTEMBER
Pale Watery	Iron Blue	Lunn's Yellow Boy	Lunn's Particular
Medium Olive	Large Dark Olive		Red Spinner
Tups	Pheasant Tail		
Blue Dun	BWO		

TROUT FOR THE TABLE

TROUT, once killed, must be eaten, and eaten as soon as possible and certainly within twenty four hours if they are to be fully appreciated. Frozen trout are not so good; they lose their delicate flavour and texture.

Every trout, brown or rainbow, after cleaning, should be sprinkled lightly with salt. Any blood that lies along the backbone should be cleaned off using salt and cold running water. Remember that every drop of water that comes in contact with the flesh washes away some of the flavour.

Here are a few simple recipes.

1 Pass the fish through milk, roll in breadcrumbs, pan fry in butter and serve either hot or cold.

2 Cook the fish in the oven for twenty minutes with butter and a little oil, covered with grease-proof paper. Turn at least once and pour half a glass of dry white wine over the fish as it comes out of the oven. Eat it as it is or later, cold, with salad.

3 Wipe the fish with absorbent paper. Season well with salt and black pepper. Heat butter and oil in a heavy frying pan and fry the trout on medium to low heat until the skins are brown. Remove the trout from the pan and keep warm. Add almonds to the pan and brown them. Pour almonds and juices over the trout, and serve.

4 Gently heat butter and in it fry chopped button mushrooms, a slice of finely chopped bacon, one tablespoon of mixed herbs and one small chopped onion. Remove from the heat and bind together with one small beaten egg. Season well and put the stuffing in the trout and sew the edges together. Arrange the trout on a greased dish, cook in a medium oven (375°F) for twenty minutes or so. Remove the stitches from the fish before serving.

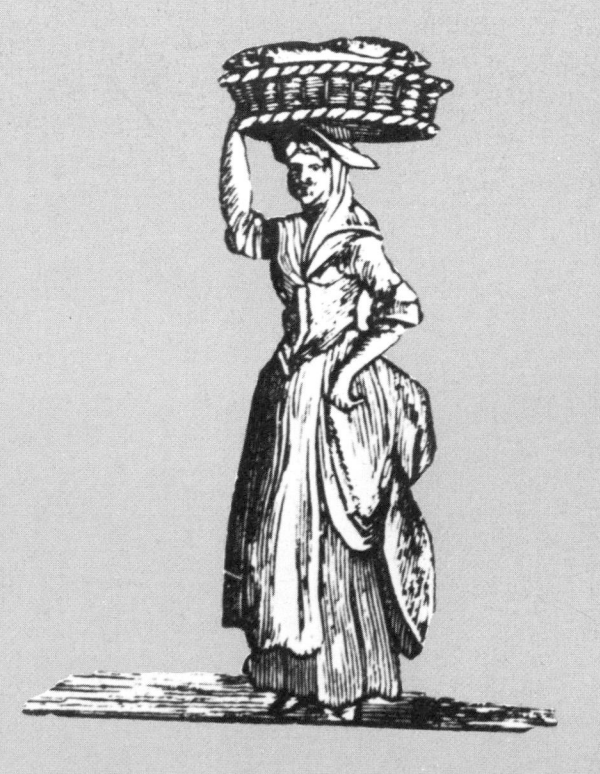

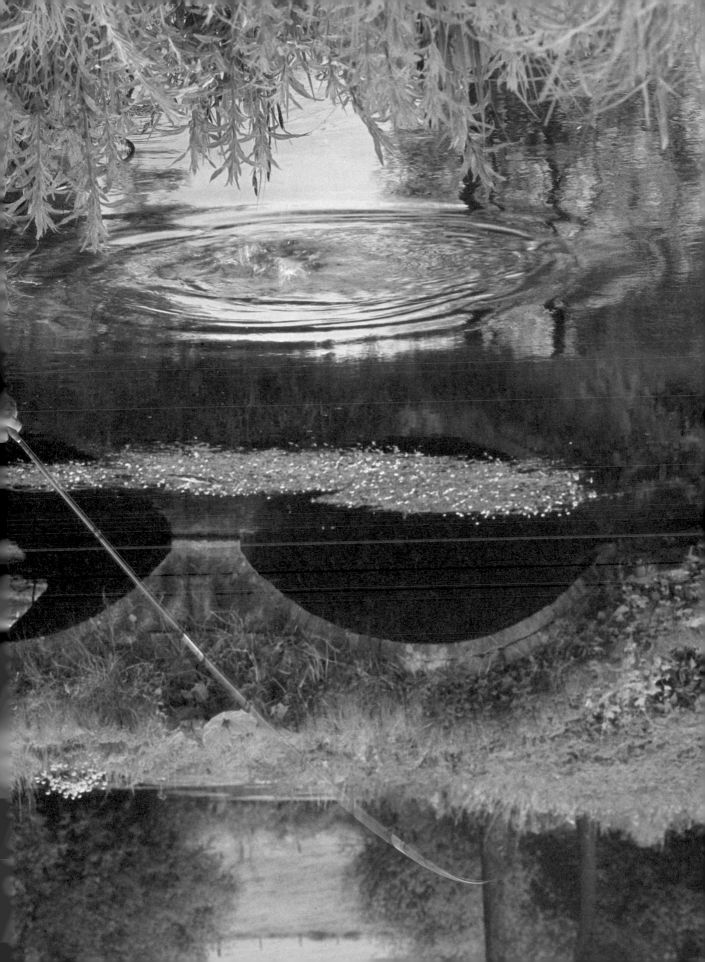

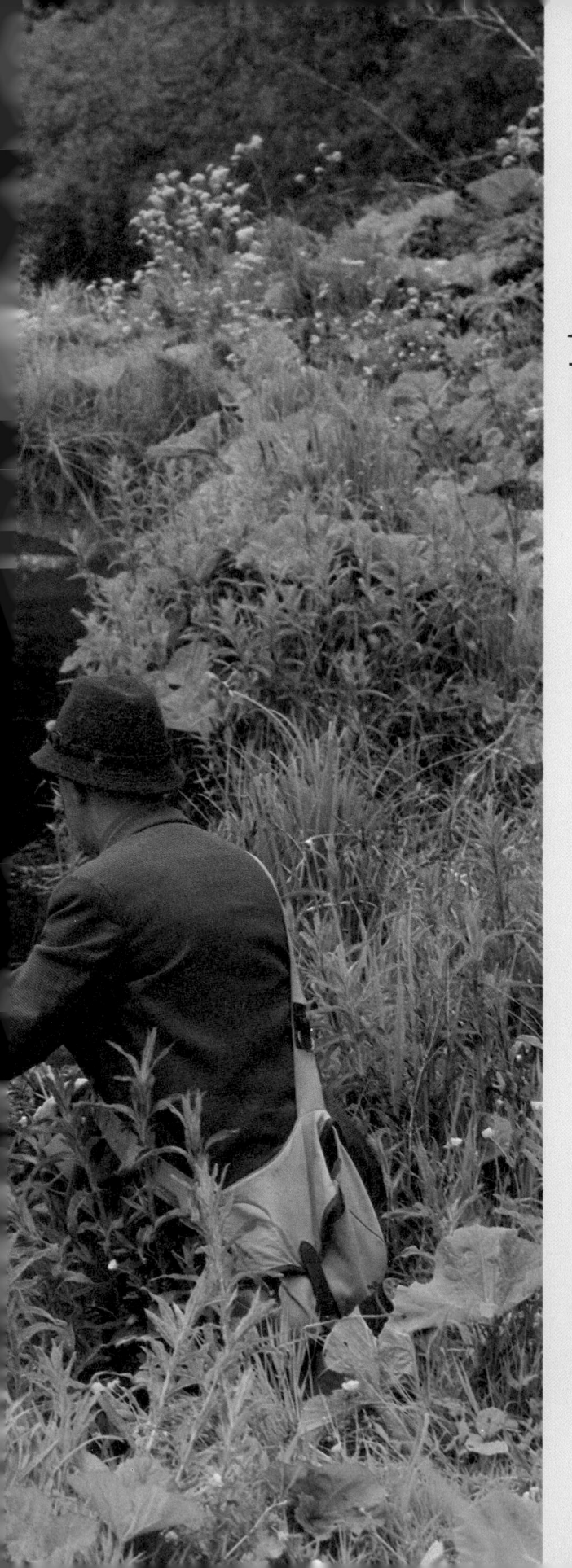

ENGLISH
WATERS

ANGLIAN AND THAMES

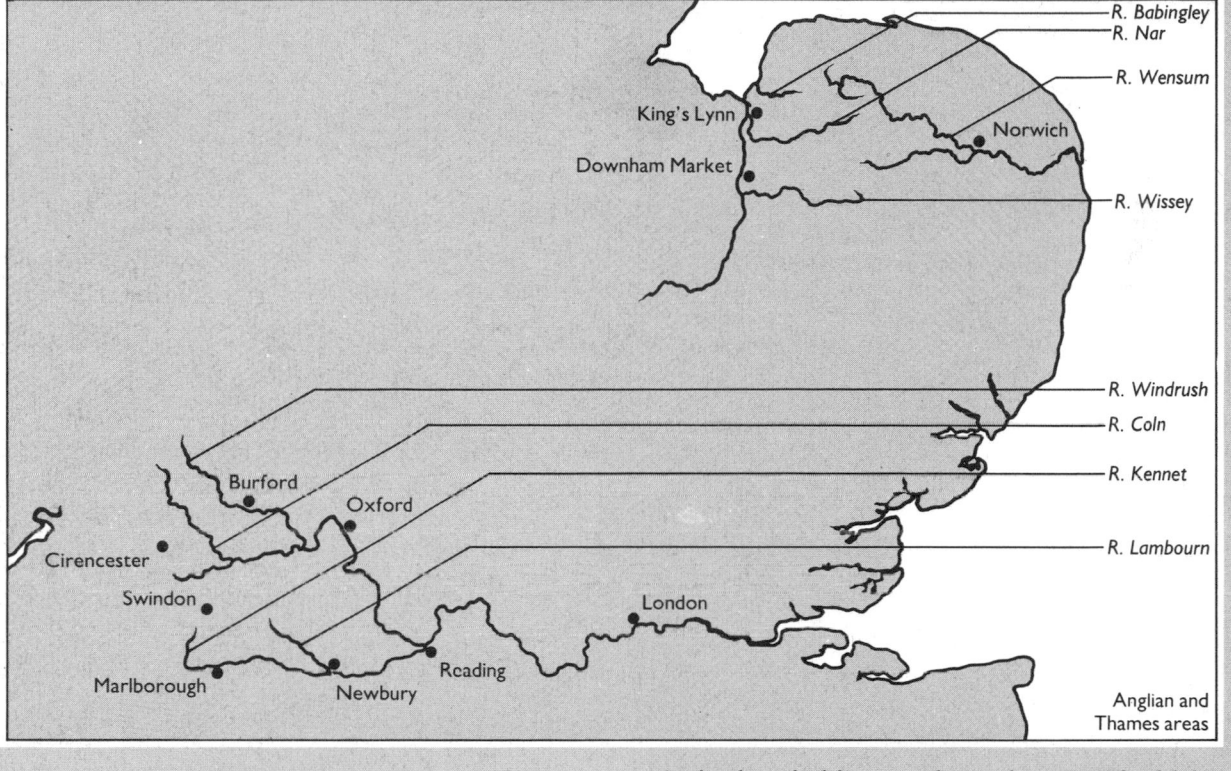

R. Babingley
R. Nar
R. Wensum
R. Wissey
R. Windrush
R. Coln
R. Kennet
R. Lambourn

King's Lynn
Downham Market
Norwich
Burford
Oxford
Cirencester
Swindon
London
Marlborough
Newbury
Reading

Anglian and Thames areas

The Norfolk Rivers

Norfolk is the county that can boast the best selection of trout rivers and streams in East Anglia, though in the main the fishing is not easily available to the public. There are trout in the upper reaches of the Bure, in the smooth flowing Glaven, in the privately stocked miniature River Burn which rises near South Creake, and in the little River Skiffkey (its name made famous by a church tragi-comedy in the thirties) which always seems to me to have potential as a small sea-trout stream. The four rivers that most commend themselves as trout fisheries are the Nar, the Wensum, the Wissey and the Babingley – the latter a river that runs peacefully from its source direct into the Wash south of Heacham.

The Nar This stream rises in the area of East Bilney and flows beneath Peddar's Way near Castle Acre, by which time it has turned itself into a pleasant free flowing clear water trout fishery, complete with attractive little fords and compar-

atively deep holding pools. It skirts Narford lake on the way to Narborough, where it flows under a bridge on the A47, then on a more sedate journey to join the Ouse at King's Lynn. The best of the trout fishing (all private) is above Narborough, but there are trout among the coarse fish between Narborough and King's Lynn – where the King's Lynn Angling Club controls most of the fishing. Just before World War II as I was making my way to the Norfolk Broads I saw the small weirpool leading to the Narborough bridge. Never – then or now – able to resist looking under bridges, I peered under the downstream side and saw the gently waving tail of a pound trout. It would have been twenty years later when I next passed – and peered underneath, and there was the gently waving tail of a pound trout. It was as though time had stood still.

The Wensum The biggest of the Norfolk trout fisheries, and certainly deserving the designation of river, its origins are to be found at Raynham; by the time it reaches Fakenham it has grown considerably in size and continues to grow in flow

Previous page: Early summer on the Lambourn   The Editor fishing the Babingley

and width (with deep and pleasant mill pools) and is a clear and highly attractive river. Trout are to be found all the way to Norwich and there are some preserved stretches that put one in mind of some of the smaller Hampshire rivers. A trout of over nine pounds was caught some years ago at Lemwade, and there are probably bigger fish in a river that is well supplied with delicious dinners for trout in the guise of minnows and even loach. There is a good head of coarse fish throughout nearly the Wensum's length. Many years ago I wrote to Lord Townshend asking for permission to fish near Raynham Hall. I looked it all up in my book on etiquette and wrote a very formal letter that began 'My Lord Marquis'. It was returned two days later with, scrawled across the top, 'Come any time and get a cup of tea if we're in.' My opinion of my betters soared mightily.

The Wissey A nice little trout river, also with a solid coarse fish population that includes some large chub that take a fly with a realistic imitation of sizeable trout. It rises in the North Pickenham area and runs by Hilborough and Bodney, through the Battle area, crossing under the A1065 between Ickburgh and Mundford and from there on to Stoke Ferry and the Ouse, passing first through Didlington Park. East of Ickburgh, where it is joined by its main tributary, is the private Battle area fishery, and from Mundford to Stoke Ferry there is a quantity of good stocked trout fishing in various hands. The private fishing at Didlington Park is particularly good and the trout grow to considerable size there. From Stoke Ferry it is coarse fishing only, though occasional trout are caught. The Wissey holds large trout as I found one day when a friend invited me to fish a hundred yard stretch that flowed through his farm, just above, I stoutly maintain, the Battle area private fishery. I lowered rather than cast a dry fly into a tiny pool underneath overhanging branches, where I had seen a tiny rise. With a sense of grave guilt I landed a few minutes later a silvery black speckled brown trout of exactly three pounds, with which I retired speedily to my friend's farmhouse as though the Norfolk police force was after me.

The Babingley Finally, the lovely little Babingley – the clearest watered stream of them all,

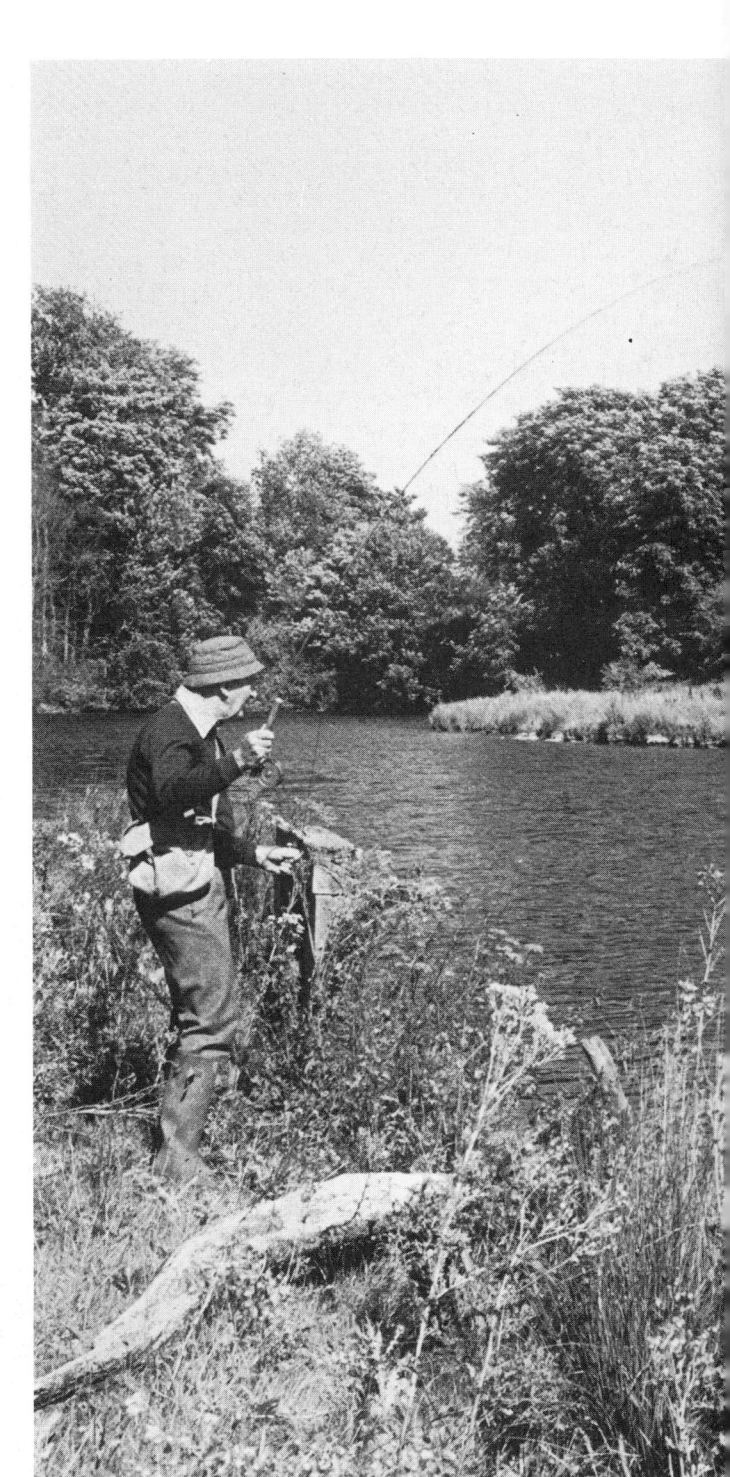

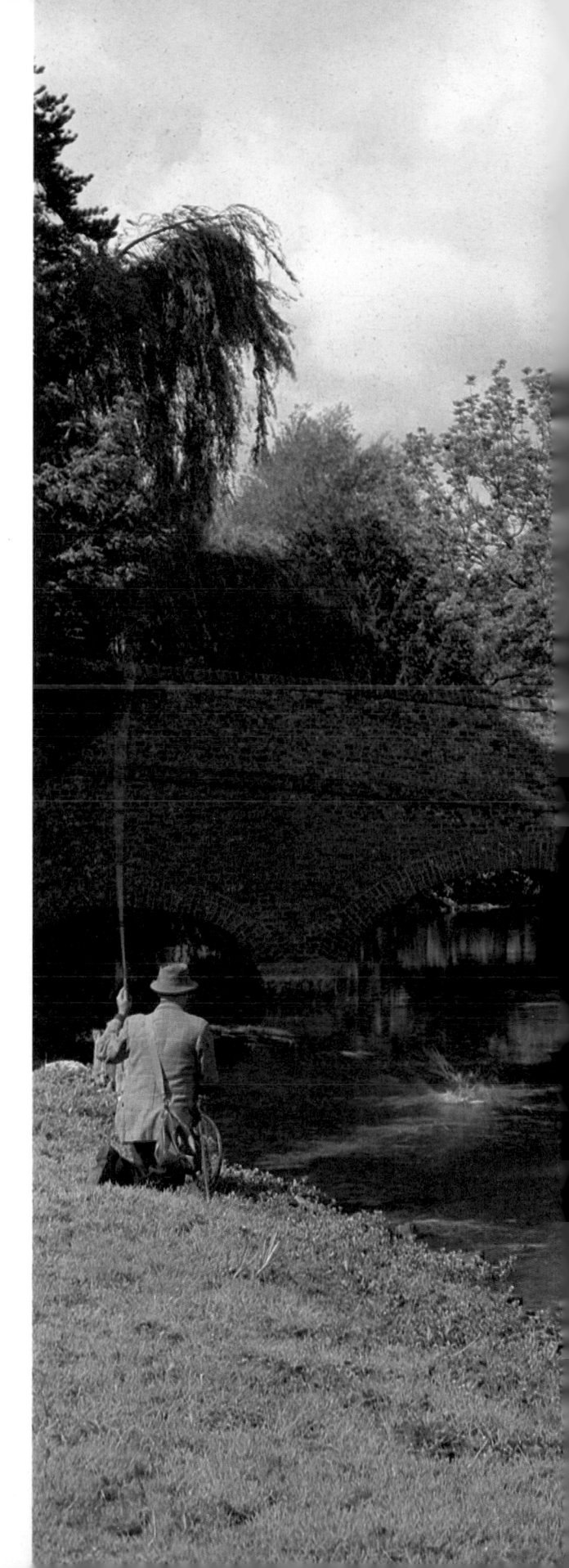

rising in a number of springs east of the B1153 and in the lake at Hillington Hall, babbling gently towards Castle Rising, under the A143, and on to the sea not far west of Wolferton. During much of its course it forms the eastern boundary of the Sandringham Estate. A famous French dry fly fisherman who was given, last summer, a day on the upper Babingley and who could not be dragged away for two, shook his head sadly and said, "There is no stream like this in France: I doubt if there's a better in England."

It is a spring fed stream, more or less impervious to storm and cloudburst, with a bottom that ranges through clay, silt, chalk and gravel. Its waters are mainly clear with a carpet of weed and a wall of cress, but, occasionally (for reasons that no expert has yet explained) it will flow for days with a grey bloom. It rises in the meadows and lows between Hillington and Fakenham. The streamlets unite, then flow into the lake (or Broadwater) in front of Hillington Hall. Here further springs supplement it and with considerably increased volume the river takes off for its five mile journey towards the sea, flowing beneath three of the roads leading to Sandringham and the coast, only hesitating at the series of pools, man made at various times during the last hundred years. Once, under the A1101 (along which the summer processions of cars push their way to Hunstanton) the river flattens out. At this point the trout are joined – for the first time – by coarse fish. It is said that there are places on the sea side of the highway where two pound roach and trout rub shoulders – or fins.

The cream of the fishing is in the top waters. Here the river runs through woods where Nature has never been checked and where the many varieties of birds include kingfishers and woodcock – and through meadows where cowslips and oxslips can still be found in creamy clumps. There is no artificial stocking; prolific breeding still takes place in the gravelly runs or up some of the small clear tributaries. The brightly marked brown trout average ten ounces with very occasional monsters from the bigger pools (or the Broadwater) that threaten the three pound mark.

In the still water the nymph is the most effective lure; in the fast water (where all the fishing is by dry fly, with the Driffield Dun capable of dazzling successes) the anglers must be ready to use breast

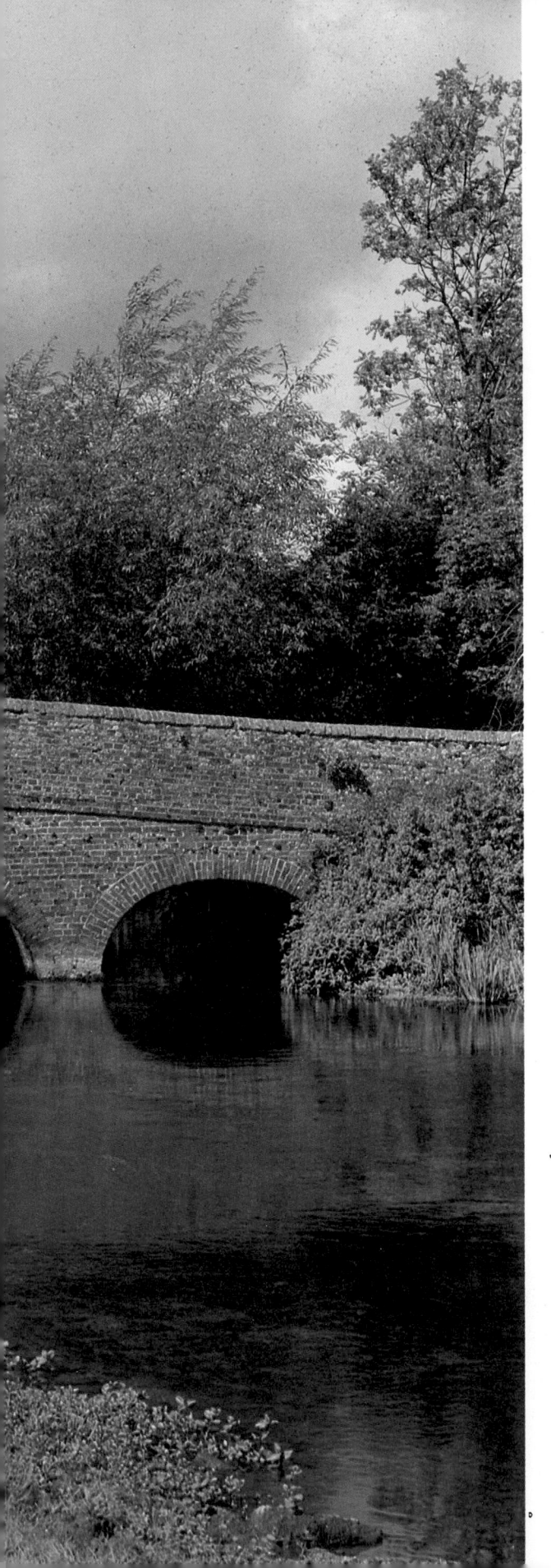

The Kennet near Hungerford

waders, casting delicately under the overhanging branches and between the bankside weed growth. Those used to the bowling green banks of the Test would regard the problems of this fishing with horror – but a really skilled fly fisherman can, particularly on warm August evenings, have some memorable catches.

There is no public water on the upper Babingley. It is all in the hands of syndicates or owner occupiers, but the King's Lynn Angling Club controls a 500 yard stretch below the A1101.

Kennet

This famous river is one of the four major chalk streams in southern England, comparable in size, quality and character to the Avon, Itchen and Test. Over forty miles in length, the Kennet rises on the Marlborough Downs just north of the prehistoric site at Avebury, Wiltshire, and flows in a general easterly direction through the towns of Marlborough, Hungerford and Newbury before joining the Thames at Reading.

During the past century or so, no river in England has produced such numbers of heavy trout, and angling literature holds many an account of exciting Kennet adventures featuring some colossal fish. The largest on record appears to be that taken by Mr Wicks near Reading brewery in 1880 which weighed sixteen pounds fifteen ounces. Mr Stephen Clifford caught a trout of ten pounds two ounces in June 1892, while W M Clifford, in 1920, landed one of eight pounds four ounces. W H Barrett, in his delightful book, *A Fisherman's Methods and Memories*, tells of his seven and a half pound trout, taken on a Mayfly pattern, which the author had spotted while on the towpath leading to Kintbury church. The fish gave him such a fight that Barrett had to go in waist deep in his Sunday best to net him, and he mentions almost as an afterthought that he picked up a trout of three pounds two ounces on the way back to his hotel! Others taken by Mr Barrett on the Kennet include fish of five pounds ten and five pounds eleven ounces.

On the Dun, a tributary stream which joins the Kennet at Hungerford, a Mr Herbert Rumball caught a trout weighing eleven pounds fourteen

Crystal water. The Kennet near Marlborough

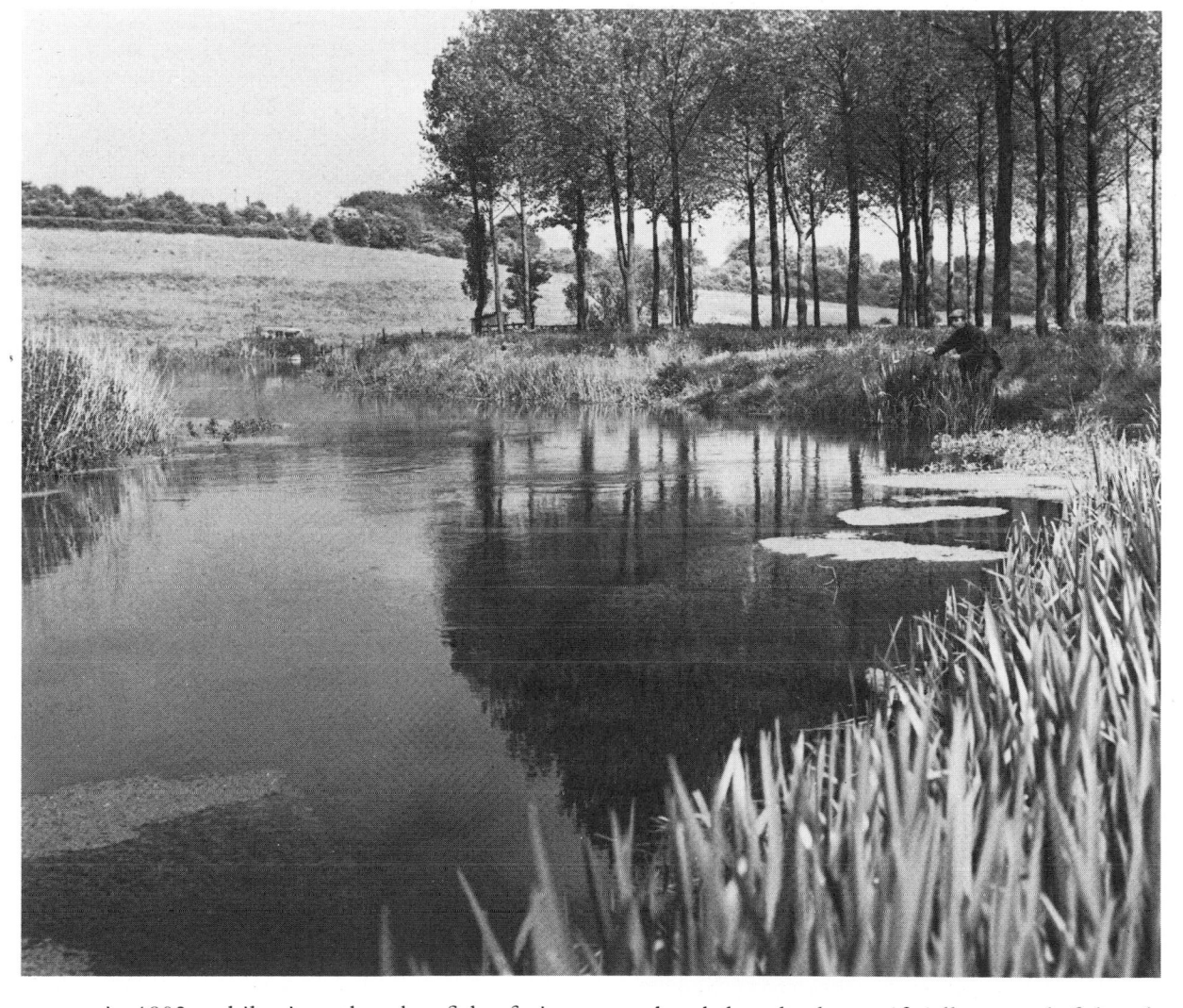

ounces in 1903, while since that date fish of nine pounds twelve, eight pounds fourteen and six pounds twelve ounces have been recorded here, and Dr R H Barker landed a brace which weighed twelve pounds six, each fish scaling six pounds three ounces.

The Kennet is renowned for very heavy hatches of mayfly, the species occurring mostly in the middle and lower reaches. Huge catches are made to this day, but this brief mayfly period is likely to be the angler's best and possibly his only chance, of catching a monster, since outside mayfly time these heavy trout seldom rise. Of course, the native trout of long ago have been replaced largely by artificially reared fish, although I am told that an occasional Kennet 'original' with no brown spots other than a few around the gill covers, has turned up in recent years. I have caught a few myself below Marlborough which have had very few spots, but these can hardly have been of the pure Kennet line, rather a mixture in which traces of the old strain still exist. Even so, Kennet fish are remarkably vigorous, quick growing, and they often cut as red as salmon.

The stretches upstream of Hungerford usually fish very well early in the season. Even during April the trout will feed avidly at the surface, for

Mayfly on the Lambourn

good hatches of large olives often occur at this time. In May, the medium olives and iron blues may come on strongly, but after the mayfly, fishing can be very dull right through the 'dog days', except on some evenings when the fish feed on sedges or blue winged olives. From about the third week of August, however, the trout resume surface feeding during the daytime, and may be seen lying up in the water, pursuing nymphs, or taking small duns when these are present in sufficient numbers. Of artificial flies which are popular on the Kennet, the following selection might be sufficient to see the angler through an average season; Rough Olive, Iron Blue, Mayfly, Black Gnat, Caperer (Sedge), Lunn's Particular and Pheasant Tail as dry flies, and for nymphs the Grey Goose and Pheasant Tail nymph.

Although this majestic river offers such fine trout fishing, it is well known also for the quality of its coarse fishing, especially below Newbury and in the Avon and Kennet Canal, which runs alongside the main river in many places. Dace, roach and chub grow large, while pike are also present in some numbers, and some barbel fishing may be had in the lower Kennet. The best of the trout fishing is privately owned, although some local angling clubs rent stretches around the major towns. The Piscatorial Society has some fishing, and rod letting syndicates exist, whose advertisements may sometimes be seen in such magazines as *Trout and Salmon*. A limited amount of day ticket water is also available.

The Kennet has suffered greatly from the effects of water abstraction, and the upper six miles or so, above and below West Kennet, are no longer fishable. Water levels on classic stretches below Marlborough which I fished in my angling youth are maintained in summer and autumn by closing down hatches, turning millheads into lakes with virtually no flow. Oxygen levels are thus reduced, spawning areas become impacted and covered by silt deposits, undesirable and unsightly water plants become established, and many forms of aquatic life are threatened with extinction.

But the next generation will accept the river as they find it. Our approach and our methods, and the flies we use will change with changing conditions, and if future Kennet anglers enjoy their sport as much as I have, albeit a different kind of sport perhaps, then I for one shall be content.

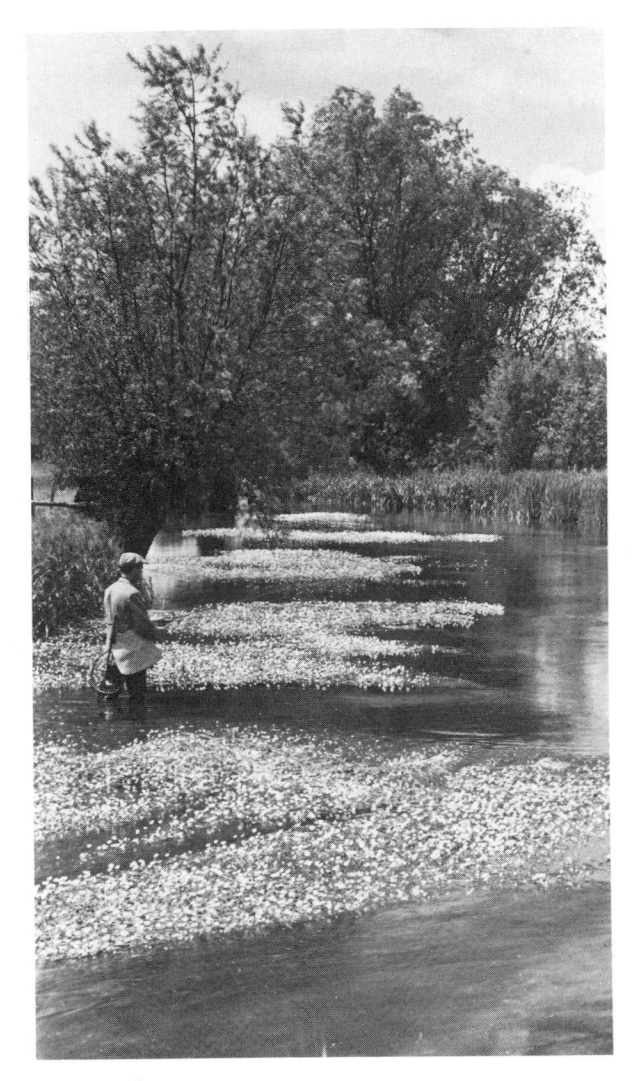

Lambourn

So beautifully does Howard Marshall, in his book *Reflections on a River*,★ paint the picture of this Kennet tributary that any words of mine can hardly do justice to this charming little chalk stream.

Of its history he writes:

Its source is in Lynch Wood near Lambourn where, said Charles Kingsley, "the dead lie looking up to the bright Southern Sun, among huge, black yews upon their knoll of white chalk above the ancient stream".

★ published by Witherby & Co Ltd   53

The strike on the Lambourn

Not far away are the White Horse of Uffington and Wayland's Smithy, where King Alfred used the Blowing Stone to summon his men to battle, and, under the steep shoulder of Sparsholt Down, the Seven Barrows mark the graves of prehistoric chieftains.

It is fitting that we should sometimes remember, perhaps when the trout are not rising, that our Stone Age ancestors stood on the very bank where we now stand, peering like us into the same river, and preparing traps for the fish which must have been an important part of their daily food. It is not difficult to imagine such things when only the water voles, the moor-hens, the dabchicks, the kingfishers, the herons and the swans keep us company, and nothing but the occasional thump of a jet fighter breaking the sound barrier reminds us of the paltry trappings of progress.

All up and down the river there are signs of man's earlier habitation — flint arrowheads, pottery, coins, and, at Bagnor, a dug-out canoe, and at Donnington, the bones of Elephas primigenius *(the mammoth) — all these and many more, show that through the ages there has been a parade of history along the Lambourn valley. Not only have the prehistoric beasts padded through its water meadows, hunted by Stone-Age man, but Cavaliers and Roundheads have fought for dominion over it and the unhappy ghost of Charles I still stumbles to defeat along its banks.*

He continues elsewhere:

Before water abstraction threatened the life of the river, it must have been a stream of perfect proportions. Nowhere was it too deep and sluggish, but throughout its length, when the springs broke in February, it went brimming through the water meadows.

Sadly, the river today bears little resemblance to the Lambourn of old, but to quote Howard Marshall once more:

However much we may try to cling to an outpost of peace in this age of progress and dizzily mounting birthrate, somehow it slips through our fingers. If our resistance is to be beaten down, there is only one answer, which is to enjoy to the utmost the treasures which still remain to us.

The little river provides sport today, between Shefford and Donnington, which can be very good indeed; rare flowers may yet delight the eye

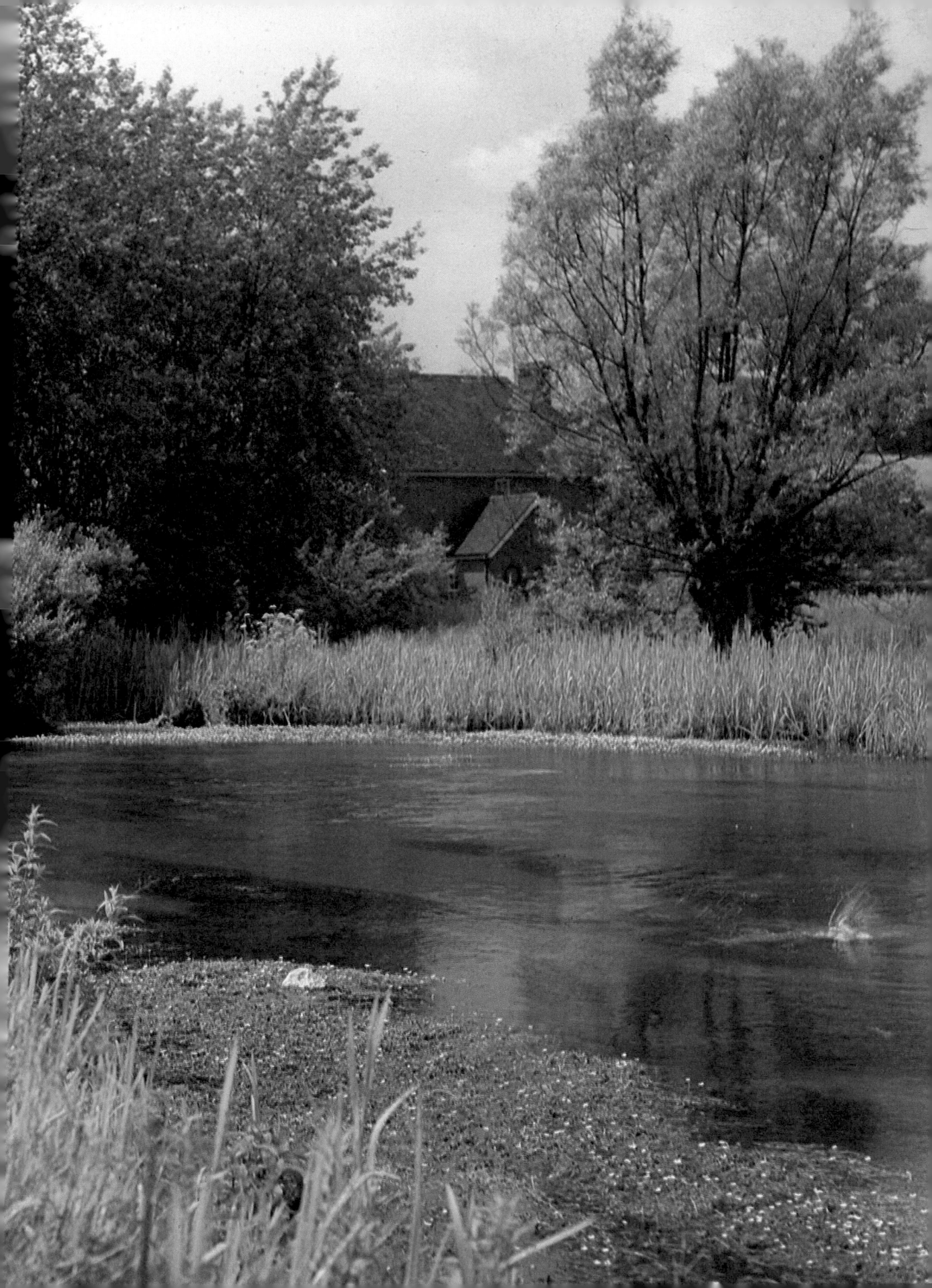

on Bagnor marsh, and the dipper still nods his greeting to you as you pass.

Most species of upwinged fly seen on other chalk streams may be found here, but hatches are not heavy today, and the blue winged olive, upon which we largely depend for evening sport after mid June, has become scarce in recent years. Very considerable hatches of mayfly occur however, which bring on strong rises of trout in early summer. Methods are restricted to dry fly and light-weight nymphs, fished upstream; favourite patterns include Pheasant Tail, Black Gnat and Pheasant Tail nymph, and of course Mayfly.

Little fishing is available to the casual visitor, since most water is private and strictly preserved by owners, some of whom let a rod or two to friends. The Piscatorial Society controls the lower one and a half miles or so, between Donnington and Bagnor, and stocks the water with small brown trout. A good head of native trout exists as well, the average weight of those taken being a little under the pound, with an occasional two pounder. Rainbow trout escape from time to time from a fish farm situated below Bagnor bridge.

The Lambourn is inhabited by trout and grayling. No coarse fish are thought to exist, save the very occasional small pike. The grayling population used to be considerable, but in recent years there has been a marked decline in numbers, leading one to suspect a deterioration in water quality. Grayling will only survive in clean, relatively unpolluted water, and abstraction may be seen as the root cause of disappearing stocks, for any reduction in the volume of pure water will automatically have the effect of increasing the degree of any pollutants which are present. This problem is not limited to the Lambourn.

Windrush

Rising on the Cotswold Hills in Gloucestershire, the Windrush flows in a general south easterly direction through Bourton-on-the-Water, Burford, and Witney, entering the Thames eight miles to the west of Oxford.

This is a most productive limestone river, offering largely mixed fishing in its lower reaches, species present including trout, grayling, pike, chub, roach and dace. It is, however, fished for trout throughout its length, and some fine catches have been made in recent years, including a brown trout of eight pounds, taken by Mr P Mayer in July 1981, which is on display at the Fox Inn at Great Barrington, near Burford. The same angler caught two rainbows in September 1973 which scaled seven pounds fourteen and seven pounds eleven ounces, while a five pound brown trout was landed by Mr Clive Perkins in 1982.

In its upper stretches, the Windrush contains mostly wild trout, although some stocking is carried out. Unlike many other streams whose higher reaches become dry each summer, there is sport to be had right up to Temple Guiting on the Cotswolds, where Temple Guiting Estate owns some good small stream fishing. Syndicates and private owners fish on the stretches from here down to Burford, and a few rods become available from time to time. Some of the best fishing is that owned by the Sherborne Estate and Barrington Park Estate. Clubs which rent waters below Burford include Burford AC, Newlands AC and Cotswolds Fly Fishing Club, and some hotels offer fishing. The grannom sedge fly appears on the Windrush early in the season, and good mayfly hatches occur on some stretches. Iron blues, blue winged olives and black gnats are also plentiful.

A remarkable story, which on local enquiry appears to be quite authentic, is that of the giant Crawley pike, which was dragged ashore by an otter as witnessed by Mr Fred State in 1913. Sadly no scales could be found which would register its enormous weight, but when it was cleaned – for distribution as food among some forty households – a pike of sixteen pounds was discovered inside that colossal fish's stomach.

Coln (Gloucestershire)

If I wished to impress a visiting fisherman from overseas or show a newcomer to the sport just what dry fly and nymph fishing is all about, I would take him to see the Coln at Bibury in Gloucestershire on a sunny day at mayfly time, or indeed at any stage of the season when the stream runs clear. Here, as you walk the riverside pathway or sit on the old stone wall, and you watch

Summer on the Coln

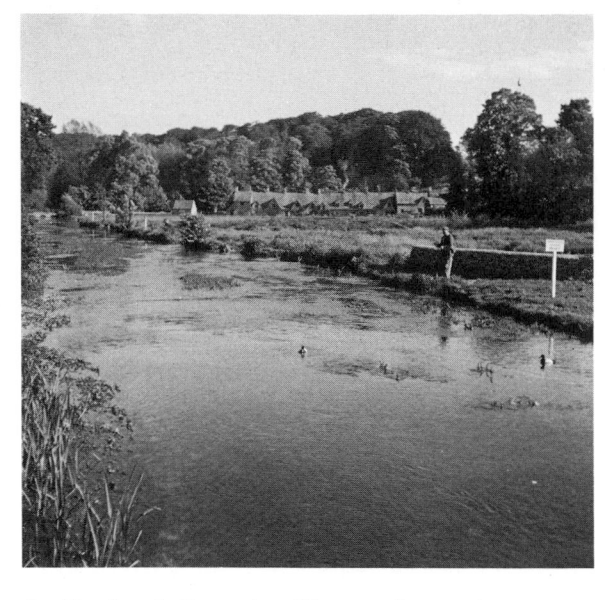

the flies hatch from the silken surface and see every movement of the fat trout as they feed, you feel somehow that you are stepping back into angling history, for this is how this famous river must have looked a century and more ago. The cottages, all built in Cotswold stone, and the beauty of the river with its patches of golden gravel and bright water plants, and the meadows beyond the stream, are evocative of all that was good about old England, and still is, in places. You might even imagine that Francis Francis, Marryatt or Halford, will at any moment emerge and cast their Red Quill or Lock's Fancy to the two pounder hovering in the crystal glide above the brilliant starwort bed.

Today, thousands of tourists visit Bibury each week in summer, all drawn to the river with their cars and coaches, and bread loaves. The crusts are scattered far and wide, and all the fowls of air and water, and the fishes which swim beneath the surface, jostle for each succulent morsel. The trout usually win the battle, for they are swift and aggressive, ever poised with keen anticipation, while the ducks and other birds appear cumbersome and ungainly by comparison. But despite this substantial fare, the trout still rise to small duns and spinners.

The Swan Hotel lets fishing from the far, right bank, and you may almost forget the camera wielding hordes, so absorbing is the sport. The fish are fearless, within reason, for they know all about the human species; indeed they welcome them! Another hotel at Bibury with fishing available for residents in more secluded surroundings is the Bibury Court, while further upstream the water is owned by the Ernest Cook Trust, which lets the fishing to a syndicate of some twelve members, and by Lord Vestey's estate. The remainder of the upper Coln is entirely private, although enquiry at other hotels along the river may prove worthwhile.

Down river at Fairford is the famous old fishing hotel, The Bull, whose one and a half mile length is let by the day to residents and non residents, the latter paying slightly more for their permits. Evening tickets are also available. The limit is two brace of eleven inches or over, and upstream dry fly only may be used. Details of all catches are entered in the hotel record book, which lists the trout which have been taken since 1946 when records began. When I opened this book I was delighted to find that the first entry had been made by a Mr Mackie, possibly my father RW Mackie, although his brother LG Mackie appears to have been a more frequent visitor at that time. Doubtless their father, Rev GE Mackie, vicar of Chedworth, fished here some years prior to this as well as at his favourite Fosse Bridge on the upper Coln, close to his parish. In Fairford the 500 year old St Mary's Church has some of the most remarkable stained glass windows in the country.

Fine stocks of native trout exist in the Coln, for it is a relatively swift flowing stream with good spawning shallows. Some stocking is carried out, however, mostly with fish of under one pound. The average weight of trout taken is about a pound, and some splendid fish have been landed recently, including trout scaling three pounds four and three pounds nine ounces, from the Bull water and Bibury Court respectively. Grayling are numerous in all middle and lower reaches, and a few perch may be found, as well as pike, in the lower stretches towards its confluence with the Thames at Lechlade.

Heavy mayfly hatches occur on many parts of the Coln, the flies appearing about the third week of May, and small upwinged flies and black gnats are plentiful. Favourite patterns include Imperial, Greenwell's Glory, Black Gnat and Pheasant Tail.

THE SOUTH

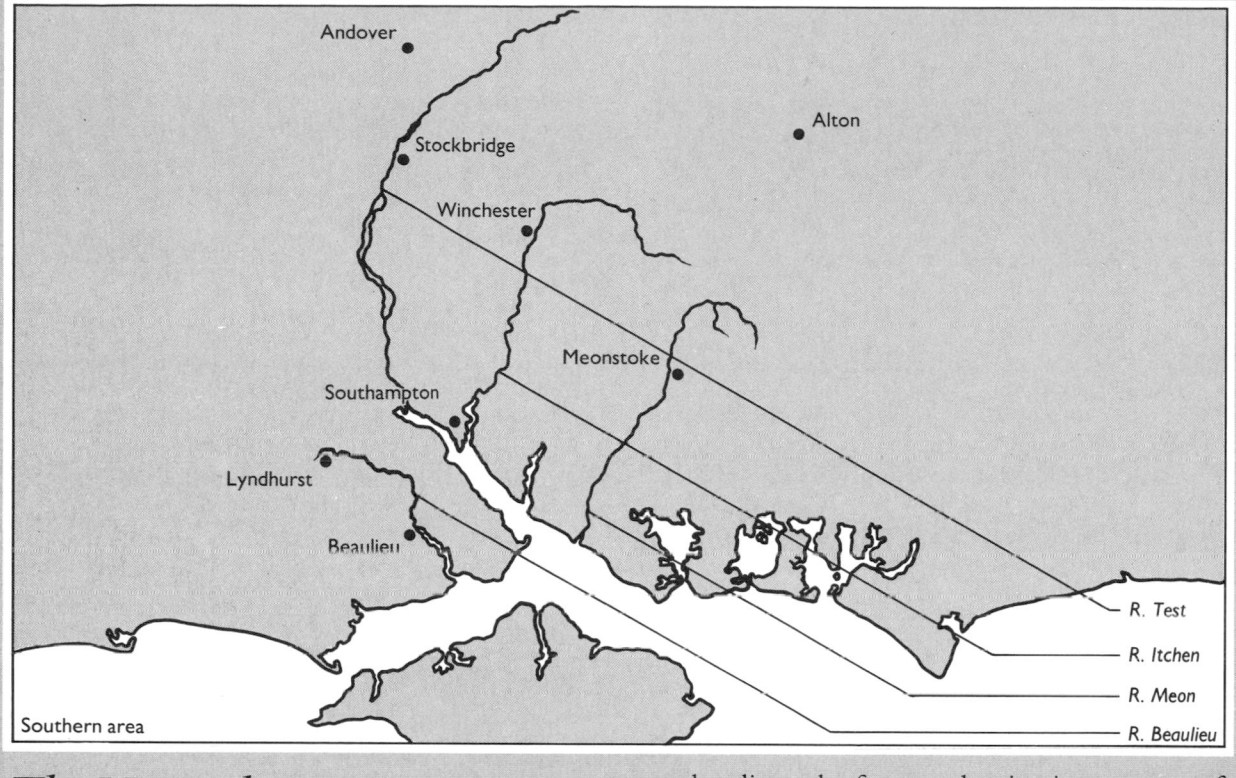

Andover

Alton

Stockbridge

Winchester

Meonstoke

Southampton

Lyndhurst

Beaulieu

Southern area

R. Test
R. Itchen
R. Meon
R. Beaulieu

The Hampshire Rivers

A great trout river is like a garden or the hair of a beautiful woman. It needs constant tending love and care.

Here follows an account of what are perhaps the greatest river gardens of them all.

The main waterways of Hampshire comprise the rivers Itchen, Test, Meon and Beaulieu. The River Avon, so famous in the past as the Hampshire Avon, now, due to the changes in county boundaries, flows through part of Dorset as well; it has been dealt with in another section.

There are tributaries to certain of these rivers and this whole water complex, together with a number of natural and artificial lakes is administered by the Southern Water Authority, with whole time and fully experienced fishery officers and staff, together with a team of water bailiffs. There are also anti-pollution detachments and a laboratory research establishment, all of which are at the disposal of not only riparian owners of specific waters but also of clubs and the general public, should need arise.

There can be no denying that between them the Test and the Itchen provide the finest chalk stream fishing in the world. However, there are many lesser rivers and chalk streams in the area which also provide truly excellent fishing; these should never be overlooked nor rejected, because they too fall into the chalk stream category.

The Test and Itchen Fishing Association Ltd was formed with the object of supporting, preserving, and indeed improving, the excellence of the Test and Itchen, and their tributaries. This association maintains an energetic practical supervisory and advisory service together with a fighting fund in support of its obligations. Riparian owners may, therefore, be assured of a constant working back-up available to them in return for a letter or telephone call to the full time secretary.

The Test and Itchen Fishing Association is always keen to increase its membership list which comprises not only riparian owners but also many individual fishermen, both from home and

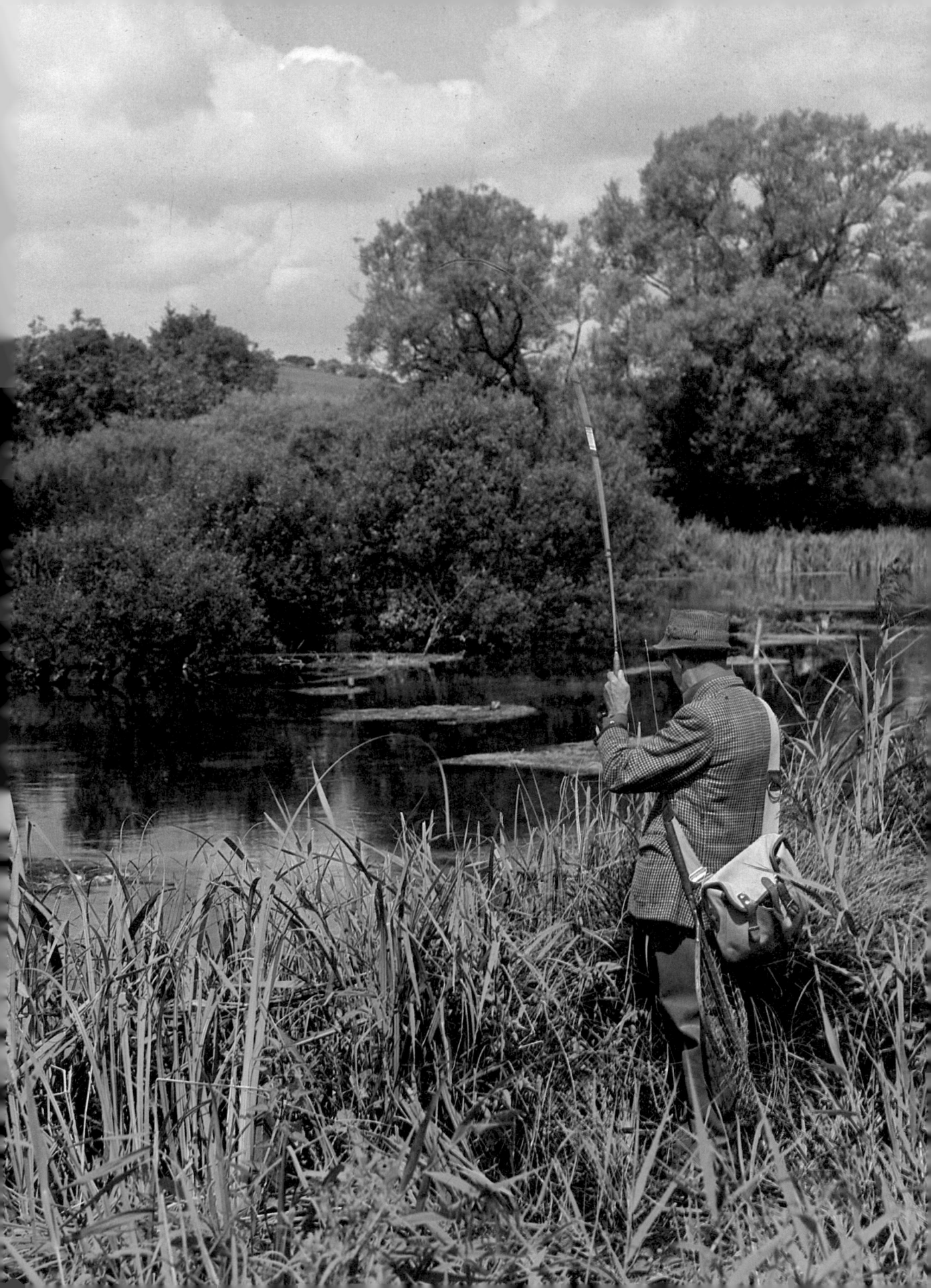

Silvan beauty near Mottisfont

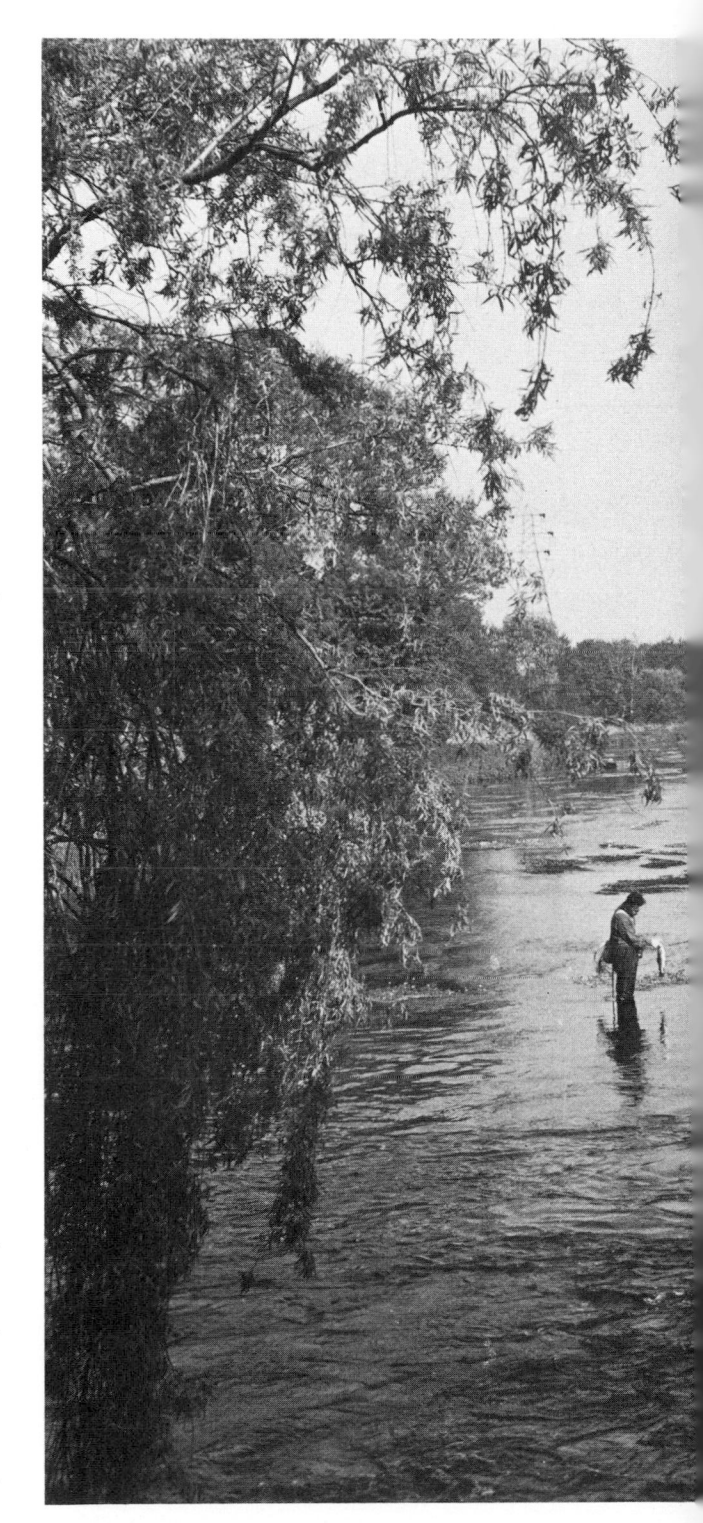

abroad, who enjoy, or have enjoyed, all that these two wonderful rivers have to offer.

In general terms the Test and her tributaries, due to the nature of the water and length of privately owned beats, are almost entirely fully keepered, whereas the Itchen, which is narrower and shorter overall, and the River Meon are adequately maintained by mainly part time keepers.

The keepers form a traditional and highly skilled body of experts to whom much of the credit for the excellence of the rivers and lakes in Hampshire is due.

The Hampshire River Keepers Association is a well organised body which, with the aid of regular meetings, co-ordinates weed cutting and other river maintenance activities together with the offering of sound and very knowledgeable advice, as and when necessary, particularly to the water keepers of the future. The Hampshire College of Agriculture runs (among others) very excellent courses for river keepers; the students have to undergo a period of practical river keepering as part of their initial training.

The results from these courses have been most encouraging and have proved to be of benefit in many parts of the country where newly trained river keepers have been readily accepted, as they have had not only practical experience but have studied the theoretical side as well.

The Test and Itchen Fishing Association, it is stressed, works in close co-operation with the Hampshire River Keepers Association, so there is a careful tie up between all interested parties, particularly in the timing of weed cutting.

Each of the main rivers will be described in some detail but it should be realised that as a general rule most waters are privately owned and looked after by full time or part time keepers, depending on the length and type of the respective stretches.

A stretch or length of water may vary from half a mile to as much as fourteen miles. As a general guide a full time keeper would be required for any length of water of over two miles, particularly if the fish for stocking the water were to be reared on site.

The rivers of Hampshire and their tributaries are jealously guarded and riparian owners take considerable pride in the maintenance and control of

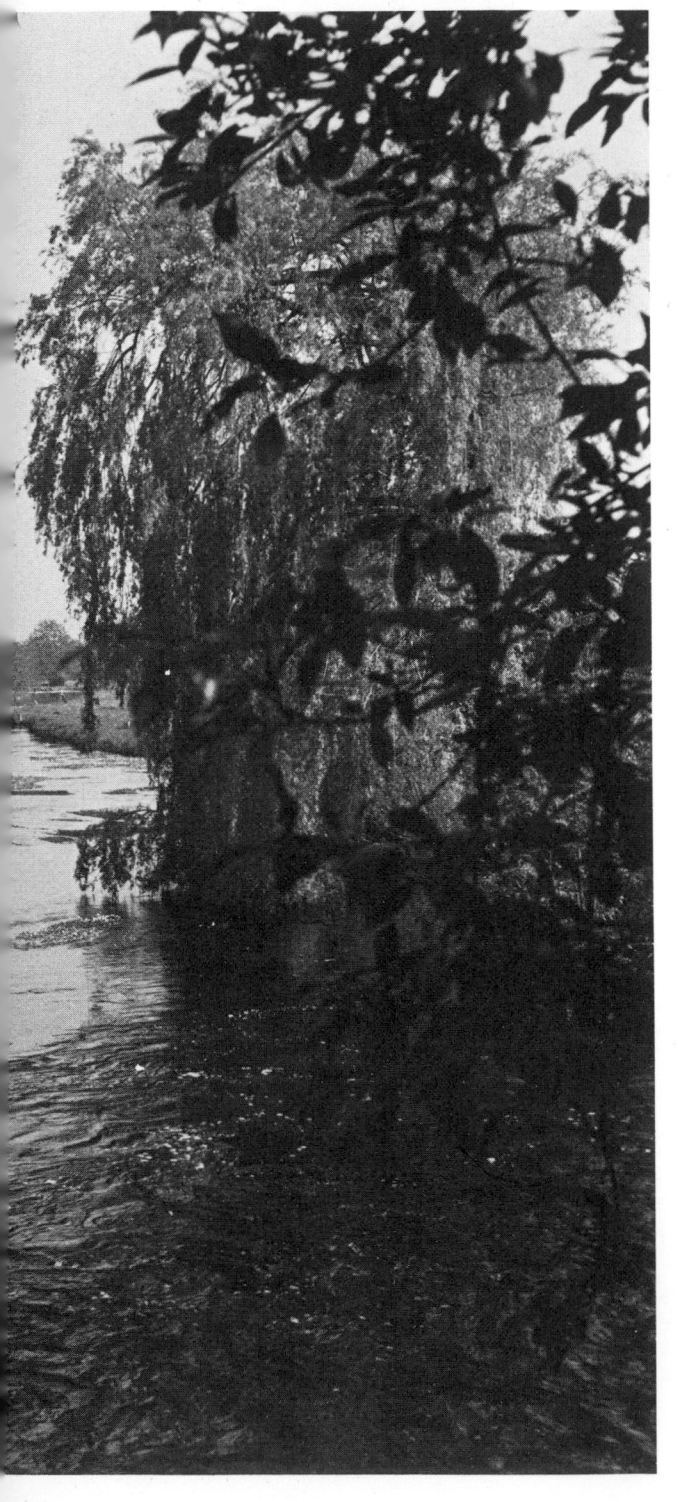

their respective stretches or beats; long stretches are divided into beats; each may be up to half a mile in length, single or double bank, as the case may be.

Fishing on these rivers is either controlled entirely by the riparian owner for his own use and that of his guests, or alternatively, the water may be let to a syndicate or with season, half season or even day permit rods. Where day permits are allowed, reservations are normally handled through an appointed agent.

Test

The Test is regarded as the queen of chalk streams, and not without justification. With her main tributaries, the Bourne (of Plunkett Green's *Where the Bright Waters Meet* fame), the Dever, the Anton and the Dun, she flows in excess of one hundred miles from the source at Deane, near Overton, to Southampton. The flow rate is some 156 million gallons per day, of which 10 million gallons are extracted daily.

The course takes a route through Whitchurch, Longparish, Chilbolton (this section is regarded as the upper Test), then on to Stockbridge, King's Somborne and Romsey (this section is regarded as the middle Test), and finally on to the lower Test flowing through Broadlands, to Testwood and Southampton Water.

The upper Test is generally shallow water from eighteen inches to four feet in depth, with a few deeper pools, usually behind mills, the most famous of these being at Overton, Whitchurch, Longparish and Wherwell.

The upper Test carries a good head of wild brown trout, which is supplemented with locally reared stock fish, mainly brown trout, but including a few stocked rainbows. These have been introduced into the Test for many years but not in such large numbers as the browns, which are always regarded as the prize fish.

The upper Test has some of the most superb shallow water fishing that can be obtained. The fish can be spotted with comparative ease, large and tantalisingly close, but great skill is needed in approaching them, quite apart from casting to them, for they spook easily.

Middle Test water is similar but is just on a larger scale, with shallow water interspersed with

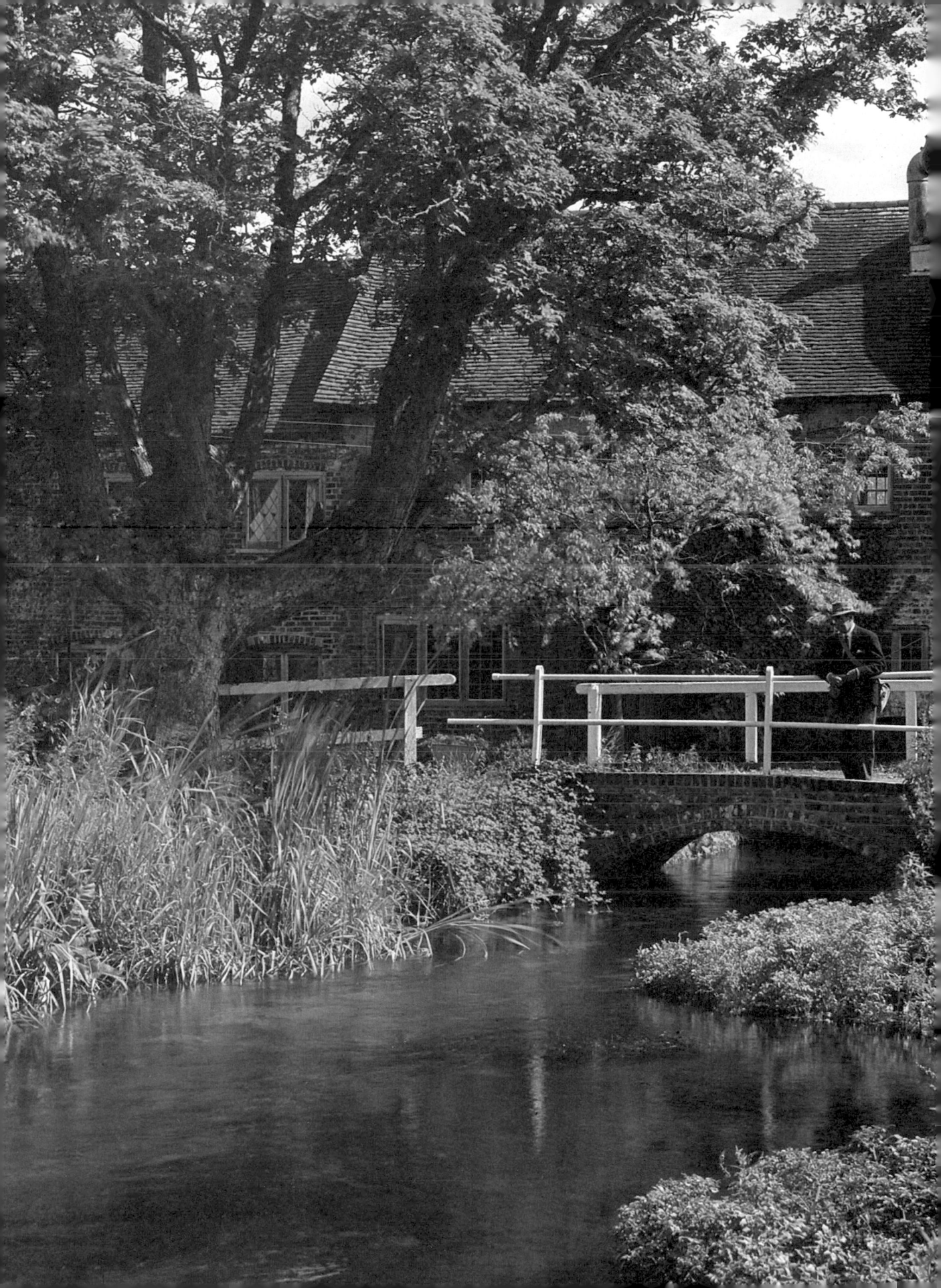

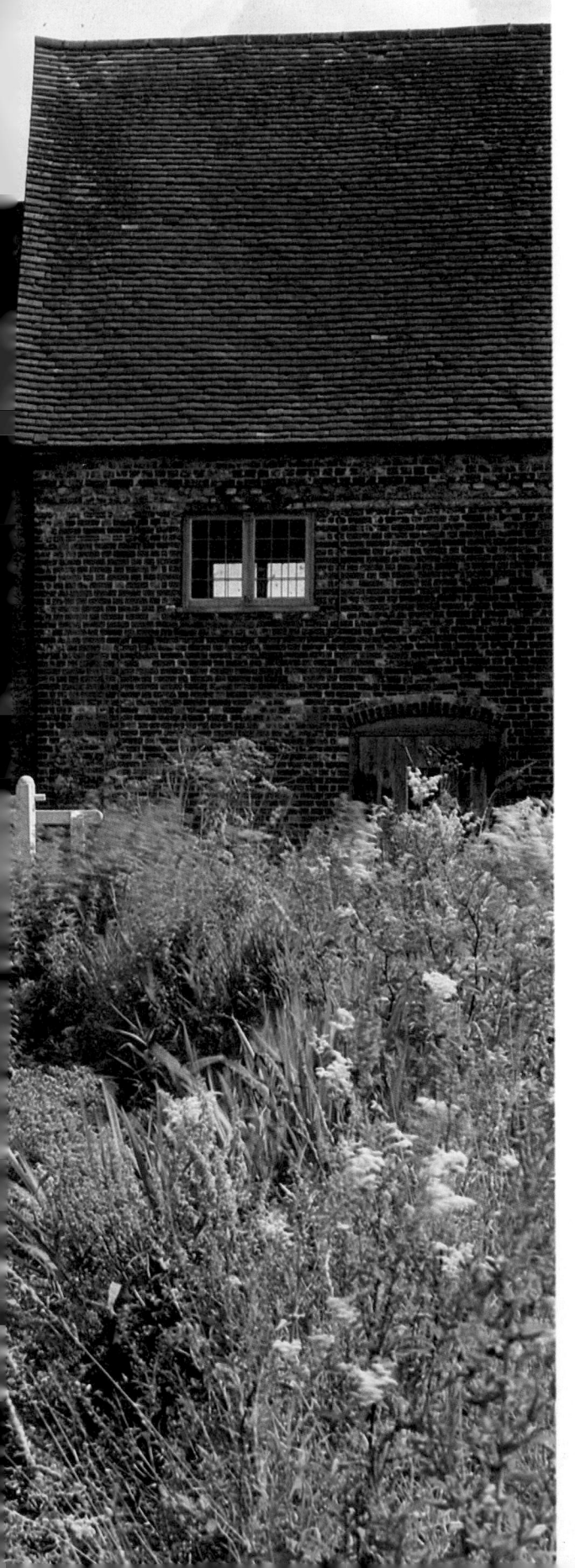

The infant Itchen at Alresford

longer, deeper pools which hold many large trout. As the water is deeper, the fish are more difficult to spot, and good eyesight and patience are of prime importance. Halford, one of the great chalk stream fly innovators, used this area of the river for his testing ground; the results of his meticulous fly dressing were one of the essential ingredients of modern dry fly tying. This area has some attractive features, as the river meanders through lush green water meadows and many beats have thatched fishing huts on them. Photographs of the eel traps at Leckford have been featured in many publications and are a reminder of the past.

The world famous and most exclusive of all trout fishing dry fly clubs – The Houghton Club★ – maintains a headquarters at Stockbridge. This is no ordinary club and is a true reminder of the traditions and conditions of the noble art of specialised dry fly fishing. Membership of the club is by selected invitation only.

The name of the Lunn family, who have worked and nursed the club waters over many generations is, of course, associated with the ever famous and successful Lunn's Particular spent dry fly, amongst many other patterns. The Lunns also perfected the modern method of rearing chalk stream trout, and their knowledge has been invaluable to the fishing world.

The middle and upper Test has a prolific mayfly hatch, which usually lasts for three weeks, sometime during May and early June; duffers fortnight or not, the mayfly is the harbinger of unforgettable fishing, with the fall of spinners being the highlight.

The lower Test is a mixture of salmon and trout water, but in the main it is the salmon that is the quarry of the fishermen. There are three salmon stretches on the river, from Romsey downstream, where anglers, as on the Itchen, catch a few springers but rely upon the summer fish and grilse runs. Sea-trout are taken in these beats but only

★ The Houghton Club stands for all that is most excellent in the world of dry fly fishermen. It was founded in 1822 and continuous records of catches have been maintained even through two world wars. The club's fishing on the middle Test is maintained and nurtured by Mick Lunn and his assistants. A day on the Houghton water is, for most fishermen, an unrealisable dream.

The cream of the Test

in sizeable numbers on the lowest stretch. These fine fish do not run high up chalk streams, due, it is said, to the water being too alkaline.

The gravel beds on the Test and its tributaries (which for the most part are crystal clear and weave their way through unspoilt countryside) with properly nurtured weed growth, allow fish to bask on sunny days and feed contentedly on nymph or fly. Tributaries are usually about twelve yards in width, whilst the main rivers cover double that distance.

In the 1920's, the Test was noted as being one of the best all round trout and salmon rivers in the country. There were excellent runs of salmon on the Test up as far as Romsey; above that, however, a few were always taken, even as far as Stockbridge. The main run of salmon has, however, declined, as in other parts of the country, and the seasonal catches have fallen off – nevertheless this fishing can provide excellent sport. On all waters fishing may be with plug, prawn, shrimp, fly or upstream mepp: the strict trout rules do not apply to the salmon fishermen.

Above Romsey, the trout fishing really starts, but the odd salmon is invariably caught on dry fly tackle, using a $4^{\times}$ or $5^{\times}$ cast and a size fourteen or sixteen dry fly. Though this is no mean achievement, there, almost unbelievably, exists a partial resentment on the part of trout fishermen when they discover the presence of salmon in their waters!

In conclusion, it is again stressed that riparian owners guard jealously and with justification, the privacy of their waters on the Test, Itchen, Beaulieu and Meon. In these vicious days of poaching, far too much trouble exists from the vicinity of Southampton, Portsmouth, London and even more locally. Close details of individual waters and their precise locations are traditionally, faithfully preserved. This to an extent, accounts for the somewhat broad nature of this description.

Beaulieu

The Beaulieu is some fourteen miles long and rises in the New Forest. It is a particularly interesting, if not very picturesque, water.

The upper reaches in common with all rivers and streams which stem from and which flow

Coming to the net

through the New Forest, are owned by the Forestry Commission. Fishing for trout can be
worthwhile on certain selected reaches but generally speaking the more serious fishing starts a
mile or so above Hartford bridge. From there
downstream the water is tidal, which as a general
rule brings in two tides in every twenty four
hours.

It is not attractive fishing scenically, but the
water in this reach can support substantial runs of
sea-trout.

Catches from this water have yielded many fine
sea-trout up to sixteen pounds! Each season a
number of six to twelve pound fish are taken, but
it is stressed emphatically that only experienced
sea-trout fishermen should consider this water,
and vacancies are extremely limited. Fly only is
fished.

Meon

The Meon rises in the area just south of East Meon
and follows a winding course through mainly
open country over a distance of some twenty to
twenty five miles to the sea.

It is classified as a brook due to the fact that it
is narrow during the greater part of its course; it
passes through West Meon, Warnford, Exton,
Droxford, and Titchfield where it joins the Solent
through a very small harbour, or yacht shelter.

The water is owned largely by the riparian
owners who farm the land on either side.

In the lower beats from Titchfield down to the
Solent there are sea-trout of up to ten pounds in
weight, the water, of course, being tidal in this
area. It is very difficult water to fish, but rewarding for the experienced angler.

Above Titchfield the water does allow a few
sea-trout up but develops mainly into a trout
water, holding wild fish of around one pound in
weight – not easy to catch – but good fishing can
be enjoyed by those who know the river. Much
of the water is let privately including a lake
through which the water flows at Warnford.

On the whole the Meon is a very pleasant little
brook which in many places is wild and unkempt.
There is ample scope for improvement but
whether the work and expense would justify it is
questionable. Nevertheless, to many fishermen a

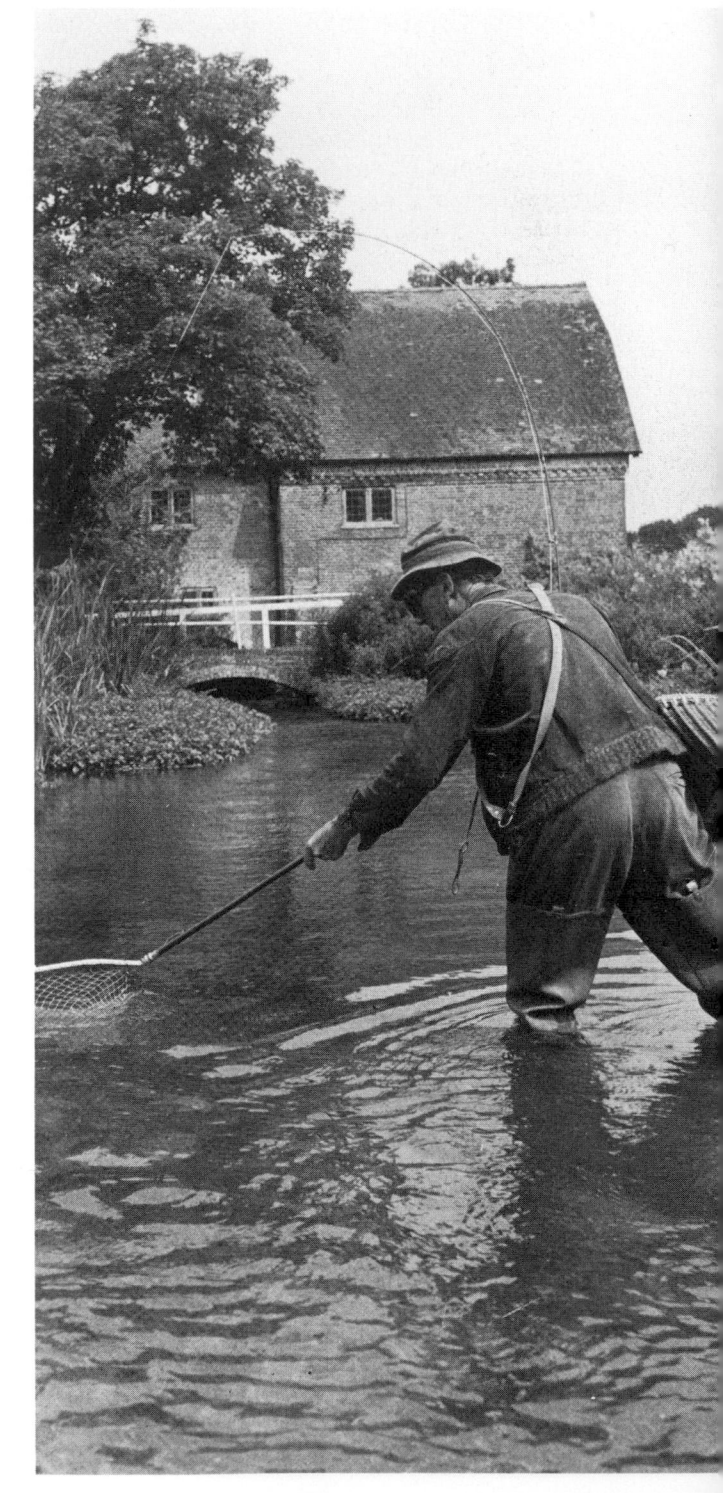

An Itchen carrier

river of brook size is the satisfaction they seek. Small wild brown trout create a challenge that gives greatest enjoyment and happiness to some sportsmen and the Meon with its added bonus of sea-trout can and does fulfil that.

The beautiful Hampshire countryside surrounds this water and it flows not far distant from the county boundary with Sussex.

Itchen

Winchester, the one time capital of England, is situated in a locality of both character and beauty, centred around the Cathedral on the east and, uphill on the west, the Castle.

As if by charm and chance, the River Itchen, so re-nowned for its association with Isaac Walton, Skues and other well known pioneer personalities in the arts of dry fly and upstream nymph fishing, flows through the very heart of this enchanted city.

The Itchen is neither a long, wide nor large river, but with its carriers and tributaries the Titchbourne and Candover brooks, together with the Arle, it flows near on forty miles, passing by or through Alresford, Itchen Abbas, Winchester, Eastleigh, then out into the estuary and Sou-thampton Water by the Swaythling weir pool.

The countryside of the Itchen valley is truly lovely and the Highways and Byeways Authori-ties in conjunction with their Footpaths and Bridleways Committees have ensured that, at cer-tain points, there are public rights of way along the river bank, which provide a delightful oppor-tunity of rightful access from which the greatest pleasure is derived by many walkers and non fish-ing members of the community.

Fishing, however, remains in the ownership and is the responsibility of riparian owners who control, maintain and keeper their waters. There are in addition a limited number of stretches in public ownership.

The Ichen Navigation Canal is still very much in existence but not as a commercial waterway. As a result, over the years the locks, sluices and weirs have fallen into disrepair resulting in the lowering of the water level and narrowing of the

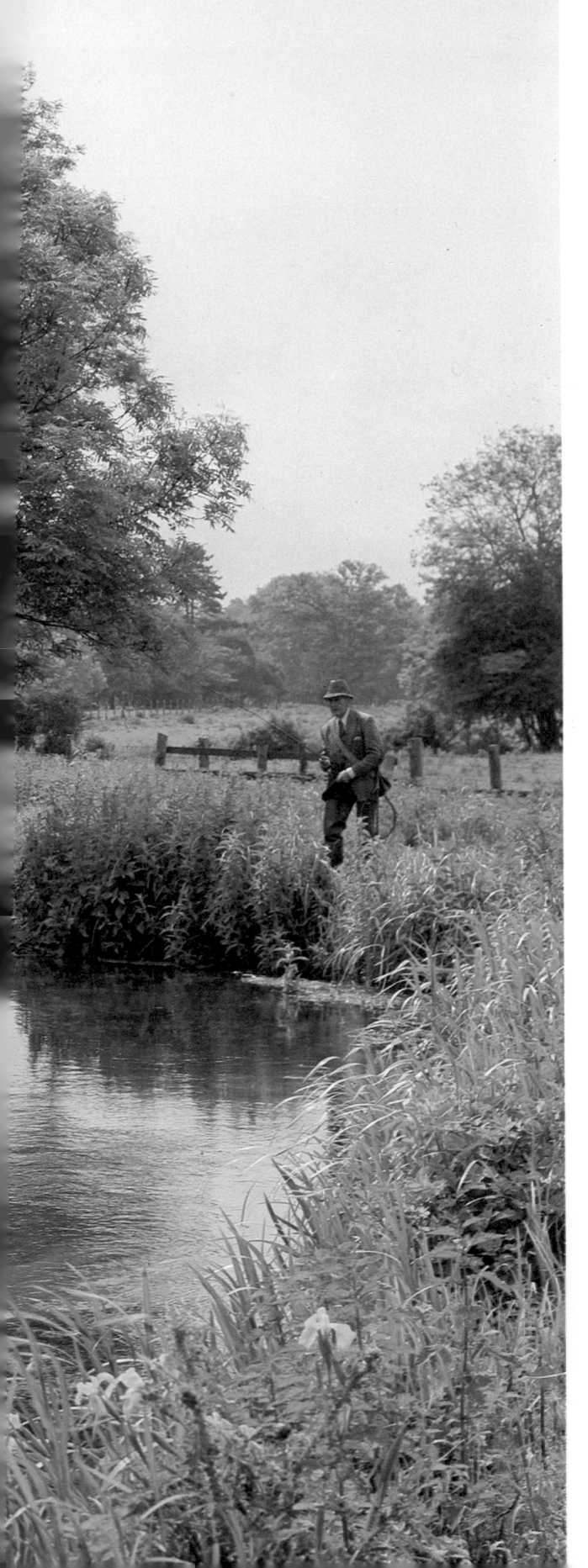

width, whilst its banks have become overgrown in many places.

Generally speaking, this interesting length of water runs from Alresford down to Swaythling and every so often leaves the River Itchen only to rejoin it again lower down.

Several 'fulling' and grain mills still exist. It was at these mills that the wool and grain were processed and loaded into barges which brought up coal and plied the canal to and from Southampton.

There is in existence the Itchen Navigation Canal Preservation Society but in view of the cessation of barge or boat traffic, together with the fact that the canal is now entirely unuseable for such purposes throughout its length, it is not used except when a riparian owner through whose land it runs, gives permission for fishing.

The flow and volume of water in the canal is controlled in certain areas on a percentage basis by the Southern Water Authority, which has the difficult task of ensuring fair distribution over a number of fisheries, all of which have a legal right to be supplied with as much water as possible.

At this juncture it would be appropriate to distinguish between the types of water found on Hampshire rivers such as the Itchen.

The main river and/or canal are self-explanatory; so too is a tributary which has a different source from and flows into the main river. A 'leet' constitutes a link of water usually feeding a mill, whilst a 'carrier' is a loop taken off the main river, rejoining it downstream.

There are many of these variations to be found along the course of the Itchen. Furthermore, the river around the area of Winchester and the fields three miles to the south at Twyford, hold clear evidence of the famous water meadow system which, dating from the last century, was in constant use until the 1939–1945 war.

These grass water meadows, which by nature are lower than the river level, were purposely flooded by controlling a number of hatches and flood gates. The water, when drained away, left a nutritious silt and this helped to produce copious growths of grass which in turn was harvested as hay. It was not unusual to get three such crops, in a season, off these quite considerable areas of otherwise normal grazing land.

Fishing on the Itchen can still be superb and it was on the well known Abbotts Barton water that

Shade on the Itchen. Ian Hay fishes

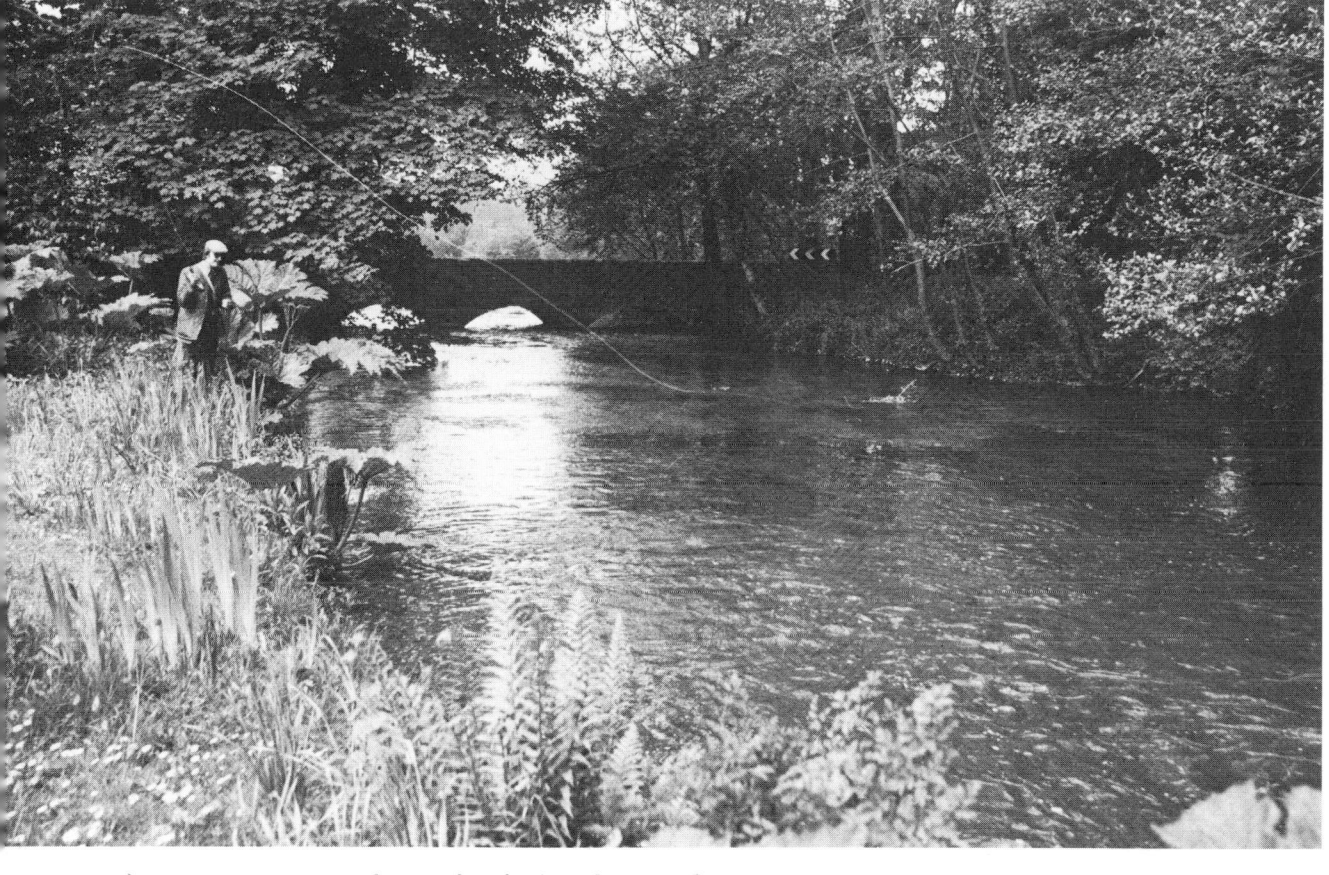

Skues spent so many hours developing the art of nymph fishing, whilst Isaac Walton★ is entombed in Winchester Cathedral, where a stained glass window above pays tribute to him. All great chalk stream fishermen past and present must surely have fished both the Itchen and the Test.

The Itchen supports a gravel and chalk bed over which flows some seventy six million gallons a day of crystal clear water provided by nature from a number of bore holes and natural springs.

The river has always supported a handsome head of wild brown trout. Beautiful deep bodied fish running down to a small head, 'Itchen brownies' are famous and notoriously hard to catch.

On many stretches above Winchester, no stock fish have ever been introduced, due to the care with which the water has been maintained and the fact that only a very controlled limit catch of these

★ Walton died in 1683. The publication of this book thus coincides with the 300th anniversary.

beautiful fish has been allowed. Furthermore, these waters are never overfished; a limit catch per rod per day may range from one to two brace.

As a very general guide, 200–300 yards of double bank fishing per rod per day suffice and constitute a beat, or if the water space allows, then a beat for two rods for a day could be 800 yards double bank.

Beats on some waters are rotated daily and the whole water is rested for at least one day each week.

There are invariably a number of pike in the Itchen below Winchester which are removed either at the end of the season in November or again when they spawn in February or March.

Grayling are found in considerable numbers and attain a weight of one and a half to three pounds. They too are removed when possible, but provide good sport when the trout are being 'dour'; they are rarely found above Easton roadbridge. The

High water at Ovingdon Mill

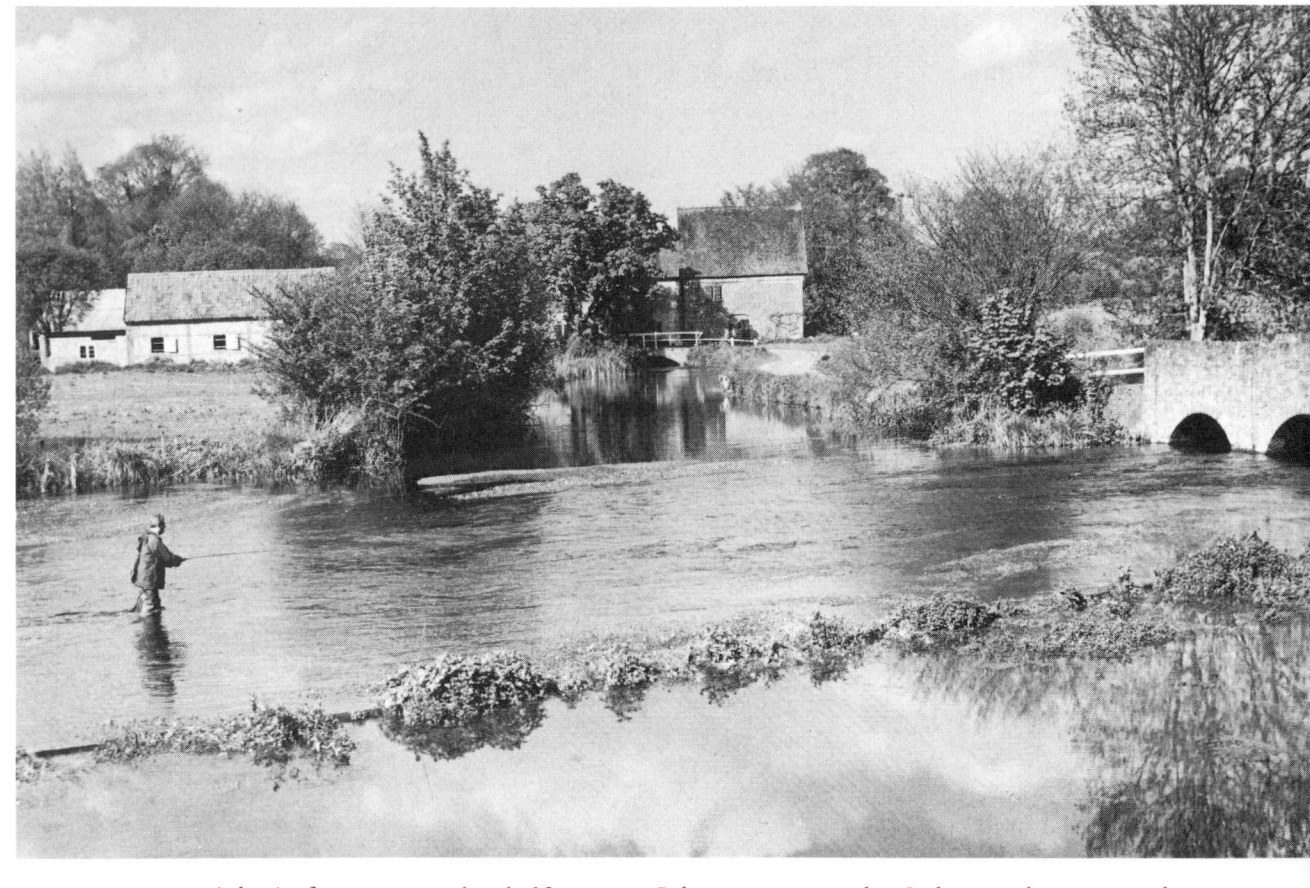

average trout weight is from one and a half to three and a half pounds.

With utmost regret it has to be recorded that the Itchen, from a commercial point of view, is suffering. Four trout rearing farms have been established, but the Test and Itchen Fishing Association maintains rigid control over such developments. Even so, dangers are always rife from the effluent release, with the inherent danger of pollution downstream.

To add to this problem, at Gaters Mill on the lower Itchen and also elsewhere upstream, a staggering twenty million gallons of water are extracted daily – much of it being piped to Portsmouth for domestic and commercial use.

To counter these abstractions, test bore holes have revealed alternative supplies, but lack of time and finance unfortunately make any such development a project for the future. But not the too distant future, we hope.

Salmon run up the Itchen and are netted at Swaythling pool, much to the annoyance of the rod fishermen. The majority of salmon fishing is below Eastleigh and in years gone by it was not uncommon for 300–400 fish to be taken each season. In common with many southern rivers, the spring run has deteriorated and fishermen have had to rely on runs of summer fish and grilse. Sadly, most of the salmon water is surrounded by the sprawling developments of Eastleigh and Southampton; and it is a far cry from the picture of a typical salmon river; nevertheless, the fish still run and good sport can be had.

The Itchen on all counts must still be regarded, with the Test, as one of the greatest of all chalk streams. Fishermen the world over marvel at its sheer beauty and the productivity that the river supports. With Winchester at its heart, here are some of the best things that England can offer.

WESSEX

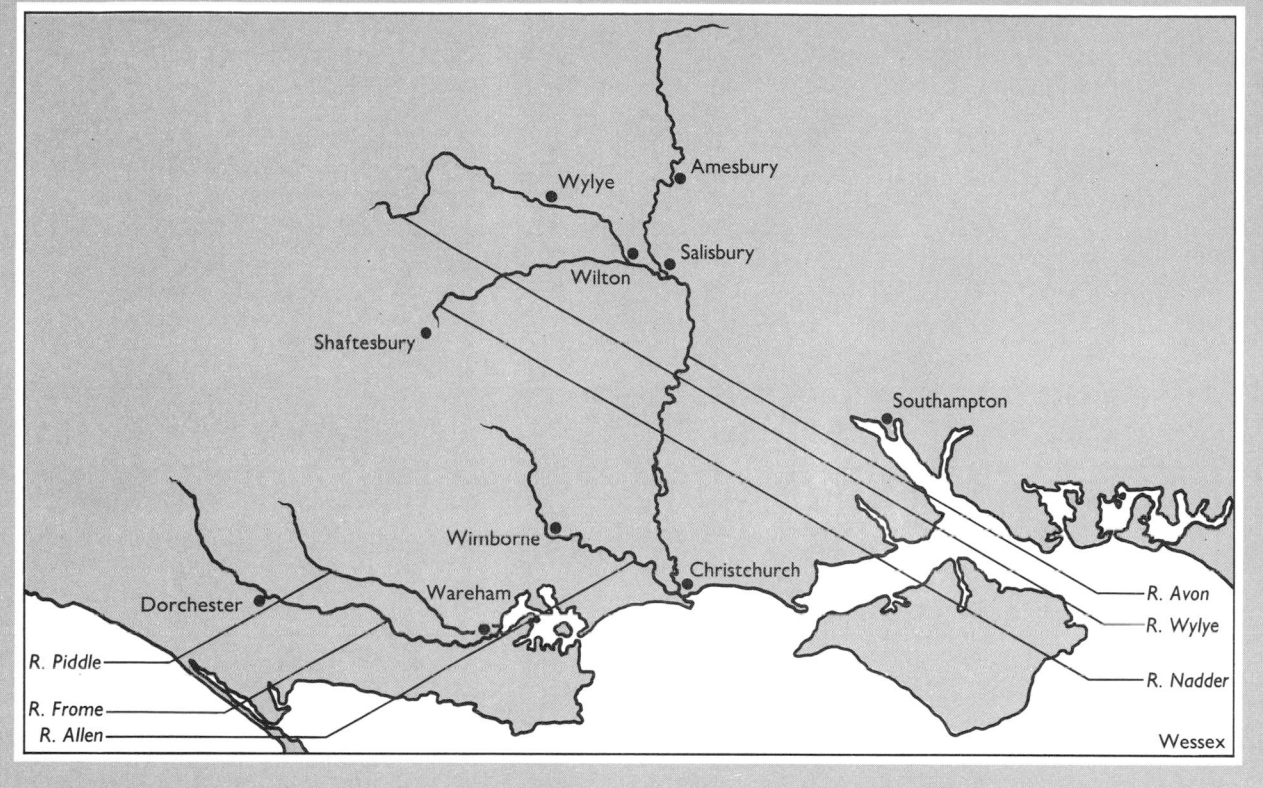

Map labels: Wylye · Amesbury · Salisbury · Wilton · Shaftesbury · Southampton · Wimborne · Christchurch · Wareham · Dorchester · R. Piddle · R. Frome · R. Allen · R. Avon · R. Wylye · R. Nadder · Wessex

Avon (Hampshire & Wiltshire)

Trout fishermen often refer to this famous chalk stream as the Wiltshire Avon, although it is also known as the Hampshire Avon or even the Salisbury Avon. In fact, it is one of the country's finest mixed rivers, which is to say that most species of freshwater fish are to be found here in abundance, but the Wiltshire stretches, particularly upstream of Salisbury, are carefully preserved as trout waters, while those below the city, flowing through Downton, Fordingbridge, and Ringwood, and on to the sea at Christchurch, are renowned for the quality of their coarse fishing and salmon fishing.

The general character of the Avon changes considerably below Salisbury, for it is here that five chalk streams, the Wylye, Nadder, Bourne and Ebble, and the upper Avon itself, join to become one mighty river. Although trout are present in some numbers on the lower Avon, stocks of coarse fish are greater than in the upper reaches

and trout do not as a rule rise as freely to the fly. Good sport may be enjoyed at times, however, especially on summer evenings with the Sedge, and on some carriers and sidestreams, but it is with the upper Avon that we as trout fishermen are principally concerned.

Rising in the Vale of Pewsey on the southern fringe of the Marlborough Downs, two sister streams, one flowing south east from Bishops Cannings, the other south west from Milton Lilbourne near Pewsey, converge at Scales Bridge, near Upavon, close to the main A342 Devizes to Andover road. Above this point, the two little Avons, particularly the five miles or so of the Pewsey branch, can provide very good fishing to those prepared to creep and crawl, stalking the shy trout with short rod and light tackle.

From just south of Upavon to the village of Enford, a stretch of some three miles, the Avon, now a wider stream but still requiring a very cautious approach, is fished by the Chisenbury Fishing Syndicate, while below Enford is the upper boundary of the Services Dry Fly Fishing Association, whose water extends for six miles from

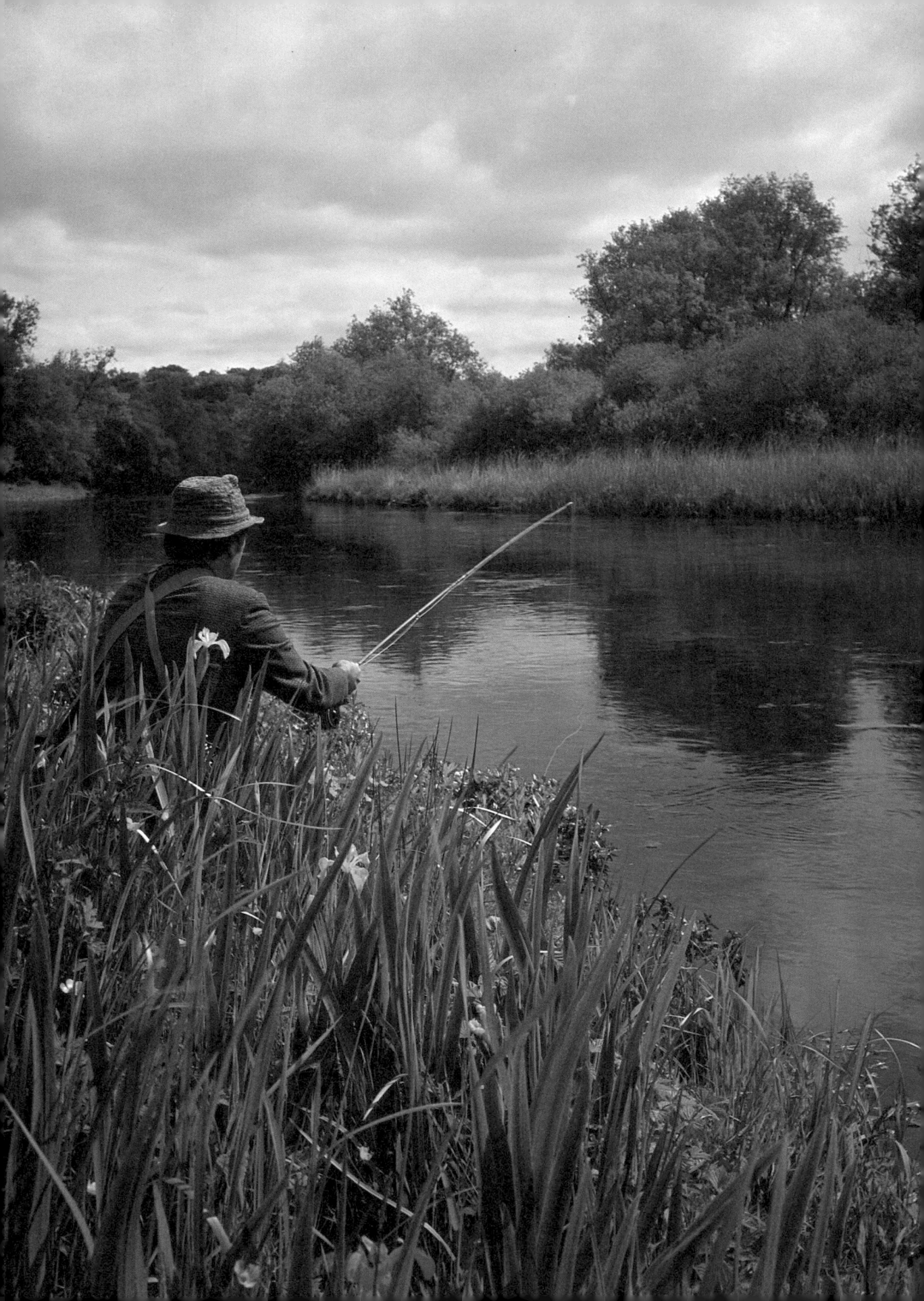

Coombe mill downstream to Bulford. This water has become well known through the writings of the late Frank Sawyer, head keeper for many years, who first developed the Netheravon style of nymph fishing in which artificials are weighted with fine copper wire. He was the designer of two of our most successful nymph patterns, the Pheasant Tail and Grey Goose nymphs. Another who fished here was the late Oliver Kite, author and broadcaster, and pupil of Sawyer. Kite wrote *Nymph Fishing in Practice*, which describes this method of upstream nymphing in detail, and produced a delightful work entitled *Fisherman's Diary*, a collection of his many articles first published in *Shooting Times* and *Country Magazine*.

Above and below Amesbury, and from Little Durnford down through Salisbury, the Salisbury and District AC have some of their best trout stretches. Members have a wide choice of waters, all very well maintained, and stocked periodically. This is a large membership club, with some 1500 members at the time of writing, approximately half of whom fish for trout. In total, the club has over ten miles of good trout fishing in the Salisbury area, and excellent winter fly fishing for grayling and coarse fishing is also available. Dry fly is the rule on most trout waters, nymph fishing being allowed only after mid summer. The fees are very reasonable and special reduced prices are offered to senior citizens and juniors.

The four mile length from West Amesbury downstream through Wilsford-cum-Lake and Great Durnford, as far as the Bridge Inn at Middle Woodford, is leased by the Piscatorial Society, which also rents stretches of the Wylye, Itchen, Kennet and Lambourn.

For much of its length, the upper Avon flows through a comparatively deep valley. In places, the hills rise sharply about the river, towering above the angler as he fishes in the lush water meadows below. The valley is well wooded too, giving a feeling of calm intimacy with the river and a sense of utter peace and tranquility.

Secluded reaches like this have two major advantages from the fisherman's point of view. Firstly, while on many chalk streams there is no escape from the winds, which often blow fiercely in such parts, here you can usually find comparatively sheltered areas in which you are able to cast a line; secondly, these conditions, by cutting

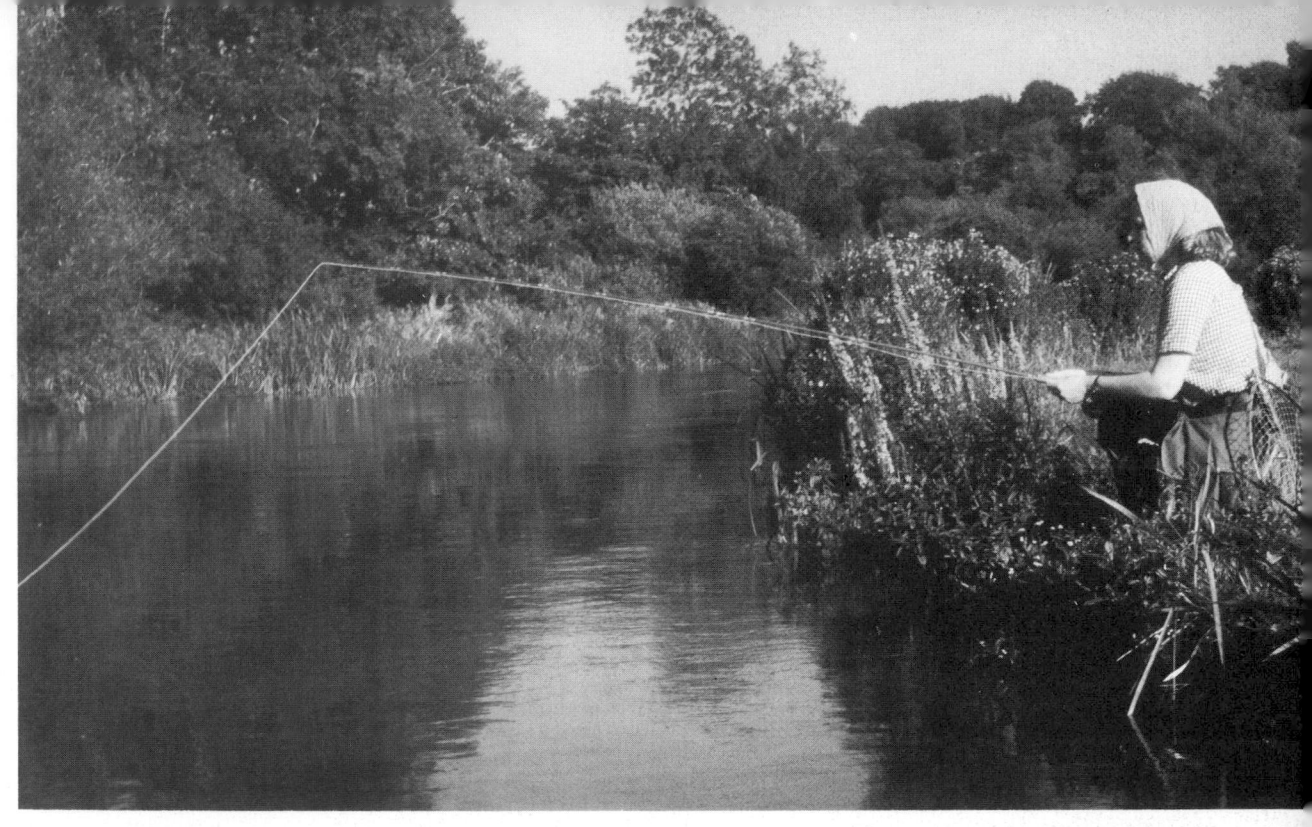

out reflected surface light, sometimes enable you to spot fish clearly as they lie in feeding positions. It is understandable perhaps that the fishing of weighted nymphs, as opposed to GEM Skues' earlier style of fishing the emergent, near surface nymph, should have developed at Netheravon, since the visibility here lends itself so well at times to the use of such patterns. Elsewhere, in reflected glare, or in water which does not have the same degree of clarity, quick sinking patterns may not be as productive as dry flies and lightweight nymphs.

Insects enjoy sheltered conditions too. Newly hatched flies can settle on vegetation without being blown away, and the delicate male dancing spinners and egg laying females are able to complete their life cycle unhindered. You may see clouds of spinners laying their eggs on wet roads, or on the roof of your car, but in deep, wooded areas a higher proportion return to the river where they belong, to provide food for the trout and sport for the fisherman.

The upper Avon is among the best rivers in Wessex for hatches of upwinged flies. Large olives, medium olives and iron blues encourage trout to rise freely in the early part of the season, while black gnats and hawthorn flies are often on the menu too. Mayflies appear quite early here, starting about mid May and continuing for about three weeks. Strong rises occur on some stretches at this time, especially during the afternoon and early evening. The best sedge fishing may be en-

joyed at late evening during June, while blue winged olives appear in quantity towards the end of the month; good hatches of them last right through until the end of the trout season and into November. Daytime fishing with dry flies is often rewarding during the 'dog days', notoriously dull on many streams in July and early August. Here you can usually find trout rising in shaded areas beneath the trees to small duns, spinners, or sundry small black flies such as reed smuts, some of which are little larger than a pinhead. If I were restricted to five flies only for the season, apart from the Mayfly, I would choose a general purpose olive pattern, such as a Hare's Ear or Greenwell, a dry Pheasant Tail, Black Gnat, Sedge and Pheasant Tail nymph.

The upper Avon is among the best rivers in Wessex for hatches of upwinged flies. Large olives, medium olives and iron blues encourage vary according to individual stocking policies, but natural growth yields many trout of between three quarters and one and a half pounds, while some native fish reach two and a half to three pounds, and very occasionally larger. A trout of ten and a half pounds, taken in 1908, hangs in the bar of the Rose and Crown Hotel in Salisbury, and a few in excess of this weight have fallen to bait over the years. The Avon is a magnificent river for grayling fishing. A good proportion of the fish weigh between one and one and three quarter pounds, and may be caught on fly well into the winter months.

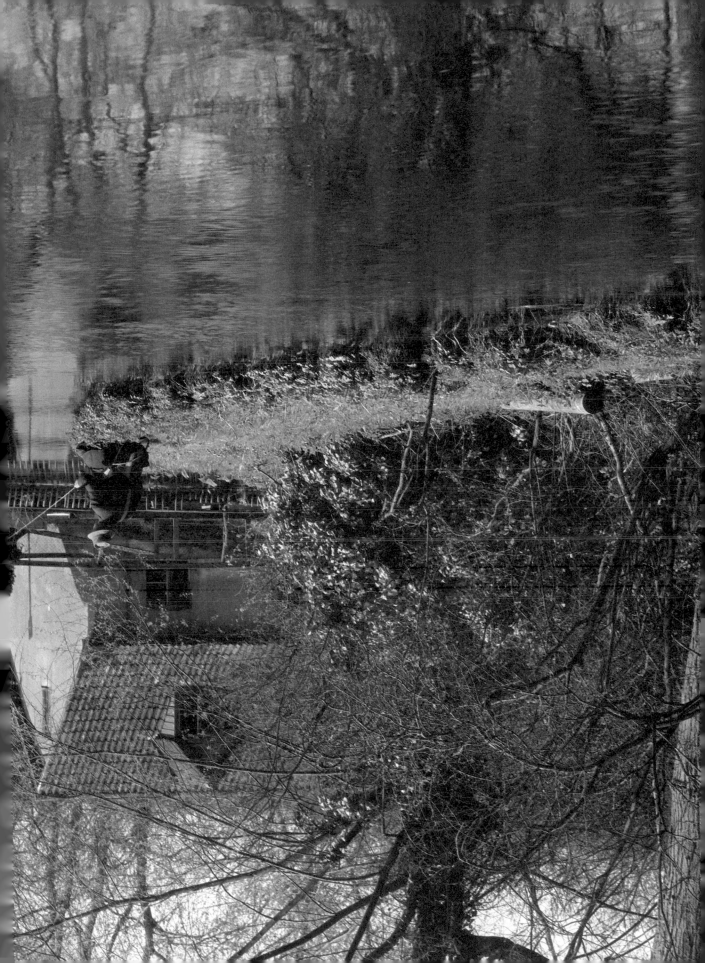

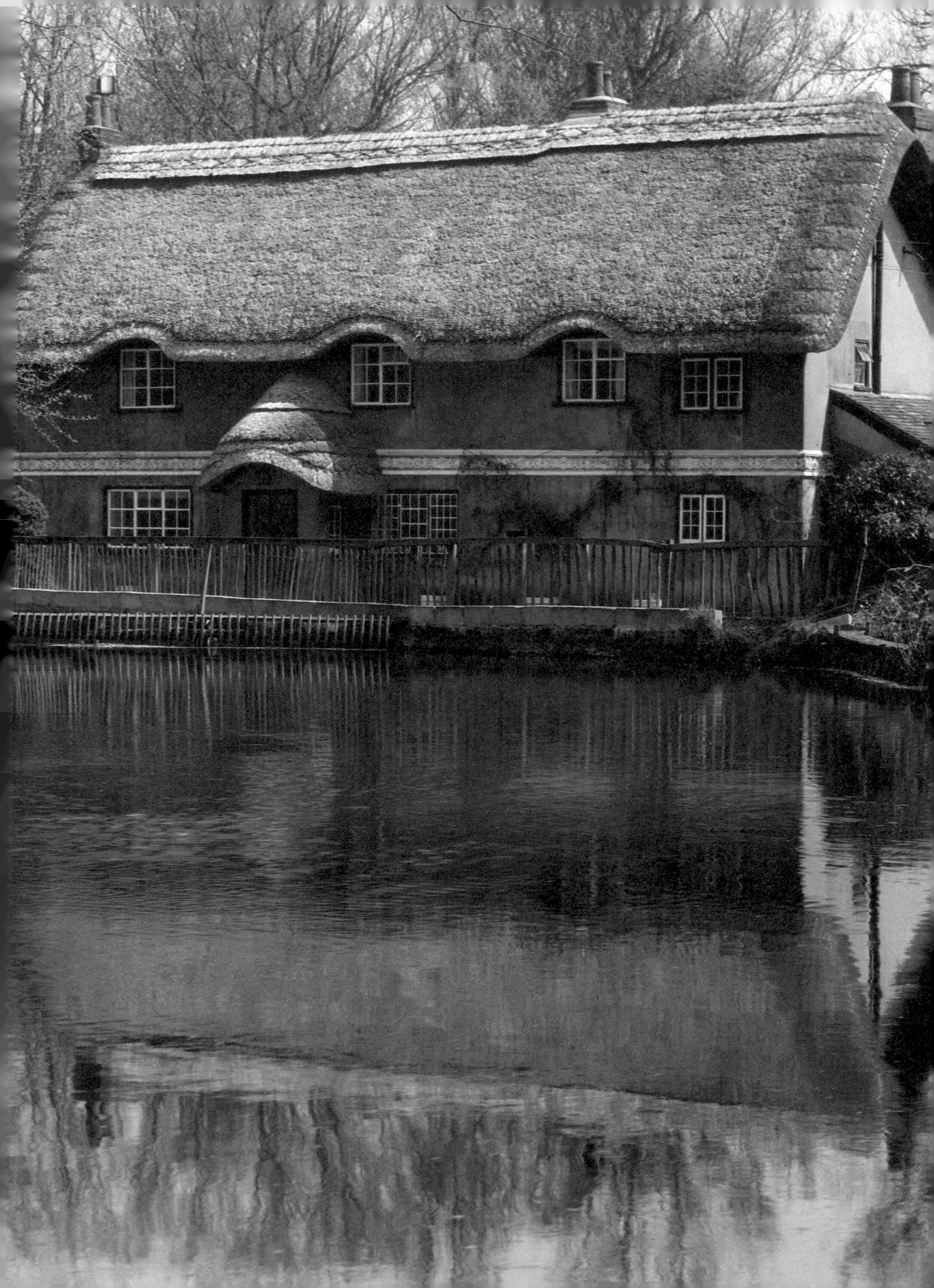

Previous page: The Avon at Lake

Below: The bright waters of the Hampshire Bourne

Tributaries of the Avon

A number of crystal clear tributary streams flow in the chalk valleys of Wiltshire which, although so small in places during late summer as to be barely fishable, are nevertheless valued highly by those who have discovered the joy and the challenge of the special kind of fly fishing which they offer. Often such brooks, ideal spawning areas for trout coming up from the major chalk streams each autumn, are full of native fish, and provide wonderful sport to the stealthy angler who is prepared to develop 'Red Indian' tactics, and use every scrap of cover. These streams are mostly in private hands and very lightly fished, but local enquiry may reveal landowners and farmers who will give an occasional day to the passing fisherman.

Of these little rivers, three are perhaps worthy of special mention.

Bourne

The Bourne, not to be confused with the famous Test tributary of the same name, is a winterbourne, which is to say that as springs cease to feed the upper stretches in summer, due to the lowering of the underground water table, these sections become dry. In fact, most of these small streams are affected in this way to a greater or lesser extent, and some are netted each year for trout which have become stranded and would otherwise die. In the case of the Bourne, of the twenty miles or so of its full length, only about six miles are fishable in a normal season, from Idmiston or Porton downstream to its confluence with the Avon.

Some of the best trout water is at Gomeldon, just above Winterbourne Gunner, where Mrs Joan Dean lets a limited number of season rods and day tickets. Here the water height is maintained by the use of a hatch which ensures that the stream is always in fishing order, with a good flow over bright starwort beds at the top, becoming slower downstream towards the hatchway. The native head of trout is supplemented by stocked brownies. There is excellent sport to be had throughout the season with fish averaging well over a pound.

The damp water meadows here remain completely wild, a paradise for birds and butterflies, and this is one of few areas left in the chalk stream country where the purple glory of the Marsh Orchids may yet be seen around mid summer.

Ebble

The Ebble flows eastward through Bowerchalke, Coombe Bissett and Nunton, joining the Avon close to Longford Castle some four miles south of Salisbury. Much of the upper water is harnessed for commercial use in the shape of watercress farms at Bowerchalke and Stoke Farthing, and a fish breeder operates near Broad Chalke, rearing

The Ebble near Odstock

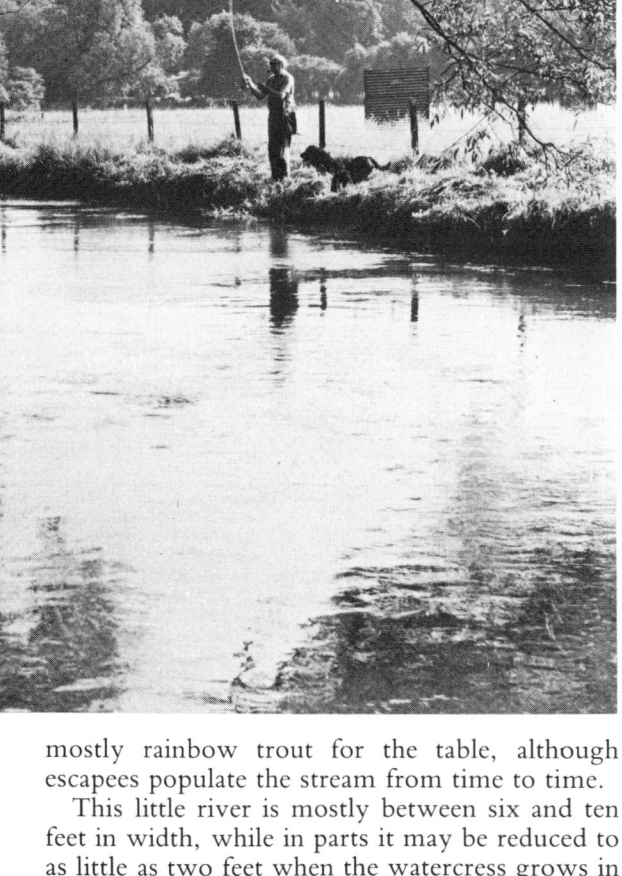

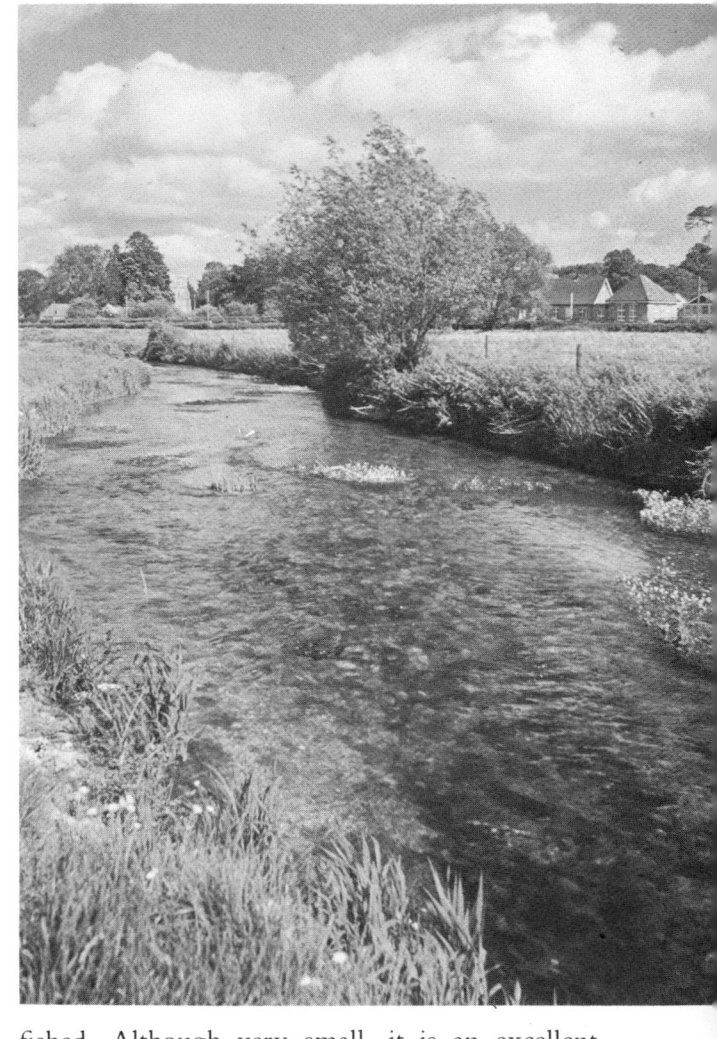

mostly rainbow trout for the table, although escapees populate the stream from time to time.

This little river is mostly between six and ten feet in width, while in parts it may be reduced to as little as two feet when the watercress grows in profusion in late summer. The lower stretch of two miles or so, downstream of Odstock, is owned by Lord Radnor, and most reaches above this are preserved by private owners, some of whom let the fishing to individuals and small syndicates.

Till

The Till, a lovely stream which flows into the Wylye at Stapleford, is privately owned and little fished. Although very small, it is an excellent trout stream, and renowned for the size and numbers of its grayling, which I understand Oliver Kite used to catch in quantity on his bare hook nymphs, while blindfolded! It has also given me some fine trout up to one pound fifteen ounces, but I had no such handicap.

All these streams have good hatches of up-winged flies in May, June and September, and during the evenings in June, July and August. The nymph is very productive since fish are often clearly visible as they lie in gravel pockets or over the green weed beds. Pale Duns do well and the angler should always have a dry Pheasant Tail and a couple of Sedge patterns in his fly box.

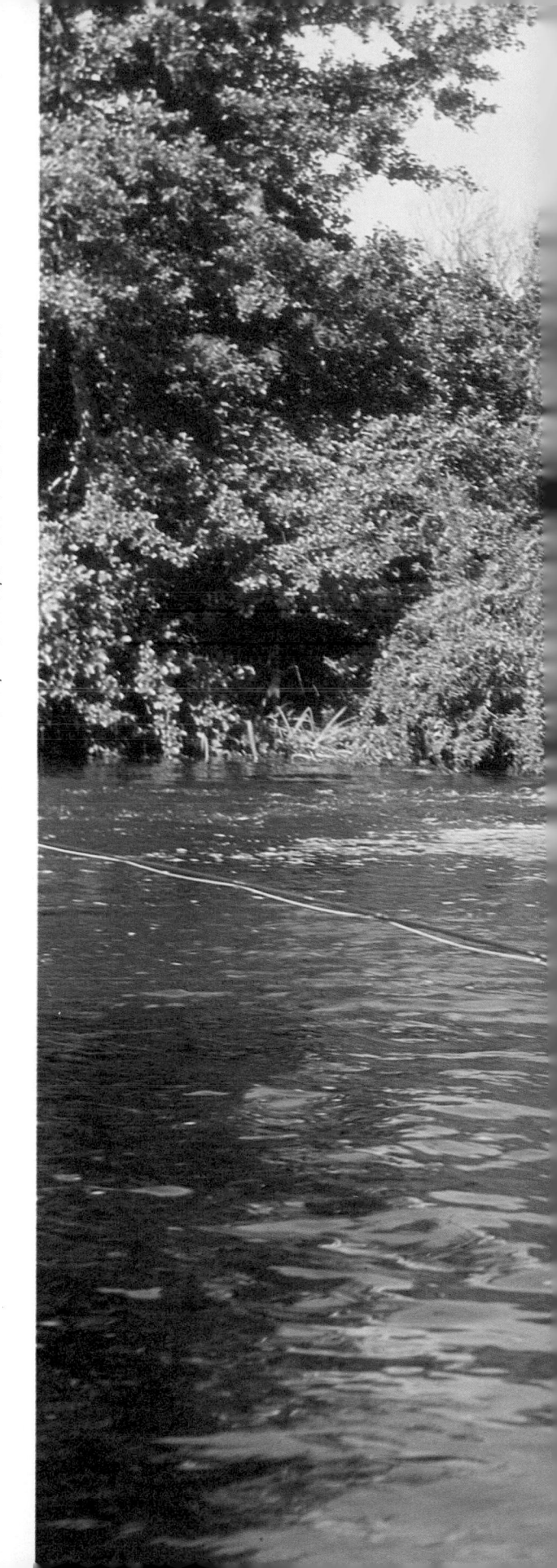

Nadder

Strictly speaking, the Nadder is not a true chalk stream, for although it is fed by springs, it also receives water from surface drainage, and is liable to rise sharply after heavy rains, and easily becomes discoloured. In fact, there is, I suppose no such thing as a true chalk stream, since all must be fed to some extent by surface water, but there are degrees of 'trueness', if you like, from the winterbournes, which rely almost entirely on spring water and remain crystal clear even after very heavy rainfall, to rivers like the Nadder, whose nearby countryside absorbs a lesser proportion of the rain water than is the case where streams are surrounded only by downland composed of porous chalk.

The Nadder has many of the characteristics of a chalk stream, flowing clear for most of the season at a good pace, and the same water plants, largely ranunculus, but some reaches, especially those upstream, are reminiscent of a rain fed brook, with alternating quick water and slow flowing pools, and with overhanging trees and bushes which create dark, mysterious corners. Nor is the fish population made up largely of trout and grayling as are the upper stretches of other streams in the Avon watershed. Although excellent fishing with these species is to be had in the middle reaches, a higher proportion of coarse fish exists upstream, in the Tisbury area, and below Wilton, at which point it becomes one with the Wylye, and flows on eastward into the Avon at Salisbury. The Salisbury and District AC has a good length of mixed fishing within the city limits, where trout may be caught by spinning as well as with artificial fly, while the Burcombe Club rents the length from Wilton upstream to Barford St Martin, and the Teffont Club from Dinton to Chicksgrove. The Tisbury Angling Club controls some of the upper water. My one experience of fishing above this was on a stretch only two to three yards in width, from which I caught three splendid trout in one hour's fishing, casting a Mayfly to likely spots. All were returned to the water, but the smaller fish weighed over one, and the heaviest well over two pounds.

Apart from the normal upwinged flies which are to be found on Wiltshire streams, the Nadder

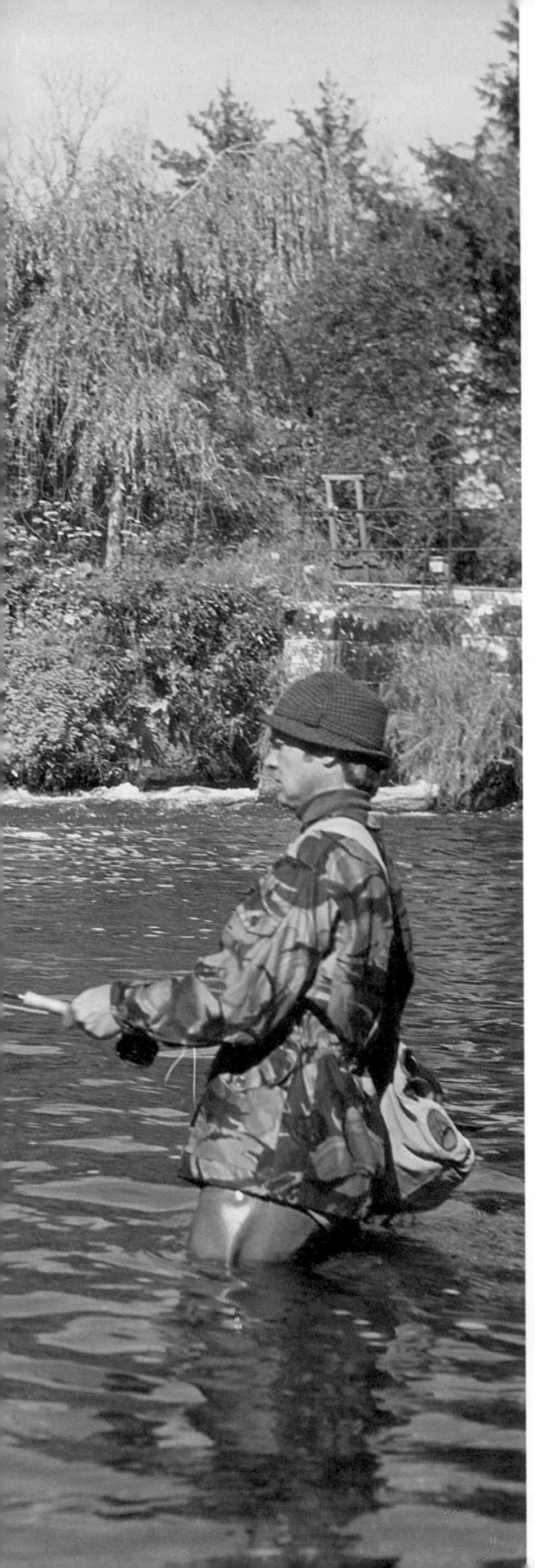

The Nadder at Dinton Mill

appears to have more land bred species, such as alders and hawthorn flies, than other rivers in this area. Black gnats are abundant, as are sedges, reed smuts and some of the midge (Chironomid) family. Mayflies here have the same habit as on the Wylye in that sparse hatches may occur throughout the summer months, instead of being confined within a two to three week period.

Native stocks are supplemented on some lengths by artificially reared trout, both browns and rainbows, and a number of whoppers in excess of four pounds have been taken in recent years. The fish rise well here during the early summer and in the autumn, and may be found feeding at the surface on the hottest days of July and August. I have found, however, that trout are slow to come on to the fly in early spring, and in some seasons are not at their best, in terms of physical condition, until well into May or even June.

Trout here are not generally very discriminating I have found, as to which fly pattern they will accept, although Black Gnats and Palmer style flies appear especially attractive, both to the trout and the grayling.

Wild flowers abound in the low lying meadows of this peaceful valley, where the kingfisher 'pips' as he passes upriver, and the barn owl silently quarters the field at dusk as the angler plies his craft, the two living side by side in complete harmony, each intent on hunting down his separate quarry in his own way.

Wylye

The River Wylye rises some four miles west of Warminster in Wiltshire, near the village of Longbridge Deverill. The stream runs in a general east to south easterly direction close to the main A36 Salisbury road, in a wide valley between rolling chalk downs, past the villages of Heytesbury, Codford St Mary, Wylye and Stapleford, to the town of Wilton, once the capital of ancient Wessex. Here the Wylye meets the Nadder to form a single river, which flows for a further four miles before joining the Avon in the heart of Salisbury.

It is one of few chalk streams which require little or no artificial stocking, due in part to the

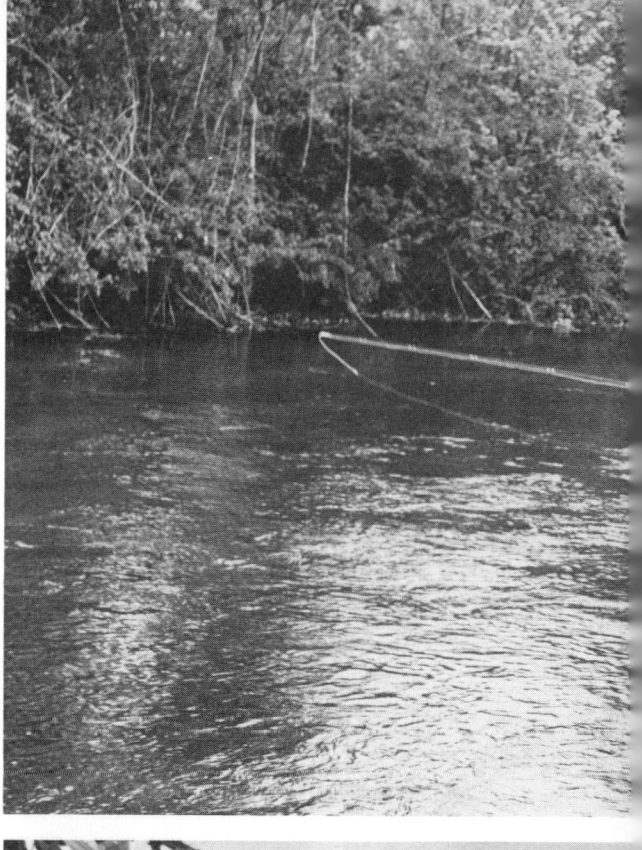

Top: Stalking on the Wylye

presence of quick flowing gravelly stretches which
make ideal spawning grounds, and partly because
for much of its length the river is managed and
fished by caring anglers dedicated to preserving
the stream as a wild fishery.

Some of the best stretches are, nevertheless,
accessible to the fisherman who is searching for
good dry fly fishing, either by joining Salisbury
and District AC for a modest annual subscription,
or by applying for membership of smaller clubs
whose fees are higher, possibly £200–£300 per
annum.

Grayling and trout are the predominant species,
but dace, roach, perch, pike and eels are also present. A few salmon run up to spawn each year.
Trout taken generally average between three
quarters and one pound in weight, although several larger fish are caught each season, from one
and a half to two and a half pounds. Occasionally,
trout of over three pounds are captured, perhaps
two or three per season. When conditions are especially favourable, as during the heavy mayfly
hatches of 1980, very big fish may rise to the fly.
On the Wilton Club length that year trout of four
pounds six ounces, three pounds six ounces and
three pounds four ounces were recorded. A number of trout over six pounds have been caught on
this water over the years, the heaviest weighing
seven pounds two and a half ounces, taken by Mr
Carlton Cross at South Newton in May 1924.

Grayling do not reach such weights as this. A
good proportion grow to between one and one
and three quarter pounds, but of the several thousand I have taken in the middle and lower reaches,
only two have topped the magic two pound mark.
As on most streams where this species is so prolific that they threaten the trout population (competing strongly for food and space) netting or
electric fishing is carried out each year to reduce
their numbers, the fish being transferred to other
rivers. Grayling are free rising on the Wylye,
glorious eating, and at their best when trout are
out of season, enabling the keen angler to ply his
craft throughout most of the year.

Methods are usually restricted to dry fly and
emergent nymph during the trout season, from
mid April to mid October, although on some
waters dry fly only is the rule. In fact this is no
great restriction, for fish generally rise very well;
they are difficult to spot lying beneath the surface,

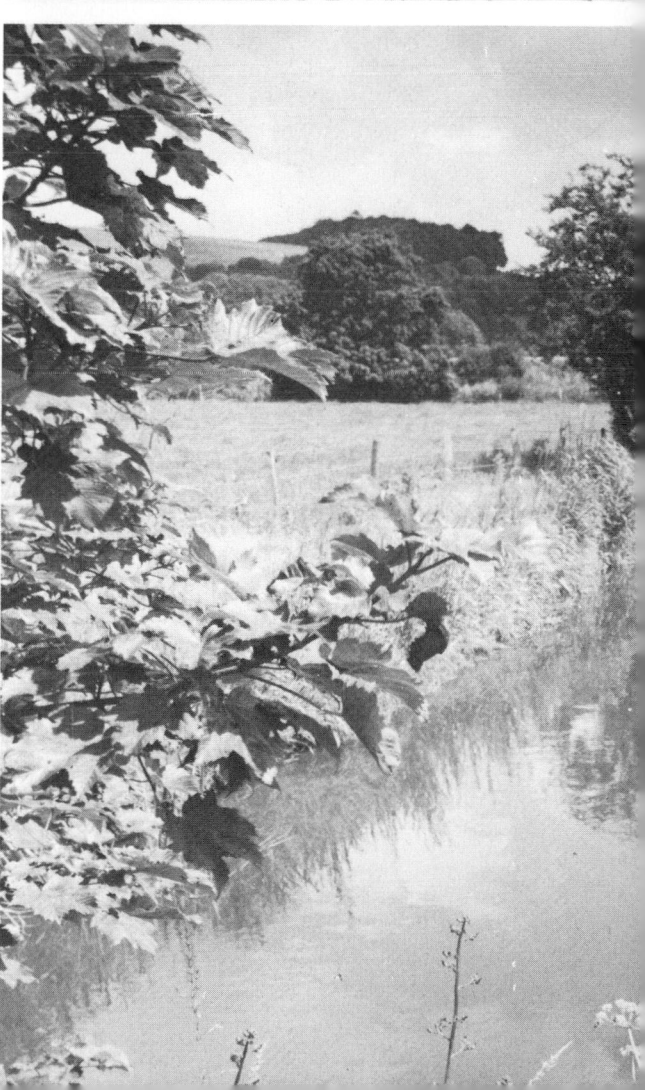

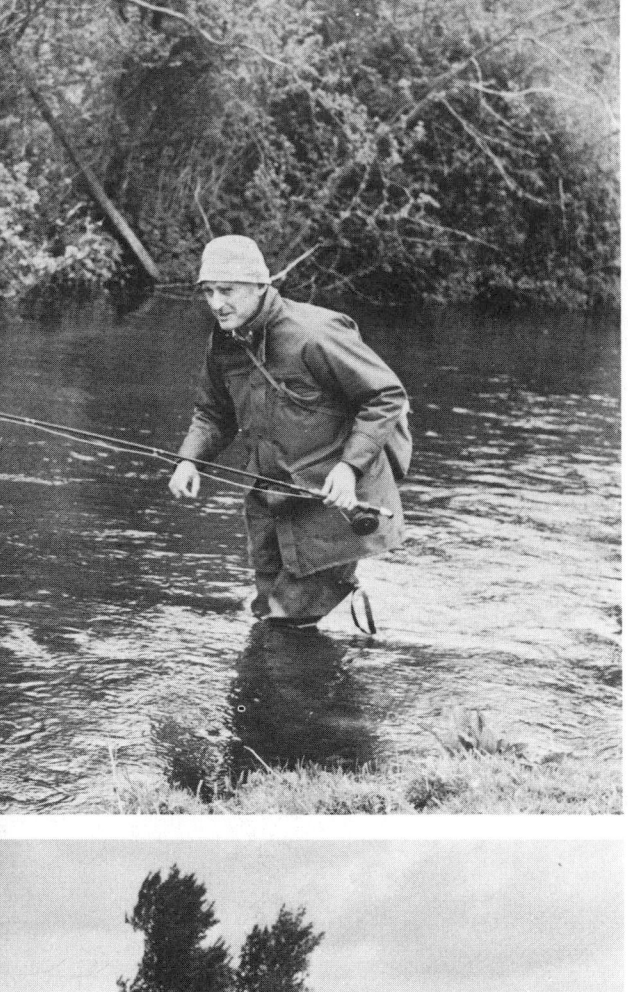

Bottom: A wild trout rises on the Wylye

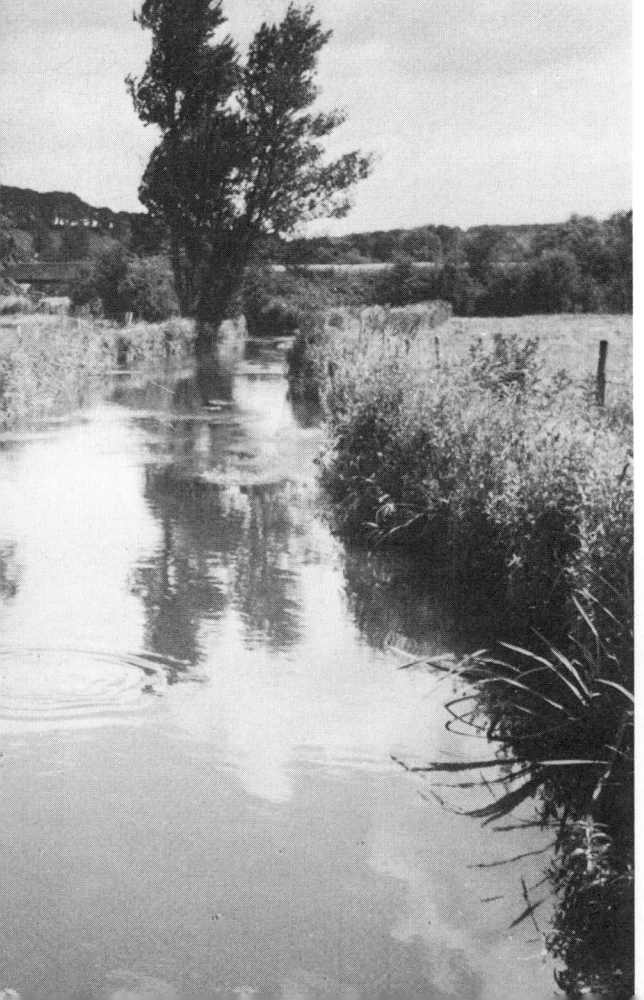

and it is perhaps only logical in such conditions to fish with floating patterns.

Daytime fishing for trout is at its best from early May until mid June. First we see the large dark olives, a winter hatching species which is nearing the end of its season, and the landbred hawthorn flies and black gnats, followed soon afterwards by medium olives and iron blues, and at mid summer by small spurwings, pale wateries and blue winged olives.

Mayfly hatches begin about 25 May and continue quite strongly on some stretches for three to four weeks, although here this species tends to trickle on throughout the summer, sometimes with a considerable increase in numbers during the early part of August.

There is often wonderful sport to be had in the late evening from early June until the end of August, since sedges, and particularly blue winged olives, usually hatch in some quantity. On many lengths of the Wylye, the angler fishes due west, looking upstream into the afterglow from the sun, which allows him to spot rises on the silver surface long after those facing in a different direction elsewhere have packed up for the day.

Favourite flies here include Hare's Ear, Black Gnat, Mayfly, a Pale Watery and Pheasant Tail nymph for daytime fishing, and a Sedge and dry Pheasant Tail for the evening rise.

Frome (Dorset)

This lovely Dorset river is over thirty miles in length, rising some five miles north of Maiden Newton and flowing in an easterly direction past the towns of Dorchester and Wareham and on into Poole Harbour. In its middle and lower reaches, the Frome is renowned principally for its excellent salmon and sea-trout fishing.

The best of the trout water may be found in the area of West Stafford, Dorchester, Grimstone and Maiden Newton, much of which is in private hands and fished by owners and small syndicates, and in tributary streams such as the Cerne, running from Cerne Abbas to Charminster, and the Wrackle, both joining the Frome just upstream of Dorchester.

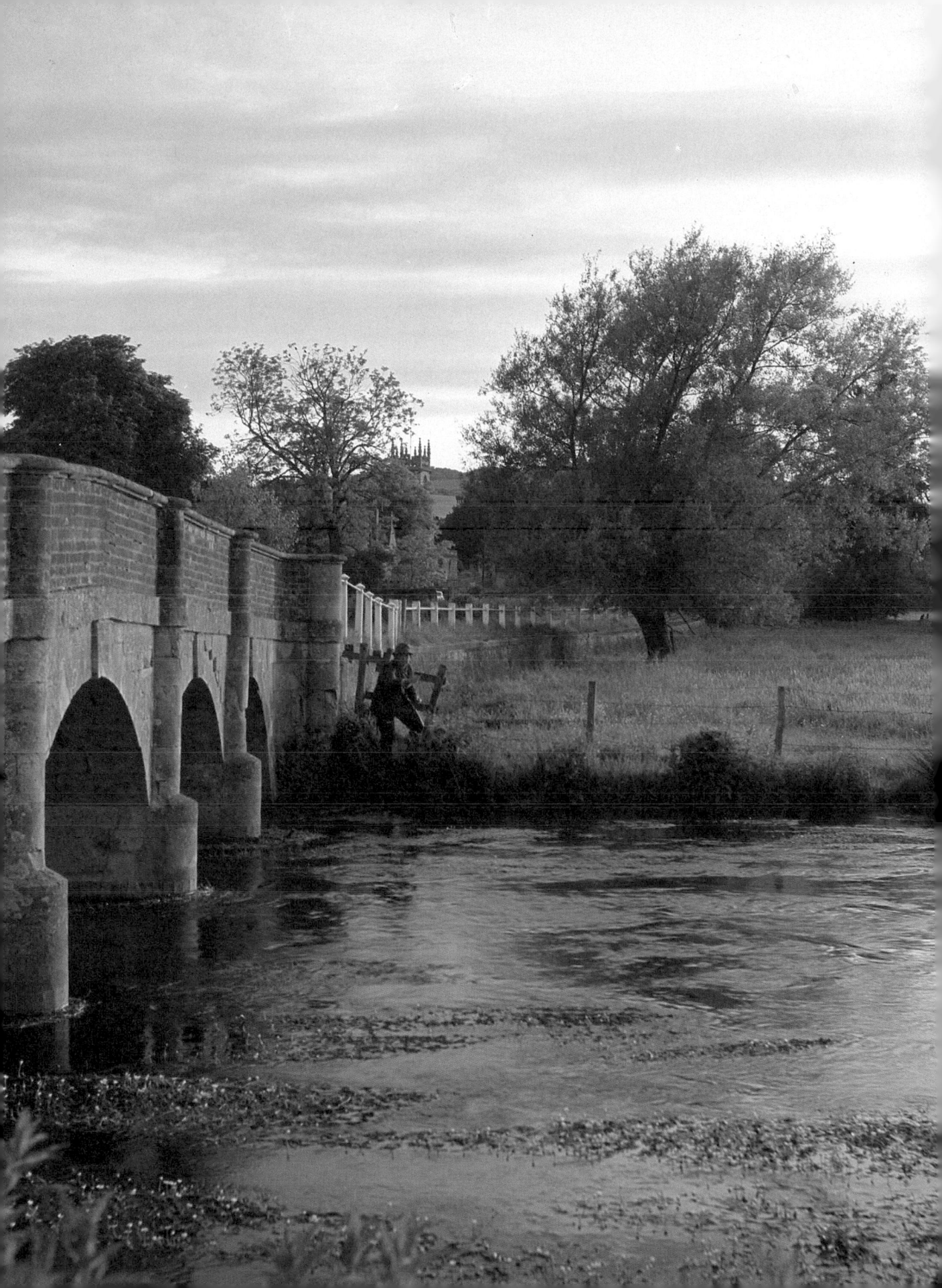

Mid summer at Stoford Bridge on the Wylye

A director of Eldridge Pope & Co, the brewers, owns a fine stretch above Gasgoyne bridge at Bradford Peverell, while the Dorchester Fishing Club controls some six miles from here down to West Stafford, including part of the Wrackle. It was in this small stream that one of the members, Mr Attryde, recently caught a wild trout weighing four and a quarter pounds. Most of the trout are native fish, although limited stocking with yearlings or second year trout takes place to provide sport in future years. The majority of fish taken weigh between three quarters and one and a quarter pounds.

This is a limited membership club, with a total of forty five members, which includes ten local people who fish by ancient right at a reduced fee. The river contains a few grayling, although these are more numerous in the lower reaches of the river near the town of Wool. Dace may be found in the lower stretches too, and pike are present in some numbers below Grey's Bridge, Dorchester. This bridge dates back to 1747 and still displays a notice to the effect that anyone found damaging the structure risks transportation!

The Dorchester Fishing Club has a waiting list for membership, and no day permits are issued. Methods are restricted to dry fly and upstream emergent nymph, for this is free rising water, especially in the early part of the season. Applications may be made to the Secretary, Mr J J Fisher, Rewhollow, Godmanstone, Dorchester. Godmanstone, which boasts the smallest pub in England, is situated on the Cerne. This stream is full of wild trout, many of which weigh over the pound. There is a fair mayfly hatch here and also on the Wrackle, beginning about mid May.

The Frome is one of few southern rivers which still has good hatches of grannom, the pale buff coloured sedge fly so beloved of our grandfathers, and the trout. These flies emerge at the very start of the season, in April. Iron blues hatch well in May, black gnats are plentiful, and pale duns put in an appearance after mid summer. Of artificial flies, the Tupps Indispensible is a famous Frome pattern, so much used by anglers in days gone by that it was once reported that the river was suffering from a form of pollution, that it stank of T I from Maiden Newton to the sea! Favourite patterns today include the Houghton Ruby, Black Gnat and small Sedges. It was in the Frome, of course, that Roderick Haig Brown, unquestionably one of the finest fishing writers of the century, had his first fly fishing experiences.

Piddle

Driving up the Piddle valley, you pass through Briantspuddle, Affpuddle, Tolpuddle and Puddletown, and above this, past little Puddle Hill, reach Piddlehinton and Piddletrenthide. Why some of these villages names should have changed from 'Piddle' to 'Puddle' – for clearly they originally took their names from that of the river – remains a mystery, although I suspect that it was for reasons of delicacy. They were a bit concerned about such things in bygone days!

This little river is an absolute gem, crystal clear, and requiring an ultra cautious approach. Generally, there are remarkably heavy hatches of upwinged duns and a good showing of 'black stuff', hawthorn flies, reed smuts, black gnats and the like, in the early part of the season and again, excluding the hawthorns, in late summer. The springtime provides the cream of the fishing, for water levels are usually well up at this time, while towards autumn the stream often runs very low. Indeed, in the upper reaches it sometimes becomes so low as to be unfishable.

There is an excellent head of native born trout here, although a little stocking is carried out to supplement the wild stock, and rainbows escape from time to time from a local trout farm. A number of brown trout in excess of two pounds are caught each season, and the average weight is higher than on many chalk streams of similar size and character.

All the fishing is privately owned, but Mr Richard Slocock of Wessex Fly Fishing, Lawrence's Farm, Tolpuddle, lets a limited number of rods on the Piddle and Frome, and on his small trout lakes. The latter are stocked with rainbows up to five pounds or so.

There is a good run of sea-trout on the Piddle, and numbers of salmon also come up to spawn. Sea-trout and salmon fishing in the Wareham area may be obtained by contacting the Wessex Water Authority, which issues day permits.

Allen

If you drive some fifteen miles out of Salisbury, to the south west towards Cranborne Chase, you meet villages with such names as Sixpenny Handley, Tollard Royal and Tarrant Gunville; and of greater significance to the trout fisherman, Monkton Up Wimborne, Gussage All Saints, Moor Crichel and Witchampton, for this is the valley of the Allen, in Dorset, one of the finest natural chalk streams in the south. It has not the world wide reputation of other rivers, possibly because it is relatively small, or because it is seldom mentioned in print, or because the Allen is a 'hidden' stream, unnoticed by motorists who stick to main roads, but bailiffs and others assure me that of the rivers in the Wessex Water Authority area, trout here are of the finest quality and display the fastest growth rate of all.

Certainly the native trout grow large, and although I have not been fortunate enough to catch any of over one and a half pounds, there are trout present of between two and three pounds, and a few are in excess of this weight. In 1982, young James Swanson caught a rainbow weighing five and half pounds, which had presumably escaped from stews on the Shaftesbury Estate. Sadly the head of wild fish has become somewhat depleted of late, and stocking has become necessary on some lengths. But natural spawning is good, and will remain so provided water abstraction does not further reduce the level and flow of pure spring water.

The Allen is a tributary of the Dorset Stour, which itself provides some trout and sea-trout fishing, although it is as a coarse fish river that it is best known. Some big brown trout, in the region of three to four pounds live in the Stour, and are sometimes taken on bait or on fly during the mayfly hatch, which is prolific here from mid May to early June. Strangely, there is no appreciable mayfly hatch on the Allen, although small flies such as medium olives, iron blues, pale wateries and blue winged olives appear in large numbers. The Black Gnat is a favourite artificial fly, as is a small Sedge, and imitative nymph fishing can be highly productive.

The upper five miles or so of the Allen are owned by the Earl of Shaftesbury, who grants permission to fish to a limited number of rods staying locally at the Bull Inn at Wimborne St Giles and elsewhere, but advance booking is necessary. This is hunter's water, where to achieve good results you have to approach with the utmost care, making yourself 'invisible' among the bankside vegetation, and cast sparingly to selected feeding fish. To do otherwise is to risk frightening every trout within range.

The water from Crichel to Stanbridge, some four miles, is fished by small syndicates, while the lower three miles is controlled by Mr John Bass of Wimborne Minster, who lets half of his water to the Wimborne Angling Club. Mr Bass also has a two mile length of the little River Crane which runs into the Stour about ten miles to the east, and two lakes in a beautiful wooded setting nearby. These lakes are regularly stocked and rods are sometimes available. The Crane, known in its lower reaches as the Moors River, is a delightful trout stream with a good run of sea-trout, and heavy mayfly hatches. A length of the upper Crane is rented by the Southampton Piscatorials, who also manage parts of the Stour.

Streams of Avon and North Somerset

Although the Bristol and north Somerset area is noted principally for its famous stillwaters, it is also blessed with numerous rivers, both large and small, many of which hold trout. The streams vary in character, but they are largely rain fed rivers, tinged with colour, and forever winding this way and that, with quick runs over stones, and dark mysterious pools. The steep banks are often overhung by bushes and trees, beneath whose branches the brown trout feed in safety, until you have mastered some more advanced tricks of casting. It can be tough going, and I have lost flies here by the dozen, and sometimes I have lost my temper, but when trudging home with a few trout for the pan the satisfaction is great indeed.

The Bristol Avon offers very good trout fishing in its upper reaches, around Malmesbury and the Somerfords, but for most of its length, through

The Parrett at Bridgwater

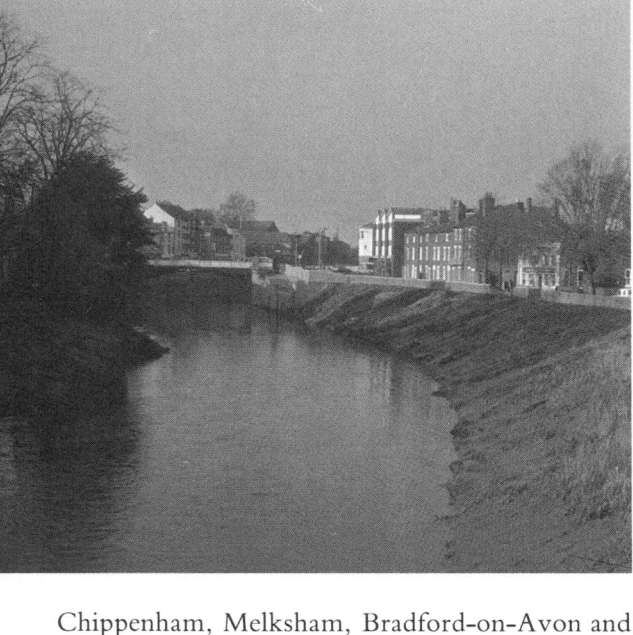

Chippenham, Melksham, Bradford-on-Avon and Bath, it is first and foremost a coarse fishing river. The upper reaches have good hatches of small upwinged flies, a fair mayfly hatch, and a good showing of black gnats and other land bred species. Somerford AC rents a stretch of a mile or so, and some very sizeable trout are taken in this area each season, around the four pound mark. The largest recent capture was of a rainbow trout weighing six pounds.

The River Chew rises on the Mendip hills and flows northwards, feeding the great Chew Valley lake, and on to Chew Magna, where it turns to the east, passing Stanton Drew and Pensford before joining the Bristol Avon at Keynsham, which lies between Bristol and Bath. There is a good head of wild trout in this little river, supplemented by some stocked brown and rainbow trout, the average weight of fish taken being a shade under the pound.

Knowle AC rents some three miles of the Chew, while Chew Fly Fishers have a short stretch at Pensford, and Keynsham AA and Bristol and District Almagamated Anglers also manage good waters. Fly hatches are fairly sparse, and few mayflies are to be seen here, but by casting a dry fly or nymph to likely spots some excellent sport may be enjoyed. Few coarse fish are present, although perch and a small number of roach exist.

The Box Brook, also known as the By Brook, joins the Avon on the eastern side of Bath, having run through Castle Combe, and the village of Box, on the A4 Bath to Chippenham road. A major part of this stream is controlled by small syndicates, and by Bathampton AA, whose water extends for about five miles, downstream of Box, and contains a very considerable head of native trout, free rising fish averaging some ten ounces.

Fly hatches are heavy at times, especially in spring and early summer, and the mayfly comes on strongly for about three weeks from 20 May or thereabouts. Some large brown and rainbow trout are introduced these days, which is hardly necessary; indeed such a policy may be harmful. In my view, man cannot improve a self stocking stream such as the little Box by 'planting' big fish, but he can, with the best intentions, upset the trout's natural environment through his lack of understanding of the river's delicate balance.

To the south east of Bath, two little rivers meet at Limpley Stoke before flowing into the main Avon. The Cam Brook, parts of which are controlled by the Avon and Tributaries AA, contains mostly trout, and is stocked predominantly with browns, the average weight taken being about twelve ounces. Fair fly hatches occur here, including the mayfly. The Wellow Brook maintains a higher average weight, and a good proportion of the trout scales between one and one and a half pounds. There are dace and roach present, and fly hatches are generally sparse, except for the mayfly, which appears in some numbers. Knowle AC, Bathampton AA and Avon and Tributaries AA also offer trout fishing on the Wellow.

Several renowned coarse fishing rivers are to be found in the Bridgwater and Taunton areas of Somerset, and some also provide limited trout fishing, principally the Brue in its upper reaches around Lydford, which lies some eight miles south east of Glastonbury, and the upper parts of the Tone, to the west of Taunton. Upwinged fly hatches are relatively sparse, but black gnats and reed smuts appear in some quantity on both streams, and the Sedge is often productive.

Further information and advice as to how to obtain fishing on these and other streams in the area may be obtained from local tackle dealers, such as Veals in Bristol, and Crudgingtons of Bath, who are invariably helpful.

SOUTH WEST

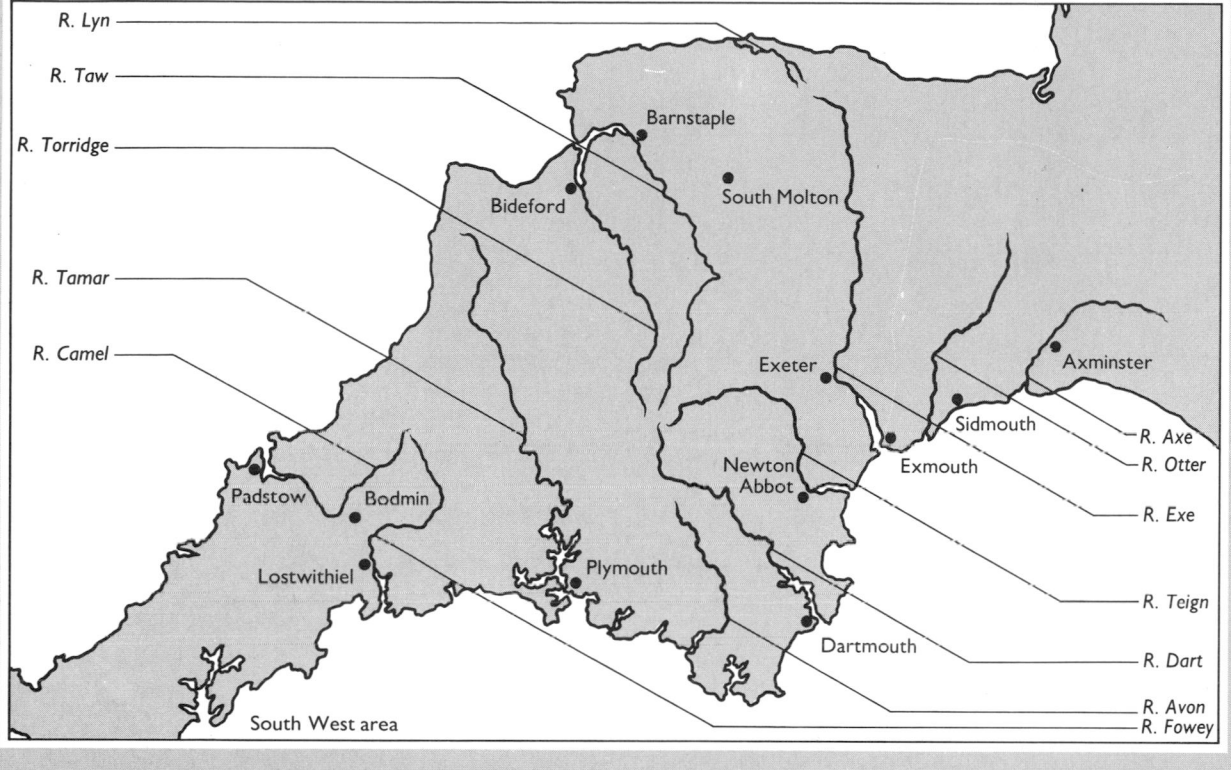

R. Lyn
R. Taw
R. Torridge
R. Tamar
R. Camel

Barnstaple
Bideford
South Molton
Exeter
Axminster
Sidmouth
R. Axe
R. Otter
Newton Abbot
Exmouth
R. Exe
Padstow
Bodmin
R. Teign
Lostwithiel
Plymouth
R. Dart
Dartmouth
R. Avon
R. Fowey

South West area

The south west offers the fisherman some of the best fly fishing for wild brown trout to be found in England – and much of it is available by purchasing a modestly priced permit. The three moorland areas, Exmoor, Dartmoor and Bodmin Moor, give rise to numerous sparkling streams where the angler can cast his fly on mile after mile of unpolluted water. In contrast, the quiet streams of east Devon provide classic dry fly fishing similar to the chalk streams of Wessex.

The trout season starts on 15 March and ends on the last day of September. The early weeks, especially on the high moors, are the time for the sunk fly, but by late April the dry fly begins to take over. Although good fishing can be enjoyed at any time in the season, the very best sport comes between the middle of May and the middle of July, when hatches of insects and rises of trout reach their peak. This is the time too when the countryside is at its best.

Some of the best known standard fly patterns were originated in Devon – Blue Upright, Pheasant Tail, Half Stone, Infallible – and these are as effective today as when they were invented, both

in wet and dry versions. Other standard patterns which are worth using are the Coch-y-bondhu, Red Quill and Greenwell. To this list you should add imitations of the more prolific natural insects, particularly the black gnat, hawthorn, various small sedges, pale watery and the dun and spinner stages of the blue winged olive.

Numerous fisheries where trout fishing is readily available are mentioned under specific rivers, but many other waters can be fished by purchasing a day or period permit. Details of these can be obtained from the South West Water Authority at Exeter.

Axe

The Axe is the only river in the south west which rises in chalk, with its source near Beaminster in the downs of west Dorset. As it flows to the south west it is, for about five miles, the boundary between Dorset and Somerset, before becoming a Devon river and running down its broad valley

The West Dart near Paradise Bridge

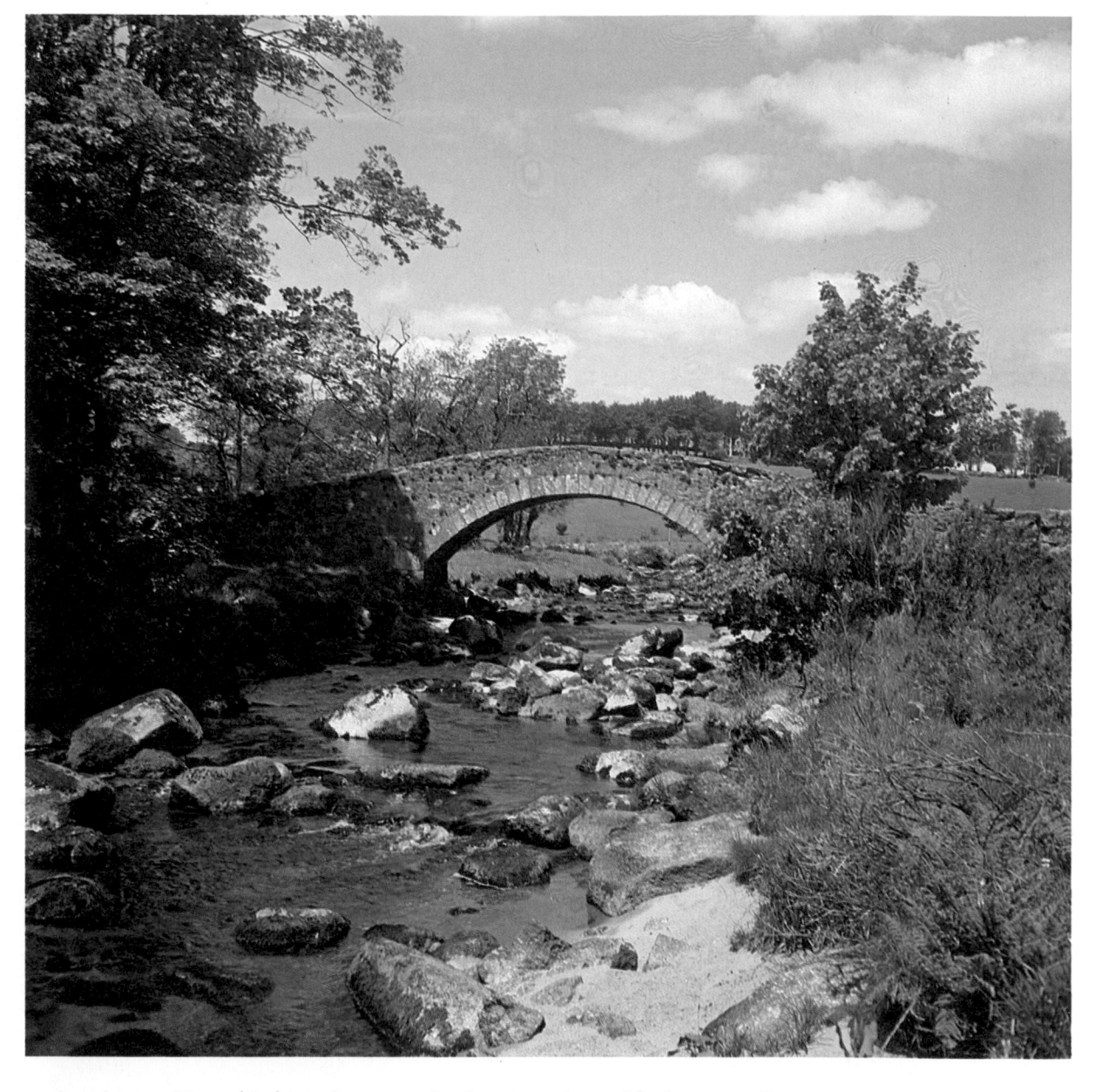

to Axminster. Near this historic town, the Axe is joined by its main tributary the Yarty, a productive little stream which rises within a mile of the source of the Otter in the Blackdown Hills. For its last few miles the Axe meanders back and forth across a flat marshy valley and becomes tidal at Colyford where the Coly flows in from the west. The estuary runs south past Axmouth to its meeting with the sea at Seaton.

The Axe is a quiet stream, often deep and slow in the reaches above Axminster, with none of the sudden floods of the moorland streams. Trout are present throughout the whole system and the Axe has long had a reputation for plump well fed fish, with plenty of eight to twelve ounce trout and the odd one up to a pound and a half. The Yarty is

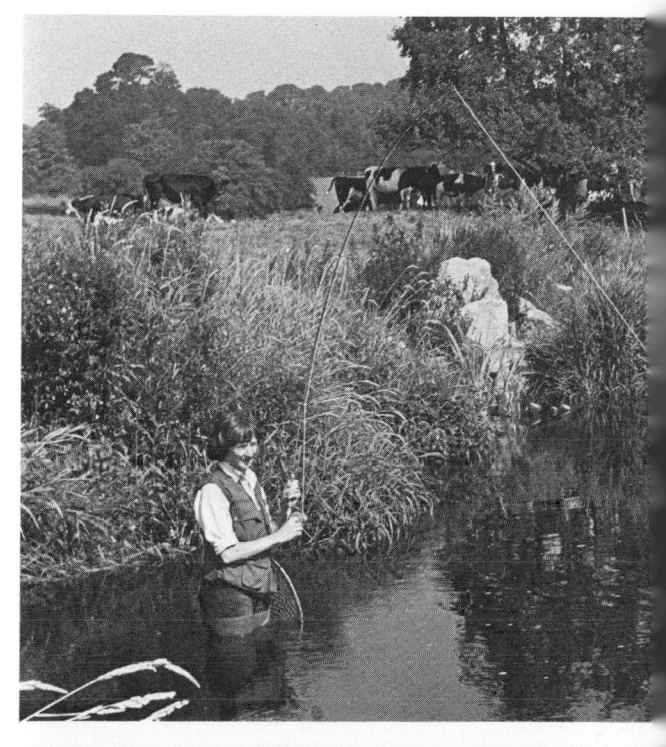

a faster stream, running quickly over its gravel bed through a series of stickles and small pools. Unfortunately, the Axe suffered severe pollution in 1982 and from Seaborough down to Axminster much of the fish life was wiped out. Prompt restocking was carried out but a full recovery is bound to take a number of years. The Axe has seen a considerable decline in its run of salmon but there remains a good run of sea-trout into the lower reaches, though most of these fish then run up the Yarty, which provides the best of the fishing. This river also continues to have a fine head of free rising brown trout, with many around half a pound or more.

Both the Axe and Yarty are essentially streams for the fly fisherman and particularly for the dry fly. Hatches of dark olive, blue winged olives and various sedges, including the grannom, are worth imitating in their seasons and the mayfly, although not prolific, can produce good sport. The traditional patterns for the Axe are the Blue Dun and a bright Red Palmer, and both are still well worth using.

The four miles or so above Axminster have usually been considered the best of the trout fishing but following the pollution and consequent restocking it is difficult to predict the best beats for the future. The Axe has always been a closely preserved stream and even today the two main associations on the river, the Axe Fly Fishers and the Taunton Fly Fishers, do not offer permits. The George Hotel, at Axminster, issues permits on nearly half a mile of the Axe and tickets are available from local farms for stretches on both Axe and Yarty.

Otter

The Otter probably offers the nearest thing to chalk stream fishing to be found in the south west and has frequently appeared in fly fishing literature in company with the Test, Itchen and Kennet. It is not, of course, a real chalk stream but its headwaters in the greensand of the Blackdown Hills give it many chalk stream characteristics – clear water, prolific insect life and plump trout which rise well to the dry fly. It drops down from the hills through Monkton Combe to Honiton,

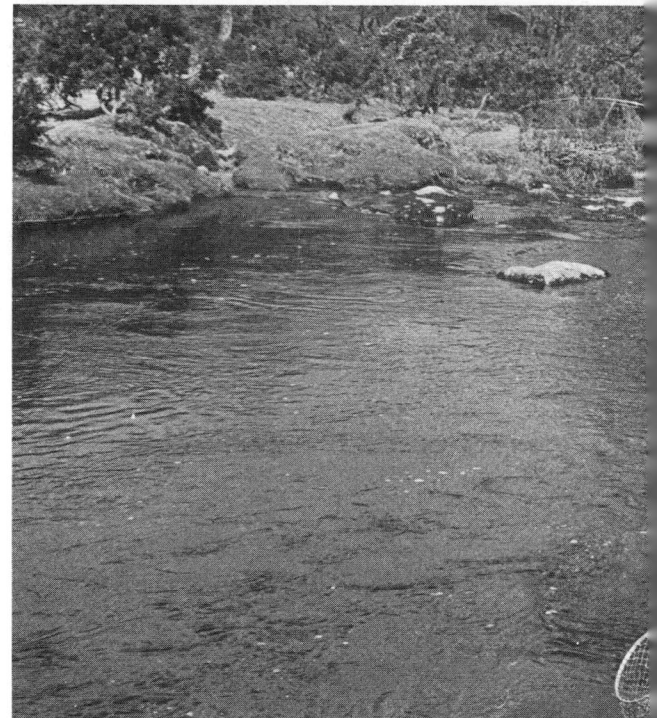

Bottom: Dermot Wilson lands a Dart trout above
Two Bridges

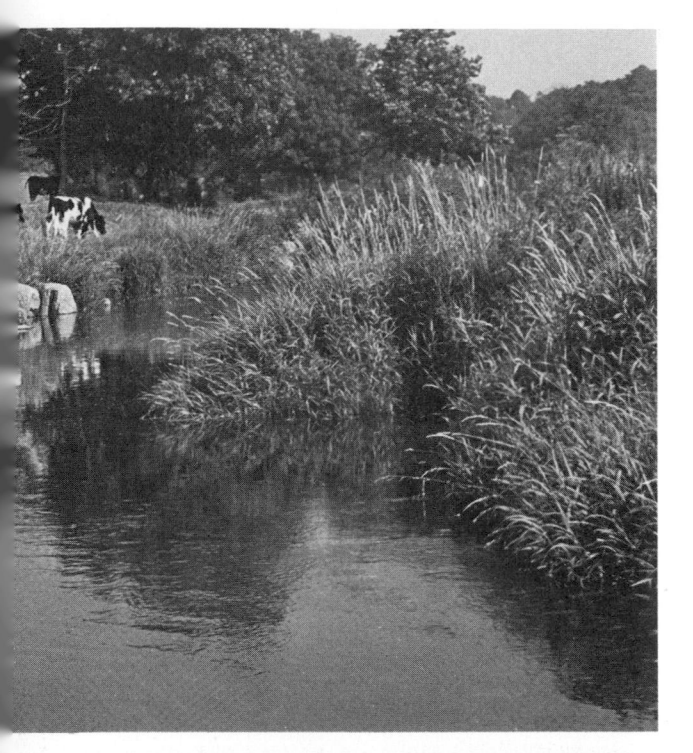

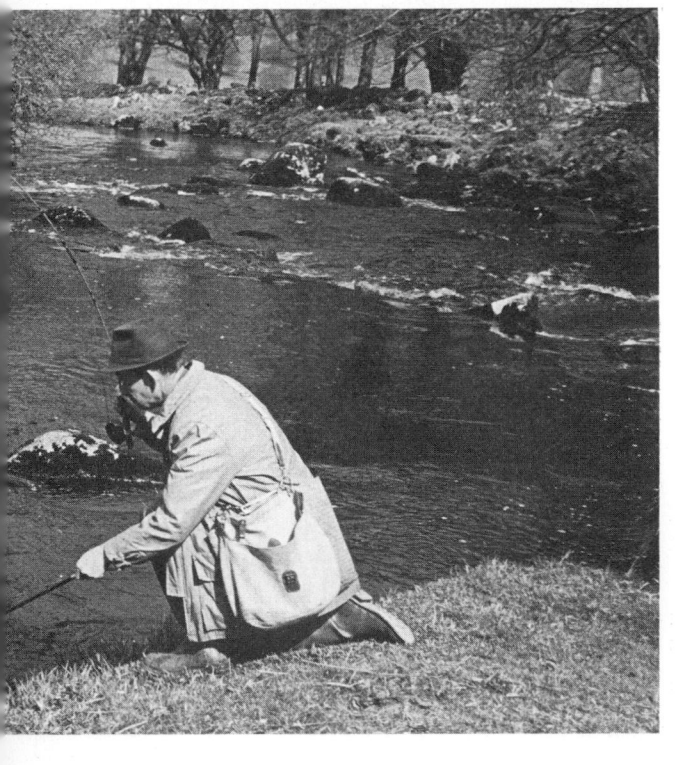

continues in a south westerly direction to Ottery
St Mary, and then south, past Newton Poppleford
to the sea at Budleigh Salterton.

Originally the Otter was not given to sudden
flooding but recent dredging and drainage of adjacent land now give rise to flash floods after rain,
followed by an equally quick return to low water
conditions. Many of the old hands on the river
claim that these changes have been at the expense
of both the fly life and wild fish population, but
the Otter still has a good head of trout as a result
of stocking on several fisheries. The native fish
are usually in the eight to twelve ounce class with
pound fish fairly common. There is also a good
run of sea-trout, though most are confined to the
lower reaches below Newton Poppleford, and
some of the slower parts of the river have a few
dace.

The Otter is essentially a dry fly river and this
is the method used by most anglers most of the
time. When there is a hatch of fly it makes sense
to match the emerging insect but a suitable range
of standard dry patterns also works well. When
the duns are hatching, a Beacon Beige is as effective here as on the nearby Culm where it was
invented. Regular Otter anglers also use a dark
Blue Upright, Grey Duster, Terry's Terror and
Palmer with good results.

With angling of the type found on the Otter,
it is hardly surprising that fishing is not easy to
find. The best bet for the visitor is one of the
hotels that control their own waters, and the Deer
Park Hotel near Honiton has been a popular venue
for many years. This hotel has a lengthy stretch
which it stocks regularly and permits are available
for both residents and non residents. The Combe
House Hotel at Gittisham and the Venn Ottery
Barton Hotel near Ottery St Mary also have fishing. The Ottery Fly Fishing Club controls an extensive fishery above and below Ottery St Mary
but fishing is restricted to members and their
guests.

Dart

The vast peat sponge of Dartmoor gives rise to
the numerous streams that come together to form
the River Dart, one of Devon's most important

trout streams, expecially for the visitor seeking inexpensive fishing. The Dart has two sources, with the East Dart and West Dart rising in the same part of north Dartmoor. Although the East Dart is probbaly slightly the longer stream, the West Dart quickly increases in volume with a greater number of tributaries and becomes the larger river. Between its source and Dartmeet, the West Dart is fed by Cowsic Brook, Blackbrook, Cherry Brook and Swincombe Brook, all miniature trout streams in their own right. The East Dart has one tributary, Walla Brook, before joining the West Dart at Dartmeet, from where the main river flows through a deep wooded valley to Buckfastleigh, and then through more open agricultural country to its estuary below Totnes.

The upper Dart is the classic moorland stream with fast boulder strewn water flowing through rolling hills covered with bracken and heather. Except in times of flood, it is a very clear stream and even after rain it turns to a peaty brown rather than becoming thickly coloured with sediment, though the lower reaches pick up more colour from the surrounding farmland after rain.

The Dartmoor reaches provide one of the great strongholds of our native brown trout with huge numbers of wild fish, whose only competition for food comes from the parr of salmon and sea-trout, both of which run in good numbers up to the high moors. As one would expect, these acid moorlands are noted for the numbers of trout rather than the high average size. However, especially on the West Dart, half pounders are common and even pound-plus trout are caught in reasonable numbers. My own best West Dart trout was only an ounce short of three pounds and even bigger fish are taken from time to time. Below Dartmeet the concentration is on salmon and sea-trout fishing but there is still a good head of wild trout which is supplemented by stocking below Buckfastleigh.

Above Dartmeet, trout fishing is restricted to fly fishing and rightly so. The broad broken stretches are ideal for fishing a team of wet flies across and downstream and, from May on, the dry fly is very effective on both branches of the Dart and their tributaries. In fact, over the course of a season I am convinced that the dry fly will easily outstrip the wet, both for quality of fishing and quantity of fish.

The traditional Devon flies do well on the Dart but the dry fly fisherman should watch out for hatches of dark olive, pale watery and especially the blue winged olive. All of these emerge in greater numbers than on other moorland rivers, particularly on the quieter weedy stretches of the tributaries like Blackbrook and Cherry Brook, and when this happens I always turn to an imitation of the emerging insect. A small hairwing Sedge or a Coch-y-bondhu is a good standby through the summer months when nothing in particular is hatching.

The Duchy of Cornwall waters on the upper reaches offer one of the most extensive trout fisheries anywhere in England, and possibly the least expensive. Nearly all of the Dart system upstream of Dartmeet is included in this fishery, for which modestly priced permits are always available in season. I have fished these waters extensively for a dozen years and always enjoyed the sense of freedom ensured by so many miles of wild river in the unspoiled country of the Dartmoor National Park. There is so much fishing that even now I still occasionally fish in new water, so the newcomer has a wonderful variety of fishing to explore.

If I were pressed to name my favourite stretches I would have to go for the West Dart for a mile or two above the mouth of the Swincombe, or the bottom mile of Blackbrook, the latter being ideal on a calm warm day when the olives are hatching. For working upstream through a series of small pools, the stretch of Cherry Brook between the two roads that cross it would be hard to beat, and the East Dart around the famous clapper bridge at Postbridge offers fine fishing, though not too close to the crowds who come to see the bridge. Permits for this lovely fishery are widely available locally.

The upper Dart is ideal country for any angler with the slightest interest in wildlife. The soaring buzzard, with its mewing call, is always present and ravens are frequently seen, especially on the high ground. By the waterside there is always the dipper and the mink is an all too frequent sight.

The best opportunity for fishing the lower Dart is provided by the Dart Angling Association, which controls much of the river between Buckfastleigh and Totnes.

Avon (Devon)

The southernmost part of Devon has its own River Avon, a small stream not to be confused with the more widely known Hampshire Avon, Bristol Avon and Warwickshire Avon. It rises in the heart of south Dartmoor, close to the sources of two other south Devon streams, the Plym and the Erme. The headwaters of the Avon are impounded to form Avon Reservoir, a bleak place on all but the most benign day. From the reservoir it drops quickly through a series of falls and pools to Shipley Bridge and on to South Brent, where it leaves the Dartmoor National Park. Above South Brent, the Avon is a small moorland stream but from here to its estuary at Aveton Gifford, its character changes as it meanders through the gentle rolling countryside of the South Hams.

The Avon can rise quickly when heavy winter rain falls on Dartmoor but during the fishing season the Avon Reservoir has a stablising effect on the lighter rainfall of summer. Even when the river does flood the upper reaches carry relatively little colour but the lower river quickly takes on colour from the surrounding farmland.

Like so many of the Devon rivers with a moorland origin, the Avon contains only salmon, seatrout and brown trout, with the latter prolific throughout its length. The fish of the moorland reaches are usually of modest size but the average increases considerably on the lower and more fertile stretches of the river, with plenty of fish over the half pound mark.

Avon trout are free rising fish so this is ideal fly fishing country, whether wet or dry. The fish on the moor are seldom selective and the usual Devon patterns all do well, but lower down it is often worth imitating the fly on the water, with the sedge, black gnat and hawthorn being far more prolific than ephemeroptera.

One of my favourite stretches of fishing on a small moorland stream is the South West Water Authority's fishery on the upper Avon, which runs from Shipley Bridge, near South Brent, up to and including the Avon Reservoir. This fishery is free to any angler holding a trout licence and offers two miles of dry fly fishing on a mixture of sparkling runs and deep little pools under small granite cliffs. A fly cast to any likely spot will probably bring a rise and good bags of brown trout of around eight to nine inches are regularly taken.

Most of the river between South Brent and Aveton Gifford is controlled by the Avon Fishing Association. Although day permits are not available for this delightful stretch of some fourteen miles, there is no difficulty in getting permits by the week, fortnight, month or season.

Teign

The Teign rises in the remote part of north Dartmoor which also, within a few miles, has the sources of the Taw, Tavy, West Dart and East Dart. For the first few miles it flows through open moorland before dropping into a wooded valley near Gidleigh. In fact, this part of the river is known as the North Teign, right down to the point where it is joined by the South Teign, a couple of miles above Chagford, the first town on the river. The South Teign is a much shorter stream and much of its water is collected by Fernworthy Reservoir.

For several miles in the Chagford area, the Teign flows quietly through meadows but just below Castle Drogo it plunges into Fingle Gorge, a deep wooded valley noted as one of Devon's best known beauty spots, especially around Fingle Bridge. The river breaks out into a wider valley at Steps Bridge near Dunsford. Before reaching Dunsford, the Teign has been flowing in a general easterly direction within the Dartmoor National Park, but here it turns south and forms the eastern boundary of the national park as far as Trusham. Near here it is joined by a small stream, the headwaters of which are impounded to form Kennick, Tottiford and Trenchford reservoirs.

After three more miles, the Teign passes under the busy A38 trunk road and is shortly joined by its only tributary of any consequence, the Bovey. This river also rises on Dartmoor and its valley is particularly beautiful around wooded Lustleigh Cleave, after which it flows through the small town of Bovey Tracey before joining the Teign. Although the valleys of both rivers are noted for their beauty, things change after they meet, with the last few miles to Newton Abbot running

Conrad Voss-Bark fishing the Taw at Umberleigh

through land which has been devastated by ball clay extraction. At Newton Abbot the river becomes tidal and the estuary joins the sea at Teignmouth.

With its Dartmoor origin, the Teign is almost always fast flowing, the only exceptions being above the weirs, which often create quiet smooth pools of nearly a quarter mile in length. It is usually clear and even in a flood it carries peat stain rather than mud, and clears again very quickly. In fact, between April and September, the Teign rarely goes into flood as much of the rainfall is collected by Fernworthy Reservoir. Although this is irritating for the salmon angler, who is waiting for a run of fish, it does mean that the river is almost always fishable for trout.

Wild brown trout are present in large numbers throughout the Teign and it never needs stocking. However, the acid nature means that the average size of trout is modest, though fish of several pounds are taken from time to time by sea-trout anglers at night. Most bags of trout will run from eight to eleven inches, with the occasional fish approaching a pound. The Teign is an excellent river for sea-trout, and has good runs of salmon when water levels permit.

When the season opens in mid March the wet fly fished across and down stream is the best method and standard patterns like the Blue Upright, Half Stone, March Brown and Greenwell in sizes twelve and fourteen do well. Towards the end of April, the dry fly becomes more effective and from early May until the end of the season many anglers, myself included, use nothing else. Although upwinged insects like the dark olive and blue winged olive hatch regularly on the Teign, they rarely emerge in sufficient numbers to produce a concentrated rise and it is for this reason that general patterns which suggest several species are effective. The most frantic surface feeding is brought about by falls of terrestrial insects, which are particularly numerous in the wooded stretches. Imitations of the black gnat, which emerges around the middle of May, and a variety of beetles, small caterpillars and the large brown wood ant can produce spectacular sport with catches of a dozen fish being taken regularly in two or three hours – especially in May, June and early July. Wading is essential and the rocky and slippery bottom makes a wading staff a real asset.

Although the whole river offers trout fishing, my own preference is for the upper Teign between Chagford and Steps Bridge, which provides a wonderful variety of pools and runs – and a large head of fish. This fishery is run by the Upper Teign Fishing Association and permits for trout are always available. There is always something to see in the wooded upper Teign valley, whether it be deer retreating to the high ground, the rapid flight of the dipper or a buzzard patrolling the top of the gorge. One of the great sights is right at the beginning of the season when the wild daffodils line the river bank. Below Steps Bridge, much of the fishing is controlled by the Lower Teign Fishing Association, but here anglers concentrate more on the salmon and sea-trout fishing, though exploring with the trout rod is well worthwhile, especially on the association's stretch of the Bovey, where I have enjoyed good dry fly fishing.

Taw

The Taw and its tributaries have their headwaters in both the main moorland areas of the south west, Dartmoor and Exmoor. The source of the Taw is in the heart of north Dartmoor but it leaves the moor while still a small stream and for most of its course flows through the rich lowland farm country of north Devon. Past South Tawton and North Tawton it wanders down its winding course through peaceful meadows, but grows to a sizable stream after being joined first by the Yeo and then the Little Dart near Chulmleigh. A few miles downstream is the mouth of the main tributary, the Mole, which flows down from Exmoor and has its own extensive system of tributaries including the Bray and yet another Yeo, one of four rivers with the name in Devon alone. The Taw, now a stately stream in a broad valley, becomes tidal near Bishop's Tawton, and enters its estuary at Barnstaple.

Except in its highest reaches, the Taw always carries a fair amount of colour and can remain unfishable for several days after heavy rains have fallen in its extensive catchment area. It is a noted salmon river, with the Mole often providing some of the best fishing. Sea-trout fishing can be very

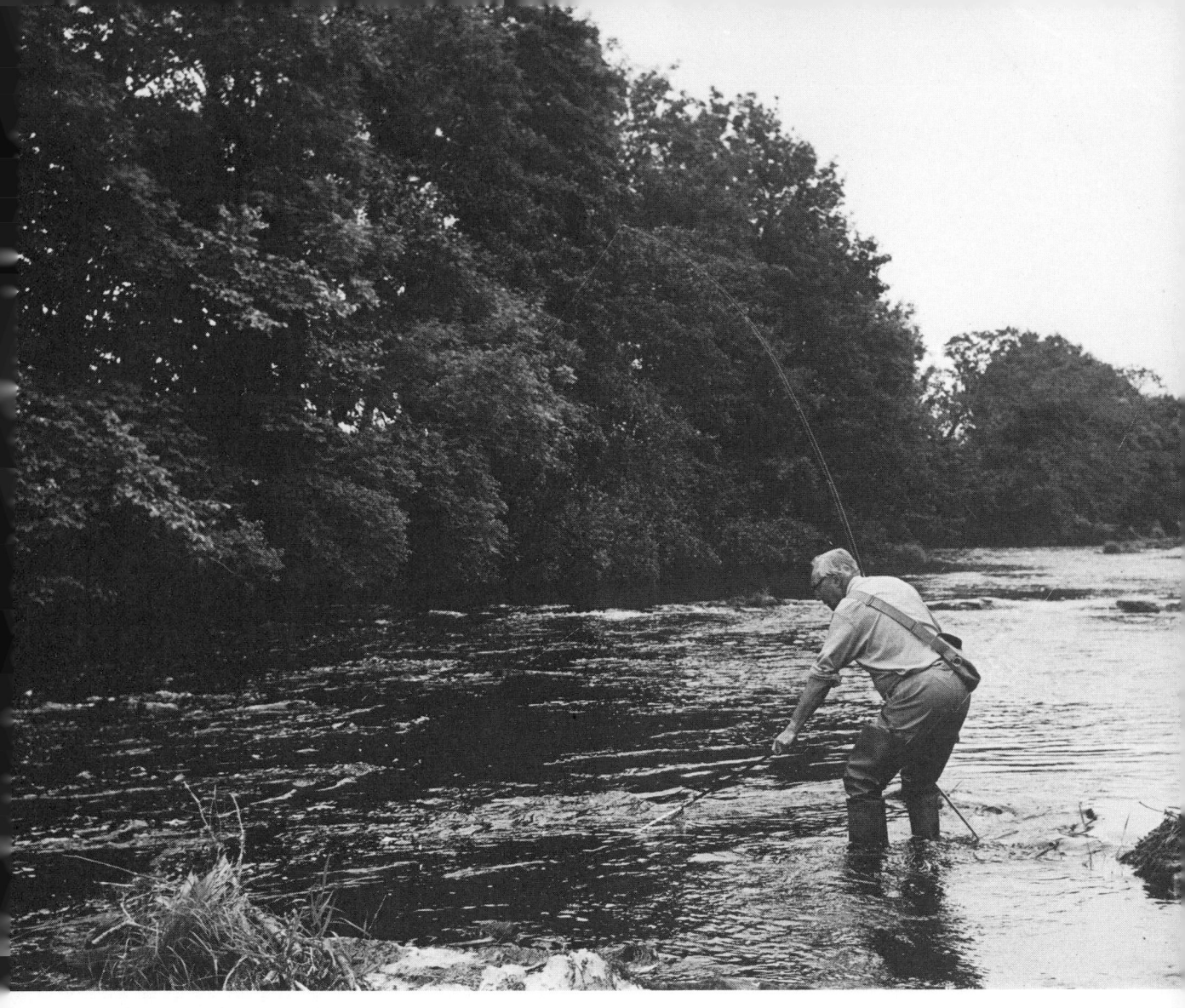

good, with some of the largest fish caught in Devon taken here in recent years. The lower Taw is one of the very few Devon rivers with a head of coarse fish in the shape of some large roach, mainly around Newbridge. Trout are to be found everywhere, though the lower river is fished mainly for salmon and sea-trout. The fish of the higher reaches, where the Taw or its tributaries are close to Dartmoor and Exmoor, are wild but some stocking has been done, especially around Eggesford.

For the brown trout fisherman, the best opportunities will be found on the upper Taw, the Mole and the Bray, where a number of waters can be fished on a day permit. The Fox and Hounds at Eggesford has several miles of fishing, with the head of native brown trout supplemented by stocking with fish of up to a pound. From here up to Dartmoor, the Taw is well worth exploring and permits can be obtained for several short

stretches. The best opportunity for fishing the lower river is at the Rising Sun, Umberleigh, but this is essentially salmon and sea-trout fishing.

South Molton is a good centre for fishing the Mole and Bray, both delightful little streams tumbling down from Exmoor and ideal for the angler who likes to work up through a series of pools and runs on a small stream with a dry fly. The South Molton and District Angling Club has waters on both of these rivers and the Bray can also be fished with a permit from the Poltimore Arms at North Molton.

Exe

Both the Exe and its first sizeable tributary, the Barle, rise high on Exmoor, much closer to the north coast than the south coast into which they

93

Below: The Exe
Right: The Barle, upper reaches

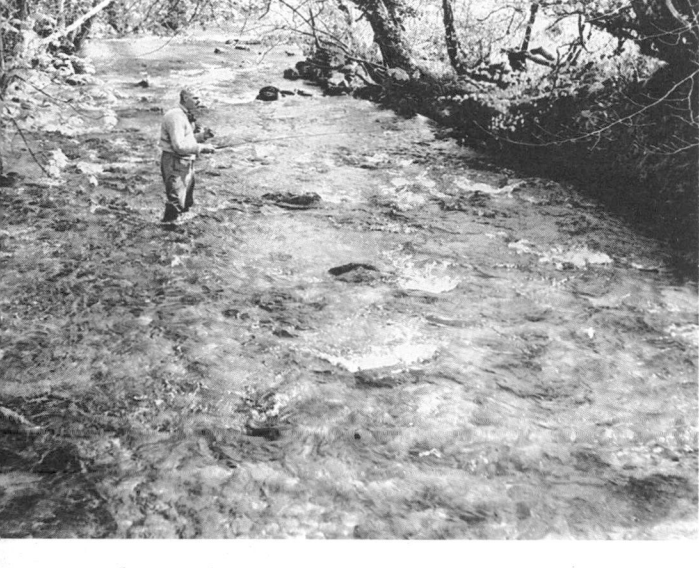

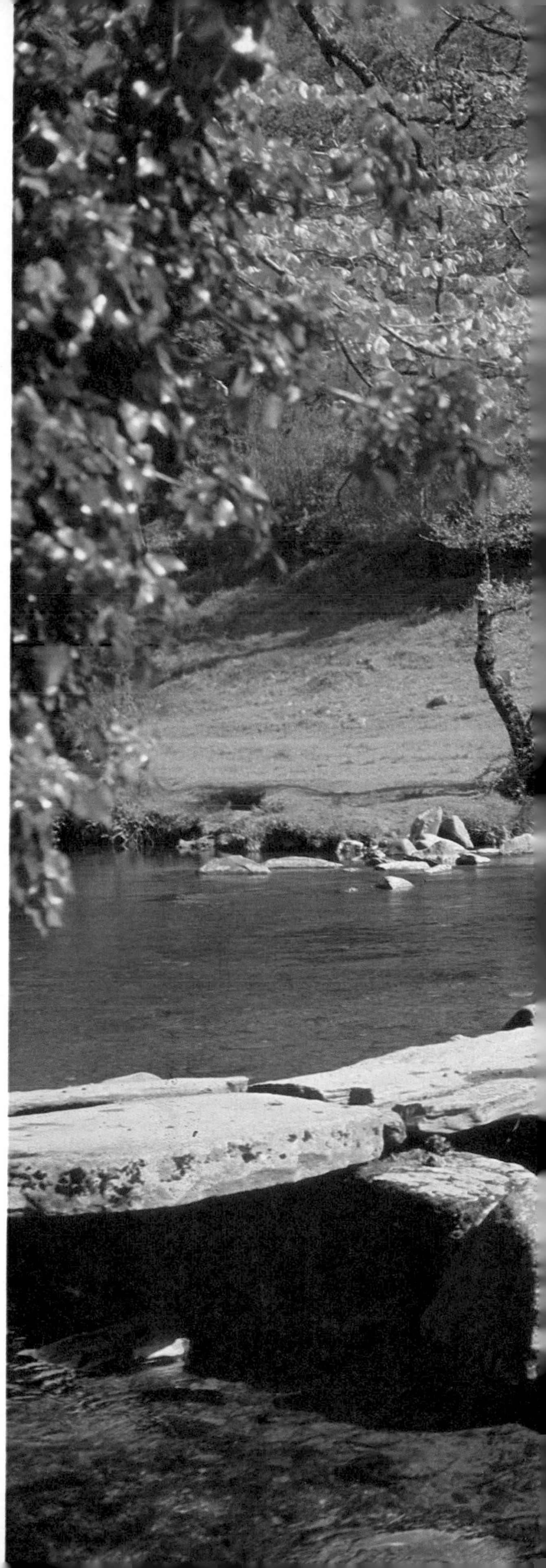

flow. They join near Dulverton, on the Devon and Somerset border, after which the Exe continues south through its broad valley, past Tiverton and on to Exeter. Shortly before reaching Exeter the Exe is joined by its other main tributaries, first the Culm and then the Creedy. The Exe becomes tidal just below Exeter and runs into its estuary at Topsham.

The Exe system probably offers the greatest variey of trout fishing in the south west, ranging from moorland trouting on small streams to classic dry fly fishing of the chalk stream type. The upper reaches of both Exe and Barle flow through Exmoor country and offer typical moorland fishing for small wild brown trout in clear quick flowing water. In its moorland reaches the Exe is always small but the Barle becomes a sizeable stream before it leaves the moor, especially downstream from Simonsbath. Even in the broader reaches below the confluence of these two streams, the Exe is always a lively stream, though below Tiverton the pools become longer and more smooth. The Culm, which joins the Exe at Stoke Canon, rises on the Blackdown Hills and is distinctly alkaline, with many of the characteristics of a chalk or limestone stream. The Creedy, however, drains an area of typical red Devon soil and in time of flood runs very thick and red.

Trout are present throughout the Exe system, varying from wild brown trout alone in the

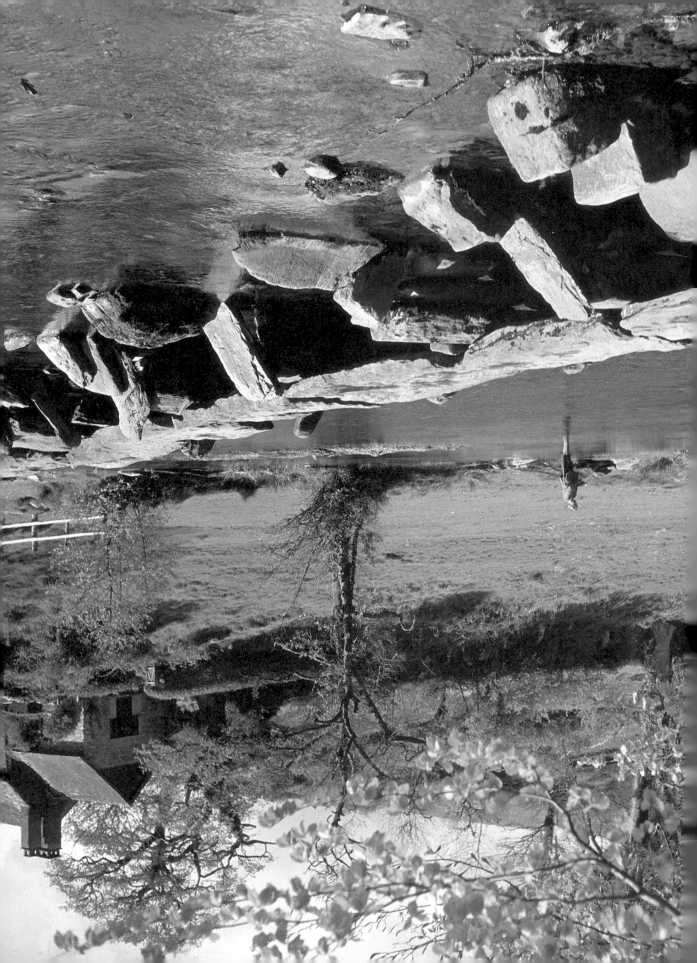

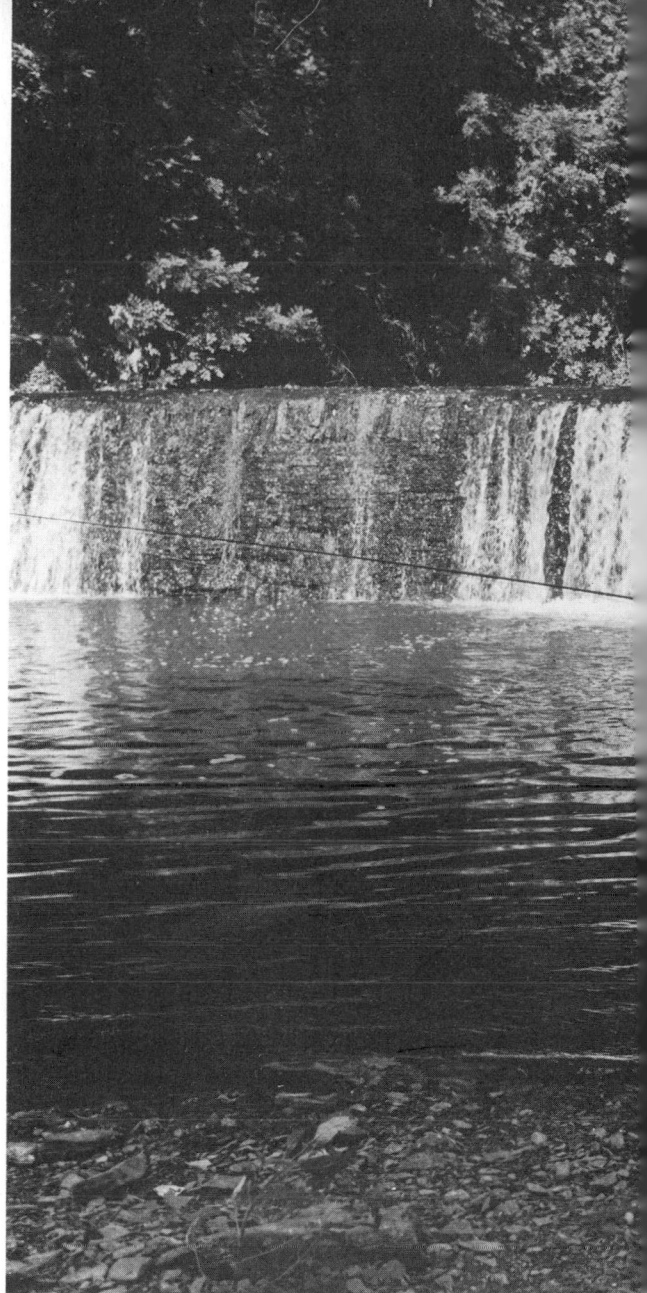

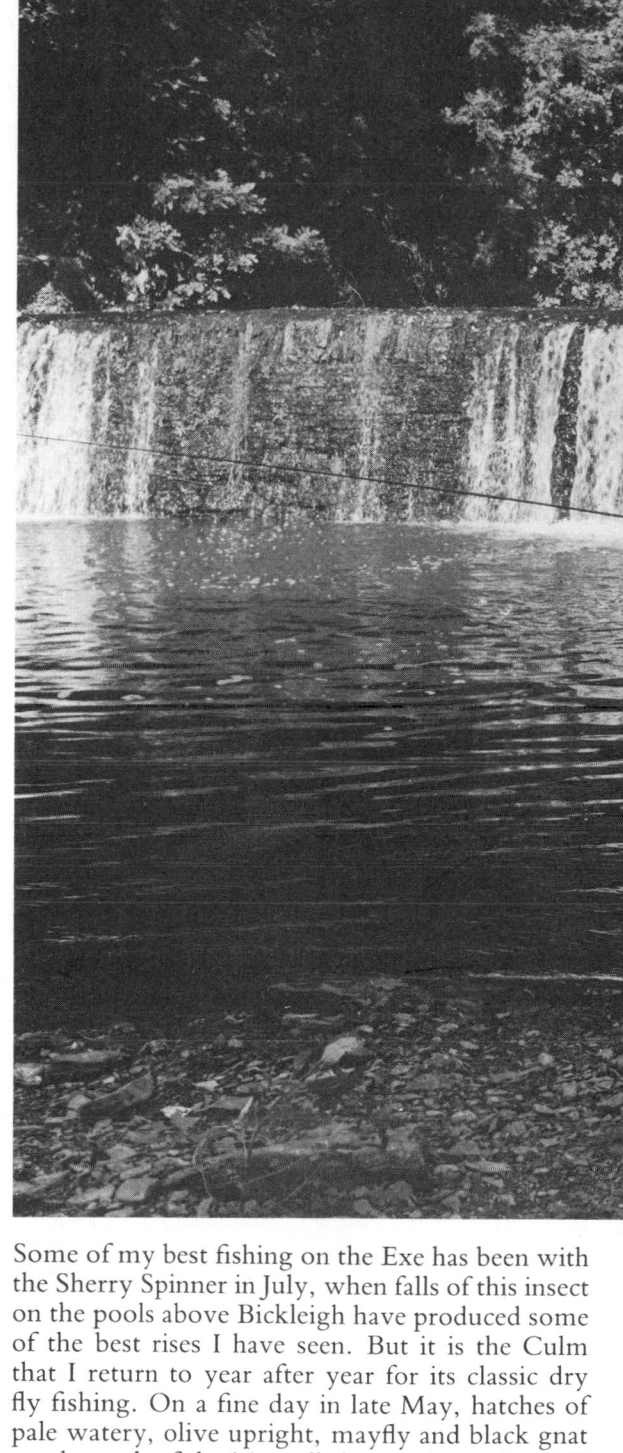

topmost reaches on Exmoor to mixed fishing with numerous coarse fish around Exeter. The middle reaches have considerable numbers of grayling, and around Exbridge near Dulverton there are numerous rainbows which have escaped from the nearby hatchery. The Exe has declined from its former glory as a spring salmon river, but still has good runs later in the season. Strangely, the Exe is just about the only river in Devon which does not get any appreciable run of sea-trout. On the Exmoor reaches of the Exe and Barle the trout are mainly on the small side but the average size increases as the streams come down from the moor and in the Tiverton area I have often averaged over the half pound with a fair number of pound plus fish. The fertile Culm, with its prolific hatches of fly, is noted for its free rising trout of good average size.

Inevitably, fishing methods are as varied as the rivers and streams of the Exe system. Fishing the water with a dry or wet standard pattern is probably best on the higher reaches, but fishermen on the lower Exe and the Culm definitely favour the use of an imitation of the emerging insect cast to the rising fish – on these stretches I never fish any other way. From May on the hatches of pale watery, olive upright, blue winged olive, and various sedges can produce really good rises. The best of the sedge hatch on the Exe can be early in the year with explosive hatches coming during late May, and at such times a bushy Sedge dragged across the surface at dusk can produce spectacular sport.

Some of my best fishing on the Exe has been with the Sherry Spinner in July, when falls of this insect on the pools above Bickleigh have produced some of the best rises I have seen. But it is the Culm that I return to year after year for its classic dry fly fishing. On a fine day in late May, hatches of pale watery, olive upright, mayfly and black gnat can keep the fish rising all day, and test the skill and knowledge of the angler as the fish change from one insect to another. If you get it right on such a day, a catch of twenty fish or more between eight and fifteen inches is well within reach – but please return most of these plump wild fish to the water. I always find a day among the lush meadows of the Culm valley a welcome change

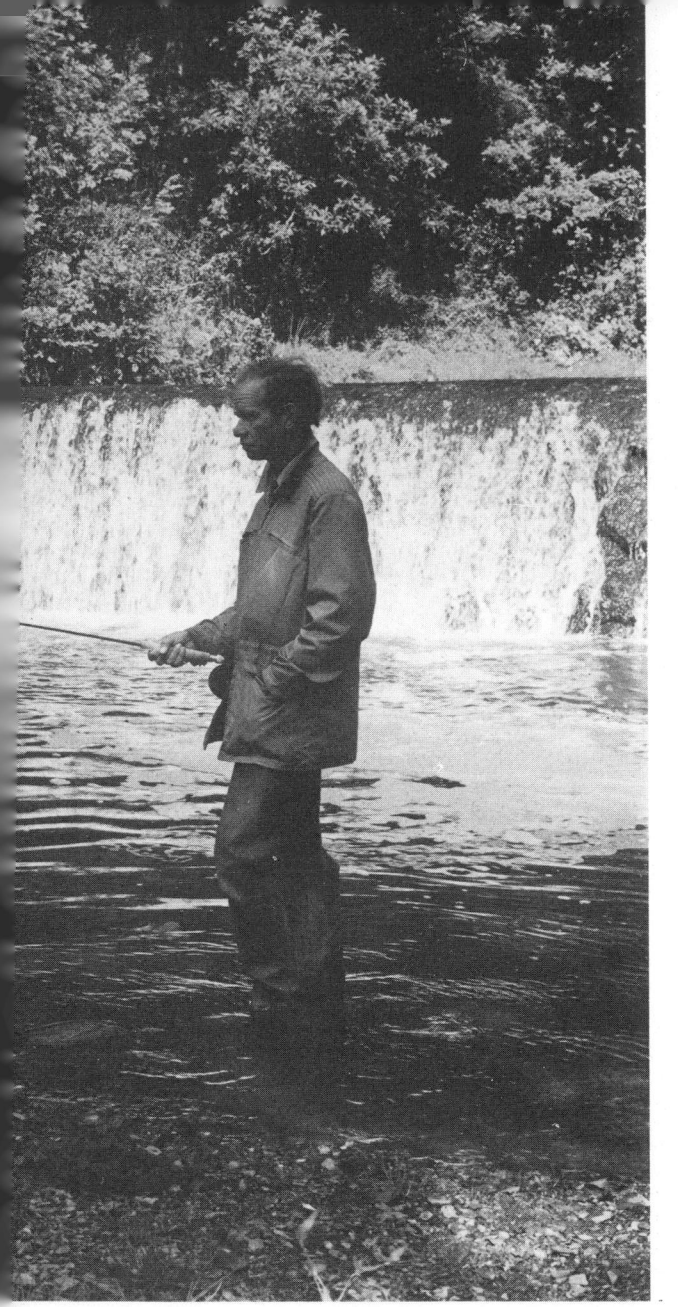

Far left: The Carey, a Tamar tributary
Centre: The Lyd, another Tamar tributary

East Lyn

Although there are two Lyns, it is the East Lyn which is of interest to fishermen, the West Lyn being a short stream which falls quickly down to Lynmouth and offers little opportunity for serious fishing. The East Lyn itself is quite a short river but it grows to a fair size very rapidly as a result of its numerous tributaries. High on Exmoor, within a mile of each other, are the sources of Weir Water and Chalk Water which join to form Oare Water at Oareford. Two miles downstream at Malmsmead, Oare Water is joined by Badgworthy Water, which itself has a large number of feeder streams, including Hoccombe Water and Hoccome Combe, the latter being the Doone Valley of legend and the novel, *Lorna Doone*. The river now becomes the East Lyn and for a further three miles, past the village of Brendon, is a quiet little stream, though always quick moving, flowing through meadows. Then, at Rockford, it plunges into its dramatic wooded gorge, past the famous beauty spot Watersmeet, where it is joined by Hoaroak Water, and on to the sea at Lynmouth. This last five miles is a series of cascades but with plenty of pools for the angler.

The Lyn is a typical fast flowing moorland river, indeed quicker than most, with a drop of 750 feet from the village of Oare to its mouth, a distance of less than ten miles. This drop can produce some dramatic floods but fortunately few to compare with the disastrous flood of 1952. At normal level the Lyn is a very clear river and even in flood has little colour.

This is a pure salmon and trout river with no coarse fish anywhere in the Lyn system. Following a flood it can produce excellent salmon fishing and it has a good run of sea-trout, but for the visiting angler, who cannot time his visits to coincide with the brief floods, it is above all a fine trout stream for those who enjoy fly fishing on an unspoilt river for wild brown trout of modest size. Stocking on the Lyn is not necessary and would certainly be undesirable with such a large stock of natural fish. In fact, the ranks of rising trout in the quieter pools above and below Rockford on a fine day in May or June, when the black gnat are swarming, offer a sight to gladden the heart of any fly fisherman. This is not a river for

from the more rugged rivers that I usually fish.

Local enquiries will reveal many opportunities for obtaining permission to fish in the Exe system. The upper reaches have several fishing hotels, including the Exmoor Forest at Simonsbath, the Tarr Steps, and the Carnarvon Arms near Dulverton; the last has an extensive fishery on both Exe and Barle. Unfortunately, it is often difficult to find fishing on the middle and lower reaches, a pity as here are many miles of first class trout fishing which are hopelessly under utilised. On the Culm, permits can be obtained from a local owner at Uffculme and the Upper Culm Fishing Association also offers permits for four miles of fishing around Hemyock.

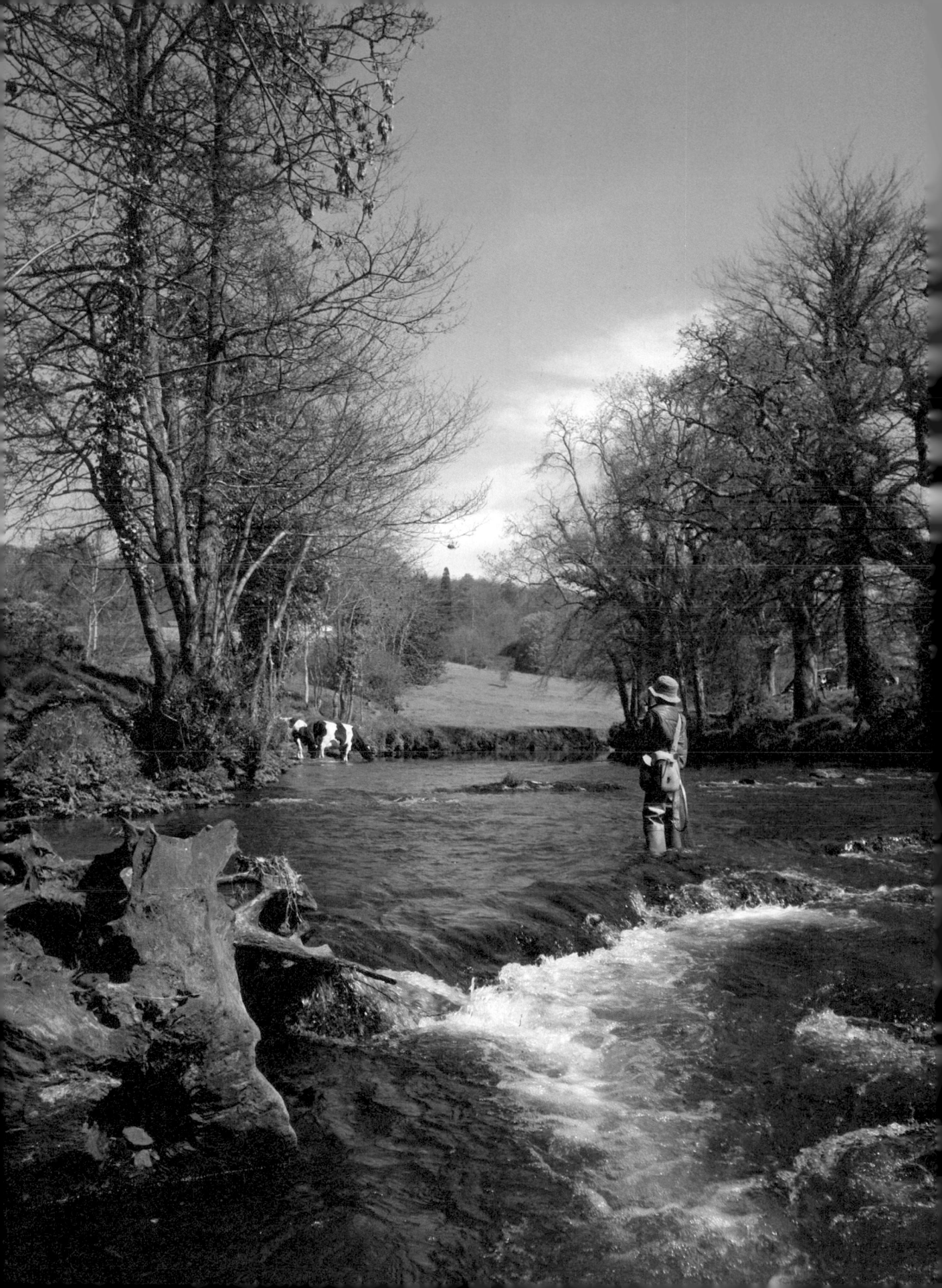

Spring sunshine on the Lyd

the big fish angler but a bag of a dozen fish over eight inches is easily come by and the best fish should top ten inches. And once they have recovered from the rigours of winter, there are few fish more beautiful than a Lyn trout.

Fly fishing, both wet and dry, works well on the Lyn and is, indeed, the only method which is permitted for trout on the main stretches. On the quieter reaches above Rockford and on the pools that intersperse the cascades lower down, my own preference is for the dry fly, as Lyn trout are among the most free rising I have experienced. In such a fast flowing moorland river, one can hardly expect a prolific population of nymphs, and hatches of upwinged flies are quite modest. However, the wooded banks bring a constant flow of terrestrial insects into the river, so suitable imitations like the Coch-y-bondhu are always worth a try. From June on there is usually the odd sedge on the wing and a buoyant hair wing imitation around size sixteen works well. Otherwise, any of the standard patterns like Blue Upright, Pheasant Tail or Greenwell will work well, in wet or dry. For me, the highlight of the year on the Lyn is the emergence of the black gnat and I always try to spend a couple of days in late May or early June fishing a size eighteen imitation on the quieter stretches around Rockford.

Fishing on the Lyn is readily available as the best of the fishing can be enjoyed with a day permit from the South West Water Authority. The authority controls both the Glenthorne Fishery, between Malmsmead and Rockford, and the Watersmeet Fishery, from Rockford to the sea. Below Watersmeet the river can be rather turbulent for trout fishing but from there to the top of the fishery there is wonderful range of varied fishing in wild and beautiful surroundings. Further upstream, day permits are available on a number of shorter stretches.

Tamar

Most rivers in the south west rise on one of the three moorland areas but the Tamar runs its whole course through gentle farm country and from its source right to the sea it drops only about 700 feet. For most of its course it is the boundary between Cornwall and Devon, and runs virtually from coast to coast. The source is only three miles from the coast of north Cornwall and after about two miles it runs first into Upper Tamar Reservoir and then into Tamar Lake, the former a trout fishery and the latter a coarse fishery. From here it continues south in its quiet way past Bridgerule and North Tamerton, always a small stream, in country rarely explored by the tourist. Around Launceston it grows rapidly in size as it is joined first by the Ottery, and then in rapid succession by the Carey, Kensey and the combined waters of the Lyd with its tributaries Wolf and Thrushel. The Lyd is the only river in the whole system with a moorland beginning, its source being on Dartmoor above Lydford. For its last few miles, before becoming tidal below Gunnislake, the Tamar runs through a deep wooded valley.

The tidal Tamar is joined by the Tavy, a river system in its own right. This river rises high on Dartmoor, flows through the historic town of Tavistock and is joined by another moorland stream, the Walkham, before flowing into the Tamar estuary.

The Tamar is never as crystalline as the moorland streams and carries considerable colour for some time after heavy rain. However, its slower pace provides a more hospitable habitat than on the high moors and this is well illustrated by the hatches of mayfly which are far superior to most streams in the south west.

Brown trout are present throughout the Tamar system but the best trout fishing will be found above Launceston and in the tributaries. Although stocking has been carried out from time to time, most Tamar trout were born in the river and fish of a pound or more are reasonably numerous, though the average would be around the half pound. The lower and middle reaches have some first class salmon fishing and there is an excellent run of sea-trout. The Tavy and Walkham both carry large stocks of small wild brown trout, as well as the salmon and sea trout for which the Tavy is noted.

Most trout fishing is done with the fly, both dry and wet, and the hatches are often sufficiently prolific to imitate the emerging insect. Some of my best memories are of the lovely little River Carey in mayfly time. The hatches here are never as prolific as on the chalk streams but, once the

Kingcup time on the Carey

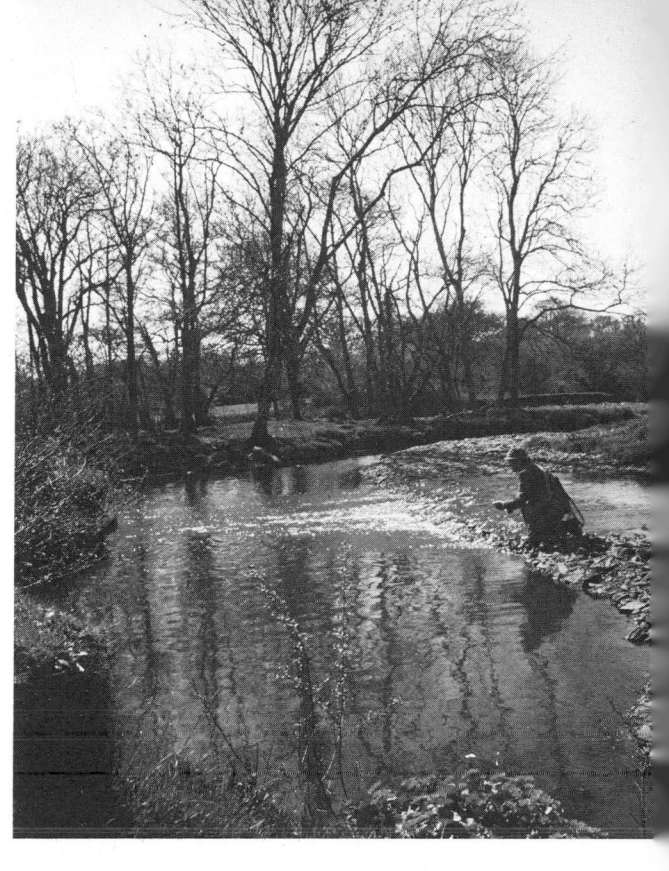

first few mayfly have emerged, the trout quickly acquire the taste for them and will take an imitation with relish, even when few can be seen on the water. My last visit was on such a day at a time when a severe drought had reduced the normally sparkling Carey to a mere trickle, yet some fine trout were taken in near stagnant water. In early season, an Imperial is well worth trying when there are a few dark olives about and later on the Black Gnat and Sedge are good in their seasons. Wet or dry versions of the old Devon favourites' like Pheasant Tail, Blue Upright and Half Stone should always be in the fly box.

Fortunately, the visiting angler has plenty of trout fishing to choose from, with permits readily available from the Bude Angling Association for the upper reaches and from the Launceston Anglers Association for the middle reaches. At Lifton there is the Arundell Arms, a noted fishing hotel with twenty miles of water on the Tamar, Lyd, Carey, Wolf and Thrushel.

Torridge

The Torridge, like the Tamar, rises within a few miles of the north Cornwall coast. Indeed both rivers have their sources within little more than a mile of each other, but thereafter their courses separate very rapidly. The Torridge swings in a great loop, first to the south and east, and then back to Devon's north coast. The upper Torridge is a quiet little stream flowing through rolling farm country past quaintly named villages like Milton Damerel, Shebbear, Black Torrington and Sheepwash. Then, near Hatherleigh, it grows rapidly as it is fed first by the Lew and then its main tributary, the Okement, which rises high on Dartmoor to the south of Okehampton. Within a few miles the valley deepens and becomes more wooded as the river winds its way through an impressive series of pools and runs to Great Torrington and Weare Giffard, near which it becomes tidal. The estuarial Torridge flows beneath the historic sixteen arch bridge at Bideford and merges with the waters of the Taw before entering the sea at Appledore.

The rich farmland through which the Torridge flows means that even when low it carries considerable colour and after heavy rain it can be unfishable for some time. However, this does have the advantage that the trout angler fishing in low water conditions will from time to time pick up a sea-trout in day time, an occurence which is rare on the ultra clear moorland streams.

The Torridge is, together with the Taw, most widely known as a salmon river, if only as the scene of Henry Williamson's *Salar the Salmon* and *Tarka the Otter*. It is also a fine stream for sea-trout. However, it is a fascinating little trout stream in its upper reaches with a large head of wild brown trout, supplemented in some places by the stocking of fish around the pound. Some of the best trout fishing on the upper Torridge is controlled by the Half Moon Inn at Sheepwash. I have always enjoyed my visits to this lovely fishery, which runs for several miles above and below Sheepwash Bridge. Just below the bridge there is a series of fast runs and shallow pools where I once enjoyed a splendid day in April. It was dull and a cold north easterly made an extra sweater essential, but the dark olives hatched off and on for several hours and a dry Imperial, size sixteen, brought fish after fish to the net. Over twenty trout between eight and twelve inches were caught. On another occasion, a mile or so downstream and on a warm day in late May, it was the turn of the Hawthorn to produce a bag of fewer but larger fish.

Another good water for trout is at the Woodford Bridge Hotel, Milton Damerel. Here the river is much smaller, with the quicker runs contrasting with very slow pools. I am always surprised by the way in which a dry fly cast over one of the slow, almost sluggish, stretches will bring a trout from out of the blue. These pools will often produce the best of the fishing and trout of over a pound are by no means rare.

Camel

The Camel rises on the fringe of Bodmin Moor near Davidstow and follows a southerly course for many miles along the western edge of the moor. Within a mile or two of its source, the infant stream flows under Slaughter Bridge, the legendary site of King Arthur's last battle, and on down its secluded valley past Camelford. Around Blisland, where the De Lank River comes in from Bodmin Moor, the river broadens and the valley becomes increasingly wooded as it skirts Bodmin before swinging to the north west and on to Wadebridge, where the main tributary, the Allen, flows in from the north. In fact, the Allen has followed a parallel course and at Camelford the two rivers are less than a mile apart.

Throughout its length the Camel is a clear quick river with a fair stock of trout, though it is better known for its sea-trout fishing and for its first class late run of salmon in November and December. The Allen is a productive little river, but some of the best trout in the area are found on the De Lank River. Near the mouth of this tributary, quarry dumping has created a rock barrier across the stream and, although the river seeps through, salmon and sea-trout are unable to ascend. The result is less competition from salmon and sea-trout parr than on the main river and the average size of trout is rather higher.

As on so many Cornish rivers, much of the trout fishing is done with the worm, as is the salmon and sea-trout fishing. However, the Camel is well suited to the fly and would probably benefit from more stretches being set aside for this method, as is the case in neighbouring Devon.

The Wadebridge and District Angling Association has some four miles on the Camel and Allen and provides permits for the visitor. Farther upstream, tickets are also available from the Bodmin Anglers Association and the Liskeard and District Angling Club. For fishing the De Lank River, permission can be obtained from local farmers.

Fowey

Deep in the heart of the highest part of Bodmin Moor is the source of the longest river completely within Cornwall, the Fowey. For ten miles it flows through open moorland in a southerly direction but after leaving the moor it drops into a heavily wooded valley and heads west to within a couple of miles of Bodmin and then south, past Restormel Castle, to Lostwithiel, where it becomes tidal. The long narrow estuary runs down to the sea at Fowey. The Fowey has only one tributary of any consequence, the St Neot River, which also rises on Bodmin Moor and runs into the main river shortly after leaving the moor at the village of St Neot.

This is a typical moorland stream, quick to rise after rain but equally quick in returning to normal level and clear water. Wild brown trout are present throughout the river, but the average size is small and in the moorland reaches the trout are far outnumbered by the sea-trout and salmon parr.

Most of the trout fishing on the Fowey is done by local anglers using the worm, with serious fly fishing largely confined to night fishing for sea-trout. Brown trout are, of course, taken on both wet and dry fly but the modest stock of fish and the predominance of worm fishing means that the Fowey is far from ideal for the trout fishing visitor who prefers fly fishing.

The best of the trout fishing is on the middle and lower river, as the moorland reaches are looked upon as nursery streams for salmon and sea-trout, and the local angling association discourages too much trout fishing in these areas. There is plenty of association water on the Fowey and permits are readily available. The Liskeard and District Angling Club has a lengthy stretch on the middle river, the National Trust offers fishing on the Lanhydrock Estate, and the Lostwithiel Fishing Association controls a stretch not far above the estuary.

MIDLANDS AND NORTH WEST

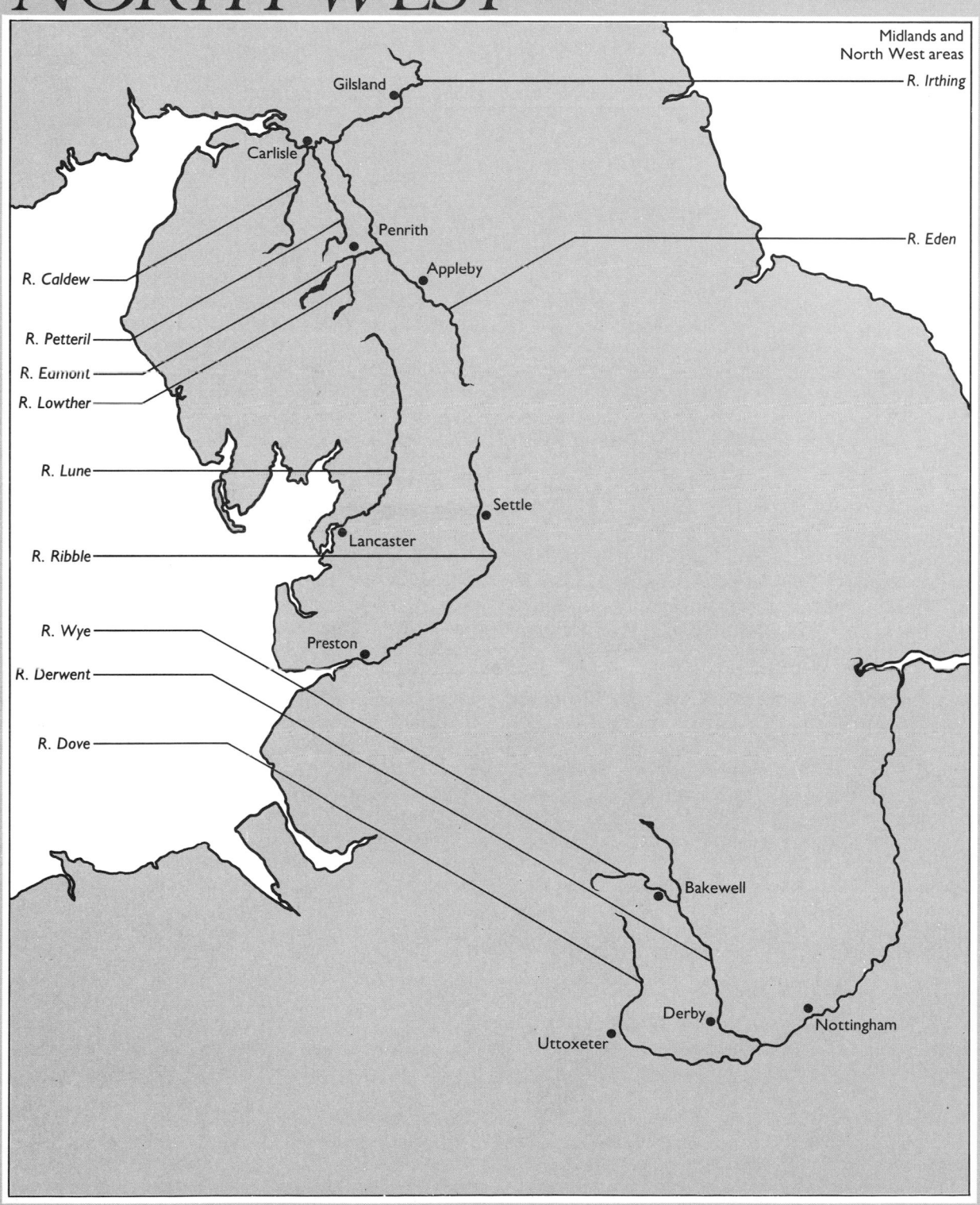

Midlands and North West areas

R. Irthing
Gilsland
Carlisle
Penrith
R. Eden
Appleby
R. Caldew
R. Petteril
R. Eamont
R. Lowther
R. Lune
Settle
R. Ribble
Lancaster
R. Wye
Preston
R. Derwent
R. Dove
Bakewell
Derby
Nottingham
Uttoxeter

The Wye at Monsal Dale

Derwent Dove and Wye

One of the choicest parts of England lies within the ambit of OS Sheet 119 (1/50000), headed '*Buxton, Matlock and Dovedale*', names that evoke all kinds of gentle countryside musings. Those green valleys and peaks spring suddenly from the Derbyshire countryside, astonishing the stranger dragging himself away from the uncompromising ugliness of the Derby ring road – or more dramatically still, as he takes the A162 from Sheffield in the direction of Bakewell.

Draining this area and north of it are the rivers Derwent, Wye and Dove – each providing many miles of good trout fishing, much of which can be made available, by negotiation, to the public

and each river so different from the others that it is difficult to realise that they are close neighbours.

Derwent
The Derwent, the biggest of the three, assumes its identity where it is joined by the Noo, south of Ladybower reservoir. There is fishing to be had in both the Bamford and Hathersage areas and enquiries are recommended to the Derwent Fly Fishers Club. Below, at Baslow, some of the Chatsworth rods are available to those staying at the Cavendish Hotel (once the Peacock). Chatsworth sits like a giant at the heart of the Derwent, Buckingham Palace dumped into the parkland surrounding it, with the same impression of empty rooms and echoing corridors. I was tempted to ask the Duchess of Devonshire about the fishing in front of her mansion, but even if I had had the courage, how would I have known

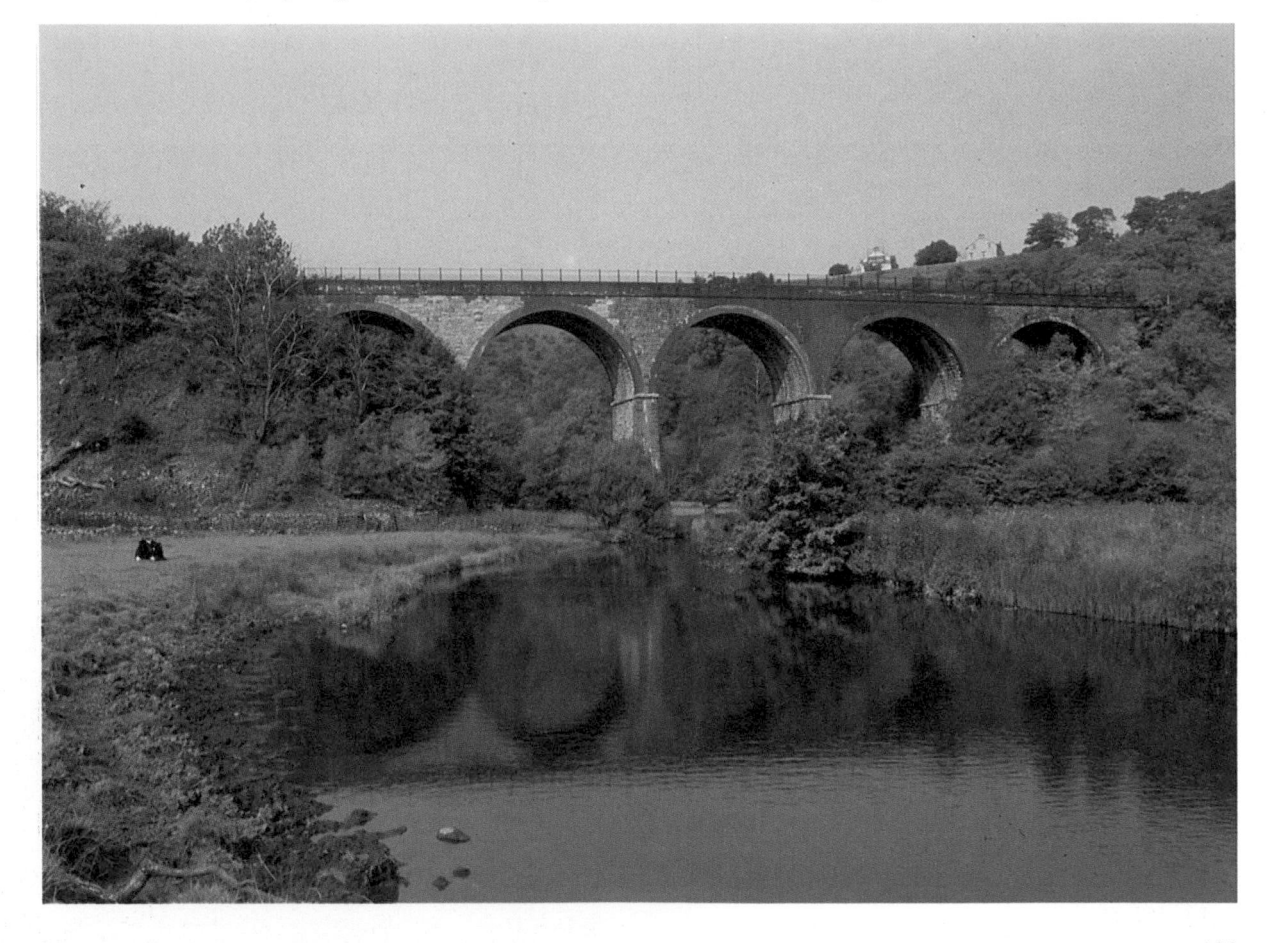

Top: The Wye north of Bakewell

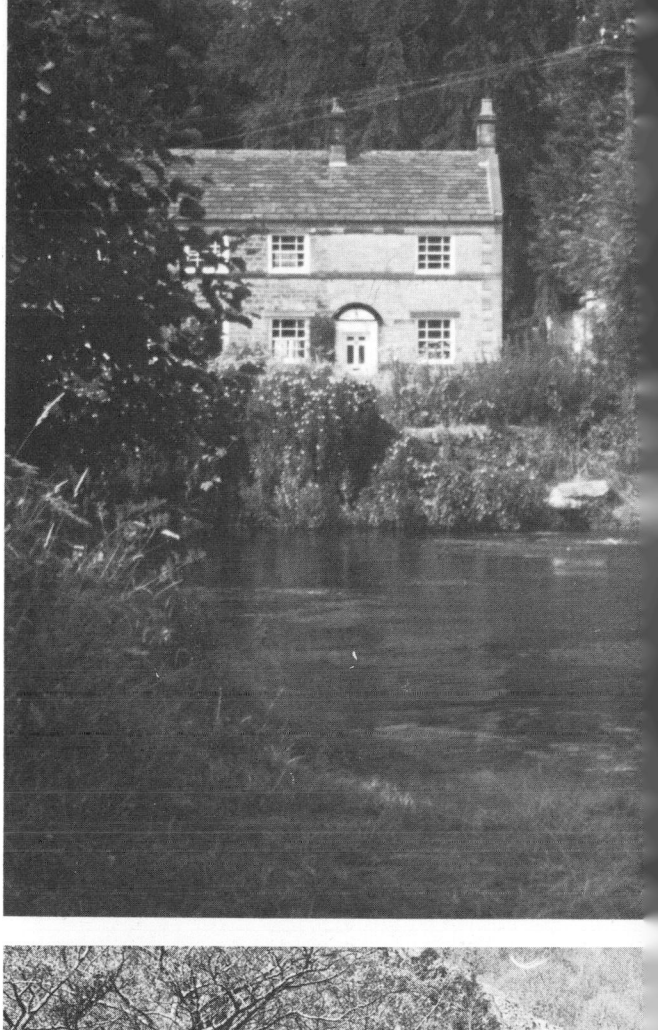

which bell to press? As on many other parts of the Derwent, the water was dammed, looked brown and slow, ducks the only sign of life. Below Chatsworth and downstream to beyond Rowsley, the fishing is let to the Darley Dale syndicate. Not so very long ago it was hardly considered worth the expense of keepering, but the syndicate taking advantage of decreased pollution has improved it considerably. The trout are mainly brown and two pounders are rare – somewhat surprising in so large a river, but no one argues about the steady increase in this fishery's virtues. The main drawback is the swiftness of the Derwent to become coloured following rain. Rainbow trout from the Wye have moved in and become indigenous in the Rowsley area. Down to Matlock the fishing is either private or controlled by the Matlock Angling Club. From there on, down to its confluence with the Trent, the coarse fish gradually take over.

Dove

The westernmost of the trio of rivers (and leaving the most interesting till last) is the Dove, clear flowing and much like a Scottish burn near its source. It is a lovely river, more famous for its past than its present, a victim, perhaps, of the old associations between Isaac Walton and Charles Cotton. Little if anything remains of Cotton's home, Beresford Hall. I could not locate the famous Cotton and Walton Fishing Temple, but I was assured that it was alive and well.

The Dove runs small and silver down to Milldale, where it is supplemented by water from further springs. From there it hurries through the most beautiful of valleys down to the Isaac Walton Hotel, via leap, cave and castle, along Dovedale. Thence, skirting Ashbourne, it makes its way supplemented by the not particularly welcome water of the Churnet, to the Trent.

There is reasonable trout fishing but in the main the Dove suffers from its own beauty and accessability. It provides impromptu picnic places, bathing pools, paddling stretches and cricket and football pitches for hundreds of thousands of visitors each year. There is not any way in which shy trout thrive contentedly when subjected to such pressures. Nevertheless the river merits inclusion here because of its glorious past, and where there's a past there may be a future.

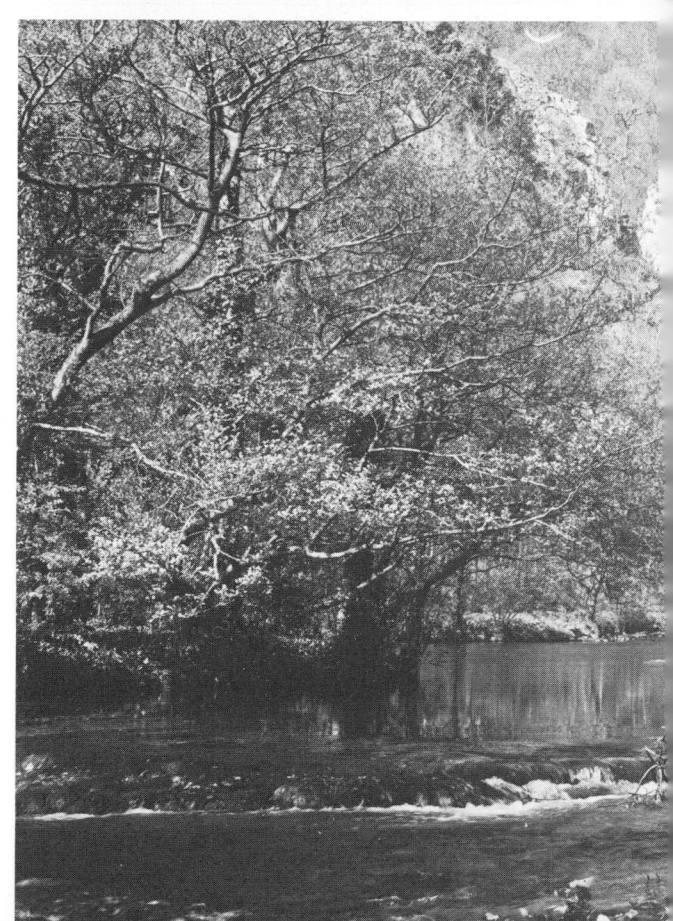

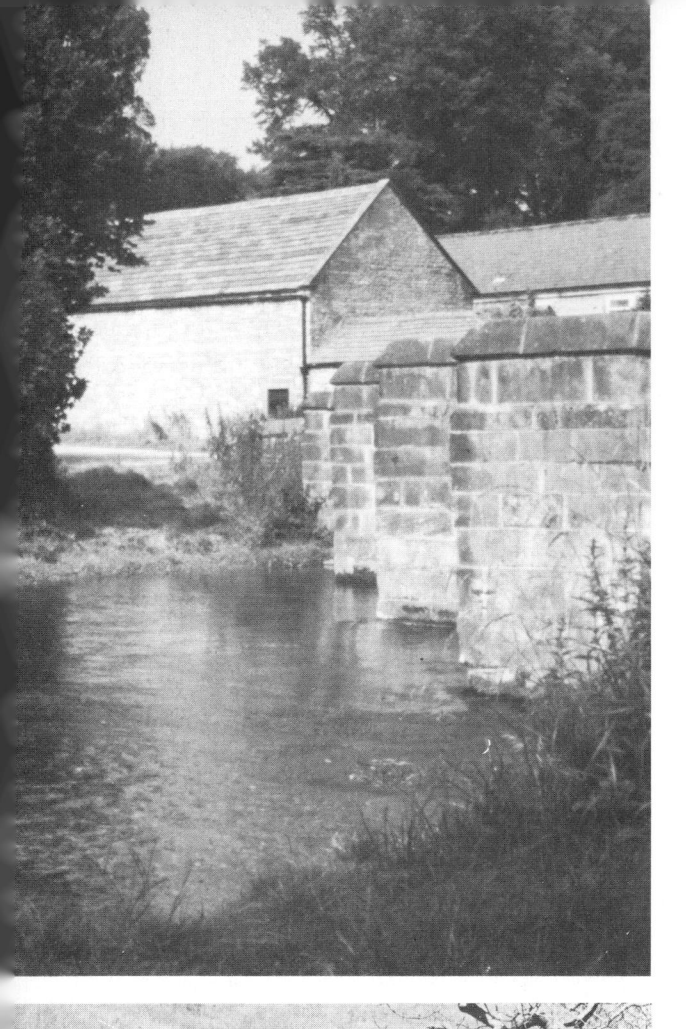

Bottom: Isaac Walton country. The Dove at Dovedale

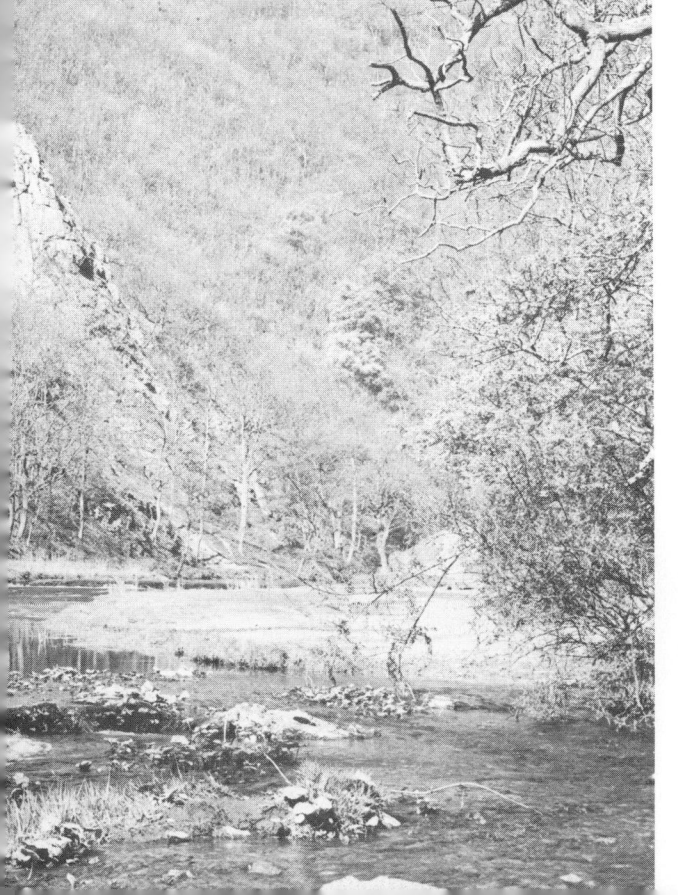

Wye

Finally (and as I have said, most interestingly) the Wye. It rises north of Buxton and is a high grade trout fishery down to Bakewell and on to Rowsley where it enters the Derwent. It is the part of the river between Rowsley and Bakewell that holds such fascination – for this is the only substantial area of trout stream in Britain that I know of where the rainbow trout breed in the wild and have done in substantial numbers for many years. Whatever it is that causes them to make the river their home and breeding ground, it ceases above Bakewell, where the brown trout take over again. The rainbows have also spread into the Derwent above and below Rowsley (where they are certainly breeding) and also into the Lathkill, two miles upstream of Rowsley, where they have spread up to but not beyond the falls at Alport Mill. These rainbows (*Irrideus* not *Shasta*) are said to have originated from a spillage from ponds near Bakewell – but rainbow trout have spilled into dozens of other rivers and been lost. What makes this part of the Wye so suitable is a matter of much speculation and many theories.

The Wye rainbows are not large. The exciting fish of over two pounds is a rarity and the three year old rainbows average no more than ten inches. Needless to say they fight as though they were twice their size and are delicious to eat. As these three year olds are the takeable fish and as they do not spawn until they are at that age, a careful balance has to be kept to maintain breeding stock.

The rainbow trout have, unarguably, an unhappy effect on the brown trout stocks. They are gay, skittish and aggressive. They move quickly and far to all passing food and maintain their places, with ferocity, in the best lies. The effect on the brown trout has been to turn them mainly into bottom feeders, competing with the grayling. This is fuel for the arguments that if rainbows bred naturally elsewhere it would be at the brown trout's expense. Some experiments are being made under controlled conditions on the Duke of Rutland's estate to see if a better growing rainbow could be developed – which would also become indigenous. A river such as the Wye that was able to support a head of large wild rainbows would be a very attractive fly fishing proposition.

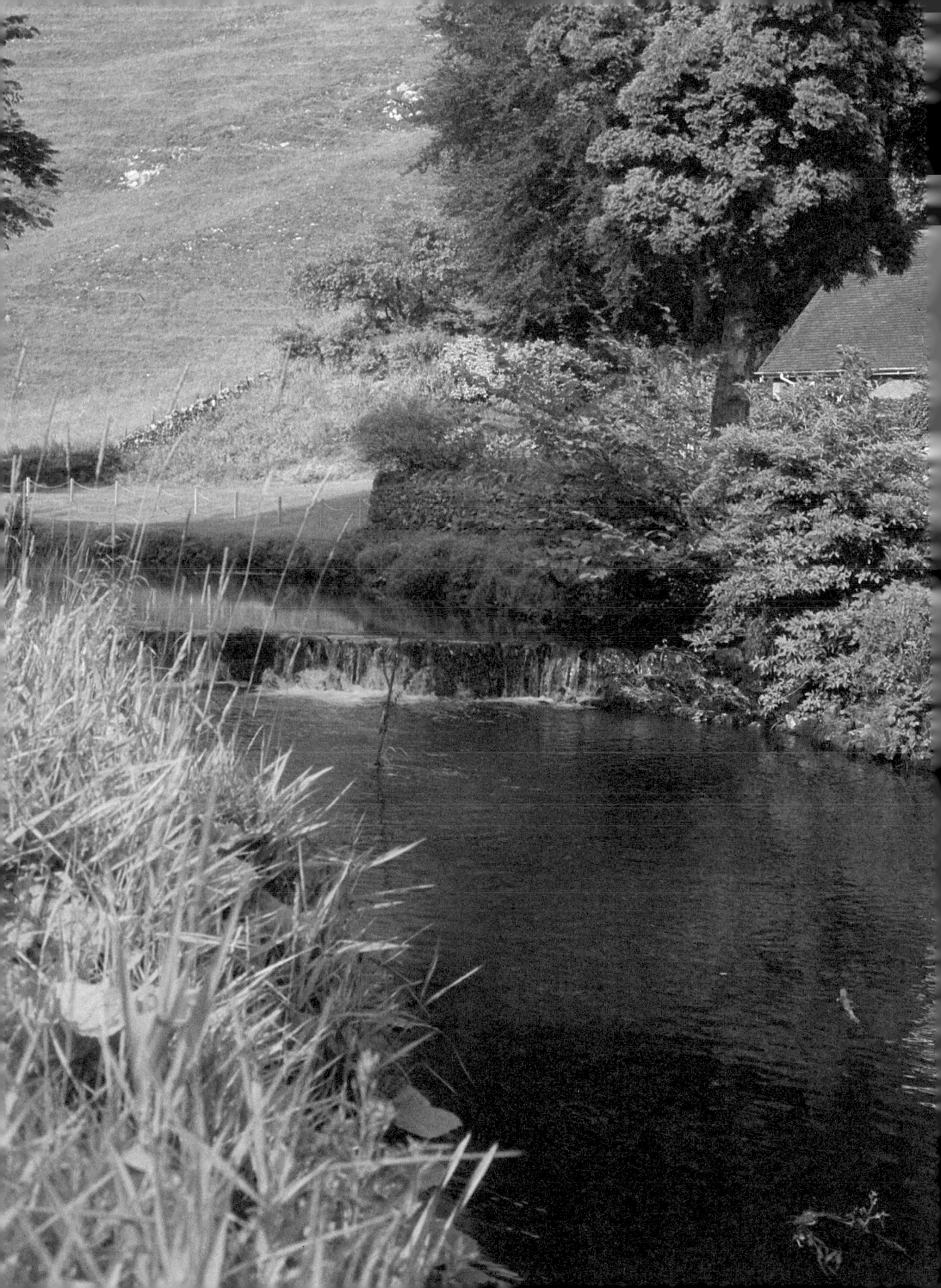

Left: The unforgettable Dove Valley

Below: A glimpse of the Wye.

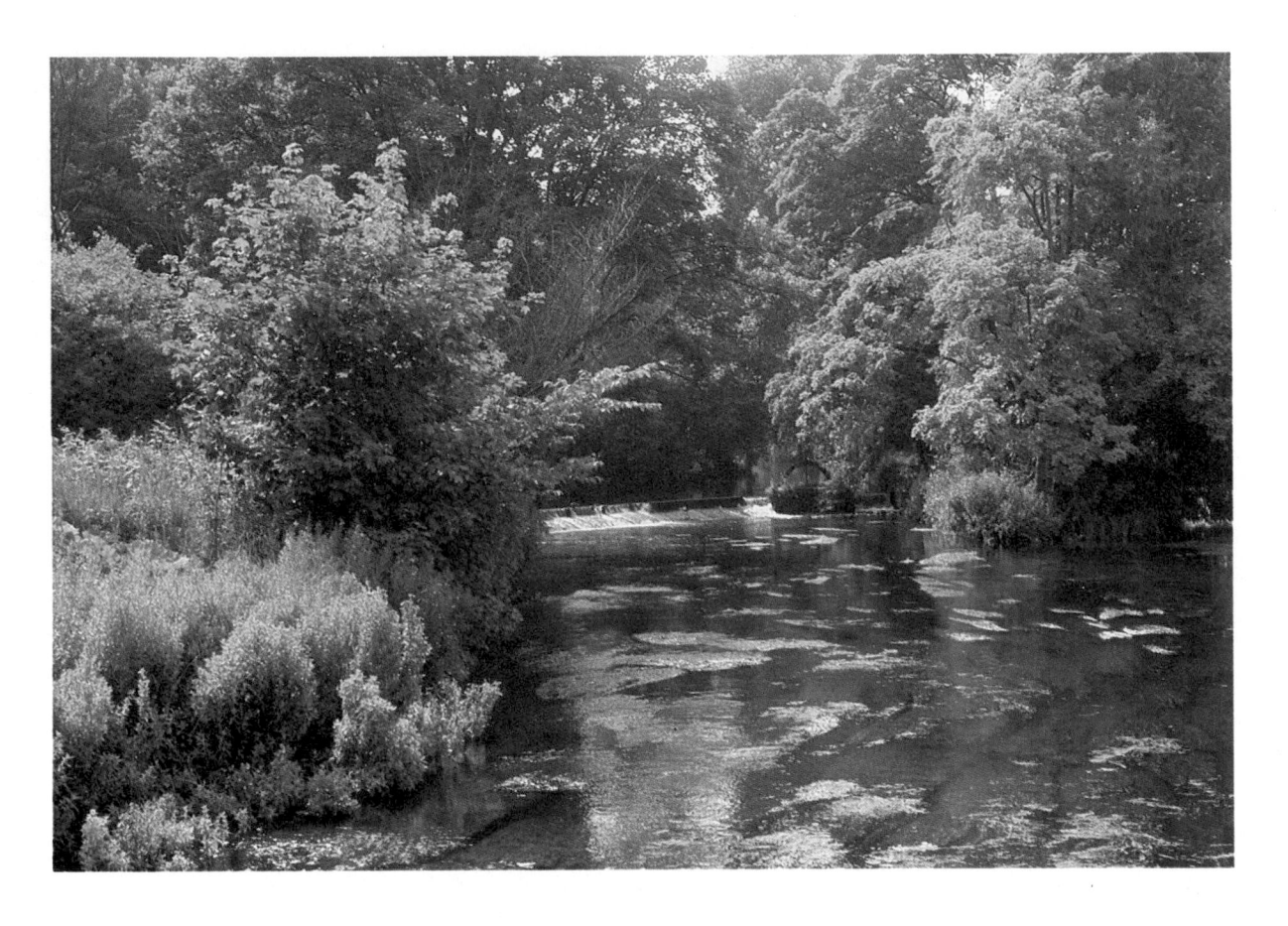

The Wye rainbow trout breed during March and April and contrary to theory do not appear to interfere with the spawning brown trout whose love life will have reached its natural conclusion several weeks earlier. One of the theories about the Wye, is that it is peculiarly suitable in terms of speed of current and composition of gravel beds to the rainbows' needs.

The whole of this unusual fishery within a fishery is in the hands of the Peacock Hotel at Rowsley whose guests get the first chance of the twelve daily rods. The fishing is not cheap but a licence to fish this winding, challenging and attractive river up to and beyond Bakewell (except for that part immediately in front of Haddon Hall) is worth the speculation involved. (Rainbow trout season, 16 May – 15 November: Brown trout 16 May – 15 October. Dry fly only). Fishermen should perhaps beware of the stretch where the river runs (more powerfully than the Windrush at Bourton-on-the-Water and more elegantly than the Nene at Wisbech) through the town of Bakewell. Some of the bigger fish there are spoiled bread fed creatures and the ladies of Bakewell are said to defend their darlings with ferocity!

It would be wrong to end this section without another mention of the upper Lathkill. This small crystal clear stream, spring fed and limestone like the Wye, flows above Alport Mill, entirely free of rainbow trout, in a series of long pools controlled by small weirs, culminating in the famous upper waters where the Duke of Rutland does his own fishing. This is a marvellous piece of water, putting me in mind of some of the prettier Hampshire rivers, where because of the enormous supply of natural food, the brown trout average nearly a pound and tiny ones are rarely seen. I was most grateful to the Duke's water bailiff, Fred Burton, for sparing me a lot of his time and giving me a most fascinating day.

Magic water on the Lune

Lune and Tributaries

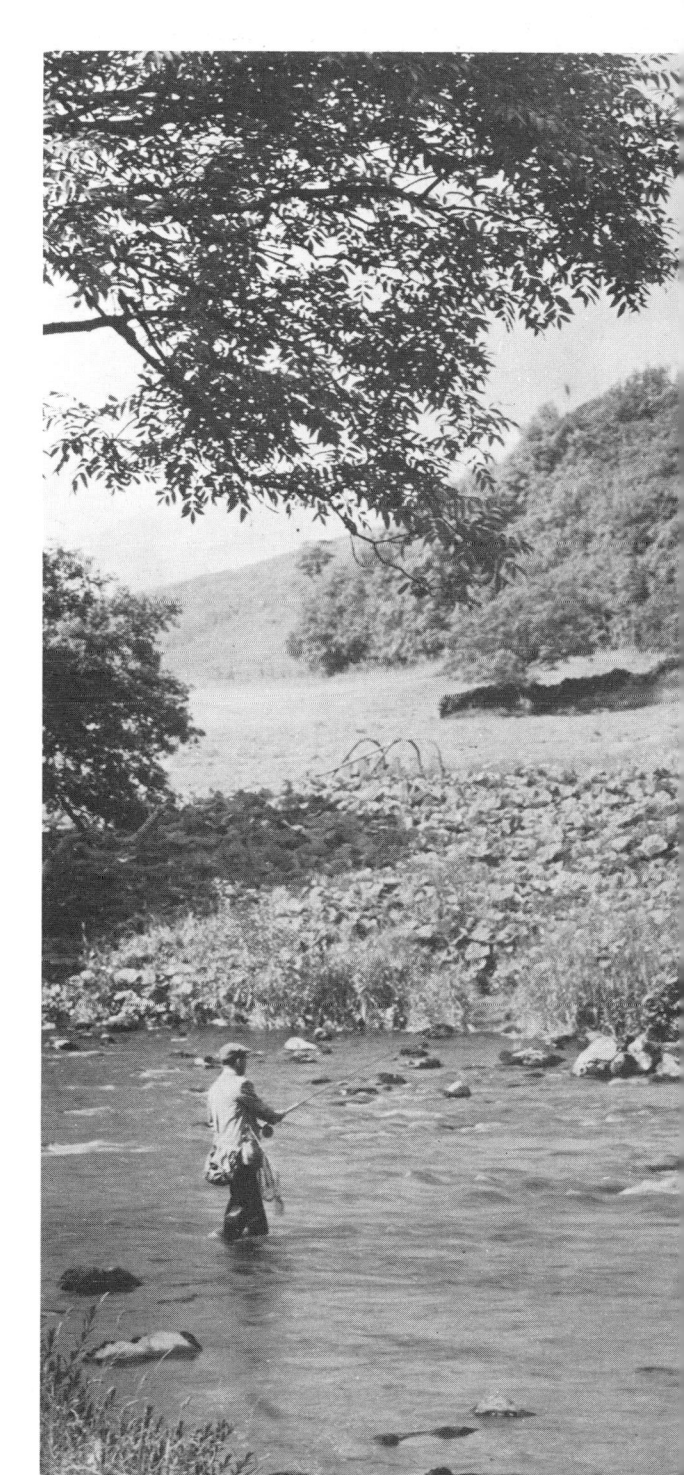

The River Lune and its tributaries, chiefly the Wenning and the Greta, offer the opportunity to catch brown trout from their origins to the sea – whether by a dry fly delicately placed into a small beck, for the fish averaging two or three to the pound, or by fishing with a lure, resembling an elver, for the large slob trout that frequent the Lune estuary.

The Lune rises on the northern slopes of Howgill fells in Cumbria, and about thirty miles from its source it enters Lancashire, south of Kirby Londsdale, and from that point it meanders across alluvial plains for some twenty miles until it reaches the sea where, like all rivers of north Lancashire, it flows into Morecambe Bay.

Near Tunstall, which is approximately twelve miles from Lancaster, the Greta joins the Lune and below Hornby, which is two or three miles south of Tunstall, the more important Wenning, which rises near Clapham in Yorkshire, also joins the parent river. Lunesdale is sometimes subject to heavy flooding. The Wray flood disaster was evidence of that, but generally the river rises and falls quite steadily after rainfall in the fells. Recent land drainage, however, has altered the rate of flooding from the days when the river would hold steady in flood condition, and then quietly recede to normal level over a period of days, to a river which can rise several feet above normal and back to summer level in forty eight hours.

The present situation does not affect the brown trout fishing too much as the river is now nearly always fishable. Even if a spate rules out fishing for a few hours in a day, there is always some method which will produce a trout or two.

The fisher who needs to catch trout might be better employed in the numerous lakes and reservoirs that the area offers, but if he is prepared to make a few inquiries he will find river trout fishing to remember in an environment which has views that border on the breathtaking to anyone who respects the intimacy of the north Lancashire countryside.

Very few local anglers fish for brown trout and when they do, it is usually prior to the arrival of

Overleaf: The Lune, where wet fly can be deadly

their migratory cousins. Therefore most stretches that are available on a day or weekly ticket basis are not fished unless the river is in spate; during the summer months that is a rare occurrence.

In the higher reaches all the becks are fishable and permission to fish is usually granted by local landowners, but it is from Tebay onwards that the Lune becomes a worthwhile proposition for trout fishing with its streams and pools alternating in succession. Many of these lower stretches are unavailable to the visiting angler who arrives on spec, but the angler who is prepared to plan his visits will find association and private water on either a daily or weekly basis. Costs may include salmon fishing, but this is rarely more than what a day's resevoir fishing would cost, and generally the trout fishing is economically priced.

Throughout Lunesdale fishing methods vary from creeper and worm fishing, fly fishing both wet and dry, to small bait spinning. The method chosen depends on several factors; river height, local rules, but above all else your own decision as to what will be the most productive. As the fishing year progresses so the method needs to change, particularly, if you are a fly only enthusiast. Early spring will provide fish for those who fish the March Brown, Dark Olive, Snipe and Purple, Greenwell's Glory and the Greenwell nymph, but as the fishing season advances one needs to change with the time of year and alter tactics accordingly.

May and June can provide very good fishing at dusk as the majority of stretches carry a good head of trout, which rise freely, and good baskets can be taken on the wet and dry fly. If the angler observes where fish are rising and presents his fly accordingly and selects the correct pattern, sport can be furious and there is always a chance of connecting with a large early run sea-trout.

Many trout over the two pound mark are taken but generally the fish average three quarters to one pound in weight in the main river with the tributaries accommodating fish in the half pound bracket and the occasional larger fish to the stealthy angler.

As the summer months continue, the trout of Lunesdale tend to spread and take up territories and then one has fishing reminiscent of a chalk stream where the angler needs to stalk individual fish. However, on most days there are still prolific hatches of fly and the trout congregate in the easy taking places until the hatch is over. Windy days rather than calm ones seem to promote fly hatches and a river running off from a spate, combined with windy conditions is ideal. Towards late August and into September the area's brown trout are in first class condition after the summer harvest that the waters provide.

Lunesdale has produced some five to six pound brown trout but these fish are usually taken by the salmon and sea-trout anglers fishing their larger lures. Evidence of these large trout is frequently indicated by minnow sprays and bow waves in the shallows as they patrol and chase their quarry. They can, therefore, be caught by emulating the sunk line fishing tactics employed on still waters. A worm fished upstream, where regulations permit, will also produce quality brown trout. Similarly the threadline minnow is another good method but the fisher may lure the trout's big brother the salmon with such tactics.

Throughout the country many of the rivers that accommodate migratory fish usually have a stunted population of brown trout, but Lunesdale appears to be one of the exceptions to this rule and the species seem to co-habit very well.

The angler who prefers to combine his fishing with other pursuits will find much to do in Lunesdale. Foxhunting is enjoyed on the Howgill and Grayrigg Forest fells, Sheep dog trials take place all over the dale, hedging, ploughing, walling and stick making competitions take place at Sedburgh, Barbon and elsewhere and these are but a few of the very many activities on offer.

Fishing tackle shops in Lancaster and Morecambe will readily supply information on brown trout fishing and they may also part with the odd 'wrinkle' as to which area is producing fish, the best methods, flies and lies, and almost any other assistance required by the angler.

The area is also very well supplied with hostelries, guest houses and the like, most of which offer the hospitality so characteristic of the Lune valley. Lunesdale's rich plant life, a valley largely unspoilt and a people who have retained their old-time independence and way of life, combine to give the angler a remarkably pleasant fishing back cloth.

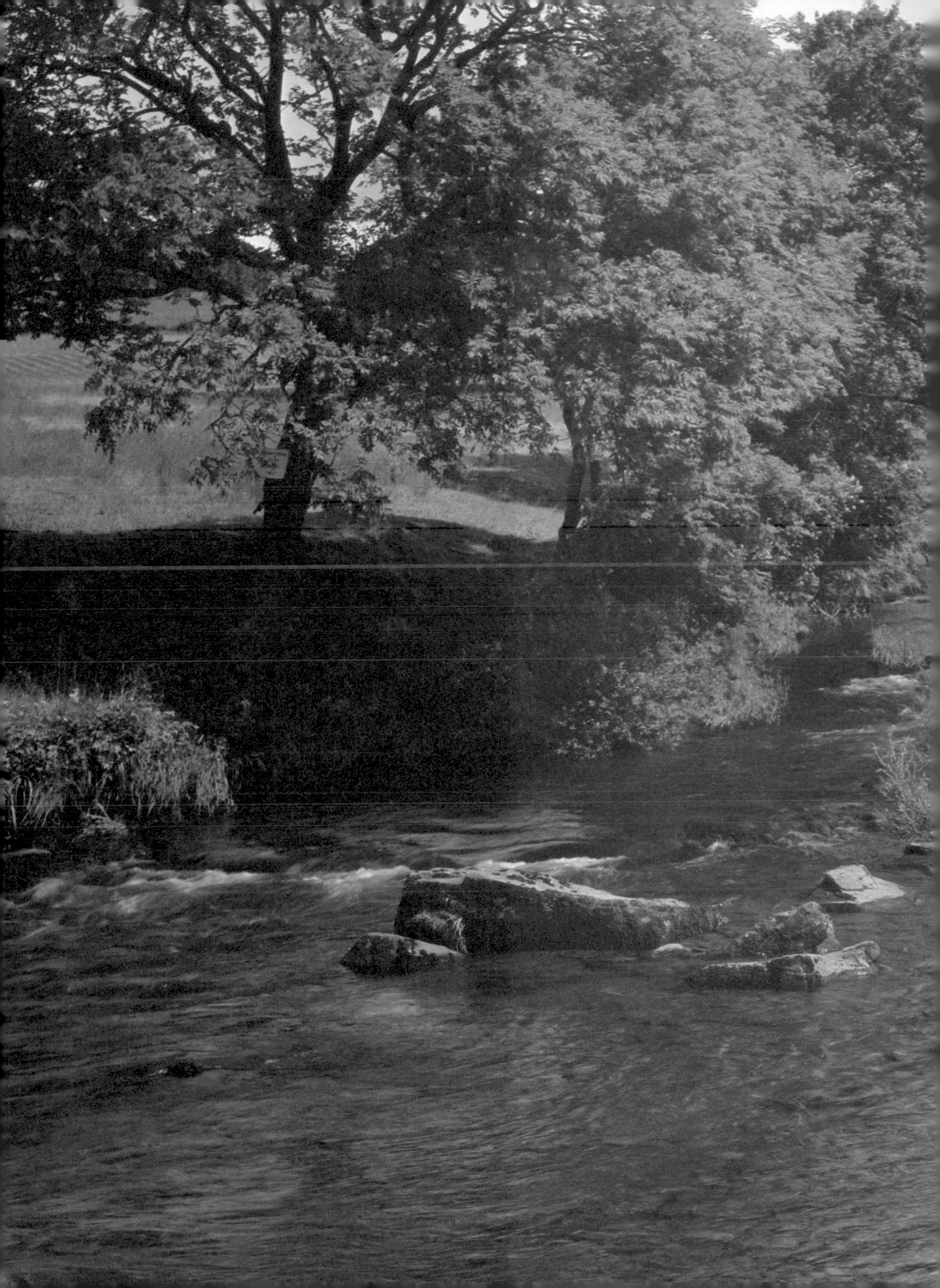

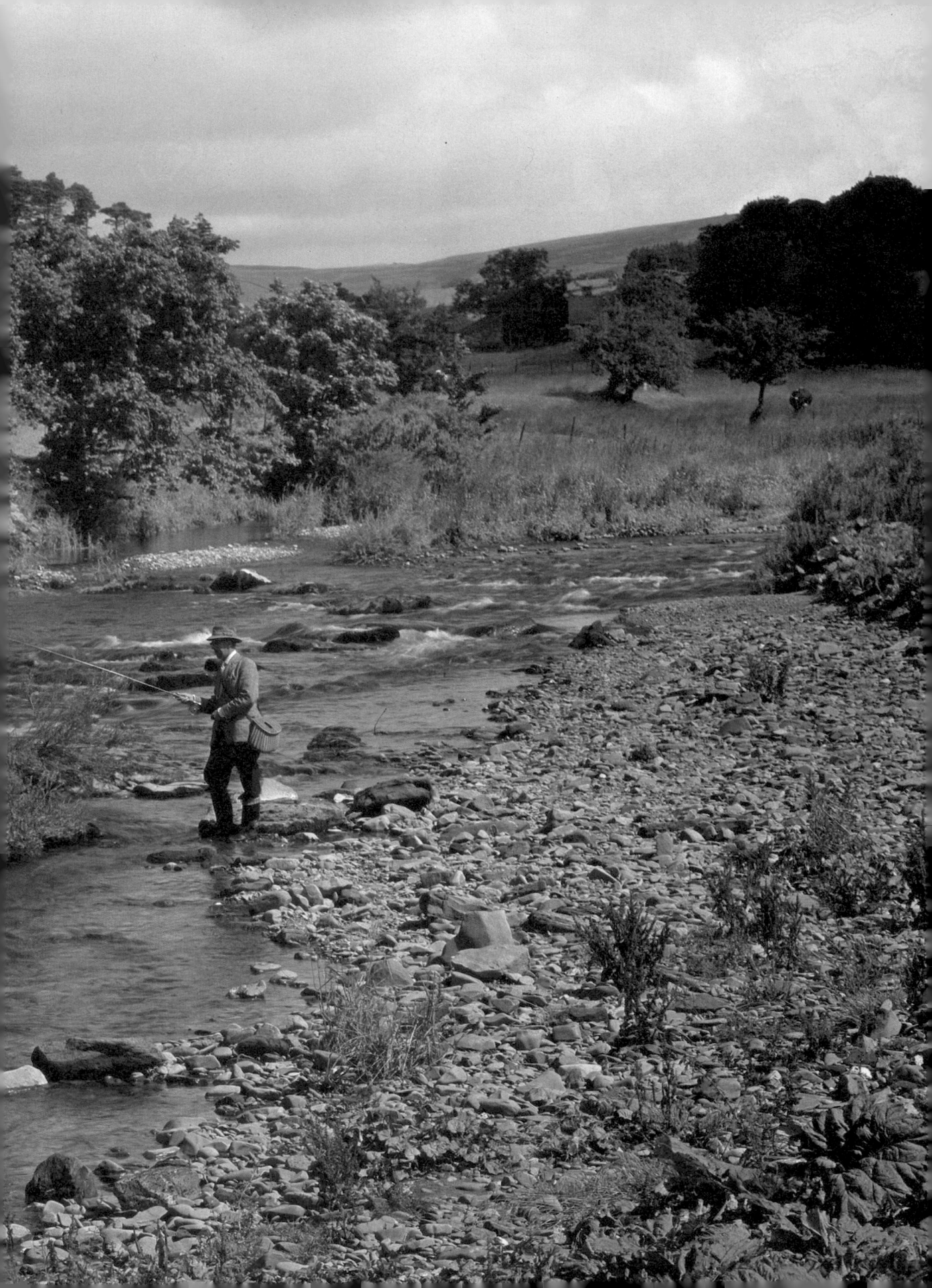

Ribble

The Ribble, like the Lune, is a river which begins from water falling as rain on the high Pennines, hills that act like sponges before releasing their water which eventually forms mountain torrents hurrying along a desolate valley.

Ribblehead, the birthplace of the river, is situated some ten miles north of Settle. After approximately twenty miles of 'glides and rushes' the Ribble enters Lancashire and divides the red and white rose counties until it meets the River Hodder.

The Hodder rises in the millstone grit fells of Yorkshire and crosses the Lancashire boundary not far from Whitewell and from there to its junction with the Ribble forms the county boundary. The Hodder spends most of its course in the heart of the Forest of Bowland, an area worthy of a visit whether one is fishing or not.

Both rivers flow through fairly high country and Horton-in-Ribblesdale and Ribblehead are dear to the sportsmen that frequent the area. At Mitton Bridge the Ribble is becoming a river of true fishing proportions and from Mitton to Clitheroe the streamy river begins to widen as it begins to meander its way to Preston. North of Preston is a zone of transition from agriculture to industry and south of Preston the river becomes estuarine for some twelve miles until it reaches the sea.

The Ribble is sweet and uncontaminated from its source to its junction with the Hodder but where it joins the Calder it used to be polluted. Recent years, however, have seen much improvement from the time when the rivers Darwen, Douglas and Calder poured about 130 million gallons of poisoned water into the Ribble every day. Preston docks have closed and the disposal of sewage and industrial waste has become better dealt with; as a consequence the fish which somehow managed to survive the days of much pollution are now increasing in number.

Above the Calder the river has always run pure through long green valleys that fall away as the Pennines stretch north and it is here that the brown trout fisher will find what he is seeking.

Upstream fishing is very much the order of the day in Ribblesdale, whether it be with wet fly, nymph, or worm. The fly fisherman will find that April and May are the big months to pursue his sport and the following patterns should prove useful. Greenwell, March Brown, Dark Olive and Snipe and Purple for wet fly fishing and for nymph fishing the Olive, Greenwell and Pheasant Tail nymphs should suffice.

Ribblesdale's brown trout average three quarters to one pound and share their surroundings with the wild deer, duck and pheasant that abound in the dale.

The angler will find ample fishing at his disposal with many association and private stretches offering permission to fish. The North West Water Authority has some fine trout fishing in the Mitton area and Settle Angling Association has several miles of fishing in the higher reaches which is available on a daily basis to the visiting angler.

In addition, many more day ticket and club subscription stretches are preserved for brown trout fishing. Local inquiry will discover their location.

The Ribble responds to the angler who has fallen for the mystical appeal of catching brown trout on artificial fly and like the Lune welcomes the angler who respects the traditions of trout fishing as a pastime.

The Eden System

Rivers of the Eden system are graded high quality, clean and clear, with a high oxygen content due to high precipitation and also to the rocky, turbulent nature of their upper reaches. They are not in the same category as the spate rivers of the west Highlands of Scotland or even the west Cumbrian streams, yet they do tend to rise and fall rapidly at times.

Despite their northerly position, anglers in the Eden district are generally able to take trout on dry fly from the season's start (15 March) in all but the worst conditions. However, most local anglers fish wet fly until about mid May. In early spring there are usually good hatches of large dark olive and a fair number of needle flies and February reds. There is also, possibly, the greatest variety of both the ephemera and the plecoptera, upwings and stonefly types, that one is ever likely

The big water. A bridge over the Eden

to encounter in Great Britain, during the rest of the season. Hatches of some upwings and sedges will not match those of some of the southern rivers, but the unusual variety should compensate and interest the visitor to Eden and its feeders.

The mayfly will hatch on several streams, but fails to provide sport; however, the artificial is effective on both Ullswater and Blencarn Lake – both are on the Eden system and close to Penrith. Under favourable conditions, there are excellent evening rises to Blue Winged Olive, Sherry Spinner and the ubiquitous Sedges; the latter are responsible, in part, for the Cumbrian practice of nocturnal angling for lake and river trout. A local wet fly pattern, the Bustard, has been evolved for this practice, but the author favours large Bottlebrush dry flies, which will also take the odd seatrout after dark. The latter are most effective on the flats and in weed channels in quiet water.

The record Eden trout weighed eight pounds and was nine years old. It was taken on a Bustard wet fly by Nathaniel Dean Lowthian on 30 May 1911, near Temple Sowerby village. A five and a quarter pound trout was taken on minnow by A T Lowthian on 30 July 1912, from a pool a little downstream of the scene of the capture of the record fish. The best trout from Penrith AA waters was a five pound fish also taken on Bustard wet fly by T Pigg in August 1960 since which time the Penrith club water has produced fish of three pounds eleven and a half ounces and four

pounds twelve ounces to local members, with trout of two pounds or over being taken most years. Big trout are taken at times on the numerous private and syndicated waters, but little is heard of these.

Eamont, Lowther and Caldew are all said to have produced trout weighing four pounds and more.

Every angler has his/her favourite selection of flies, but the following are particularly popular in this area and should form a sound, working nucleus on which to develop.

Wet Flies

EARLY SPRING: Greenwell's Glory, Olive Dun (or similar 'Olive' pattern), Partridge and Red, Snipe and Purple.

LATE SPRING: Greenwell's Glory (or similar), Red Spinner, Goldribbed Hare's Ear, Snipe and Yellow, Little Woodcock (a local pattern) Hawthorn or Black Gnat.

SUMMER: As for late spring, plus Wickham's Fancy, Red Sedge or similar Sedge pattern, Treacle Parkin (a good, local beetle pattern).

Dry Flies

EARLY SPRING: Greenwell's Glory, Blue Upright, Olive Dun.

LATE SPRING: Greenwell's Glory (or similar), Pheasant Tail, Iron Blue Dun, Hawthorn or Black Gnat.

SUMMER: As for late spring, plus Knotted Midge, Blanchard's Abortion (a local Sedge pattern), Ginger Quill and Treacle Parkin (a local beetle pattern which is good on bushy streams).

Eden

Rising high in the North Yorkshire moors, near the source of the Ure, and flowing north for most of its sixty-odd miles through the old counties of Cumberland and Westmorland, the Eden and its tributary system drain a large area of Cumbria. On its right flank lies the massive Pennine chain with its numerous small becks, stony and fast-flowing, a breeding ground for the Eden salmon, sea-trout and brownies. None of these Pennine

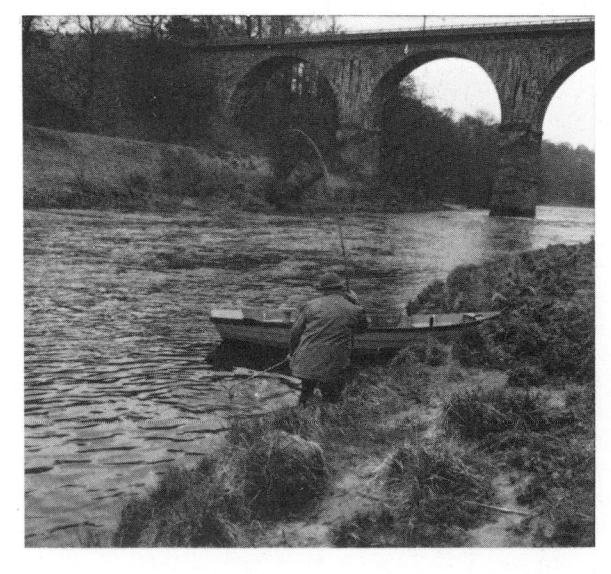

September evening. The Eden near Lower Sowerby

tributaries of the upper and middle Eden is of great size, although all provide enjoyable fishing in beautiful hill country for wild brown trout weighing about three or four to the pound. There are a few better quality fish in the bigger pools, and the lower reaches of these feeders provide both a higher average weight and the chance of the odd grayling. The latter were once both numerous and widespread throughout the Eden valley, but their decline began with that of the Eden salmon in the 1966/67 winter.

Above Kirkby Stephen, the first town on the Eden, trout fishing is similar to that in the larger upper Eden tributary becks, but below the town, Eden soon fills out into a sizeable river. From here onwards, the trout will average two to the pound or better. Regular re-stocking of the water by the Kirkby Stephen Angling Association has improved sport with fly considerably over the last ten years, and one hears of the occasional two pound trout being taken on its preserves.

As Eden descends towards the wide, fertile plain to the north, the river becomes enriched with a mixture of dissolved calcium from the limestone hills, dissolved lime from the arable farmlands and with the various fertilizers, leached out by those infamous Cumbrian rains. Between Kirkby Stephen and Appleby (county town of old Westmorland), weed becomes first evident and then luxurious in growth. In an average season, following on a normal winter (1981/82 was exceptionally hard on the river), ranunculus can cause problems for anglers. However the numerous weed channels, if properly exploited, will provide the competent upstream fly fisher with excellent sport. Such weedy conditions as were seen before the 1982 winter, also provided a natural harbour for a host of ephemera and other aquatic insects. In the Kirkby Stephen – Appleby stretch, the first of the bigger Eden pools is encountered. Some of the pools on the lower river will measure 100 to 200 yards of flat, slow moving water, often of considerable depth; but even the middle and upper Eden provide large pools, connected in places by surprisingly shallow streams. The face of the river changes continuously and provides a wealth of varied fishing – fast streams, often boulder strewn; slow, silty flats, stony glides and, further downstream, in the Langwathby to Armathwaite stretch, some impressive falls and

gorges. At Langwathby and Edenhall villages, we have reached the upstream limit of the serious salmon fishing preserves, the upper boundary of which is Waters Meet, the confluence of Eamont, the major tributary, with the mother river.

The left bank of Eden receives water from the Shap and Orton fells and, via Lowther and Eamont, the waters of the eastern Lake District hills. These left bank streams are less precipitous than the Pennine becks and are, generally, more fertile and more productive of good quality trout. Crayfish, for example, are more numerous in such streams as Lyvennet, Lowther and Eamont than they are in the majority of the Pennine tributaries and, whereas the former have a minor mayfly hatch, mayflies are rarely heard of on the east fellside becks. However, the latter, high rising becks do have medium stonefly, a high altitude species, so each type has its own character and peculiarities – the more silted, gravelly pools will be found on left bank streams, whilst the Pennine becks are essentially rocky.

From Langwathby onwards the Eden becomes more and more a salmon river, with sea-trout and brown trout as a consolation to be sought when sport with *salmo salar* is slack. Most of the water is fished almost exclusively for migratory fish by either private owners, syndicates, hotels or the angling clubs of lower Eden – Carlisle Angling Association and the Yorkshire Flyfishers' Club. Trouting is permitted, of course, but it tends to take a third row seat the nearer one approaches Carlisle, the Solway Firth and the Irish Sea. One finds, also, that more coarse fish are encountered as one nears the city. Chub may be found in the Appleby area, and dace have been caught as far upstream as Culgaith village, but the really big shoals of both species are met on beats below Armathwaite. Eden pike are relatively few and far between, but the odd eighteen to twenty pounder has been caught and the record for the river is twenty nine pounds. Again, most pike are seen below Armathwaite, the highest upriver pike being hooked and lost at Culgaith some time ago.

The major tributaries of lower Eden are the Irthing, which rises on the Spadeadam fells and which is the main right bank feeder, entering Eden at Warwick on Eden; and lastly, Petteril and Caldew, which join the left bank of Eden at Carlisle itself. Petteril flows north from its course in

Greystoke forest, running parallel with Eden for much of its length, while Caldew drains the fells in the vicinity of Blencathra (Saddleback) to the south west of the city. Petteril is a gentle, meandering stream, while Caldew is a stony, brawling river; but both provide good trout fishing in their middle reaches in particular. Trouting at Carlisle can be good, but the better fishing is found in the upper reaches of the Carlisle AA water on Eden, that is, upstream of the mouth of the Petteril. In recent years the Carlisle club waters have become better known for the excellent chub and dace fishing which has provided a match weight of sixty four pounds and a top weight chub of six and three quarter pounds. Grayling, now relatively few and far between, are of a good average weight, fish of two to three pounds having been taken on lower Eden on several occasions during the past fifteen years, mainly by visiting coarse fish anglers.

Enquiries for available trout fishing should be made from Kirkby Stephen Angling Association (Appleby). Upper Eden (Appleby) fishing: Appleby Angling Association. Lazonby fishing: Lazonby Estate Office. Warwick Hall fishing

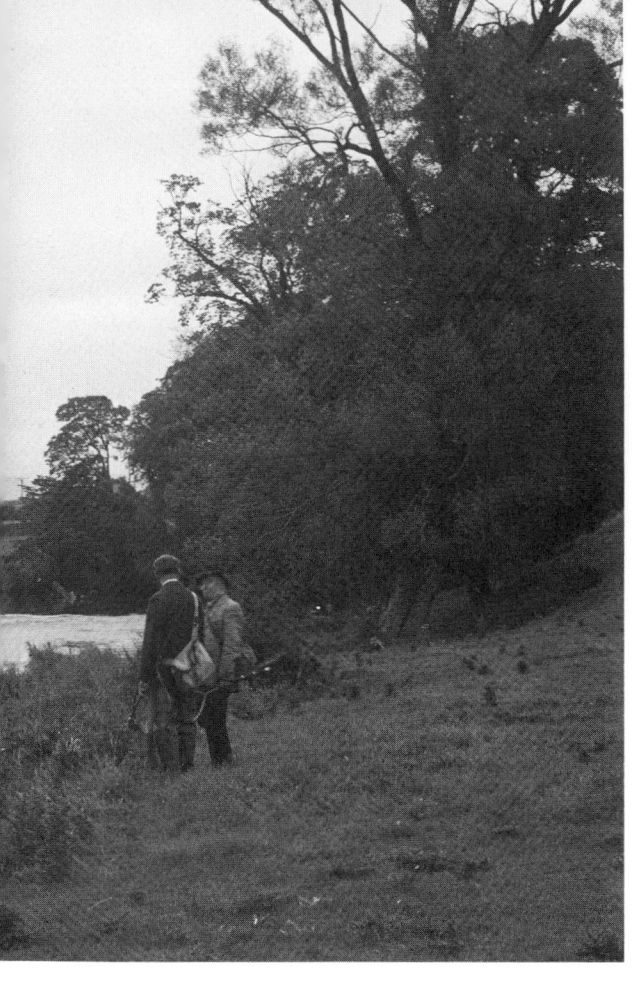

Brown trout country on the Kent near Kendal

duced brown trout of two pounds fifteen ounces (summer 1981) and two pounds twelve ounces to one local dry fly enthusiast in June '82.

Eamont would be more precipitous but for several weirs which are seen between Pooley Bridge and Brougham Castle on the A66 road. At the castle is the last of these weirs, down which Eamont cascades to be joined by the River Lowther. Above this weir the fishing is, with the exception of several rather short stretches, mainly controlled by the Penrith Angling Association, whose restocking of the upper Eamont, in particular, has provided fairly consistent, quality brown trout fishing. The only other sport species encountered above Brougham are rainbow trout (escapees from two fish farms) and migratory fish.

From Brougham downstream, the river widens and deepens considerably, forming numerous large pools, most of which hold salmon in their season and provide sport for rods of the Yorkshire Flyfishers' Club, which controls most of the left bank fishing. The right bank below Brougham is entirely privately owned and is strictly preserved as a fly only fishery. In lower Eamont, chub, pike and grayling are found, each species becoming more numerous as one nears the confluence with Eden, where occasional dace are to be seen.

Eamont is essentially a flyfisher's stream. It is a very clean river, judged by today's standards, and, being backed by Ullswater, it has a good, steady flow. Usually it is the last of the Eden area rivers to drop in level following a spate, and will provide a good fishing height and pace even when Eden itself has fallen. The upper half, above Brougham, is over treed in places, but these trout sanctuaries are necessary on a river which receives a steady rod pressure, as the upper Eamont is for a couple of miles a casual ticket water – hence the annual re-stocking. Really deep pools are few and far between, and the greater percentage of water is readily accessible and wadeable. Below Brougham a number of large red sandstone scars may be seen, and under these, pools up to ten feet in depth have formed. One in particular, the salmon pool at Udford, has at its neck a narrow gulley which is sixteen feet deep. This deep water is the result of an earth fault, however, and not due to erosion. Throughout most of its length Eamont sports weed growth of varying density. Rarely is it a problem on the upper river, but

(Carlisle): Carlisle Angling Association. Yorkshire Flyfishers' Club (Leeds). Tactful local enquiries produce other limited opportunities.

Eamont

For the volume of water which it carries annually from Ullswater to the Eden at Waters Meet, the Eamont must be almost unique, since its total length is roughly ten miles, and yet it is the major Eden tributary. First seen at Pooley Bridge, where it is a broad and shallow gravelly nursery for Eden salmon, the Eamont offers inviting glimpses of itself through the heavy growth of deciduous trees which clothe its valley, running almost parallel with the A592 Windermere – Penrith road. A mile or so south west of Penrith, Eamont swings west to Eamont Bridge, where it is spanned by a bottle neck bridge carrying the old A6 road to Kendal. On its journey, the river collects Dacre Beck, the only stream of significant size to swell its upper reaches, a stream, incidentally, which has pro-

below Brougham it can cause headaches for wet fly anglers after May in a normal season; but, as with Eden, the weed channels provide the cream of summer evening fishing with the dry fly, and without them, day time angling would be very difficult in low water. Average weight of trout taken on the entire river must be better than eight ounces; and on lower Eamont it is possible to 'farm' an average of almost one pound by selective fishing. Trout of two pounds or over are reported from beats between Pooley Bridge and Brougham weir every season. Best brown trout up until June 1982, for example, was two pounds two ounces, but the water holds fish well in excess of this. A personal best for 1982 was a catch of four brown trout, taken on dry fly in May, for a total weight of five pounds four ounces.

Lowther

Once a prolific trout stream, Lowther has never really recovered from the shock it received when its headwaters were impounded by the construction of the Haweswater Reservoir. Since that time, Wet Sleddale Dam, near Shap village, has been built and several of the upper Lowther feeders have been impounded and tapped by the old Manchester Corporation Waterworks. The minimum acceptable flow was, in the opinion of most local anglers, inadequate. However, the Lowther provides fair sport, generally, results being better on the middle and lower reaches, and it has produced several cup winning trout for the fly fishing enthusiasts of Penrith AA over the years. The crayfish population of Lowther is the highest of any local river and no doubt accounts for the better trout found in some of the larger pools.

Chub are found throughout most of the river's course, and pike were once common from Bampton to Brougham, but are rarely encountered now. Grayling also inhabit lower Lowther, which has fewer obstructions than Eamont to impede their movement, and the river attracts late running salmon to the redds in its upper half.

Trout fishing above Bampton is typical 'beck fishing' for truly wild, game little fighters with the chance of the odd heavier fish, but, below the village, much larger pools offer a better average weight of fish. The Lowther provides numerous streams and runs, alternating with some surprisingly big pools for so small a river, but it flows less urgently than Eamont, thus producing generally slower moving flats and glides. Although less popular than Eden or Eamont, Lowther comprises several miles of uncrowded, meditative angling in beautiful surroundings, and it is an improving river, mainly because the Penrith AA has been running an annual re-stocking programme on upper Lowther, Askham area, in conjunction with the owners, Lowther Estates, since 1977.

Insect life is similar to that found in Eden and Eamont, but ephemerids are not quite so evident and ranunculus, troublesome only on the lower reaches, is much less of a problem.

Irthing

The River Irthing, which rises in the Northumbrian Pennine hills, enters the Eden below Warwick Bridge on the A69 Carlisle – Newcastle road. Much of the fishing is controlled by the Brampton Angling Association which has rights extending from the remote hill country above Gilsland down to the lower reaches, including the tributary Gelt. Upper Irthing provides typical beck fishing for small brown trout without competition from the migratory species, since an impressive waterfall near Gilsland prevents progress beyond that point.

Below Gilsland, Irthing changes steadily in character; having fallen quite dramatically through some outstanding rocky, forested terrain, it becomes a more placid trout stream. Grayling, chub and dace are found in the lower river, and the Brampton club has taken steps to improve this water both by removing the unwanted coarse species to other rivers and by supplementing natural trout stocks by regular re-stocking. Weed is evident in the lower beats, which provide the better trout fishing. This is not of the standard met with on Eden and Eamont, but the river has a fair grayling population, and it receives a higher proportion of the Eden sea-trout.

It should be possible to catch trout at about two to the pound on fly, and the bigger pools of the lower river will provide better fish. Closer to the

confluence with Eden, the river holds pike, and it is thought that the Eden record pike of twenty nine and a half pounds was taken at or near Irthing foot. The moors which form the Irthing watershed are presently being prepared for afforestation, and it is likely that the river will be subjected to more flash flooding as a result of the extensive drainage work involved.

Petteril

This little river has the gentlest of flows. It rises in Greystoke Forest, not far above the village of Greystoke, and follows a leisurely course roughly parallel to Eden; it is flanked by the M6 motorway on its left and the A6 trunk road on its right – a sheltered river. By nature it is warmer than its neighbours, and very fertile; its trout come into condition more rapidly than those of any other north Cumbrian stream (but closely followed by the fish of the Lyvennet, an upper Eden feeder). In times of heavy rains or fast thaws, Petteril is subject to flooding, but it is usually the last of our rivers to flood and the first to drop in level.

As it is generally very clear and mainly quite shallow, Petteril is a dry fly man's river, but wet fly fishes well when the water is slightly coloured or clearing yet running a little above normal height. It was during flood conditions in October 1968 that spillage from a tanker (involved in an accident on the nearby A6 road) killed the animal life in an eighteen mile stretch between Plumpton village and Rickerby Park, Carlisle – scene of the confluence with Eden. Some official re-stocking was carried out in the 1970's, but only on beats below Plumpton. In the three miles of fishing above that village, Penrith AA has practised annual re-stocking since March 1977, and the river has been recovering steadily since this began.

The trout caught on the Penrith AA preserves run to an average weight of about eight ounces, with a fair percentage of three quarter to one pound trout taken. On the private waters below Plumpton, the bigger pools hold even larger fish and the odd, good rainbow may be taken on the river between the village and Carlisle. As with the Eamont fish, these rainbows will have escaped from a nearby fish farm. Above the Penrith club preserves, again, the fishing is privately owned.

After mid May, Petteril begins to fill with ranunculus on its shallows and this weed can be most troublesome during the summer months, but it is always possible to take trout by adopting the upstream method of fly fishing. Insect life on Petteril is similar to that in neighbouring rivers and, in a good season, the medium olive dun hatch is the best in the area, considering the size of the stream.

Caldew

A rocky river for much of its length, fast flowing, with a fair overall gradient, Caldew rises on the eastern slopes of Skiddaw and drains that area and the northern side of Blencathra, finally entering Eden in Bitts Park, Carlisle. From its headwaters to Sebergham village, the river provides mainly typical upland fishing – small wet or dry fly on light tackle – but develops into a sizeable river as it approaches Sebergham on the B5305, Penrith – Wigton road. From here onwards, the fishing improves and provides good fly fishing in the numerous streams and pools between Dalston and Carlisle. There is no competition from migratory species, for an impassable barrier at Holme Head, Carlisle, prevents salmon and sea-trout from ascending the river, although they spawn annually on the gravel below the dam, within the city.

From Holme Head to Bitts Park and the confluence with Eden, chub and dace are encountered in increasing numbers, while trout become less numerous, as the lower Caldew is subject to pollution due to industry within the city. A recent report on the river stated that chub and dace exist above Holme Head, which suggests transportation of ova by water fowl or coarse fish or by some other means.

Weed is rarely a problem on Caldew, due mainly to its stony nature, and is restricted to the lower reaches, which are slow running. More silt is found towards the river mouth, resulting in a greater midge population. In spring time, especially if cold weather deters the large dark olive hatch, a preoccupation with midges and smuts can make morning fly fishing difficult but sport is usually pretty dependable, and Caldew has the best March brown hatch seen on local waters.

119

YORKSHIRE, DURHAM AND NORTHUMBERLAND

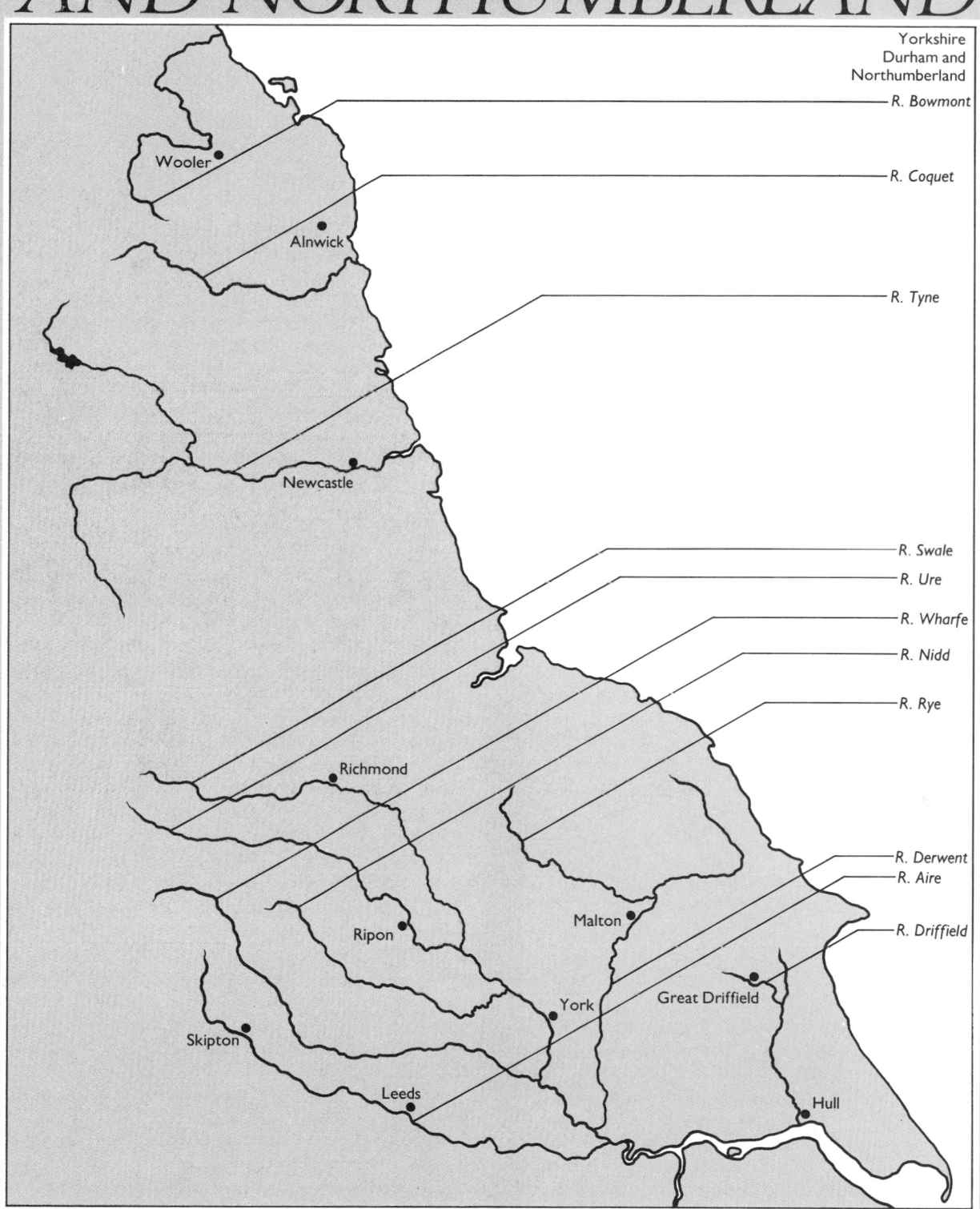

Yorkshire Durham and Northumberland

R. Bowmont

R. Coquet

R. Tyne

R. Swale
R. Ure
R. Wharfe
R. Nidd
R. Rye

R. Derwent
R. Aire

R. Driffield

Wooler

Alnwick

Newcastle

Richmond

Ripon

Malton

Skipton

York

Great Driffield

Leeds

Hull

Early days on the Wharfe at Ilkley

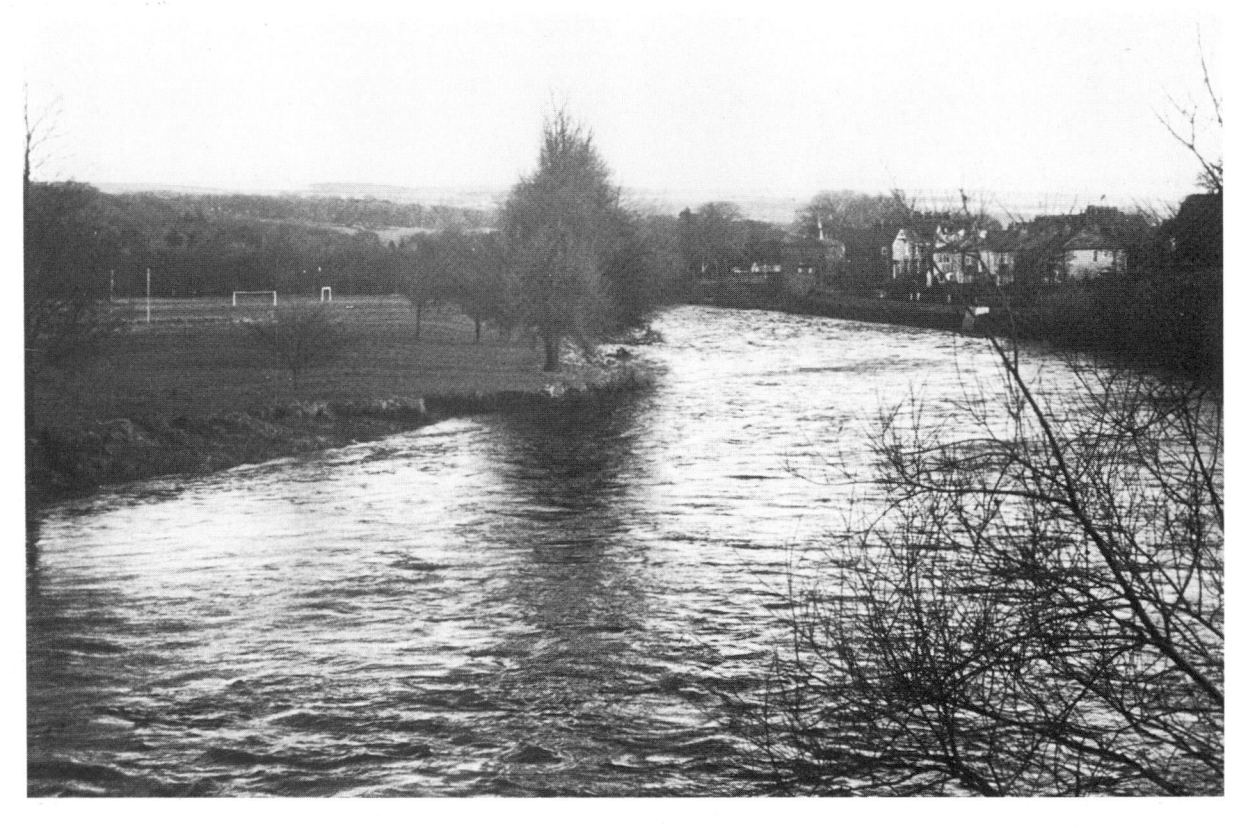

Wharfe

The Wharfe is typical of the broad shire. From start to finish it is a Yorkshire river. It first flexes its sinews on Cam Fell on the high side of Oughtershaw – about 1,000 ft above sea level – and from Beckermonds downstream through Deepdale, Yockenthwaite and Hubberholme it provides good beck or burn fishing during or after a flood. By the time the Wharfe is joined by its tributary, the Skirfare, just upstream of Kilnsey, it is a river of lovely dimensions for the trout fly fisherman. From there it flows south east through the principal parts of Wharfedale skirting such colourful villages and towns as Grassington, Burnsall, Appletreewick, Bolton Abbey, Beamsley, Addingham and Ilkley. Burley-in-Wharfedale and Otley follow in the long chain and it is about at this point that the river ceases to be primarily a game fish river. From here on down to its confluence with the river Ouse at

Cawood it is a good mixed fishery. Tributes have been paid to the Wharfe since the days of the Romans. In more recent times, Wordsworth got from it some inspiration for his finest verse while Turner found that it would yield subjects for his matchless drawings.

Like its near neighbour, the Ure, the Wharfe is a rain fed river and is subject to searing floods. Occasionally a virtual tidal wave, resembling the Severn bore, sweeps down the river and has been known to carry off a few wading anglers. The water, however, tends to be slightly more alkaline than some moorland rivers – particularly in its lower reaches. During its early and formative course it is very much a spate river – running brisk and clear over sparkling gravel. As with the Ure it is also a renowned grayling river, but the wild trout are not to be scorned and one of the best managed clubs is to be found in the Kilnsey Angling Club which also has fishing rights on the Skirfare. Here again it is customary to augment the stocks of natural trout with injections from

hatcheries. Even so the trout tend to run small and a fish of one pound must be considered a specimen. Traditionally the Wharfe must be regarded as a wet fly trout water, although both Pritt and Walbran thought it every bit as good as the Ure for grayling. For those who appreciate the sheer beauty of the landscape, however, the Wharfe may have a slight edge on other dales rivers. Sadly, there are now parts of Wharfedale which attract vast numbers of day trippers, campers, caravaners and canoeists and a fine summer weekend may not be the best time for the angler to seek his sport. Stick retrieving dogs and stone throwing kids all contribute their own brand of mayhem.

As with other Yorkshire Dales rivers there are sections where bait fishing is permitted. Upstream worming is a popular method; but there are more clubs insisting on a fly only rule, even if only for the first part of the season. As with the Ure the most popular flies tend to be the sparsely dressed patterns such as the Waterhen Bloa, Snipe and Purple, Partridge and Orange and the Dark Needle. But fish of the '80's are more catholic in their tastes and anglers find that a wide variety of patterns will now catch fish provided their presentation is done with the stealth of the hunter.

While the wet fly retains its dominance over other methods there are places and occasions when the dry fly will take fish – particularly in the lower water of late spring and summer. One of the most attractive and accessible beats of the Wharfe is that owned and administed by the Chatsworth Settle-ment Trust. The Estate Office in Bolton Abbey issues tickets for that lovely stretch of river and in recent times the stock of natural trout has been augmented by frequent injections from their own hatchery. Guests staying at the newly renovated Devonshire Arms Hotel may fish the water at a much reduced rate. Close by is the 'Strid' or 'Stryth' of saxon times. It was here, as the story goes, that over eight centuries ago, the Boy of Egremond, the heir to the Romillys, perished in a flood while out hunting. Indeed, it is here that the river narrows to a seemingly easy jump and even to this day there are severe warnings about the dangers of drowning in the Strid.

Of all the Yorkshire trout streams it is the opinion of many anglers that the Wharfe is the most attractive. It may not produce the biggest or the most prolific bags of fish; but it is a captivating dale and a visit to it is made much more enchanting if it may be undertaken when the entire population of Yorkshire do not share the same idea!

Ure (or Yore)

The Ure (from the celtic 'ur' or 'brisk') rises on the mountainous boundary line of Yorkshire and what used to be Westmorland and has its source 2,000 ft above sea level on the North Yorkshire moorland of Lunds Fell. By the time it has reached the diminutive township of Hawes it is a sizeable stream. It then continues to grow in volume and girth as it passes through Bainbridge, Aysgarth, Wensley, Middleham, Masham and Tanfield. At Ripon it is a good mixed fishery and just below Boroughbridge it undergoes its final metamorphosis to become the river Ouse and ultimately the Humber. It is essentially a rain fed river, but with comparative low acidity – particularly in its lower reaches. The upper reaches are subject to flash floods and most people have heard of the great flood damage which occasionally happens at York. It is virtually free of pollution and is not over abstracted. Most of the small feeders also provide water of high purity and low acidity; but the trend is to higher acidity – as it is almost everywhere in the country – where catchment areas are downwind of big industrial connurbations with the consequent fallout of acid rain.

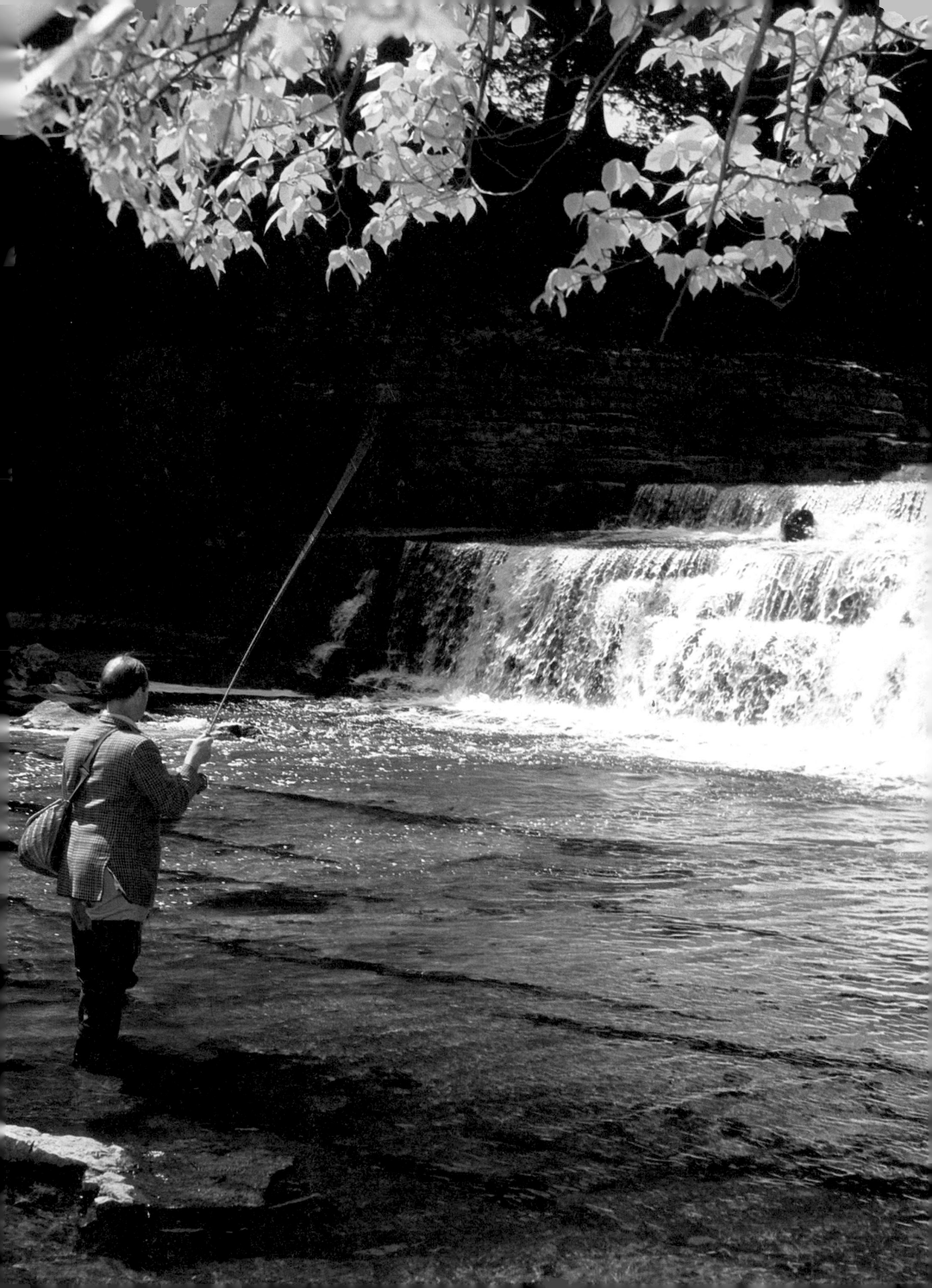

Mayfly time on the Nidd

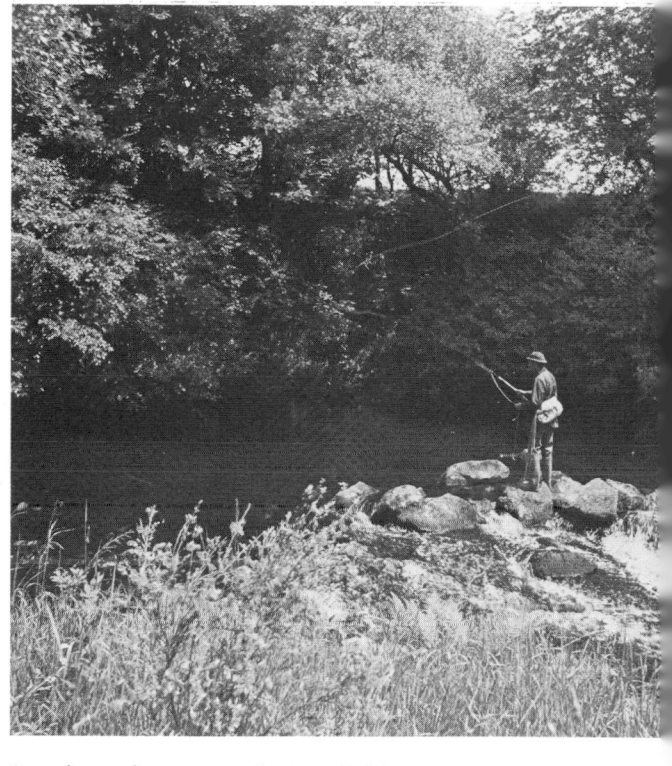

In its upper reaches the Ure and its tributaries provide some noted trout and grayling fishing. Those two great Yorkshire anglers of yesteryear, T E Pritt and Frances Walbran, both extolled the virtues of the river. Both might have been slightly biased in favour of the grayling; but there is a good head of wild brown trout in the water with more clubs and syndicates augmenting the stock by frequent releases of hatchery fish. Some headway has been made in reclaiming the Ure as a salmon fishery and there is rarely a year which passes when salmon may not be seen at Aysgarth Falls – the ultimate point on the river to which they migrate. Coarse fish are not seriously encountered much upstream of Tanfield, but there are occasional pockets of barbel and chub in the deeper sections near Middleham.

Although the wild trout tend to run small and will do well to top the twelve inch mark there are now several clubs and syndicates which stock with larger fish. The Tanfield Anglers Club has one of the most prolific sections of the river, but there is a long waiting list and only accompanied guests may gain access. Similarly disciplined, the Yorkshire Flyfishers have excellent water at Clifton Castle, but there are no facilities for day tickets and club membership is not easy to acquire. Some of the clubs now stock with rainbow trout as well as the native browns. This gives a larger average size of fish, but must be detrimental to stocks of resident brown trout and thus injects a deal of artificiality into the sport. One supposes it is part of the price we must pay for a more plentiful supply of larger fish for an equally more plentiful supply of anglers.

While fly fishing retains its long standing domination as a prime method on the Ure, there are sections on beats where bait fishing may be allowed. For instance, there are places where the upstream worm may be permitted after July 1 – as may the use of the natural minnow. The maggot is usually frowned upon, as is spinning, and undoubtedly the best of the sport with Ure trout comes on those sections which are stocked and where there is a fly only restriction. Popular Yorkshire flies tend to be slimly dressed in wet fly style and for early season fishing there is little to beat that Yorkshire trio, the Waterhen Bloa, Snipe and Purple and Partridge and Orange. The Sturdy's Fancy, a fly named after a forbear of the present

Sturdy – a keeper on the Tanfield water – is always worth a try; but trout are much more catholic in their taste than they were in Pritt's and Walbran's time and it may be that presentation of the fly is of much more importance than exact imitation of the natural.

Although the wet fly is the traditional method of fishing most of the Yorkshire Dales rivers, there is an increasing tendency to go for some of the bigger fish with a dry fly. This is best used after the high waters of spring and when the river starts to run at summer level. It could well be late May or June before the best of the dry fly fishing gets under way; but even then it is often a mistake to fish with dry flies which are too large. Small representations of the ephemerid family will often do better than the bigger ones and it always makes sense to have a few ultra-small facsimiles of the various smuts. As with most rain fed rivers, the Ure fishes best when fining down from a recent rise. There is a deal of day ticket water and the casual visitor may well find access from one of the many hotels in that general area of the Ure valley known as Wensleydale.

The Nidd's rocky runs

Nidd

The Nidd first sees the light of day at Nidd Head Spring on Great Whernside, some 2,000 ft above sea level in North Yorkshire and the headwaters then drain into the Angram reservoirs. At Croydon Pot the river goes underground, but reappears shortly and becomes a sizeable beck or stream until it runs into Gouthwaite Reservoir just below Ramsgill. The reservoir then presumes to become the river again near Wath and it flows on down through Pateley Bridge, Glasshouses and Summerbridge where it assumes more sizeable proportions as a good trout stream. Next in line come the prime trout waters near Darley, Birstwith, Hampsthwaite and Killinghall. By this latter time, however, the river has become a good mixed fishery and by the time it gets to Knaresborough, with its castle dating back to Henry I and its memorial of Mother Shipton, the game fish population is in decline. Below Knaresborough the river continues in a series of wide 'S' bends until, crossing the A1 at Walshford, it adopts a more meandering pace until its junction with the River Ouse at Nun Monkton.

Much of the water flow which comes down into the main area of the Nidd is controlled by the Yorkshire Water Authority from the outfall at Gouthwaite. Most times this spares the main valley from searing and damaging spates and it is rare to find flood damage as devastating as it might be elsewhere in Yorkshire. Conversely, the river rarely gets down to its bare bones; and angling may be interrupted by the effects of an artificial rise in the water when the reservoir gets too high. In its upper reaches the Nidd is very much like any other north country trout beck or stream. The trout run small and most forms of bait fishing are allowed after 1 July.

Along with the native trout population there is a thriving stock of grayling. In some situations these grayling may well be present in greater numbers than the trout. Indeed, Gouthwaite Reservoir is said to be one of the few stillwater sanctuaries of grayling to be found in Britain; but this may be little more than hearsay. Stocking with trout at Gouthwaite has certainly improved the average size of the trout encountered there and may be responsible, in some measure, for a decline

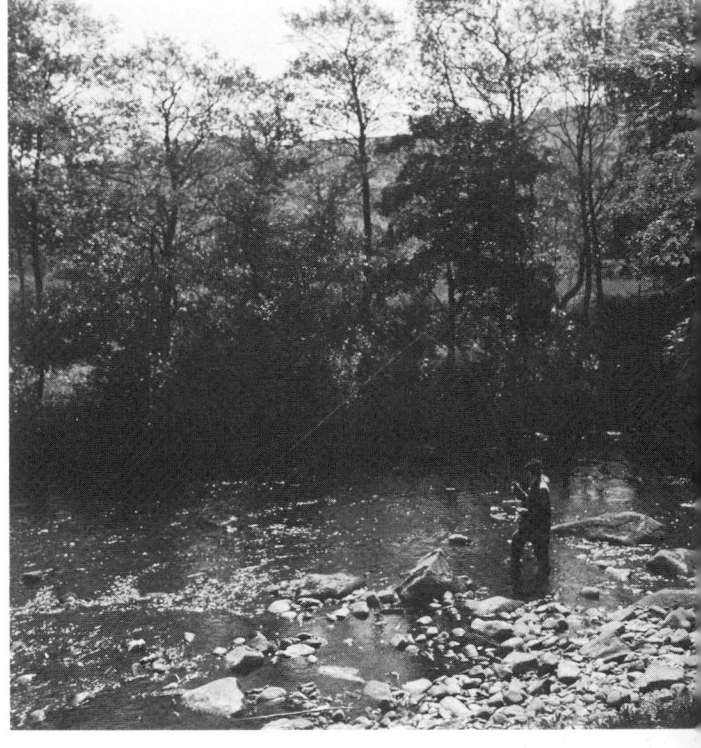

in grayling stocks. Elsewhere on the river, however, grayling are plentiful if not very large. Indeed, a grayling over the one pound mark must be regarded as a specimen. Little trout fishing of consequence is to be found below Killinghall and the best of the river fishing is undoubtedly in that section between Hampsthwaite and Pateley Bridge.

Here again wet fly techniques dominate. The three principal clubs in the area, the Birstwith Private Anglers Club, the Harrogate Fly Fishers Club and the Nidderdale Angling Club all insist on fly only rules for most of the season. Perhaps the Harrogate Fly Fishers have the best preserves and they have been most prudent in making outright purchases of some of their water when it has come onto the market. While most of the trout caught tend to be stock fish there are a few wild brown trout and large stocks of small grayling. Just occasionally a large brown trout of the order of two pounds is encountered; but they are not plentiful and the angler has to be content with trout bordering on the one pound mark. One popular method of taking difficult fish involves

The late Eric Horsfall Turner menacing trout on the
Yorkshire Derwent

the angler casting a long line downstream and
stripping off some residue. Then the line is slowly
retrieved and it is during this period that the fly
may be taken by a better than average fish.

A rare event these days on many Yorkshire
waters, is the late May/early June arrival of the
mayfly. 4 June sticks in the mind as a day when,
most years, the trout of the Nidd may be seen
taking mayfly in good numbers. It is a time when
trout throw caution to the wind and rise well to
the floating fly. At other times of the season they
may be reluctant to do this. This is an occasion
when fishing with small wet flies or smuts may
be the only way to catch fish. The popular Yorkshire patterns all have their time and place on the
Nidd; but the Snipe and Purple and the Greenwell's Glory are special favourites.

Most of the clubs and syndicates on the Nidd
have waiting lists, so good water is hard to find.
Tickets are available on the Nidderdale water; but
the Harrogate and the Birstwith stretches are only
open to members and accompanied guests. All in
all the Nidd must be regarded as a fascinating
river to fish, if only by virtue of the fact that by
the time spring has turned into summer, the fish
are not among the easiest trout to catch.

Yorkshire Streams

It would not do to assume that the Ure, Wharfe
and Nidd represent the best of north country trout
rivers. Yorkshire is undoubtedly blessed with
more trout streams than any other county in Britain and certainly of greater variety. The Swale
for instance, (probably from 'swale' the Teutonic
'gentle') rises in bleak surroundings just south of
Kirkby Stephen in Cumbria at the confluence of
the Great Sleddale and Birkdale Becks. From there
it flows almost due east to Keld and Muker. Here
its course is down a steep, rock girt dale hemmed
in by high hills. From Muker down to Gunnerside
and Grinton several tributaries add to the river's
girth, but it is not until Reeth and Grinton, with
the addition of Arkle Beck, that the river assumes
reasonable proportions. From here it flows on
down through good trout country to Richmond.
Thereafter it becomes a mixed fishery with occasional good trout, continuing thus until it joins

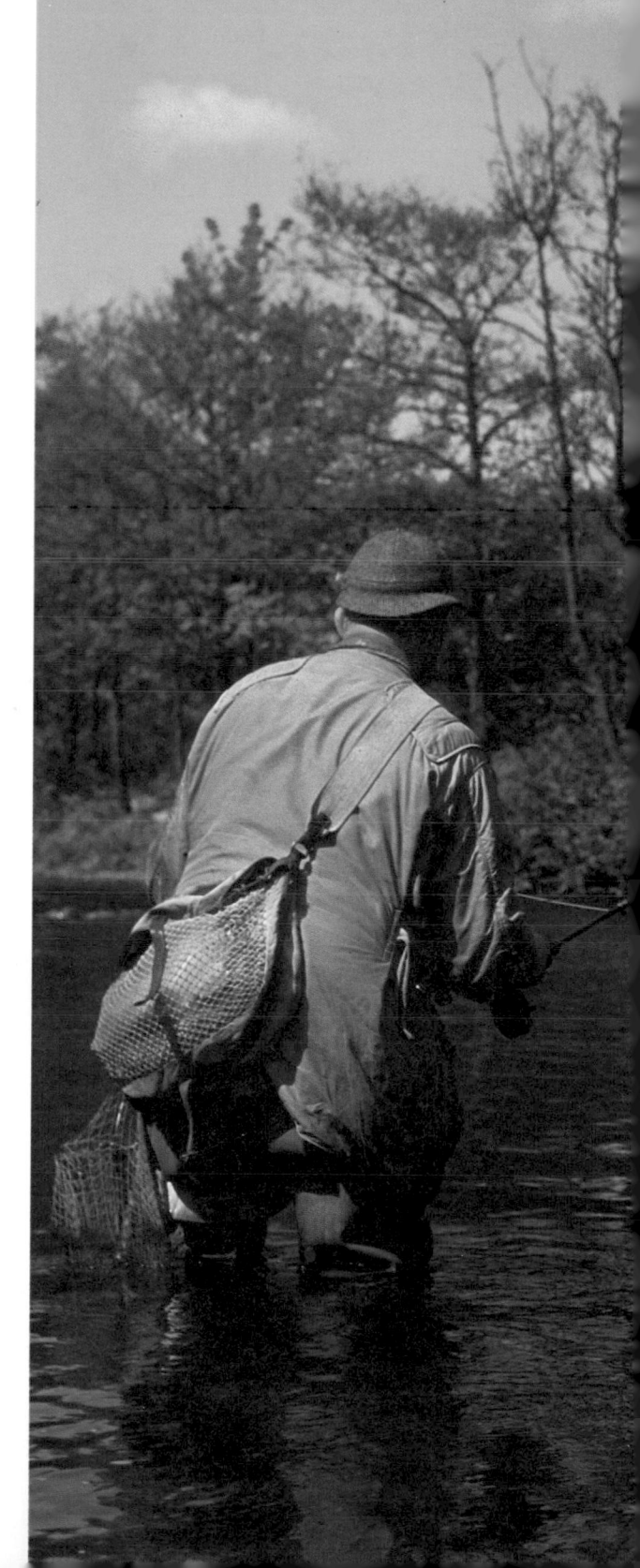

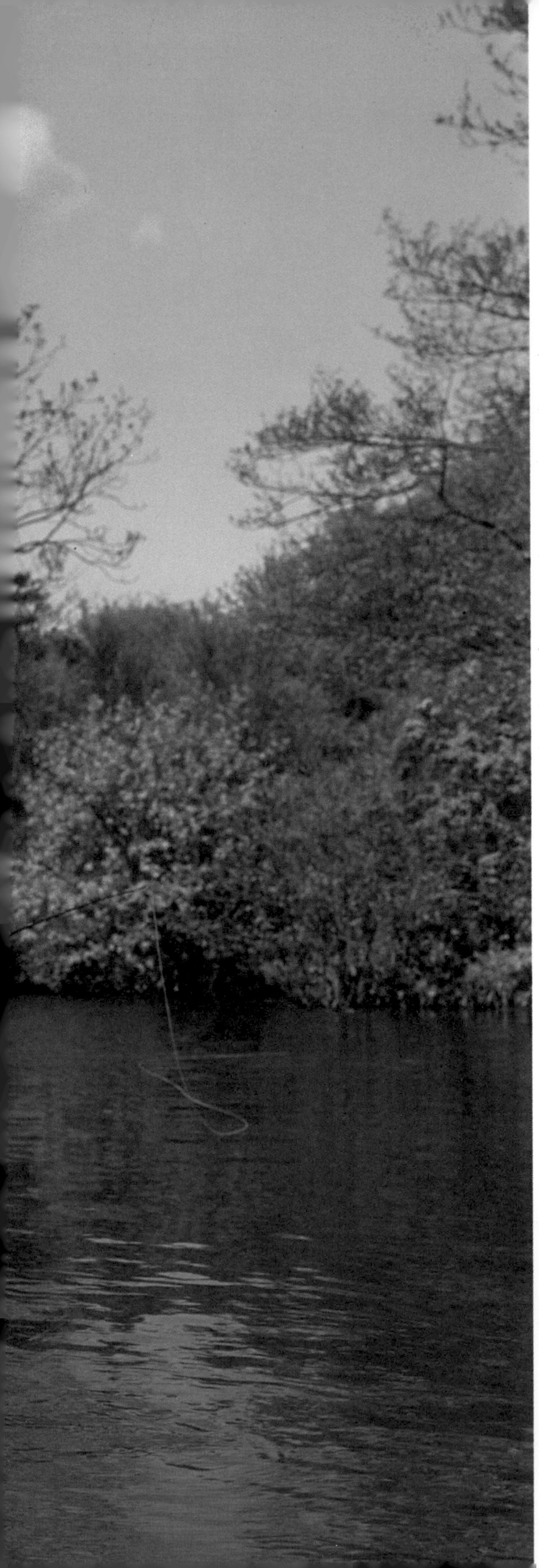

Below: Donald Overfield fishing the West Beck near Driffield

the Ure at Myton on Swale near Boroughbridge – almost sixty miles from source to junction.

As with most non-reservoir controlled Yorkshire rivers the Swale is subject to rapid flooding. In its upper reaches it is principally a brown trout river with fish averaging three or four to the pound. Despite its staunch disciples it lacks the charisma of the Ure and Wharfe and does not produce such good trout preserves as either of these waters. Grayling are frequently encountered lower downstream, as are specimen sized barbel and chub; but the trout of the lower reaches are hard to tempt even if they do grow to goodly proportions when allowed to survive.

Most of the upper Swale is either fished with small, traditional Yorkshire flies or with upstream worm tactics. Occasional spinning is permitted but this is usually limited to a single hooked lure. Wet fly is again the most popular style but there are occasions, as elsewhere in Yorkshire, when trout rise well to the dry fly.

Of lesser dimensions, but of great note as a delightful little fishery, the Yorkshire Derwent has its source on Wykeham High Moor near Fylingdales in North East Yorkshire. Here the Derwent Anglers Club – one of the oldest in the county – administers ten miles of superb water in the vicinity of Hackness. This represents the prime stretch of Derwent trout fishing and offers a great kaleidoscope of scenery and variety of river

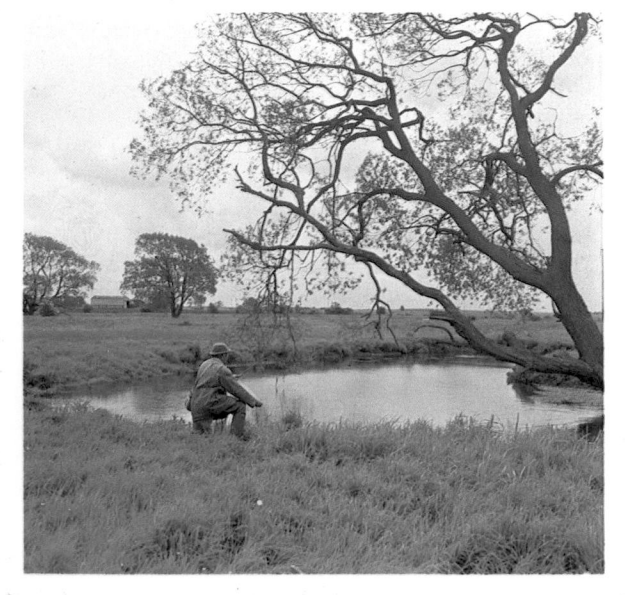

Where the trout are returning. The North Tyne

flow; from the babbling streams at Langdale End to the tranquility and semi–chalk stream effect of Forge Valley – at the bottom end of the club's preserves. Below West Ayton the river becomes a good mixed fishery and continues thus down through Yedingham, Malton, Kirkham Abbey and Stamford Bridge until its junction with the Ouse near Long Drax. Occasional salmon run the river as far as Kirkham Abbey, but they are very unpredictable.

Most of the best Derwent trout fishing occurs in the vicinity of Hackness (about four miles due west of Scarborough) but the native brown trout run small and the water has to be regularly stocked with larger brown and rainbow trout from the club's own hatchery. This water holds particular attraction for the writer. It was the first fly fishing club he joined immediately following the second world war. On one far off May day it yielded fifty five trout to him, but that is another story. In times past it was possible to catch a very large number of small wild trout on a variety of artificial flies. There was always a good hatch of mayfly and some nice trout to be caught in Forge Valley. Today, though artificially reared, the fish are much larger but the upper Derwent valley has lost nothing of its magic as a consequence. There is a fly only rule in operation throughout the season.

Like most of Yorkshire's rain fed rivers, the Derwent is subject to rapid rises following heavy rain. Just downstream of Hackness, however, there is a sea–cut to the nearby saltwater at Scalby. This takes the excess of flood water and thus eliminates any flooding in Forge Valley, but it does not always ensure clear water.

While in that area of North Yorkshire it is as well to remember a myriad of smaller streams and rivers where good trout fishing may be found. The Rye is a principal tributary. It rises on the Cleveland Hills and joins the Derwent just north of Malton. There is excellent fishing near Helmsley where the water is administered by the Ryedale Anglers Club. At Nunnington there is good day ticket water and there are several lesser tributaries such as the Riccal, Dove, Seven and Seph which all hold native brown trout and where access is largely confined to members of the various clubs. Most insist on a fly only rule and one of the most popular flies in that area is the John Storey – a fly which had its origins on the Rye

from a well known river keeper of that name.

Travelling further east there is a little known chalk stream which has its source from springs near Pickering. Titled the Costa, it eventually joins the Pickering Beck and ultimately the Rye. In pre-war times the Costa was a noted fishery. Just prior to the war, however, the water was stocked with fly larvae imported from Hampshire's River Test. Nothing was ever seen again of the blue winged olive it was hoped would thrive, but the weed on which they were transported (*ranunculus fluitans* or water buttercup) quickly took root and eventually choked the stream to such an extent that it had to be dredged to overcome flooding problems. Since then it has never regained its legendary reputation although

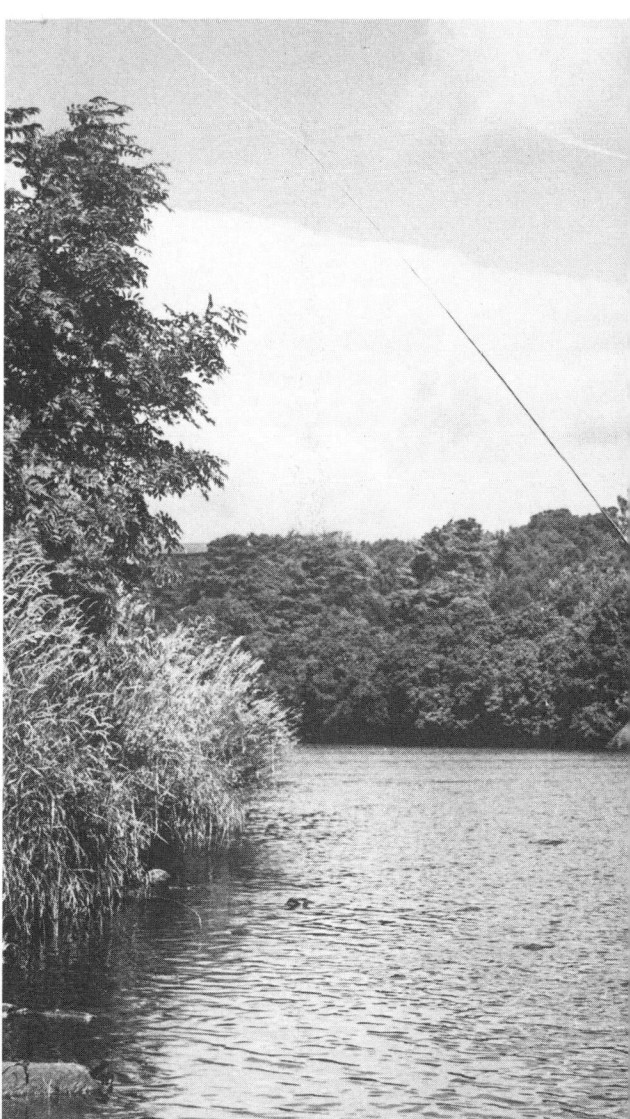

it still produces the occasional specimen trout and grayling.

Going south east from Pickering we come to the little market town of Driffield, in what used to be known as the old East Riding. Here the much revered Driffield Anglers Club has excellent preserves on the upper portion of the Driffield Beck. This is yet another true chalk stream having its principal source from springs at Kirkburn, on the edge of the Yorkshire Wolds. The club has the distinction of being the oldest angling club in the county and is run very much on traditional lines with only members and their guests being permitted access. As elsewhere the river is liberally stocked with fish from the club hatchery; but there is abundant natural food in the form of fresh-

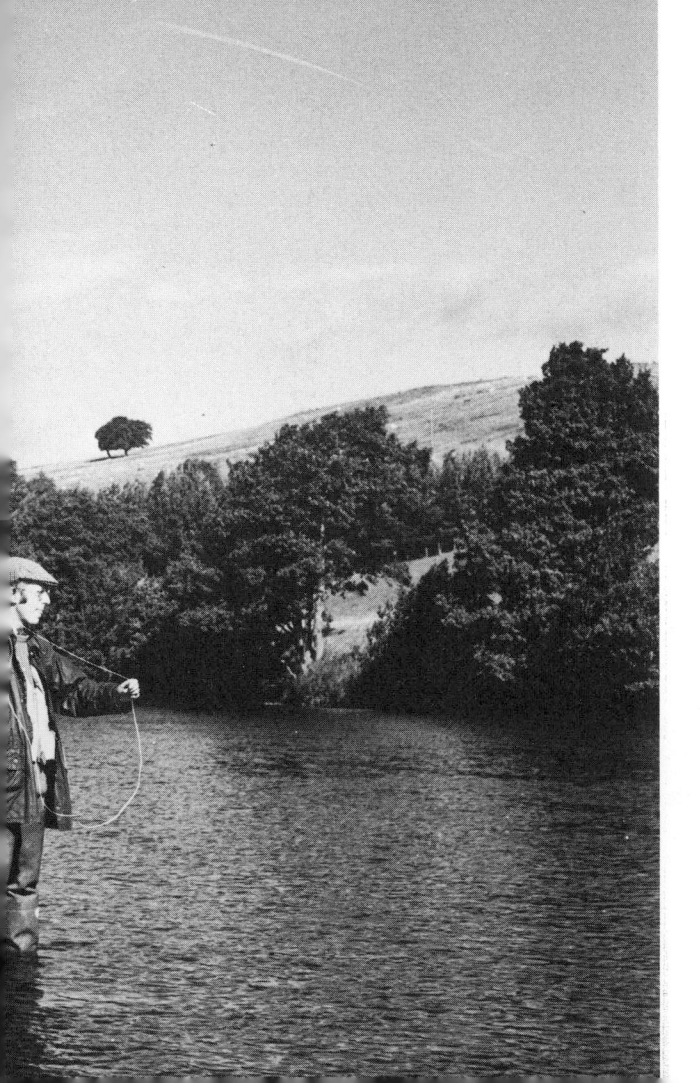

water shrimp and natural aquatic flies and some specimen fish are taken every year. Perhaps it does not need to be recorded that there is a fly only rule. Below the Driffield club water there is further excellent fishing on the Golden Hill water and on that administered by the West Beck Preservation Society. Thereafter the water becomes an excellent mixed fishery and continues thus until its junction with the River Hull.

Adjacent to the Driffield Beck is the Foston trout stream. This has its source from springs at Kilham and is yet another chalk stream containing excellent wild brown trout. The Foston Fishing Club controls the best section from Bracey Bridge to the mill at Foston and the water is perhaps unique in that only brown trout are to be found in the club's preserves. Just a few specimen trout are taken from this water every year and the late H Cholmondeley-Pennell, commenting on the Governor fly, wrote, 'The heaviest take of large trout which ever came to my knowledge – though, alas, I was not the captor – was made with this fly on the upper waters of the Foston Beck.' The writer had the privilege of being secretary of the Foston Fishing Club for ten years and in one September day in 1959 he took eight trout weighing fifteen pounds ten ounces all on the upstream nymph.

Below the mill at Foston there is good trout water administered by the Millhouse Beck Fishing Club. This consists of a short stretch before the water becomes a good mixed fishery. Much has been done to augment the stock of trout and it is now liberally replenished with both specimen brown and rainbow trout. As with the Foston Fishing Club there is a fly only rule and fishing is for members only.

Although in this short summary it is impossible to cover all of Yorkshire's excellent trout waters; it would be unfair to leave the county without some mention of the River Aire. This has its source at Aire Head half a mile south of Malham village near the little town of Settle in North Yorkshire. It flows on down through Gargrave and Skipton before it is reduced to sewer like ignominy in the middle of Bradford and Leeds and its final demise at Ferrybridge. In its upper reaches it is an excellent trout water where perhaps the best portion is controlled by the Aire Fishing Club. This fishing is strictly reserved for members

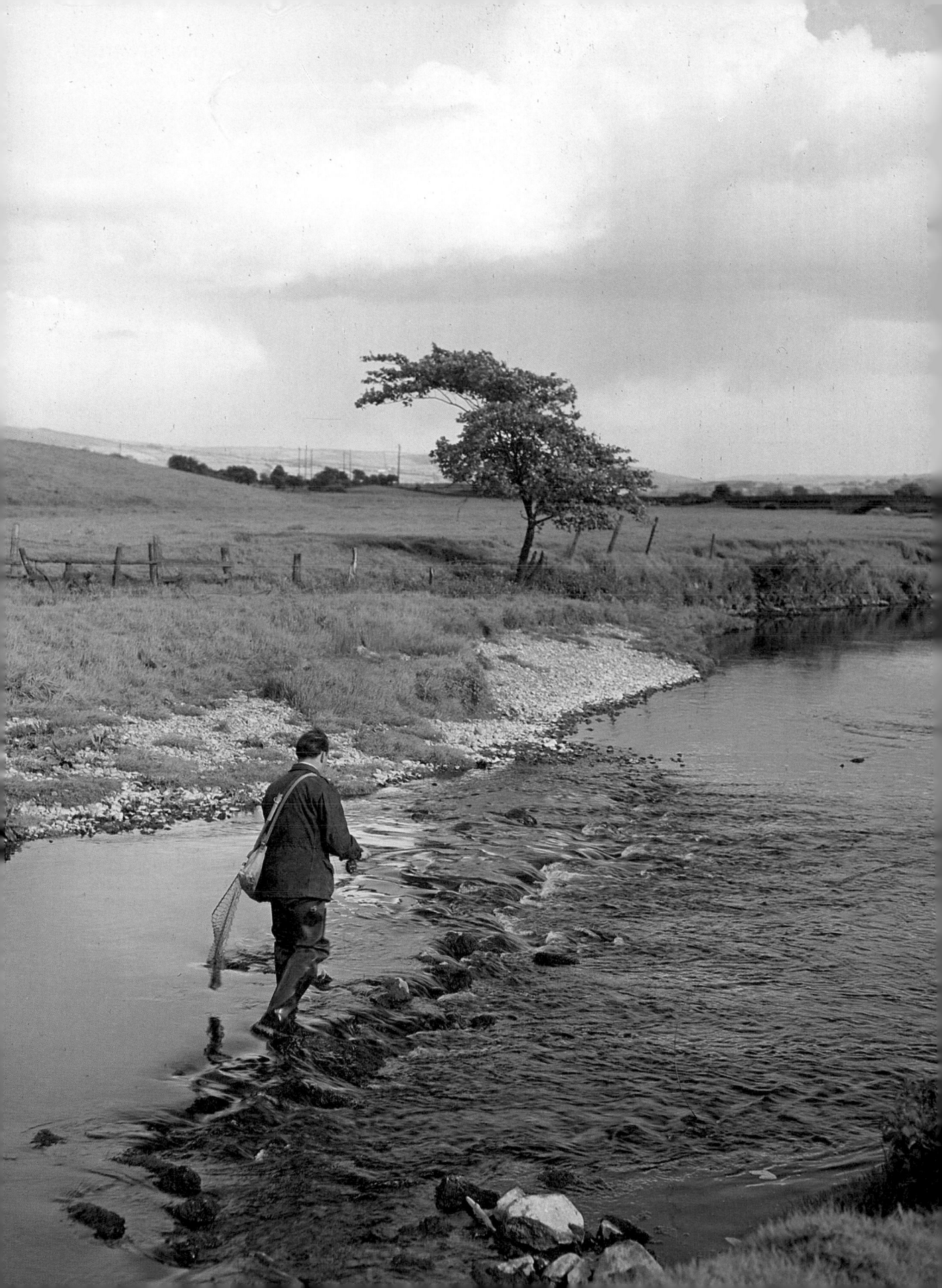

Left: Peter Tombleson on the Yorkshire Aire   Below: Arthur Oglesby gets another Foston trout

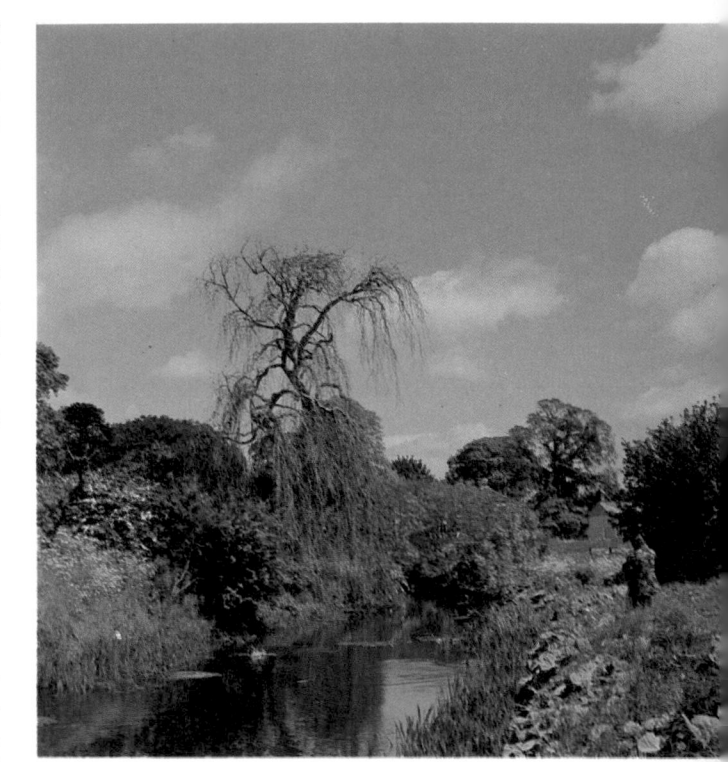

and is among the best of its type in the north of England. The water is stocked annually but it also contains a vast natural minnow population. These provide wonderful food for the trout and some natural minnow fishing is permitted after 1 July. For the most part, however, it is fly only

Within the space alotted it has not been possible to do any more than give but brief mention to some of Yorshire's better known waters. Despite the inferences of dark, satanic mills there is a wealth of lovely country in Yorkshire with hundreds of miles of unpolluted waters. An earlier writer on angling in Yorkshire once commented, 'Yorkshire has the lot!' Most certainly he was right when it comes to varieties of trout water!

Tyne

The River Tyne rises at Tynehead in the hills above Alston, five miles beyond Garrigill, the highest point in England. It supports a great variety of fish, including salmon and sea-trout and their offspring. The Tyne sea-trout are not in fact sea-trout but bull trout, and the argument about when a sea-trout is a bull trout and vice versa is an endless and fascinating one.

The main Tyne also holds dace, roach, perch, gudgeon and pike – and in the not too distant past the native brown trout (known as the yellow trout) were evident in most stretches of the river. In those good old days it was quite common to creel a dozen in a day, average size between half a pound and a pound, with the occasional two pounder.

The Tyne has suffered severely from pollution and, sadly, deserved to be described as an open sewer. All kinds of new sewerage systems have now been installed and, with the multi million pound sewage work at Howdon below Newcastle, the river may well return to its old glory. It is hard to realise that as recently as 1927 more than 3,500 salmon and sea-trout were killed in the Tyne on rod and line.

The trout population also suffered in the '60's from UDN but, thanks to the energies of a dozen clubs and syndicates, and intensive stocking with two year old brown trout, excellent sport can be enjoyed once again, and will, we hope, continue.

The Tyne is served by the South Tyne which flows from above Alston and joins the Tyne one and a half miles above the market town of Hexham. In company with many rivers in the area, disused mines are to be found among its headwaters. In the area of Featherstone Castle the river runs over deep ledges and moves into some magnificent deep pools, with a background of sycamore, larch, oak and beech. The headwaters of the North Tyne are above Kielder village where the valley has been flooded down to Falstone village to create the vast new Kielder Reservoir.

The Tyne is also fed by the River Rede which flows below the A68 and which joins the North Tyne at West Woodburn, near Otterburn. The Rede is an attractive little river rising near Carter Bar at Catleugh Reservoir. It eventually reaches the Tyne after passing under the A68 just on the northern end of that stretch of blind summits and switchbacks that enliven the journey to Scotland. Rede trout can attain three quarters of a pound or even more, particularly where the river has grown and is running through deep pools and by deep

131

Evening rise on the Coquet

ledges. It is a stream for which a seven foot rod is ample.

Another little river, the East Allen, which rises at Killhope Law reaches Allendale after a journey through lovely and lonely valleys. It meets the West Allen, west of Whitfield, and joins the Tyne just below Bardon Mill on the A69 road. In the early part of this century many lead mines and slate quarries were in operation near its headwaters – but only one mine is still working. There is also a small underground stream which runs beneath Allendale and emerges from the hillside just below Allendale where it joins the East Allen. There is surprisingly good 'yellow trout' fishing in this river – and fishing tickets can be obtained at the Allendale Post Office.

The most successful flies in the Tyne area (early season) are the Greenwell, Wickhams Fancy, Pheasant Tail (with a smoky grey hackle) and (later on) Ginger Quill and Snipe and Purple, all tied sparsely.

Permits for the main Tyne are obtainable from the Corbridge Riverside Sports Club, Corbridge, from the Haltwhistle Angling Association and from the Hexham Anglers Association. For the East Allen, from the Allendale Angling Association; for the North Tyne, from the Black Cock Inn at Falstone and for the South Tyne, at Haltwhistle.

Bowmont

The Bowmont rises in the Cheviots and flows down to Kirk Newton in Northumberland where it meets the College Burn where, in the magic way that rivers have, it turns into the River Glen, eventually joining the Till below Wooler. Like most of the Northumberland rivers and streams it is peaty and acid and the trout do not average more than half a pound – but a wild moorland half pounder makes a very tasty and adequate breakfast. Later in the season much bigger brown trout run from Tweed to the Till (Tweed is such a river that custom has denied it a definite article) and from the Till into the Glen or Bowmont. As is almost universal in the area, the main fly in the local angler's armoury is Greenwell's Glory and the authentic story of the origin of this fly is worth

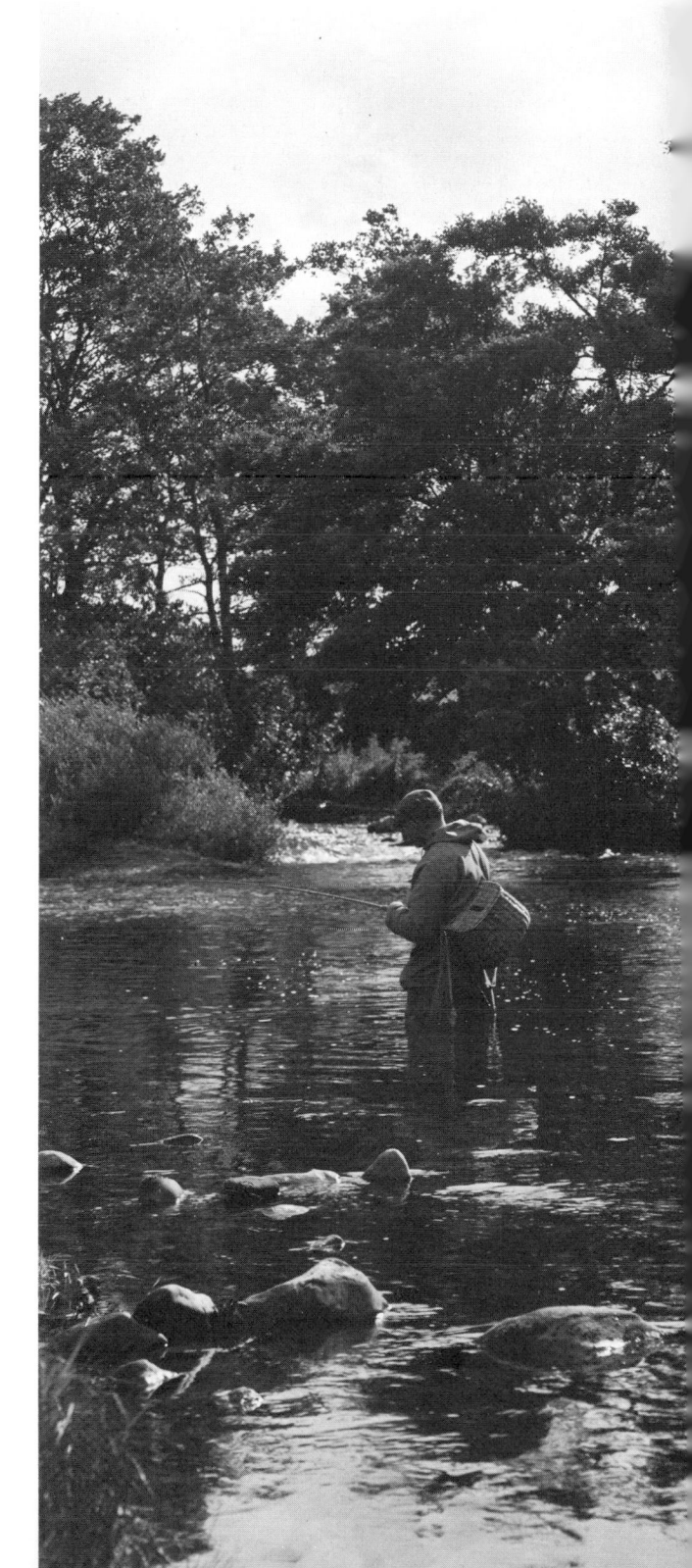

Dry fly water at Felton

grey one is rarely seen. Tickets for the Bowmont fishing can be obtained in Newcastle and Wooler.

Coquet

The River Coquet rises in the Cheviot Hills at AD Fines Roman camp, above Rothbury and reaches the sea at Warkworth flowing through Coquet Dale and then under the A699 and the A1. Although it is primarily famous for its salmon and bull trout (it was on the Coquet that early members of the Hardy family sharpened their teeth) there is also excellent brown trout fishing, with fish running from half a pound upwards, and monsters of up to four pounds giving anglers pleasant surprises every year.

It is a slow running river, winding through beautiful Northumberland countryside, flowing from heather covered moorland down to rich farmland and meadows. The native brown trout population (similar to the Tyne's yellow trout) is more prolific than on the Tyne system – with wild fish spawning in the many upstream feeders. This meandering river (not unlike the River Eden) is tailor made for the dry fly man ready to fish with a cast tapered down to three pounds breaking strain. Curlews, oyster catchers, herons and dippers are plentiful along the Coquet's banks – so, unfortunately, are gooseanders in great quantity. Bird conservation has its proper place but the growth in the gooseander numbers is threatening trout stocks in the Coquet. It was not all that long ago that the corncrake could be heard in the meadows – and in some tyings of flies its primary feathers were used. This harmless and attractive bird would have really deserved protection.

The best Coquet flies include Cairns Fancy, Greenwell's Glory, Grey Wolf (fully palmered) and the tying by Tom Stewart of Dumfriesshire of Withians Fancy: early flies include February Red, March Brown and Tups Indispensible.

Much of the fishing is controlled by the Northumberland Angling Association and the Rothbury and Thropton Angling Association also has good ticket water. The Chairman of the Northumberland Angling Association, appropriately enough, is Mr J L Hardy, of The House of Hardy at Alnwick.

recording. Canon Greenwell, Mr Henderson and Mr Foster were a trio of friends who fished Tweed for trout. Every time they fished it was Mr Henderson who had the best filled basket – something he took pains to remind the others about.

One evening in 1854 after a day's Tweed trouting, Canon Greenwell called at the workshop of a local fly tier, Jimmy Wright, bringing with him a little box of natural flies taken from the river and asked for imitations to be made. Under a strong light the flies were laid out on paper and copied. The result was nearly miraculous. Suddenly it was the Canon who ended the day with the biggest catches and after discussion with his friends the elated Canon christened it 'Greenwell's Glory'.

The Bowmont valley is one of the few places where the red squirrel runs free and where the

133

STILL WATERS

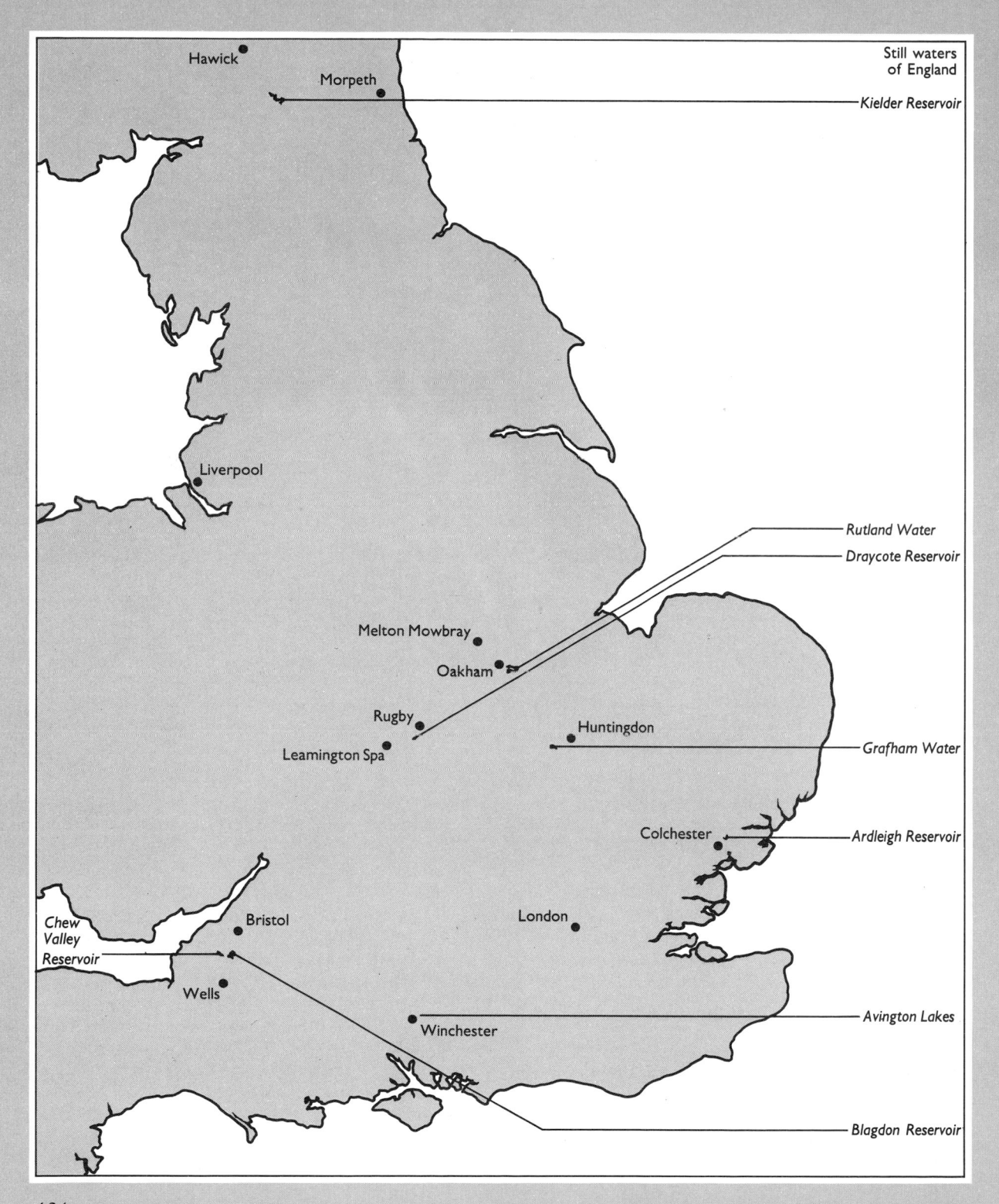

Hawick

Morpeth

Kielder Reservoir

Liverpool

Rutland Water

Draycote Reservoir

Melton Mowbray

Oakham

Rugby

Huntingdon

Grafham Water

Leamington Spa

Colchester

Ardleigh Reservoir

Chew
Valley
Reservoir

Bristol

London

Wells

Avington Lakes

Winchester

Blagdon Reservoir

Top: The Grafham skyline
Bottom: Into a big one at Draycote

Grafham

It was Grafham Water's 1600 acres, unlovely as they are, that provided the spark which touched off the boom in stillwater fly fishing.

Its fairy tale opening in the middle sixties was fashioned from events of which only fishermens' dreams are made. Highly experienced fly fishers waded ashore bewildered, as rainbows of unbelievable strength had torn away their lines and backing. A dozen fish scaling an arm aching half hundredweight were commonplace captures. Such happenings spawned a special breed of fly fishermen. The exploits of Dick Shrive, Cyril Inwood, Bob Church and that wizard of the stillwater nymph Arthur Cove, became part of the new sport's history. Now their innovations, revolutionary at the time, are considered the standard approach by the new and rapidly growing army of stillwater fly fishermen.

But, while these immense catches are now part of our angling folklore, Grafham is still regarded by many as our premier stillwater trout fishery. Each new season sees its own recently set records, eclipsed. Grafham, the mainspring of ideas a decade and more ago, has, much to the delight of former fishery manager, David Fleming-Jones, become the Mecca for the traditional style fisher who deftly plies his three small wet flies in front of a broadside drifting boat. Gone to a great extent are the boats sent skimming on a curved course aided by a drift control rudder, with the occupants casting their specially designed lures at right angles to the speeding boat in what became known as the Northampton style. The talk is now more of Wingless Wickham's, Grenadiers, Soldier Palmer's and the like. There has too sprung up in the footsteps of Arthur Cove, a new breed of nymph fisher such as Dave Barker and Robert Ince who have developed the style he invented into a method demanding an extensive knowledge of entomology, intense concentration and prodigious casting ability.

The northern shore still produces the most consistent fishing for the shore bound angler with Church Cove proving a magnet for both trout and anglers. The south west winds of summer bring an awkward right to left problem but long distance casting is usually unnecessary as the rain-

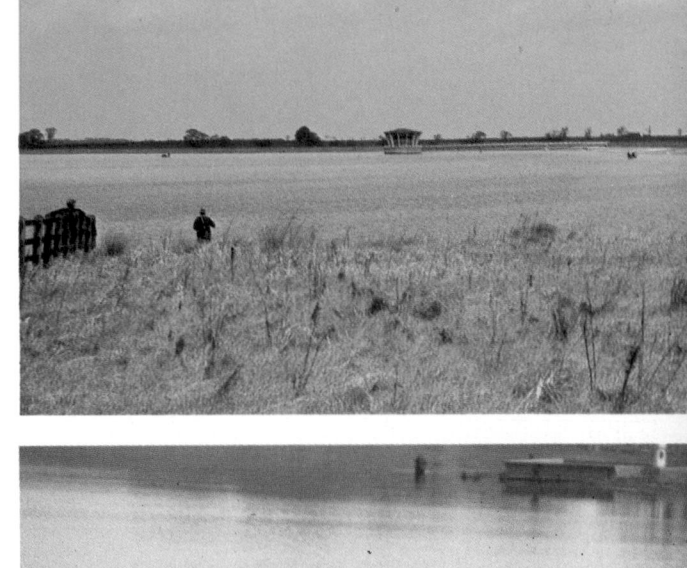

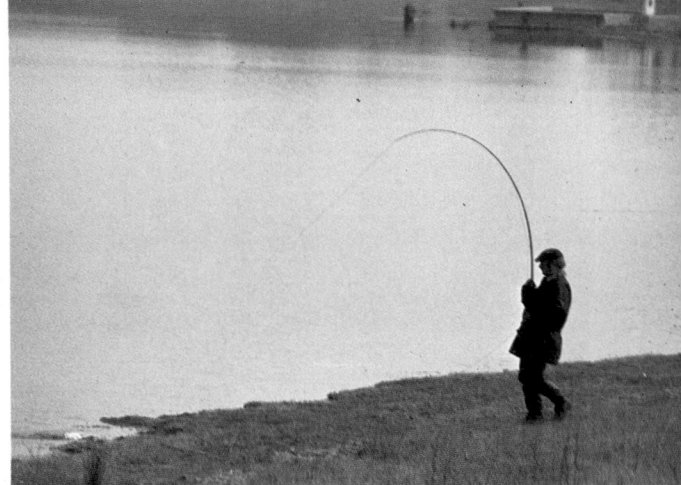

bows, which provide by far the highest proportion of the reservoir's stock, tend to hug the shallow northern shoreline. Savage's Creek is the place to be at the season's ending as both rainbows and the big brown trout which have left the safety of the deeps move into the narrow inlet to crash into the dense shoals of roach and perch fry. Grafham's bigger fish in the four to six pound range are quite common at this time mostly falling to floating imitations of the small perch and roach.

The Dam Wall, inhospitable place that it is, provides a constant bounty for the bank fisher. A high proportion of the reservoir's biggest fish are taken from within yards of the sloping concrete

wall, especially on the calm days following a storm which has sent high waves crashing onto the dam face. The best fish recorded is a brown trout, an ounce under thirteen pounds, which oddly enough accepted a tiny nymph offered in the dawn light by Barry Capener from Nuneaton. Big as that trout, was Grafham holds far larger: the bailiffs find trout of fifteen pounds and more each winter in the nets they lay to snare Grafham's unwanted pike.

Draycote

After major setbacks in the middle seventies, Draycote Water has now regained its rightful place amongst Britain's premier stillwaters.

Situated close to Birmingham, Coventry and other large conurbations Draycote can boast the most consistent attendance records of all stillwaters. Much of Draycote's early problems can be put down to the stocking policy which saw massive injections of small stockfish in autumn and in spring. Sadly the bulk of these failed to survive the hard winter months; this gave visiting fly fishers too small a head of trout to hold their attentions through the summer months. However, a timely switch to weekly stocking solved this problem and anglers can expect their intended quarry to be present in good numbers. Draycote has recovered too to a large extent from the devastation of its renowned brown trout stocks from a tragic tapeworm infestation which struck in 1973. Again it was a change of stocking policy, which now sees a far higher number of less vulnerable rainbows being introduced, which appears to have broken the chain of infestation.

The hatches of chironomids, or 'buzzers' as they are better known, are without equal anywhere. The timing of these have-to-be-seen-to-be-believed hatches, on this 600 acre fishery controlled by the Severn Trent Water Authority, can be calculated to within days of each new season. For devotees of nymph style fishing then the third week of April is the time to head for Draycote's shores. John Snelson, from Daventry, who probably accounts for more stillwater fly caught trout than anyone in the country has his own special

chironomid patterns which he uses to devastating effect.

John finds little use for the now traditional buzzer pupae where the dressing is carried around the hook bend. Instead he favours a tapered black wool tied fly, ribbed with coarse brown thread; he finishes his simple nymph with just two turns of a black hen hackle. A brown version which he finds highly effective near the season's end has its brown wool body ribbed with silver and a tiny claret hackle.

The considerable hatches of sedges which Draycote once boasted have dwindled in recent years. Incidentally, it was at Draycote that Northampton's Bob Church designed his famed Black Chenille lure after catching numbers of brown trout gorged on sedge larvae which had fashioned their mobile homes from inch long fragments of rotting black straw.

As the chironomid hatches thin out, the trout's attention is centred on the immense shoals of tiny sticklebacks. In recent years these concentrations have been joined by myriads of immature roach. The usual stickleback imitating patterns rarely seem to work their magic at Draycote. A small Silver Invicta fished near the surface and retrieved in long slow pulls brings far better results.

The second phase of the stickleback feeding spree occurs in mid August when the new adult fish shoal over the deep water. Now a specially designed lure is the winning medicine. This fly has a white, silver ribbed body and sports a bright yellow goat hair wing. Its inventor John Snelson fishes it in exactly the same way as he does the Silver Invicta. Of all the Midlands reservoirs Draycote has the most convenient ease of access, with a metalled road following the whole five mile perimeter.

Draycote is unusual too in that although a man made water storage reservoir, its bed is anything but a flat clay place but a series of underwater islands which rise to within six feet of the surface. These islands, bounded by depths of up to forty feet, provide Draycote's finest boat fishing. This was confirmed by competitors in the 1981 international event who caught more fish than had ever before been achieved in any international fly fishing event anywhere.

The daddy of them all. A corner of Rutland Water

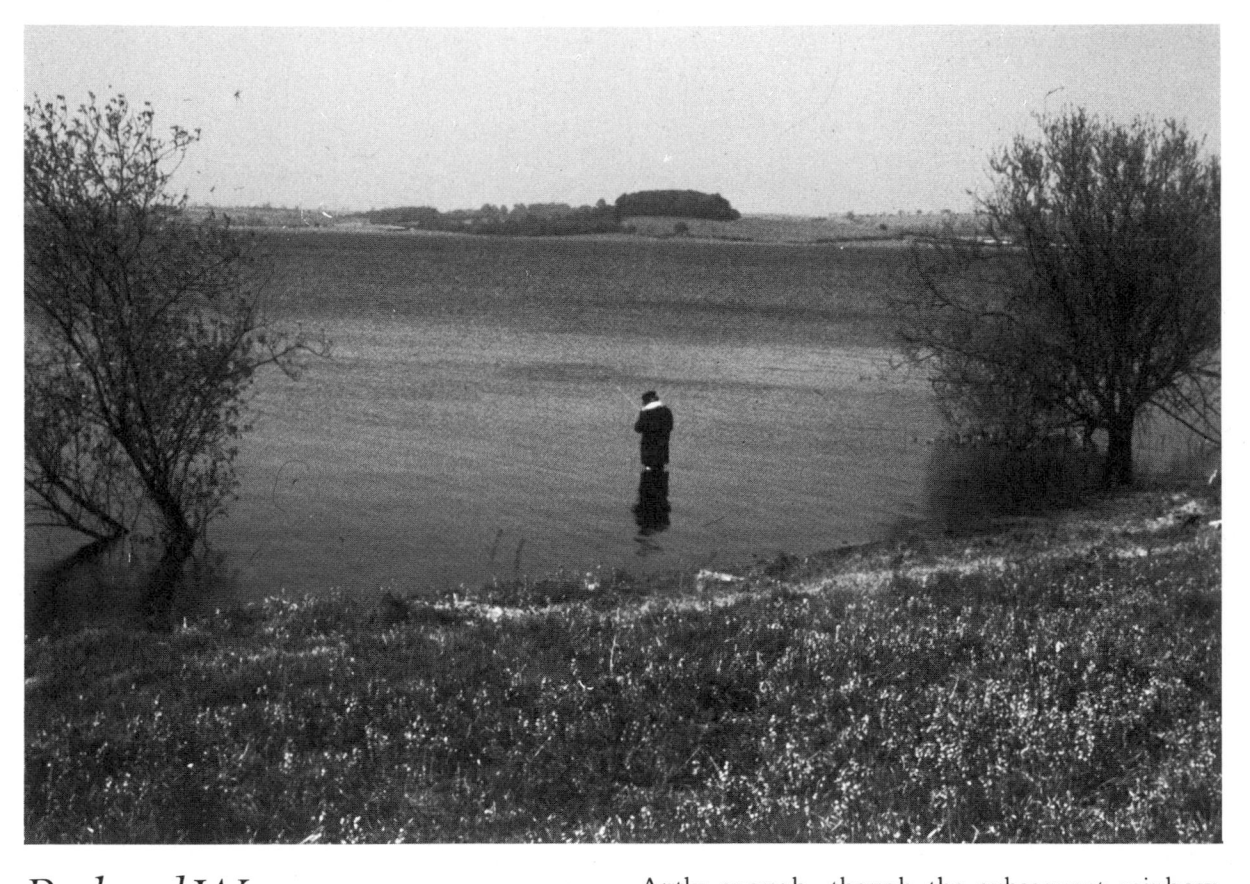

Rutland Water

The opening of Rutland Water, which spread like an ever growing giant inland sea across what was once England's smallest county was possibly the most exciting thing ever to happen to the sport of modern still water angling.

But the fishery promised by planners as an angler's dream very nearly turned out a dreaded nightmare. Attracted by the anticipated repeat of the Grafham opening a decade before, fly fishers came in thousands from all corners of the country in search of the lusty, fighting mad rainbows.

But these rainbows, bitterly, had died the previous winter, victims to eye fluke; the day, and Rutland Water's reputation, was saved by the brown trout which had thrived unaffected by the disease which had ravaged their cousins.

Despite that early setback Rutland Water's 3,100 acres have now fulfilled all the early promise.

Aptly enough, though the subsequent rainbow stockings have done well, it is the brown trout which have made the fishery's considerable reputation. Its twin arms, shared amicably enough by sailors and other water sportsmen, are expansive enough to accommodate the multiplicity of fishing styles and methods employed to catch the browns, rainbows and the small head of American brook trout which sadly have failed to thrive in the rich environment. Rutland Water has followed almost exactly the pattern set by other large stillwaters. In the first season the rapidly growing trout gorged on the millions of earthworms drowned in the rising waters. The earthworms gone, the items highest on the menu were the carpet of water snails which had bred by the million on the rotting vegetation. Then it was the seething hatches of chironomids which towered in teeming pillars above the bankside hedges which drew the fishes' attention, as they still do. But it was the long awaited explosion of daphnia

137

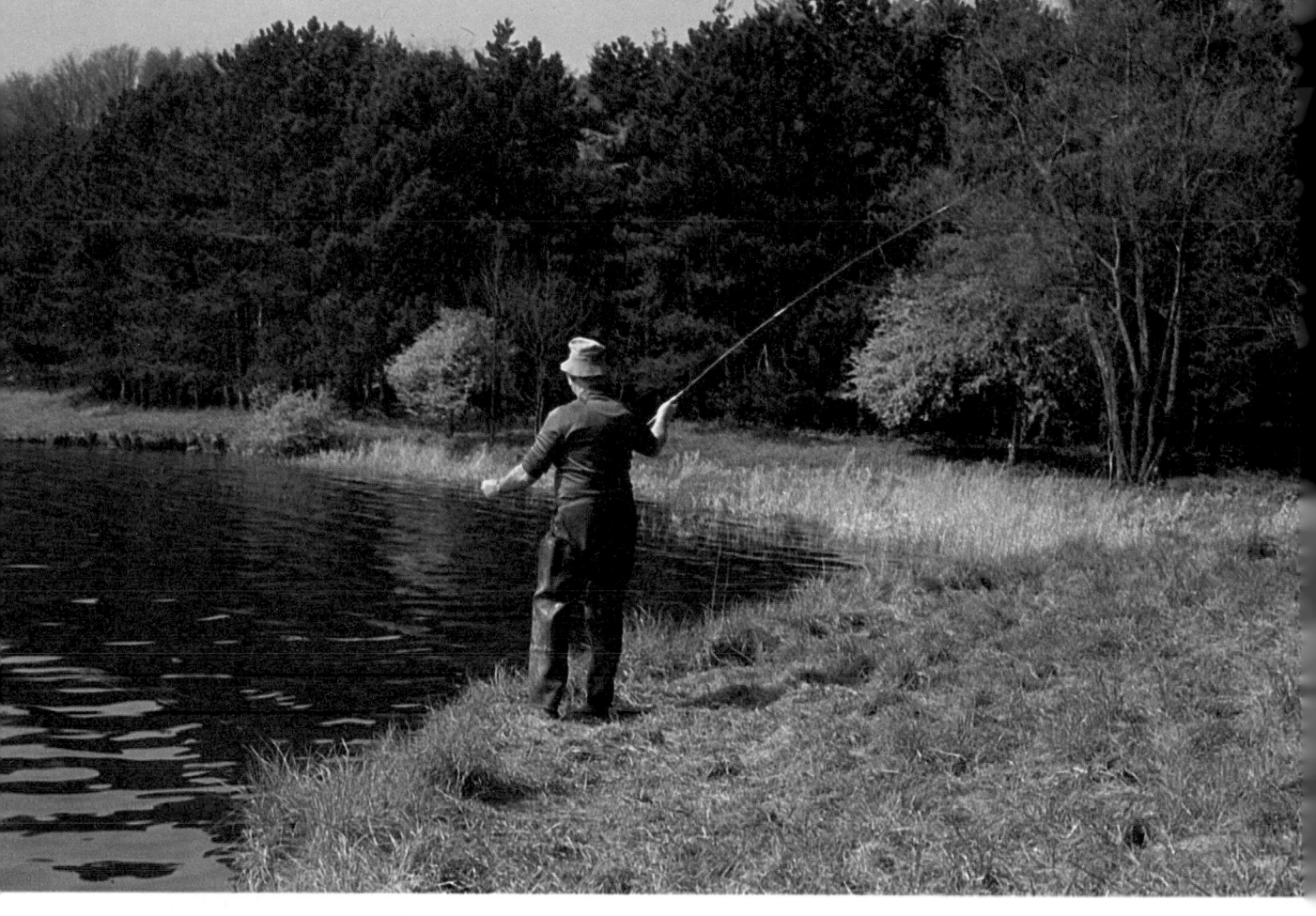

which accounted for the growth rate which turned a twelve ounce stock rainbow into a silver bar two pounder in a season.

Then, as at Grafham a decade earlier, the progeny of the teeming perch shoals contracted a killer disease which saw both seagulls and trout fighting for such easy food. Large lures designed to imitate these stricken fish were floated and twitched near weedbeds. Such tactics brought the record forty eight pound, eight fish catch of brown trout and a handful of double figure browns that had grown on from the original fingerling stocking five years previously. It should be recorded that the numbers of such fish taken on fly anywhere in Britain are very small indeed:

Rutland's facilities are arguably without equal. Its sturdy diesel powered boats are perfectly adequate to endure the long long journeys and ill handling.

While 'always' and 'never' are unwise words for anglers, a fly fisher's calendar at Rutland Water could follow this sequence. Chironomid patterns and Pheasant Tail nymphs fished in the sheltered bays bring a fair share of early season fish as will small black or white biased lures. The warmer water sees the sedges in profusion and a team of imitations of both pupae and adult insects brings rewards. It should not be forgotten though that, for some reasons best known to themselves, Rutland's trout will often prefer buzzer pupae in a sedge rise, nor should it be overlooked that the seemingly lost art of fishing a well hackled fly with some hurry in the gloaming is worthwhile too.

The cooling waters urge the bigger trout into looking for more nourishing food as if in preparation for the lean months ahead and that suggests the use of the small fish imitations around the dying weedbeds.

Avington

Avington, nestling in a lush Hampshire water meadow holds pride of place among the countless small fisheries which have sprung up in profusion to satisfy those anglers whose aim is a trout fit for a glass case.

By English standards Avington's three spirit clear lakes are the ultimate in put-and-take style fishing. Trout caught one day are replaced with

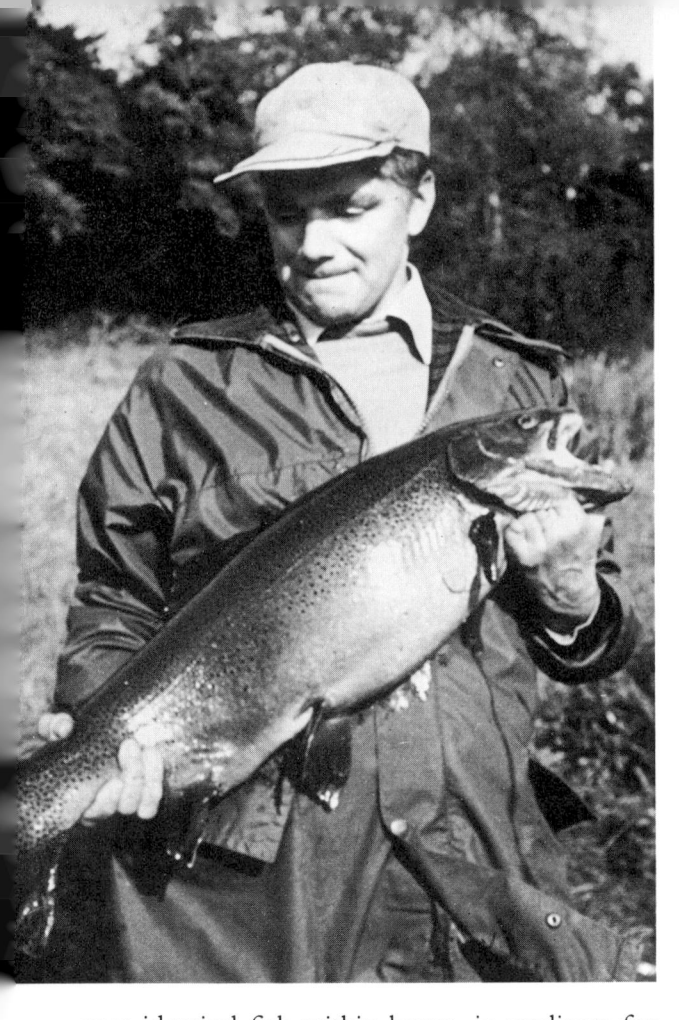

Far left: The pleasures of Blagdon
This page: A fourteen and a half pound Avington rainbow

nymph of different size and colour and so the hunt, which can be likened to a sophisticated game of Space Invaders, continues.

The high standard of fishery management which ensures that so many giant fish are available daily has brought its critics. True the stock are guileless when first introduced but the attentions of a score of fishers soon sees a return of their natural instincts. Those that have escaped capture for a week or more have seen and rejected many hundreds of nymphs. Such a fish is a prize indeed. Once again it fell to Dick Walker's ingenious mind to come up with the answer for the capture of large fish in deceptively deep waters. His weighted Mayfly Nymph, an incredible mirror of the natural beast, has accounted for thousands of large fish at Avington and elsewhere.

But while such big patterns dressed on size eight long shanked hooks still work their magic, Avington's rainbows have in recent years shown a preference for much smaller patterns and dry flies too are taking more trout than ever before.

So even should the idea of such fishing not be your cup of tea, try it once, for Avington is a very special place to be and, by the way, take a large landing net.

Blagdon

With his natural eye for beauty the American Indian would undoubtedly have called Blagdon, a jewel like lake set deep in the green Mendip Hills, 'Mother of all the Waters'.

Blagdon, which opened when the new century was just a year old was the Rutland Water of its day and more. The Mecca for the infant breed of stillwater fly fishers for half a century, it is still reckoned by many not to have lost anything of the quiet charm of those early halcyon days, when anglers were few and the trout large and plentiful. Those early trout, immense by even today's exaggerated standards fell at first to traditional salmon flies and gut casts with strength sufficient to bring a horse to its knees. Silver Wilkinson's, the Doctor's and others, all dressed on the great irons of the day were regarded as essential for the immigrant rainbow which was to have such a profound effect in later years, but was then a little known fish.

near identical fish within hours, in readiness for those anglers yet to come. And come they do, for Avington has, with owner Sam Holland, earned the reputation for trout of leviathan size which a mere decade ago would have existed only in an angler's elastic imagination.

It is taken for granted that when the rainbow record is broken, Avington will provide both the fish and the scene. The capture of such massive fish – Avington provided a hundred rainbows of double figures and more and a handful of brown trout of similar proportions in a single season – has led to the evolution of a special style.

While normal blind casting will bring average sized fish, the biggest demand the approach of a determined sniper. Once spotted, the cruising fish must not be disturbed or it will flee to the cover of the many algae umbrellas. The speed of the fish judged, its angle of movement decided and the depth of the water gauged, the heavily weighted nymph is pitched to a spot where its destination will coincide with that of the trout's arrival. If the offering is acceptable it will be taken with grace. If not it will be totally ignored. The disdainful trout is then allowed to potter on and the angler left to wait until its return this time to offer a

The moment of truth on Chew

Two men, alike only in their love for Blagdon were each in their different way responsible for much of what followed on the specialised still-water fly fishing scene.

One, Captain J J Dunn turned away from the salmon flies of his contemporaries to invent the now world famed Missionary lure. Originally designed to tempt Blagdon rainbows feeding on small fry, it proved irresistible to the truly wild rainbows of New Zealand's Tongariro River where the new lure accounted for a bag of seven fish averaging twelve pounds in a single morning's fishing. His Missionary underwent a cosmetic change years later at the expert hands of Northampton's Dick Shrive. Dick turned the original Missionary's wing on its side; that way it fluttered down to imitate well the struggling of an injured fry. Another of the Captain's designs was the oddly named Reckless William. That too worked well at Blagdon as did its partner, Reckless William's Mate. While the Missionary is a

household name, both these latter patterns have been forgotten. While few of today's army of stillwater fly fishers know of Captain Dunn few do not have admiring regard for the legendary Dr Bell.

A quiet man, he saw further than the methods and flies of his day. An observant entomologist, his fly dressing mirrored well the natural insects he had observed at Blagdon. His studies brought the first truly imitative chironomid or buzzer pattern. His Amber Sedge too is still a first choice fly.

A complex water, its bed is a pattern of ridges and hollows with the deepest part lying near the dam on Blagdon's western end. This, together with Home Bay and the deep water stretch running along the northern shore into Butcombe Bay, are first choice early season places to fish. Rainbow Point, Holt Bay, Peg's Point, Orchard Bay, Rugmoor Point and of course Bell's Bush are locations whose names are part of the sport's

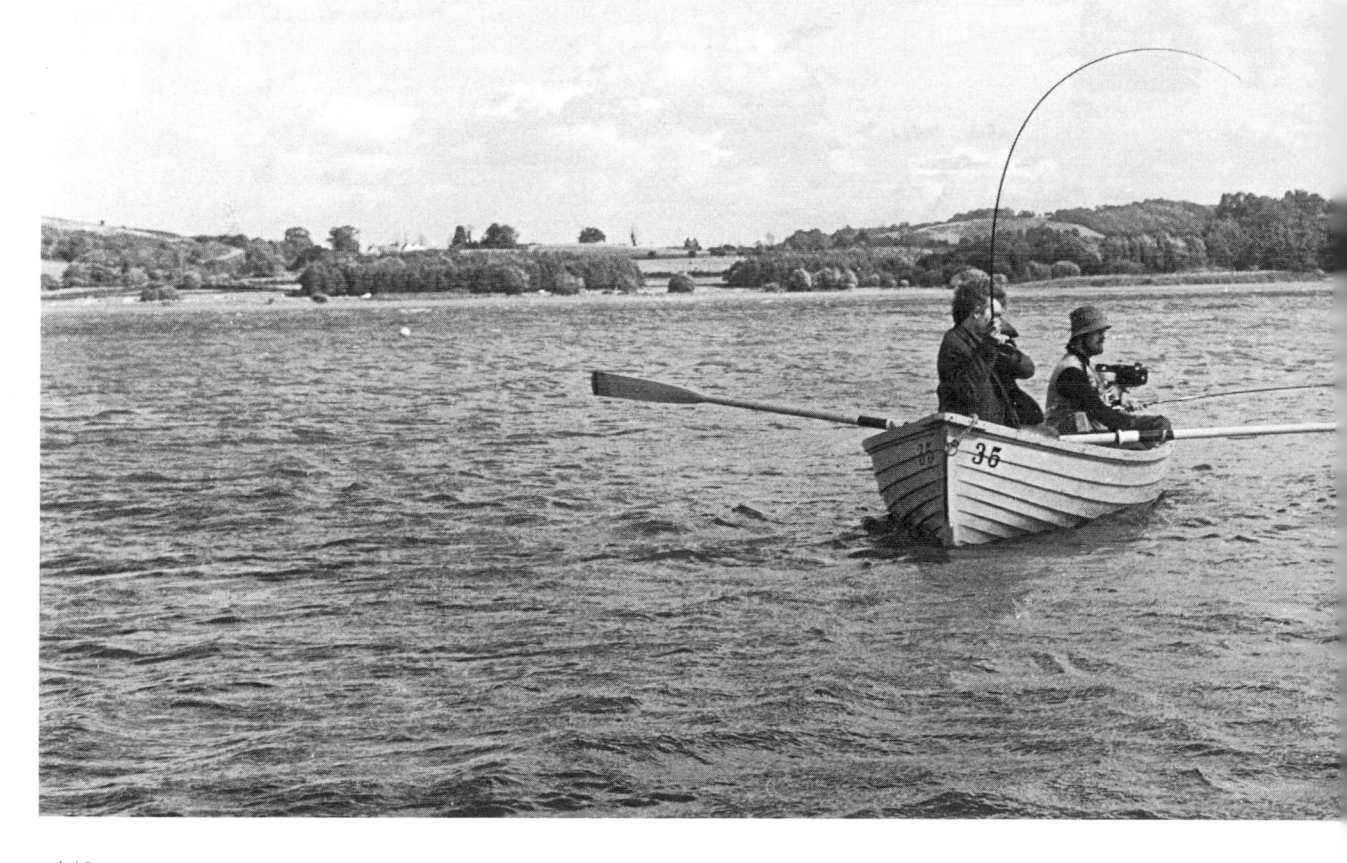

short history. Patterns for Blagdon would include Bell's Buzzer and Amber Nymph, the striking emerald green Blagdon Green Midge and a corixa imitation, especially if the fishing choice is Home Bay and the month late August or September. A small selection of fry imitating lures (and what better than the Missionary?), a black lure to imitate Blagdon's many leeches and a dry fly or two are more than sufficient choice with which to enjoy a day on beautiful Blagdon.

Chew Valley

Apart from being nearly treble the size, Chew Valley offers a much wider scope to the fly fisher than is afforded by its little sister Blagdon.

The reason lying behind this fact are the teeming shoals of roach which it has in abundance, whereas Blagdon has yet to cope with this

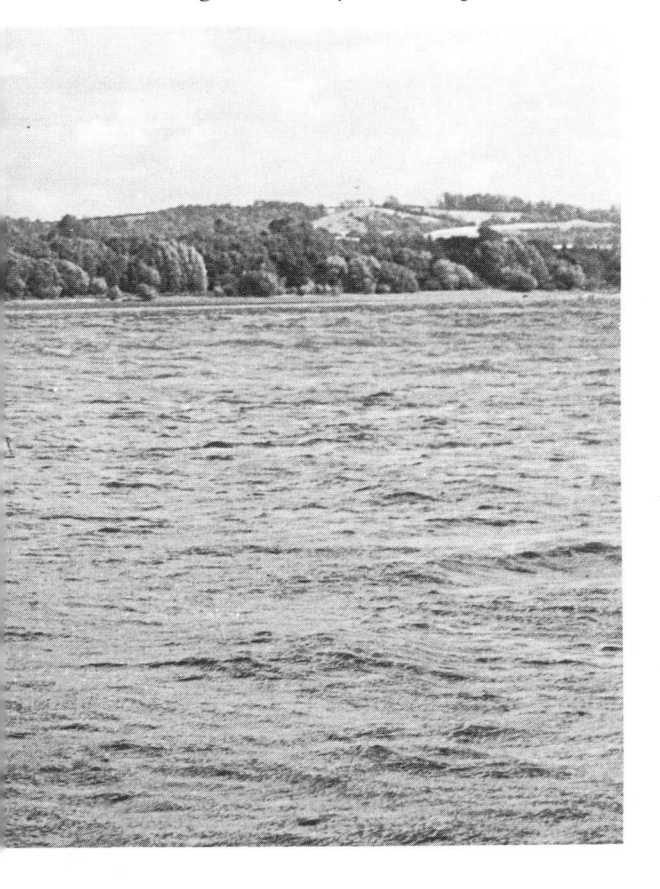

problem, if indeed a problem it is. When Chew Valley opened its 1200 acres in 1956 it was heralded as Europe's finest stillwater fishery. The prophets were not too wide of the mark either, with the first two seasons nothing less than unforgettable. Two pound rainbows were average, four pounders commonplace and fish even more, little to write home about.

This high standard could not be expected to continue but neither was there a sudden slump. Rather a gradual settling occurred down to a position where Chew can justifiably be ranked among the top four fisheries in Britain. Unlike the major reservoirs which have opened since, Chew holds onto its anglers. For them fly fishing means only Chew Valley with just the odd trip to nearby Blagdon thrown in by way of a change.

The Bristol Waterworks Company which controls both Chew Valley and Blagdon can take all the praise for this happy state. Ragged tailed stockfish of dubious parentage are unknown at both waters.

The trout produced by the company are by far the weightiest and certainly the most handsome introduced into any stillwater fishery. Even Grafham stalwarts have been heard grudgingly to admit that Chew Valley rainbows are the equal of theirs. High praise indeed.

Chew's coarse fish, although controlled by the fishery management are possibly the greatest factor contributing to the rapid growth rate. Whereas at some other water the trout seem hesitant to accept the newly hatched fry as a readily available food source, Chew Valley's browns and rainbows can be seen slashing into the terrified shoals within weeks of the new season's opening. For the first few weeks the usual lures take their expected toll but then even the more gullible rainbows become wary of the gaudy lures retrieved at breakneck speeds. A far more effective representation of the tiniest fry is a Pheasant Tail nymph dressed on a standard length size ten hook which mirrors well the profile of the newly hatched fry.

The Worm Fly, its origin lost in time is probably used more at Chew and Blagdon than anywhere else. Chew fly fishers dress theirs on size ten or size twelve long shanked hooks instead of the normally accepted tandem hook style. Trickled slowly across the bottom on a long sunken leader in early season, or greased and retrieved

141

Below: A Chew trout comes to the net   Right: From Ardleigh's productive banks. . .

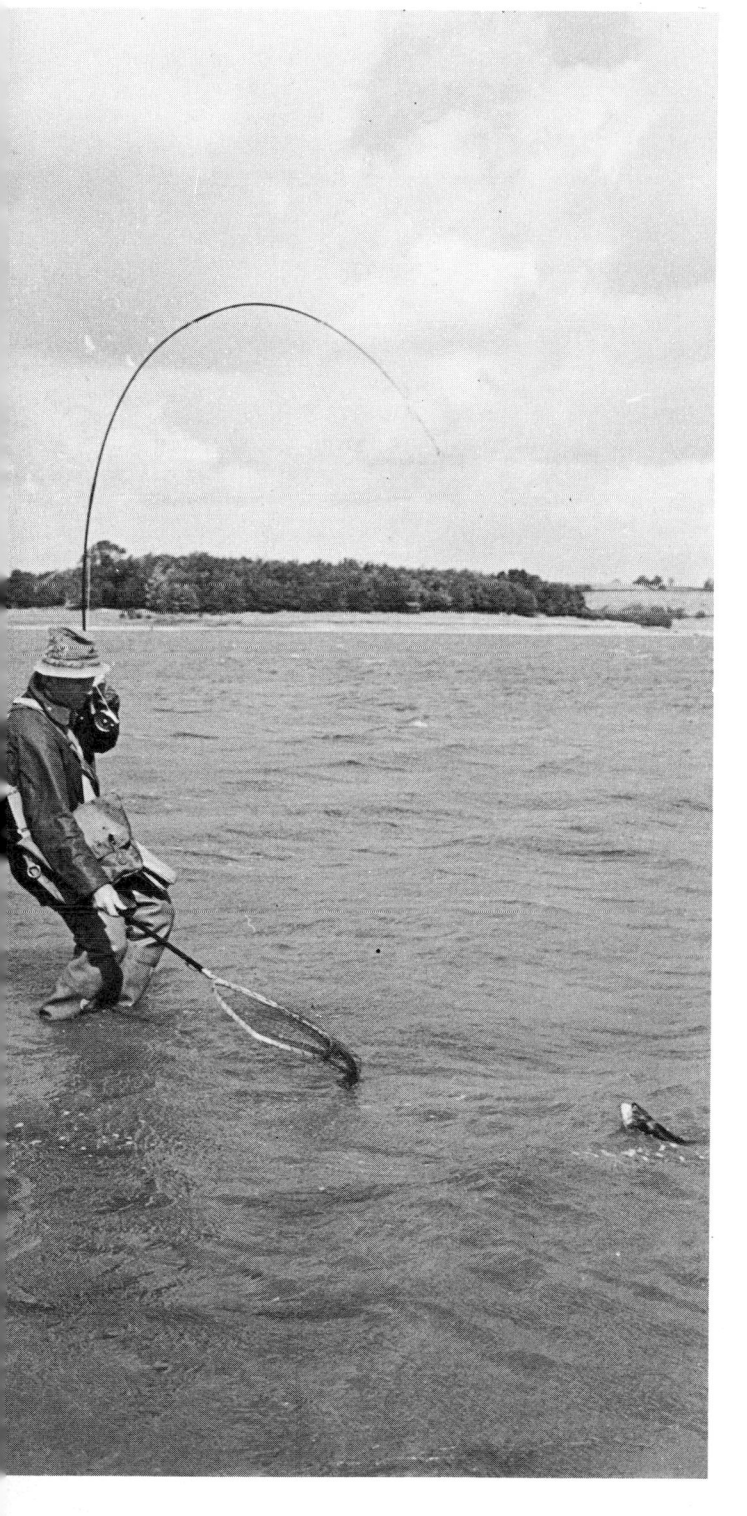

with a wake in high summer, it is a pattern not to be without on Chew Valley.

Like Blagdon, the bed of Chew Valley is anything but level, more a series of depressions left by rotted away hedgerows, old ditches and roadways. Old hands, who watched the reservoir flood across the rolling pastures know the locations of these fish holding areas well and head for them when a favourable wind allows their flies to be offered in these now hidden places. In the opening weeks, a consistently productive area runs from Nunnery Point, across the mouth of Villice Bay and along the Woodford Bank and down to the down, probably because here lies the deepest water available to the angler restricted to the bank. The strengthening fly hatches see an armada of boats heading for the Roman Shallows, with Wick Green Point and drifts aiming for Stratford Bay and Moreton Point providing a wealth of rising fish depending on the prevailing wind direction. The very shallow area bordering Herriots Bridge, choked in high summer with dense weed beds and reedmace beds, is Chew's answer to the dry fly enthusiast, particularly in late summer when the still evening air is clouded with swarming sedges.

Recommended patterns for Chew Valley must include the Bell's Buzzer which for many retains its place as a top dropper fly the season through, the Amber Nymph, a lightly dressed Green Nymph, the Welsh originated Diawl Bach, Pheasant Tail nymph, and the flashing orange Dunkeld.

Mention must be made of the orange Grenadier without which no Chew Valley angler would dream of going afloat in mid summer. Lures to imitate the roach fry, which are acceptable up to three inches long, include the Baby Doll, Badger Matuka, Whisky Fly and a large black lure sporting darting jungle cock eyes.

Ardleigh

Blessed as it is with a host of small sheltered bays and prominent headlands, Ardleigh Reservoir certainly provides far better fishing for the shore bound angler than its more expansive rivals.

Although totalling about 160 acres, the Essex fishery, which is not much more than an hour's drive from London, has five miles of fishable bank

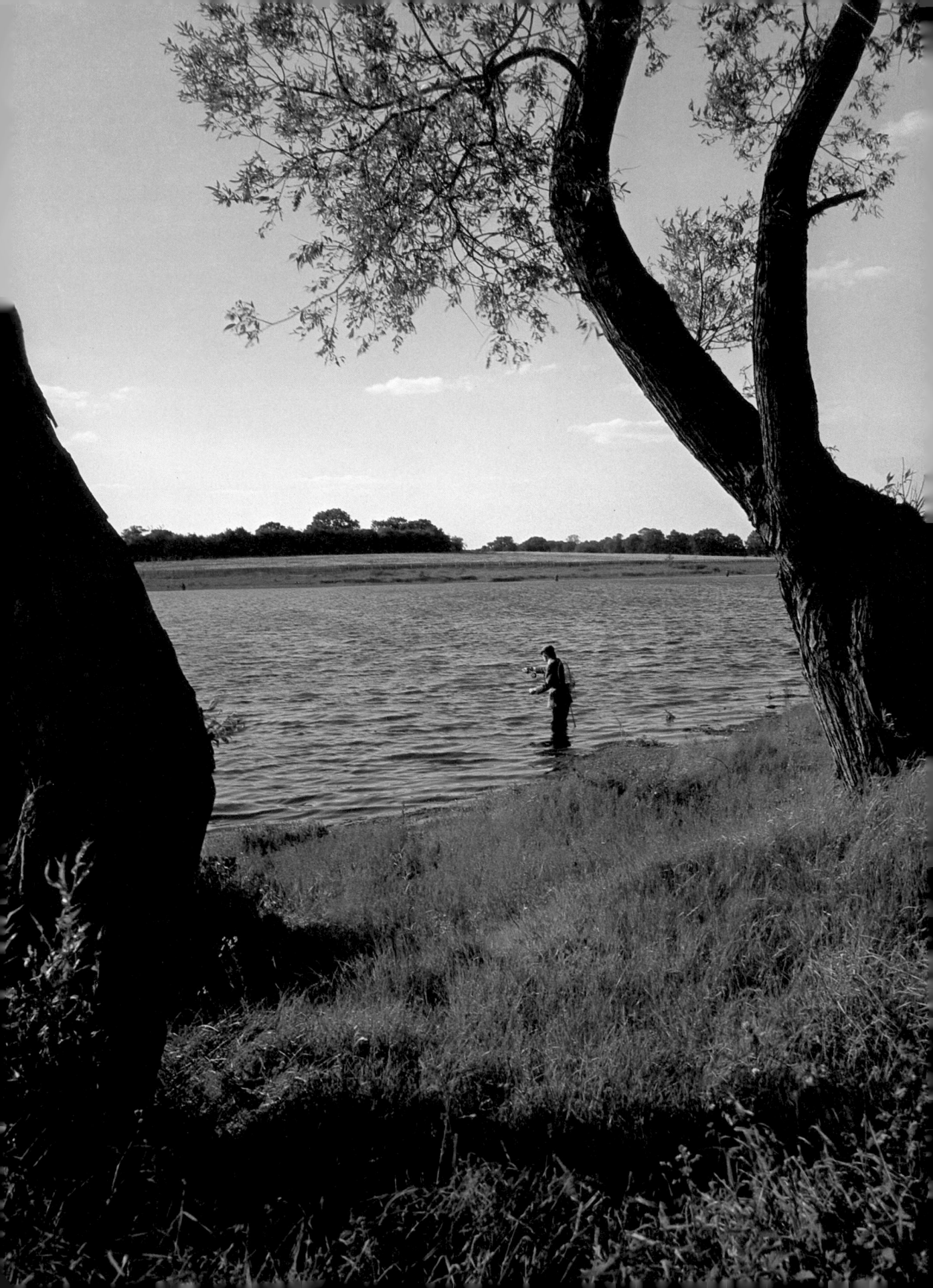

Evening lights on Ardleigh

space. Five miles of excellent fishing.

By modern standards Ardleigh's trout are not huge, with the average running at a little over the pound mark. That said, the fishery provides plenty of rainbows in the four pound range and just now and again a brown trout or two even weightier.

The reservoir is unusual in that it has not followed, much to many local anglers' delight, the now universally accepted path of stocking with vast numbers of rainbow trout, with just a sprinkling of brown. Fishery Manager, Richard Connell, being a Scot, has a soft spot for the native trout and his firm ideas of stocking are a complete reversal from the normal, with the splendid brown trout he rears himself being by far the most dominant species.

Indeed such are Richard Connell's fish farming skills that not only does he provide all his own stock fish but has sufficient left over to sell to less enterprising fisheries. He broke new ground late in the 1981 season by allowing any method of fishing on his reservoir for the last month. Although arousing a little early animosity, the experiment turned what had been a poor financial year into a profitable one.

Ardleigh is known to fish particularly well at the season's beginning with bank and anglers afloat taking about equal shares of the sport.

The sedge hatches which dominate sport to a large degree during the warm months can occur very late on in the day. Indeed on such evenings (which may have followed a difficult day) Richard will turn a blind eye to his own fishery rules and allow his anglers to enjoy the late rise and to fish on into the darkness. At such times it is perfectly possible to take a good bag of fish in a frenzied half hour session. It is generally accepted that Ardleigh is a small fly water. Recommended flies include Mallard and Claret, Wickham's Fancy, Greenwell nymph and the various chironomid and sedge pupae imitations.

Richard Connell's own invention, the Ardleigh Nymph, is a reliable standby. A variation on the ever popular Pheasant Tail nymph theme, Richard's fly has a peacock-herl thorax and a tiny Greenwell hackle. The dry fly works its slow magic at Ardleigh too as do the various lures, the better of these being the Black Chenille, the various Muddlers and the white Baby Doll.

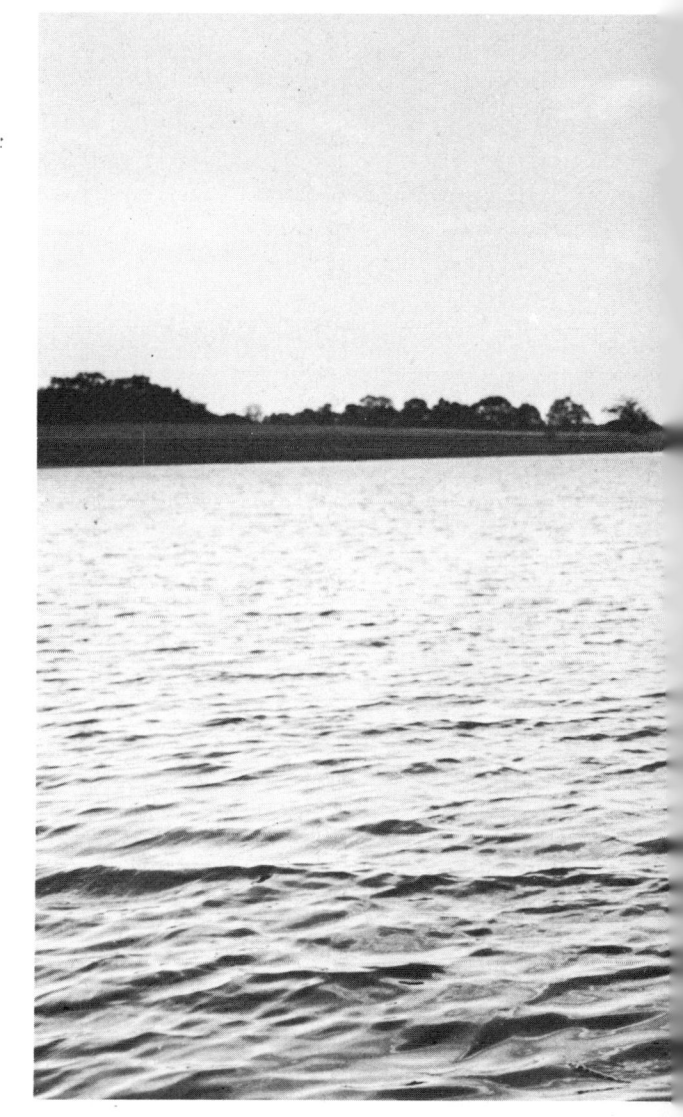

Kielder

Bigger by a shade than Windermere, Kielder's 2684 acres lie hidden in Europe's largest man made forest not a long cast from the Scottish border.

It would be inapposite to think of grouping Kielder with the English reservoirs. Better to class it more as a sort of Scottish loch for it was carved from the acid forest peat and so, as yet, boasts none of the teeming insect life which thrives in its

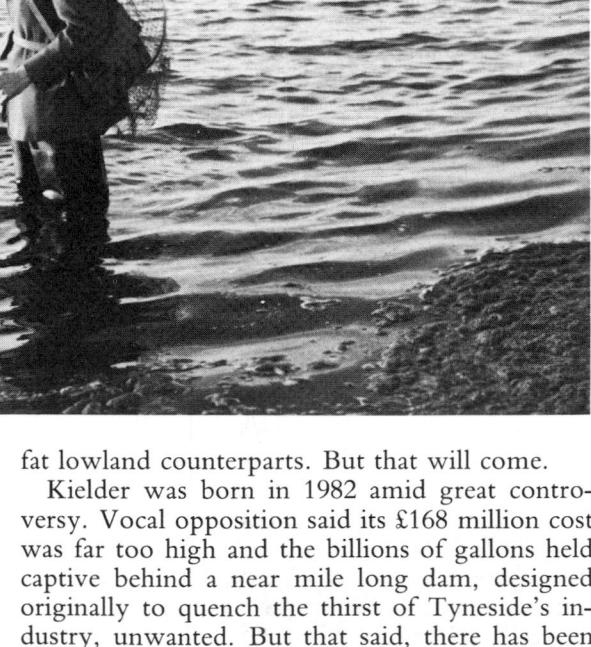

heavy stocking, anglers will experience that rare satisfying feeling that they will be seeking not stumpy tailed rainbows but truly wild brown trout, born in the reservoir's countless feeder burns.

With the natural insect life confined as yet to sparse hatches of small chironomids, much of the trout's menu is provided by terrestial flies blown onto the water from the surrounding forests making the fish, which average something under a pound, enthusiastic surface feeders.

This eagerness to rise, coupled with the provision by the Northumbrian Water Authority of twenty five clinker built, dory style boats capable of a safe North Sea crossing, makes Kielder a heaven sent fishery for the fly fisherman who considers his quarry worth something better than the pulling of a two inch gaudy flight and a lead cored line.

To enjoy Kielder's brown trout, little more in the way of tackle than a long limber rod, light floating line and a book filled with traditional patterns is required. The most rewarding flies at Kielder are the Mallard and Claret, Peter Ross, Black and Peacock Spider, Black Gnat and William's Favourite. A heavily hackled Zulu sporting the addition of a fluorescent orange tail has proved a deadly bob fly fished in a steepish wave. But while eager, Kielder's brown trout are not foolish. The golden rules which apply to all wild trout apply here, in that the flies should be small, certainly nothing larger than a size ten fished quickly, and with hooks and strike kept sharp.

In their willingness to please all the region's anglers the authority allows worm fishing along much of Kielder's twenty seven mile shoreline. While not denying that this decision has certainly attracted thousands of anglers, it has provided a thorn in the flesh of the reservoir's fly fishers. They claim that the spawning fish are being lost unfairly to the legions of wormers who crowd the feeder stream mouths.

The authority is aware of this problem and has increased its bailiffing force to ensure that the bait fishers do not exceed their eight fish quota.

If Kielder's wormers can be considered a nuisance then its famed midges are a menace. Lapland's biters are as nothing compared to the Kielder variety which can, if not guarded against, drive an angler screaming from the water.

fat lowland counterparts. But that will come.

Kielder was born in 1982 amid great controversy. Vocal opposition said its £168 million cost was far too high and the billions of gallons held captive behind a near mile long dam, designed originally to quench the thirst of Tyneside's industry, unwanted. But that said, there has been little acrimony amongst its anglers, 8000 of them accounting for 25,000 of the original half million stockfish in its first season.

Kielder is different too from the souther reservoirs in that in the years following the initial

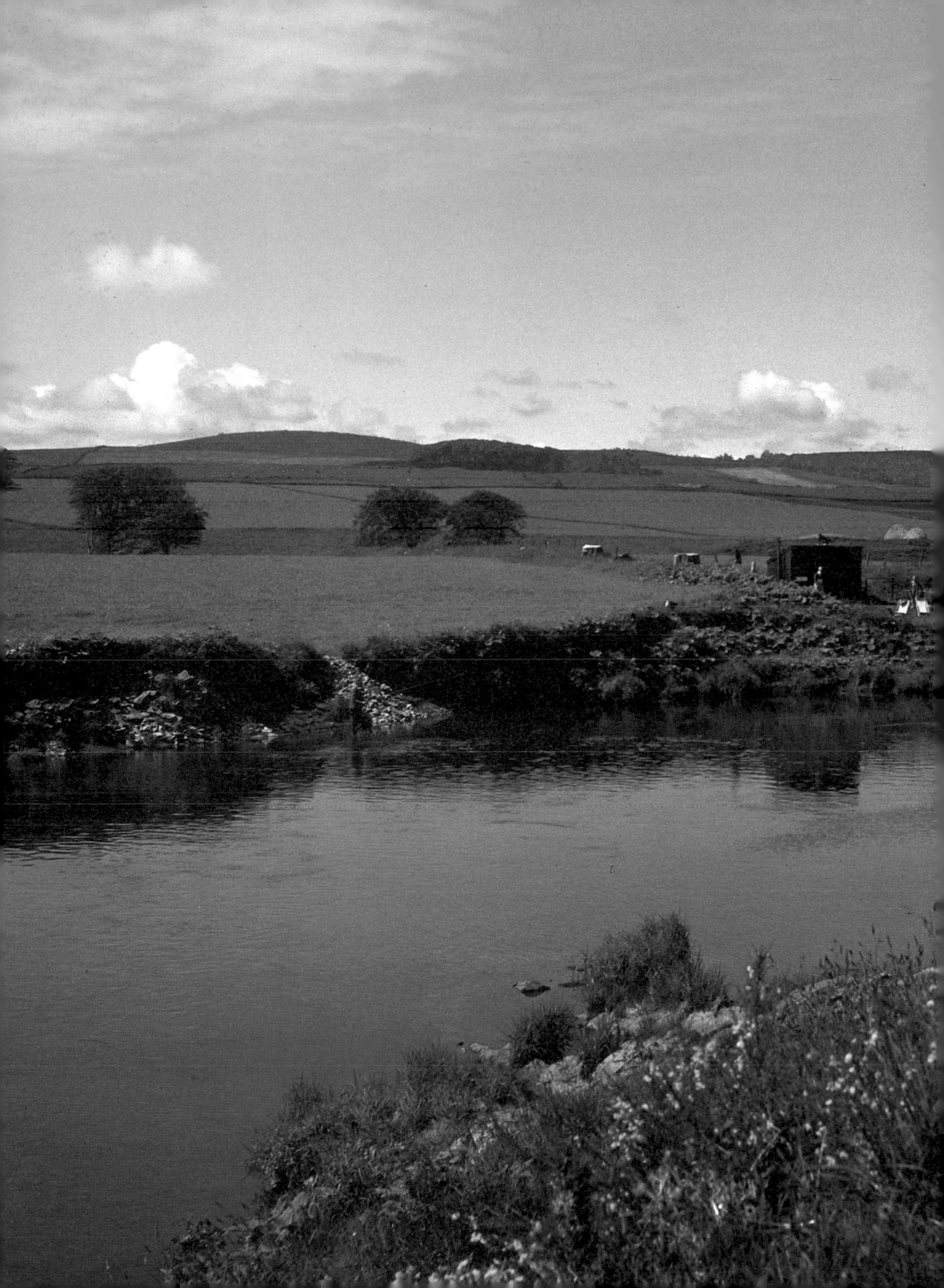

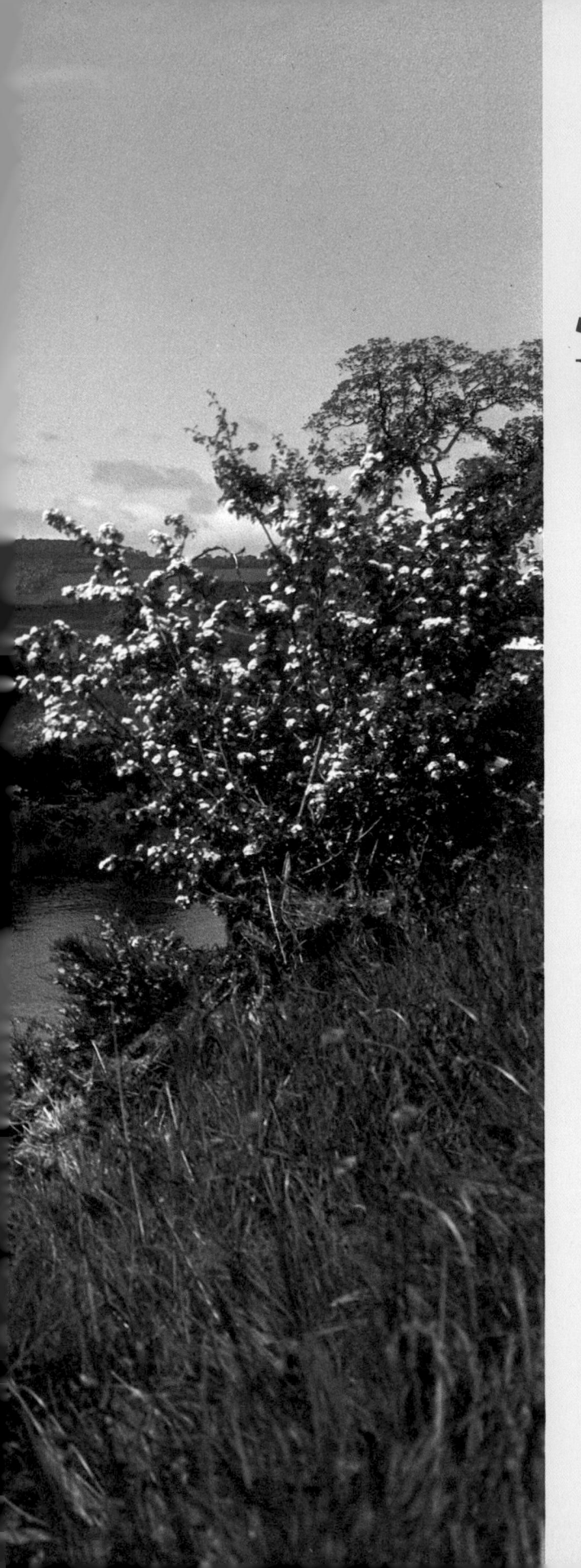

SCOTTISH WATERS

SCOTTISH RIVERS

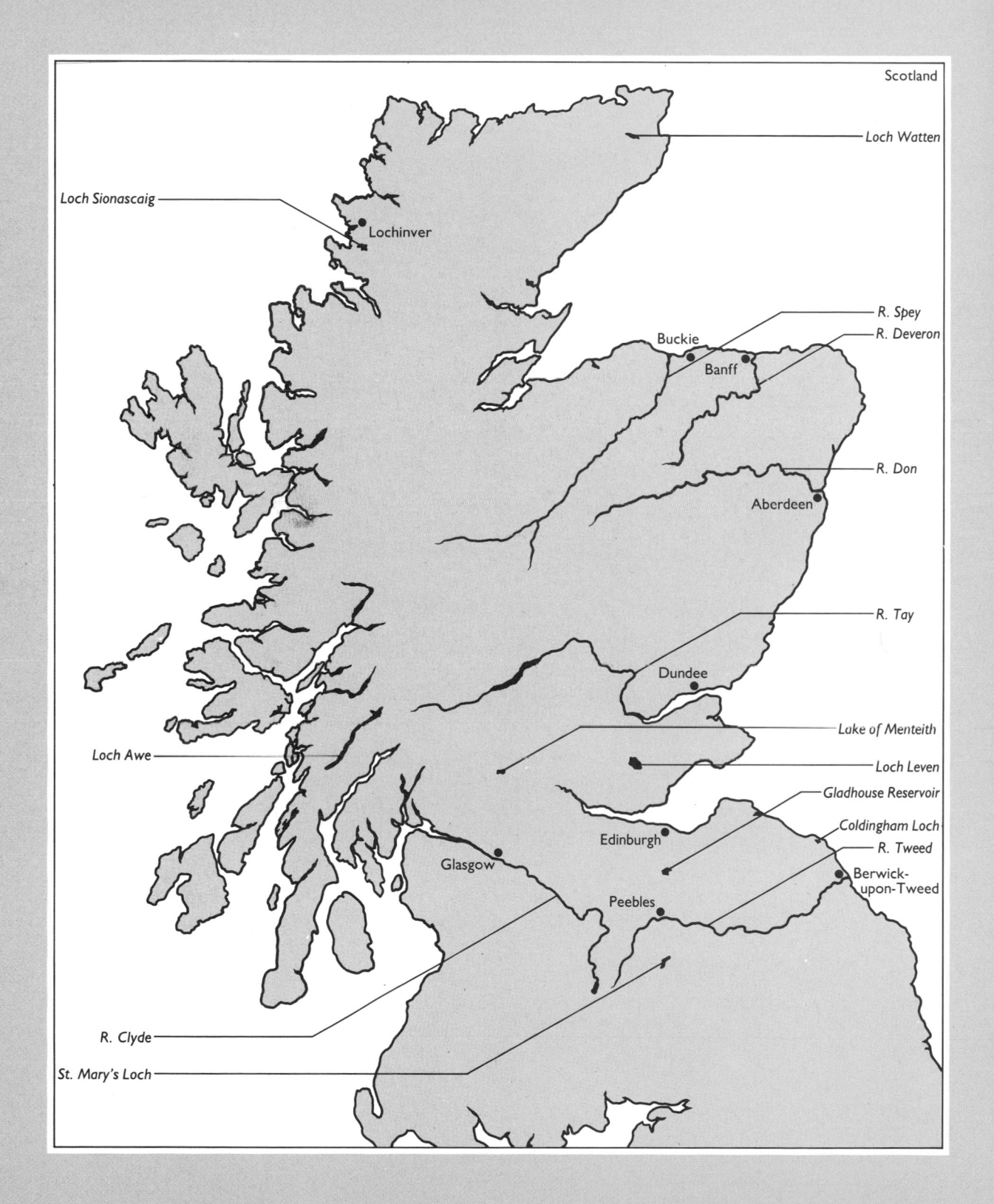

Scotland

Loch Watten

Loch Sionascaig

Lochinver

R. Spey

Buckie

R. Deveron

Banff

R. Don

Aberdeen

R. Tay

Dundee

Lake of Menteith

Loch Awe

Loch Leven

Gladhouse Reservoir

Coldingham Loch

Edinburgh

R. Tweed

Glasgow

Berwick-
upon-Tweed

Peebles

R. Clyde

St. Mary's Loch

Previous page: By Deveron's bonnie banks

The silver Tweed by Roxburgh Castle

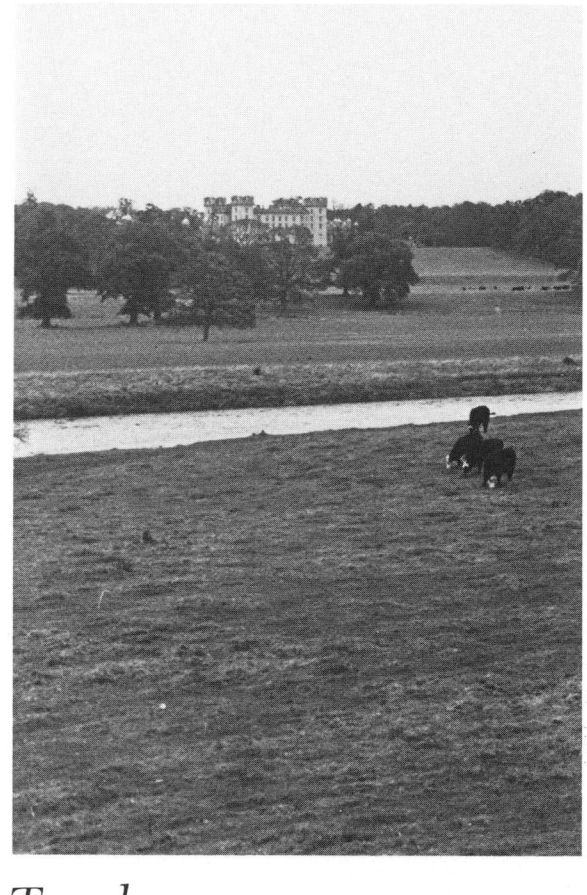

Tweed

Never surely can Railways and Rivers run more lovingly together than the North British and its Branches and the Tweed and its Branches
'BORDER ANGLER' 1858

These words from the famous *'Guide Book to the Tweed and its Tributaries and the Other Streams – Commanded by the North British Railway'* published in 1858, epitomise the special position of the River Tweed as the cradle of popular trout angling in Scotland. The earliest recorded angling club was formed at Ellemford on the Whiteadder in 1828. Angling stalwarts like Stoddart and his friends made the journey down from Edinburgh by coach and foot during the 1830s. However it was the coming of the railways in the 1850s that brought the Tweed within easy distance of the lawyers,

clerks and artisans of Edinburgh. The railways and their small stations have gone, but a good road network has replaced them and the Tweed is still very convenient to the urban parts of Scotland. The tradition of access remains but the Tweed was the first river system to seek controls through a protection order under the Freshwater and Salmon Fisheries (Scotland) Act of 1976. This was granted in 1980 for a trial period of three years and it is now a criminal offence to fish for brown trout without permission within the catchment area of the Tweed and its neighbour, the River Eye.

The Tweed rises high in the rolling sheepwalks of the Southern Uplands, at Tweed's Well, and the infant river gathers the runoff from the highest massif in south Scotland, Broad Law (2754 ft). It is a sizeable stream by the time it ripples down the gravel beds of Stanhope and swings east through the woods and parklands of Drumelzier and Dawyck. Down through Peebles, Innerleithen and Walkerburn the Tweed traverses one of its most picturesque stretches in its deep valley flanked by the forestry plantations of Glentress, Cardrona and Elibank before emerging into the basin of Melrose. Here it collects its tribute from the rivers Ettrick and Yarrow, draining the Ettrick Forest from the south, and the Gala and Leader waters running off the Moorfoot and Lammermuir Hills to the north. The growing river curves around the Eildon Hills, squeezes itself through the canyon of the Gateheugh at Bemersyde before spreading into the rich farmlands of the Merse at St Boswells. From here it is a stately river, winding its ample proportions through the fields of history past burghs, abbeys, castles and stately homes redolent of the country's past, in deeds and in literature. In this lower part of the river lie the world famous salmon casts of Rutherford, Makerstoun, Floors, Hendersyde and Birgham. Before the river reaches the sea at Berwick-upon-Tweed, it gathers the Teviot at Kelso, the Till from the south and the Whiteadder from the north.

The Tweed is a classic example of a Scottish river habitat and has been designated a site of special scientific interest. It illustrates the regular transition from a small upland stream, through moderately flowing gravelly sections to a large meandering lowland river. It is a rich river, described as 'eutrophic', and drawing its minerals

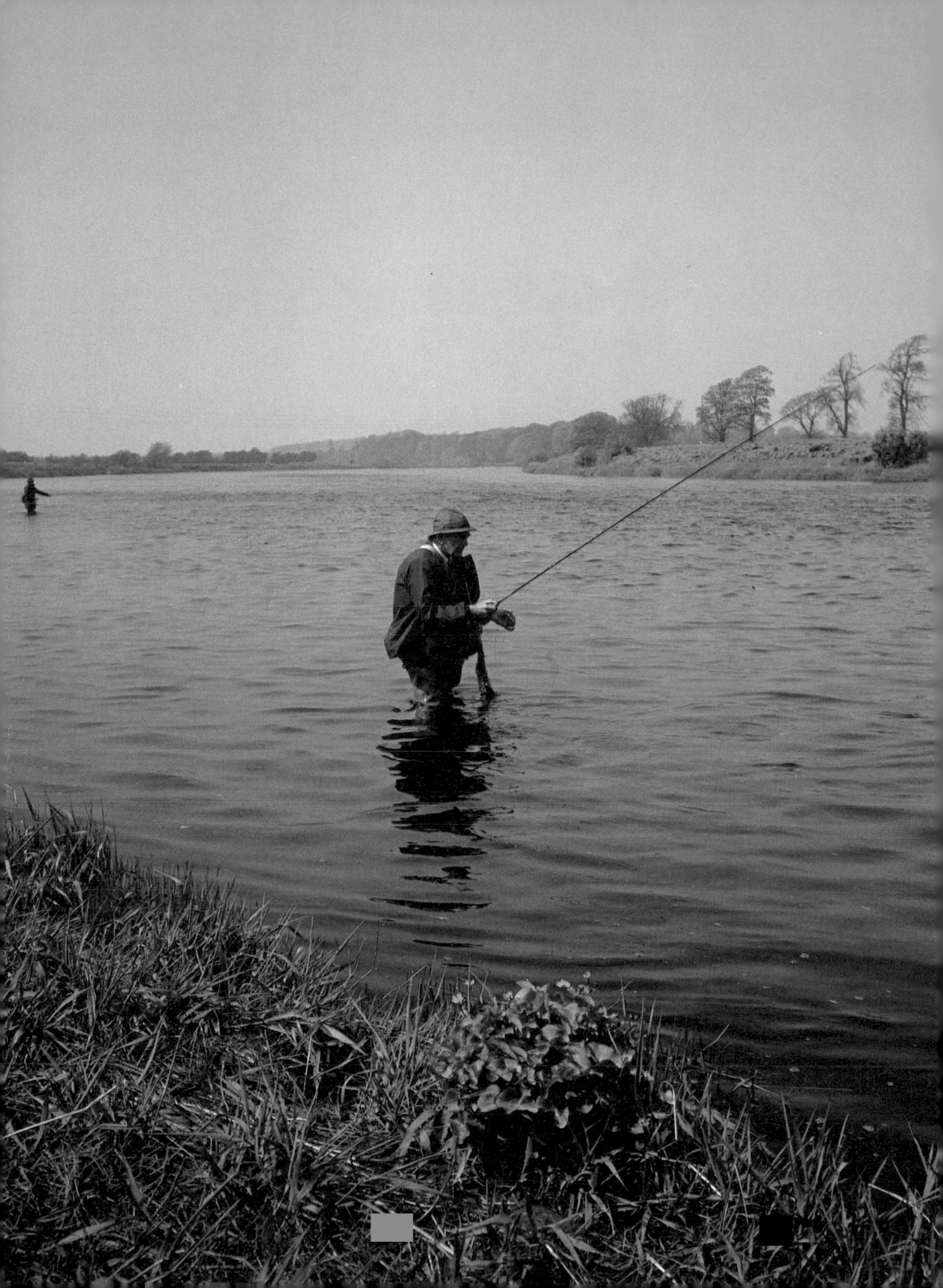

Opposite: Robert Scott fishes the Tweed for trout near
Coldstream
Below: Marvellous wet fly water. Tweed at Selkirk

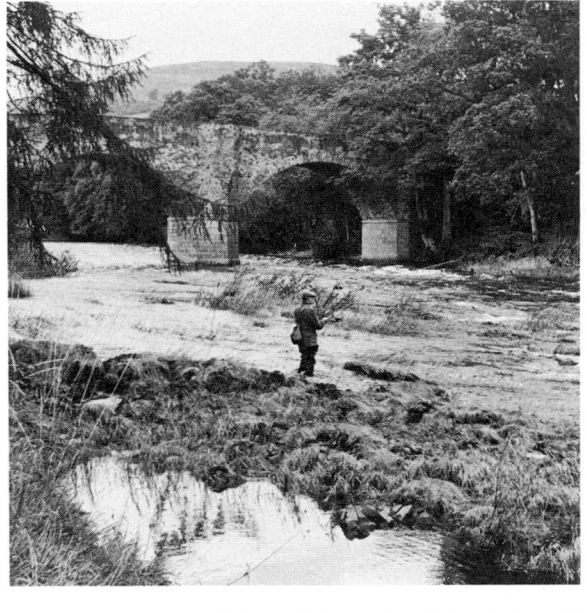

from the Silurian shales of the uplands and the old
red sandstone and carboniferous sediments of its
lowlands. It supports a rich and varied vegetation,
a wide range of invertebrate food items and a
number of fish species which include dace, roach
and gudgeon. It also carries a healthy stock of
wild brown trout.

True, the Tweed will no longer produce the
huge baskets of Stoddart's day when the catch was
measured in dozens, but then perhaps he and his
friends are partly the reason for this state of affairs.
However, there are plenty of trout left. In the
tributaries fish of half to three quarters of a pound
are normal but on the main river fish of a pound
to a pound and a half are common and two pounders are not unusual. The average size improves as
one goes downstream and the stretch between
Melrose and Kelso reputedly holds the biggest
trout up to five pounds in weight.

The river is not without its environmental
problems. The watersheds and uplands have been
extensively drained for agriculture and forestry so
water levels rise and fall more quickly than in the
past. The river drains a well farmed catchment
and receives the treated effluent of several thriving
settlements along its course. The already
eutrophic water thus gets additional doses of
nutrients which in low water conditions can lead
to growths of blanket weed. However despite

these problems, the Tweed remains an excellent
trout river and this is reflected in the number of
clubs and associations which actively conserve the
fishing.

There are at least twenty clubs and associations
together with individual estates and farms offering
permits to the visiting angler. Tickets are available
on stretches of the main river from Stanhope
down to Norham and on the tributaries of Lyne,
Ettrick, Yarrow, Gala, Leader, Teviot, Black-
adder, Whiteadder, Jed and Till. The tourism di-
vision of the Borders Regional Council has
regularly produced a comprehensive guide, *Angling in the Scottish Borders* which is a must for
visiting anglers. It gives all the details on where
to buy permits, the prices and the rules of the
water. These rules vary from water to water as
each club and association have their own regulations. Most of the best fishings are fly fishing
only.

All types of fly fishing can be effective. Traditional downstream wet fly fishing is popular and
Tweed is the source of W C Stewart's classical
treatise on the upstream wet fly. Patterns are numerous and varied. The Greenwell's Glory was
invented on the Tweed and remains a popular fly
along with Blae and Black, the Partridge Spiders
and the Woodcocks. Among the dry flies, the
Badger Hackles and the Grey Hen series of 'grizzle' hackle flies are successful. Where night fishing
is allowed in summer, a big night 'moth' fished
wet, downstream, accounts for some good trout.

Clyde

Fish fair an' free
An' spare the wee anes

This dedication on the monument to Matthew
McKendrick, 1848–1926, one time postmaster of
Abington in Clydesdale, symbolises in many
ways the particular place held by the Clyde in the
traditions of Scottish trout fishing. Reputedly
fished by the patriot William Wallace who lived
in Lanark, the river has been the nursery for many
famous Scottish anglers and has been formally
managed as a fishery since 1887 in the best traditions of access and conservation.

151

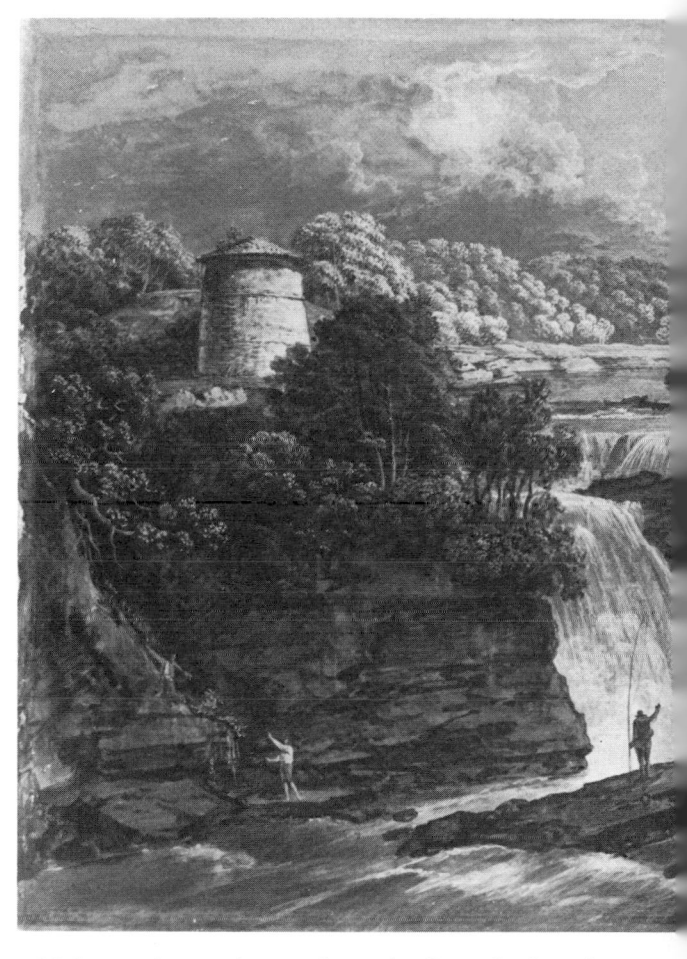

As it was. Nasmyth's famous painting of the Clyde at Bonnington Linn

Like the Tweed, the sources of the Clyde lie high among the Silurian shales of the Southern Uplands. Although there may be local disagreement as to the recognised 'source' of the river, the 2400 ft ridge of Culter Fell, Coombe Dod and Clyde Law forms a watershed between the two river systems. From there, the Clyde catchment swings west, past Beattock Summit round the head of the Daer Valley Reservoir, up into the massif of Green Lowther sheltering the high villages of Leadhills and Wanlockhead and on up to Cairn Table in the west. By the time the river reaches Roberton it has collected its headwaters from the Camps, Daer, Potrail, Elvan and Duneaton waters and a sizeable stream issues from the flat bottomed upland valley into the neat pasture and farmland of Clydesdale. Here, in a landscape dominated by the peak of Tinto, a sparkling river ripples over gravel fords and smooth glides, past the villages of Lamington, Symington, Thankerton and Quothquan, whose musical names echo the ghosts of the famous steam engines which used to power the 'Royal Scot' up the valley from Glasgow to Beattock and on to Carlisle and London. The line is still there. The small stations are all closed, but the coaches behind the electric expresses still provide cheery waves for the angler.

In the middle of this stretch, as the river passes Symington, it abruptly changes course and the curious eye will trace the shallow, flat valley of the Biggar Water leading over to Broughton on the upper Tweed. Much of the geographical evidence suggests that, at a time not too far distant, the upper Clyde did in fact form the headwaters of the Tweed until it was 'captured' by the more active downcutting Clyde. Now below Symington, the whole river flows north westwards, collecting the Medwyn and Douglas waters before throwing itself over the spectacular waterfalls of the Bonnington and the Cora linns at Lanark. These impressive falls, together with Stonebyres Linn just downstream, mark a significant change in character between the upper and the middle river and would form a formidable barrier to any migratory fish which might try to defy the pollution in the estuary. Below the linns the river continues in a deep sheltered valley between the orchard laden slopes of Kirkfieldbank and Hazelbank. This is a colourful market garden area which continues down through Crossford and Dalserf before emerging into industrial Lanarkshire at Wishaw, Motherwell and Hamilton where an increasingly sluggish river loses its trout appeal.

Because of its accessibility the Clyde has always been heavily fished. The river has been managed as a trout fishery since 1887 and the United Clyde Angling Protective Association was formed by the amalgamation of the upper and lower parts of the river in 1920. This association, in conjunction with the Lamington and District Angling Association and the Lanark and District Angling Club now manages virtually the whole river and very reasonably priced permits can be obtained through local outlets.

The river carries a good stock of trout which varies from place to place depending on fishing

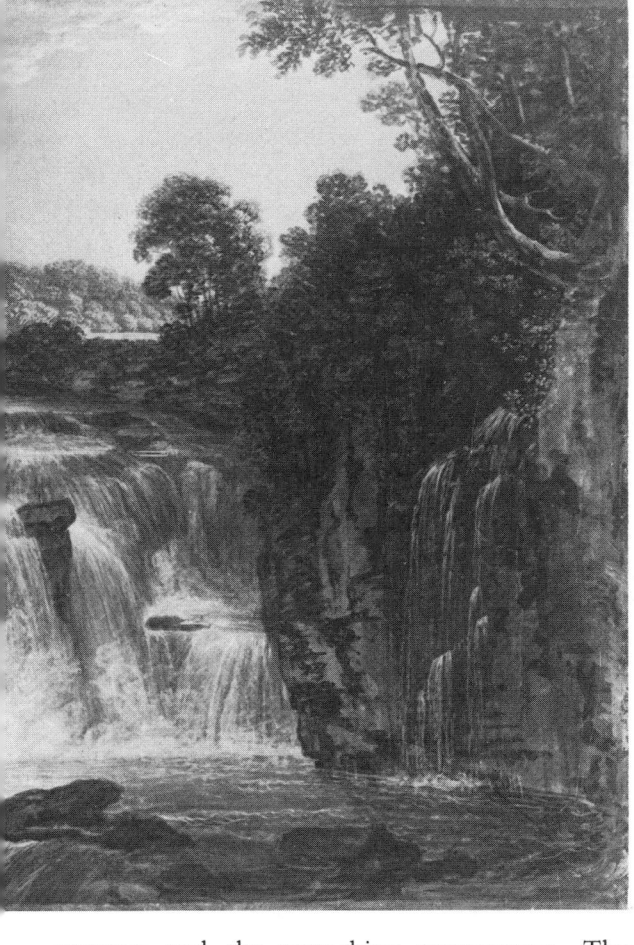

of the natural insect and the materials, patterns and techniques have been refined over generations of anglers. In addition to familiar patterns such as Greenwell, March Brown and Blae and Black, the Clyde has its own patterns whose poetic names are lost in the mists of time. Such names as Blae and Hoolet, Corncrake, Hen Blackie and Waterhen Bloa obviously refer to the source of the feathers, but what of Greensleeves, Edmead and Downlooker? The Clyde patterns can be dressed as wet fly, dry fly and nymph and although not normally obtainable outside the local area they are equally effective in other waters even as far away as the Falkland Islands.

The traditional local fly fishing technique is downstream wet fly with a team of three or four Clyde patterns fished across and down the streams and runs. The upstream dry fly is also popular and effective. Clyde style dry flies are as delicate and lifelike as the wet patterns and may be of the hackle or winged variety. Favourite hackles are the badger or the 'grizzle' hackle which give a whole range of Grey Hen patterns with different body colours. Apart from fly fishing, at the right time of the year, the stone fly nymph, or 'Gadger', the upstream worm and natural minnow are expertly handled by the locals.

Tay

The trouting of Tay is a great Scottish potential, for at present, it is almost wholly ignored by the tenants on most of the salmon beats.
W B CURRIE 1972

This assessment of eleven years ago reflects both the neglect of trout fishing in the past and its prospects for the future on Scotland's greatest river. Since it was written some of these prospects have begun to materialise. There is a much greater awareness of the merits of the trout of the Tay with active management and development by many clubs. Proposals for the third Scottish protection order have been submitted for the Tummel-Garry part of the Tay catchment.

As the Tweed and the Clyde 'rise on ae hillside', so do the Tay and the Spey share a common watershed. In this case the common divide lies

pressure and the restocking programme. The United Clyde Angling Protective Association stocks the river regularly from its hatcheries at Rigside and Abington. The average size of trout ranges from half a pound to one pound but monsters of up to fifteen pounds lurk in the deeper holes and are caught from time to time. The trout share the water with shoals of grayling which are looked on as a mixed blessing. They compete with the trout for food and space yet provide the angler with a worthy adversary.

The clear water and the heavy fishing pressure has led to a wary and educated population of trout. This has demanded the development of a particular style of fly dressing known as the Clyde style of fly. This has characteristics of a very sparse dressing, on fine, small hooks. The aim has been an accurate imitation, both in scale and delicacy,

153

Below: Fishing Grantully on the Tay

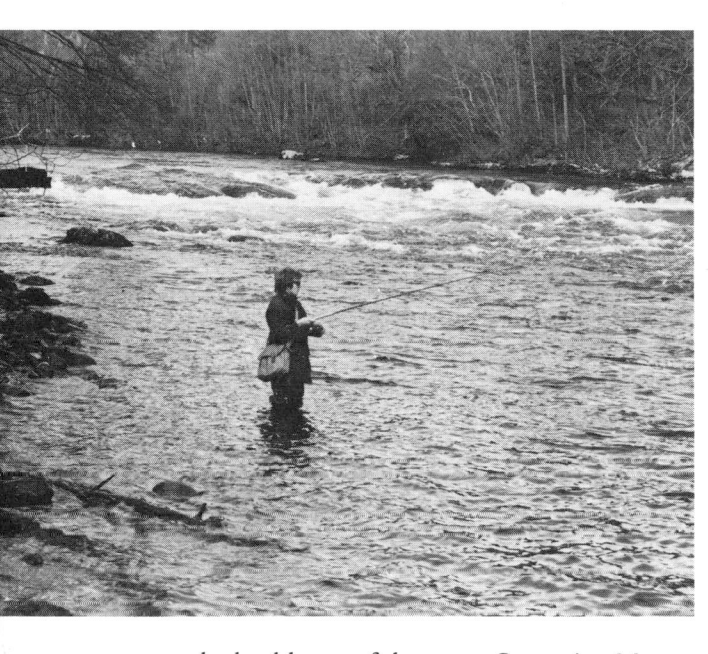

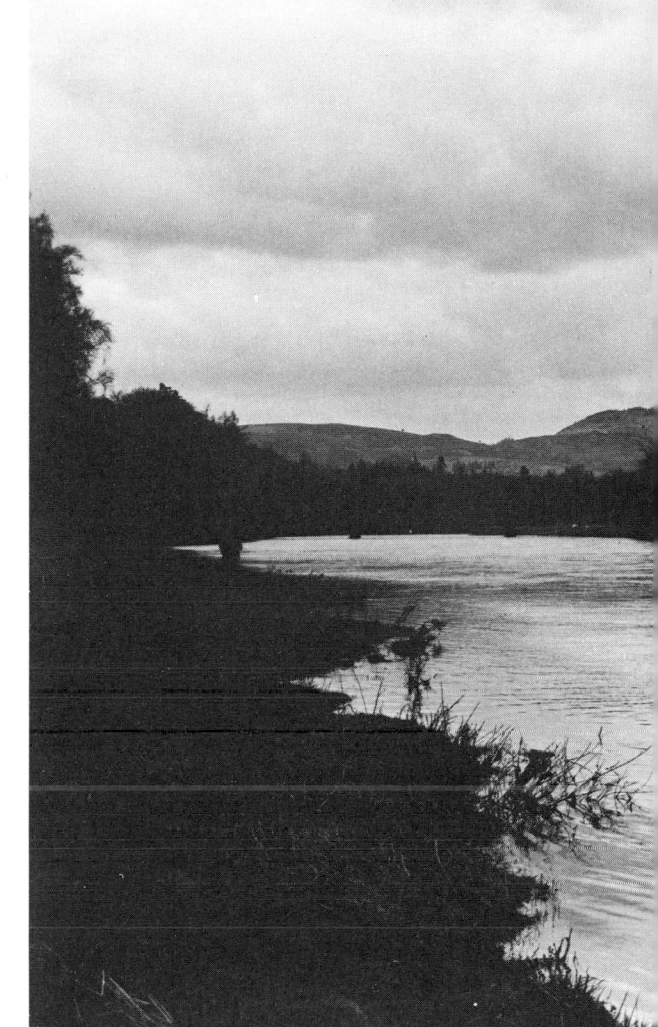

across the backbone of the great Grampian Mountains in the wild deer forests of Atholl and Gaick. In the heights of the Forest of Atholl rise the infant Garry and Tilt which running southwards join the River Tummel at Pitlochry and the Tay itself at Ballinluig. The River Tay proper is the longest Scottish river and covers some eighty five miles from its source near Ben Lui to the tidal water at Perth, and a further thirty miles to the open sea. The headwaters reach low ground near Tyndrum in Strathfillan and flow north eastwards as the River Dochart to tumble over the Falls of Dochart at Killin and enter Loch Tay, alongside another major tributary, the Lochay. Fourteen miles to the north east the loch outflows into the Tay proper at Kenmore. Here it is joined by the River Lyon and traverses the Strath of Appin, past Aberfeldy to pick up the Tummel at Ballinluig. The now impressive river sweeps through Strathtay to break out of the mountain wall at Dunkeld into the rich and fertile farmland of Strathmore. At Meiklelour it is joined by the Isla, draining the large eastern catchment of Glenisla, Glenshee and Strathardle, and alters direction to the south west wending its way through the famous salmon beats of Ballathie, Stobhall, Stanley and Scone to the fair city of Perth. Below Perth the estuary collects its last tribute from the River Earn, bringing its waters from a large catchment in the western

mountains and fertile Strathearn.

Tay trout first attracted the attention of the visiting angler in 1786 when Colonel Thornton, during his famous *Sporting Tour* sampled Loch Tay and complained; 'But the morning was so intensely warm I could scarce get a rise in five minutes, I however killed a brace'. Despite such a slow start to his day Thornton later adds: 'In the course of two miles sailing, however, hooked a trout of about a couple of pounds, which I killed and afterwards two more, weighing about four pounds each'. Heady sport, indeed! By the 1830s however when Thomas Tod Stoddart was carrying out his rambles in this part of Scotland, he was disappointed. Despite catching baskets of trout totaling up to fourteen pounds in one day, he was satisfied that: 'In point of abundance, as well as size, the trout of Tay will not bear comparison with those of Tweed.' But then, perhaps Stoddart was biased!

Certainly today the main river carries a good stock of wild brown trout averaging about three

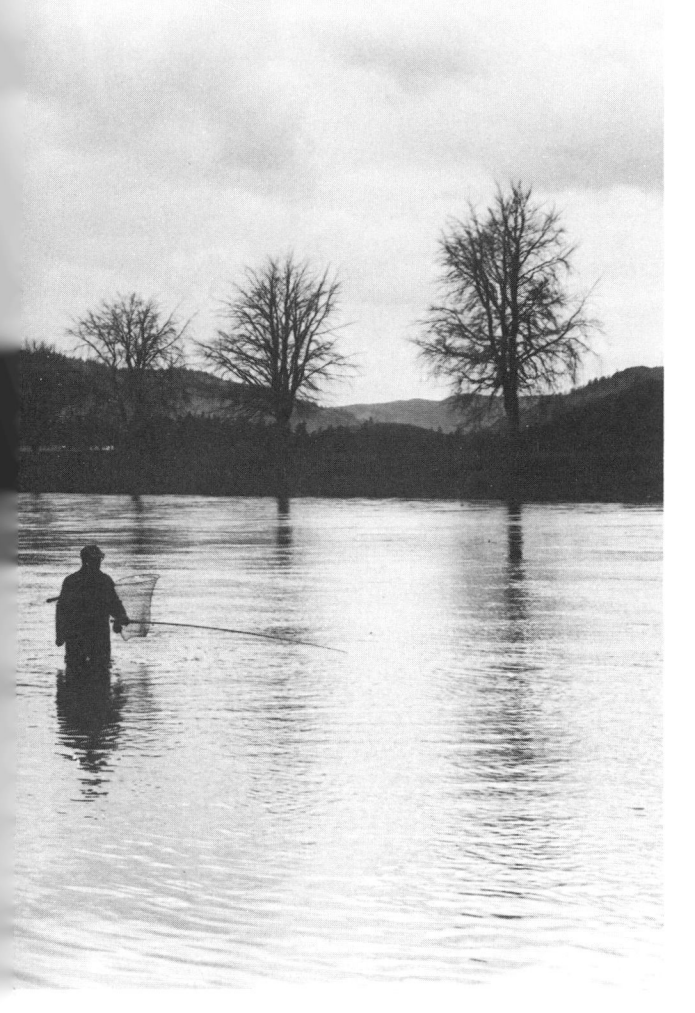

Left: Dusk falls on a Tay Sunday
Below: Where the brown trout lie

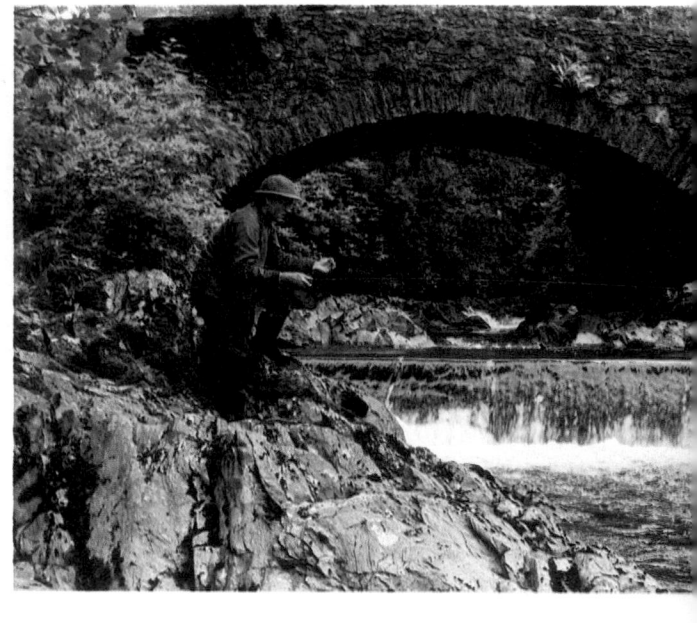

quarters of a pound in weight, with some fish of three and four pounds caught each year. Permits for the main river can be obtained from the Aberfeldy Angling Club, the Dunkeld and Birnam Angling Association and the Perth and District Anglers Association while the hotels at Dunkeld, Grandtully and Logierait can all arrange trout fishing for visitors. Although Loch Tay may be most famous for the opening of the salmon season on 15 January each year it also produces good trout up to two pounds and the hotels of Ardeonaig, Clachaig and Killin can provide boats. Permits for the Dochart can be obtained from D & S Allan, tackle dealers, Killin.

Apart from the main river the Tay system offers a great range of trout fishing opportunities within the tributaries and lochs. The Department of Recreation and Tourism, Tayside Regional Council, have regularly produced a guide *Tayside for Fishing* which gives all the essential details for the visitor.

The Tummel is a marvellous trout stream and regularly yields fish in the three to four pounds category. Pitlochry Angling Club issues permits for the five miles of both banks from the junction of the Tay up to Pitlochry. Up the Garry tributary, the Atholl Angling Club issues permits for part of the rivers Garry and Tilt while further up the main Tummel branch the Loch Rannoch Conservation Association has many local outlets for permits around the loch.

Loch Rannoch itself introduces another aspect of trout fishing in the Tay catchment and in Scotland in general – the 'ferox' trout. Despite the attempts of last century to classify these large cannibal loch trout as a separate species, they are now recognised as large and usually old specimens of ordinary brown trout whose longevity and diet of fish allows the attainment of double figure weights.

In the large eastern part of the catchment area, drained by the River Isla and tributaries, much of the water is managed by the Strathmore Angling Improvement Association whose efforts have achieved many improvements on the Isla and Dean. Further upstream, trout fishing on the River Ericht is offered by the Blairgowrie, Rattray and District Angling Association while other parts of this river and the neighbouring River Ardle can be fished through several of the hotels in these glens.

The River Earn drains the southern part of the Tay catchment and flowing into the tidal estuary

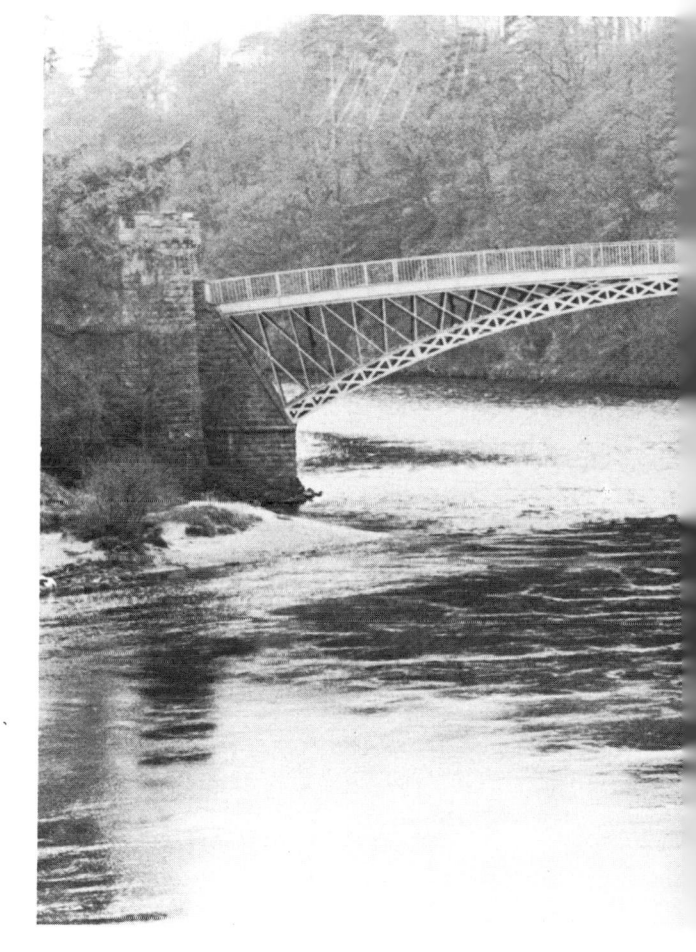

The Telford bridge over the Spey at Craigellachie

itself it almost forms a separate river system. It is primarily a sea-trout river with a good head of grayling as well, but has little fame as a trout water. This does not detract from the efforts of the angling clubs on the upper river to improve this reputation. The St Fillans and Loch Earn Angling Association issues permits for Loch Earn and the upper part of the River Earn and further downstream the Crieff Angling Club controls a good piece of the river.

The vast water resources of the Tay system were early harnessed for hydro-electric development. A complicated system of dams and tunnels had channelled the water to a network of power stations of which Pitlochry is perhaps the most famous. Although the effects on salmon are mainly adverse, the trout fishing has benefited from the creation of many new or bigger lochs behind the dams.

It is also significant that the Tay is the centre for research in freshwater fisheries. The Brown Trout Laboratory was established at Faskally, Pitlochry, in 1948 and carried out comprehensive research into Scottish brown trout populations and habitats. Subsequently it was renamed the Freshwater Fisheries Laboratory and now concentrates more on salmon research.

Spey

The Cairngorm water is all clear. Flowing from granite, with no peat to darken it, it has never the golden amber, the 'horse-back brown' so often praised in Highland burns.

NAN SHEPHERD 1977

This water which nourishes the Spey makes it world famous for two important commodities – whisky and salmonid fish. The whiskies require a separate treatise but the fish are relevant here. The Spey's main claim to fame is as a salmon river and in this it is in the very top class. Perhaps the most adventurous of its trout decided to follow the salmon as it is also a first class sea-trout river. However behind the glamour of the migratory fish, it is also a very commendable trout river and while in the lower river they may be neglected in favour of the migrant fish, the middle and upper

Spey offers much good and accessible trout fishing.

As the tributary Tilt drains the Forest of Atholl soutwards into the Tay, so the rivers Truim and Tromie drain the Forest of Gaick north into the Spey. Further downstream the 4000 ft massif of the Cairngorms feeds the Feshie, Luineag Nethy and Avon and the summer snowfields keep the water running full and cold for most of the year. The main river rises in the bleak wilderness of the Corrieyairack Forest and from the tiny Loch Spey this fast flowing river sets out on its hundred mile journey north east to the Moray Firth. The upper river gathers the run-off of the Monadhliath (or Grey) Mountains to the north and the tributaries of Trium, Tromie and Feshie from the south. Two large, important lochs, Laggan and Ericht, occupy the upper part of the catchment although

The middle Spey below Grantown

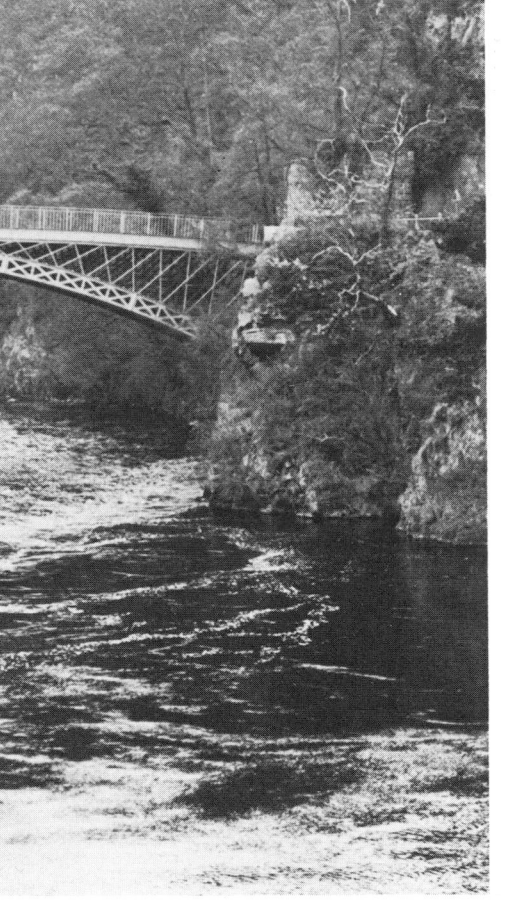

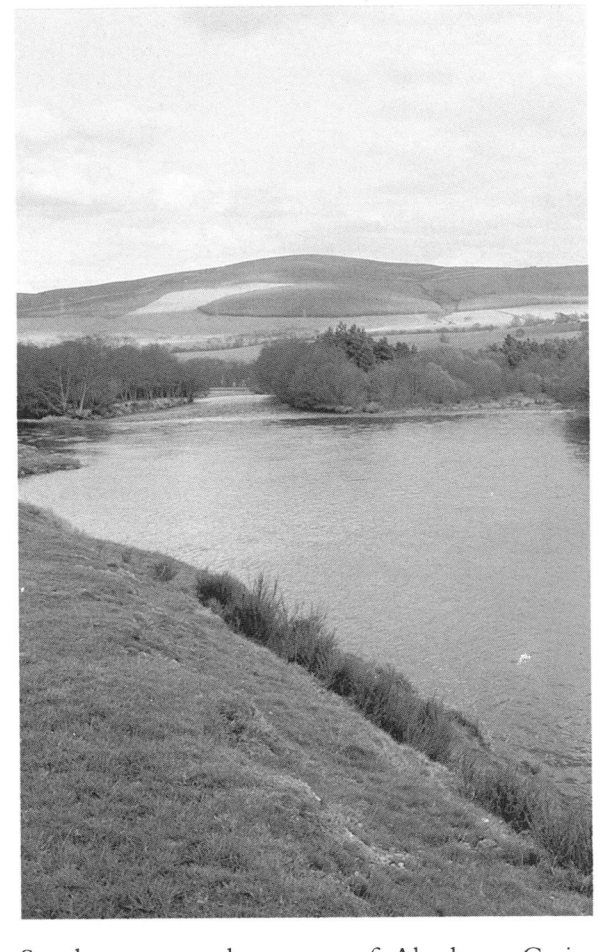

diversion of waters for hydro-electric purposes tends to confuse the drainage pattern in this area. By Truim junction the river Spey swings across a wide flat strath in streams and pools, past the towns of Newtonmore and Kingussie in the historic lands of Badenoch. Below the poorly drained basin of Loch Insch and the nature reserve of Insch Marshes the river enters the main holiday part of 'Spey Valley' around the centres of Aviemore, Carrbridge and Grantown-on-Spey. Here it collects the snow-melt off the Cairngorm (or Red) Mountains to the east and joins with the River Dulnain from the west.

Within this lowland area lie a series of smaller lochs – Loch Alvie, Loch an Eilean, Loch Morlich, Loch Pityoulish, Loch Vaa and Loch Garten of the ospreys. Below Grantown, the river, in full majesty, makes its way down the lower part of

Strathspey past the towns of Aberlour, Craigellachie and Rothes and through the famous salmon beats of Tulchan, Elchies and Ballindalloch. Here the Spey collects its major tributary, the River Avon (pronounced A'an) draining the whisky country of Tomintoul and Glenlivet, before passing on through the beats of Delfur, Speymouth and Gordon Castle to the Moray Firth.

Although there are splendid trout stocks throughout the River Spey it is in the upper and middle reaches that the most management has been carried out and the best opportunities for access have been arranged.

In 1982 the Badenoch Angling Association was granted Scotland's second protection order, covering the upper catchment of the Spey as far downstream as Loch Insch and including the lochs of Laggan and Ericht. Much of this water is avail-

157

A pastoral scene on Speyside

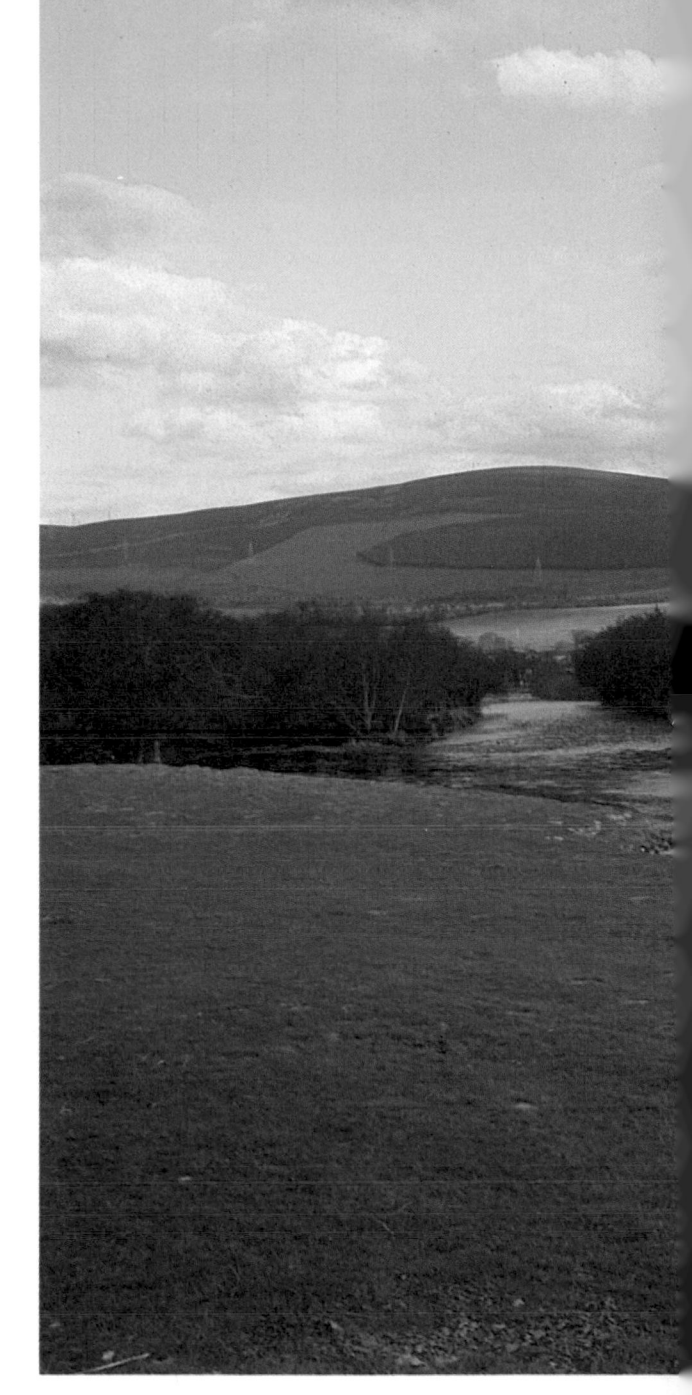

able on permits from the Badenoch Angling Association and can be obtained from local outlets in Newtonmore and Kingussie. The higher stretches of this water are typical of a Highland river, flowing off hard, granitic rocks and low in dissolved nutrients. It flows fast through shallow riffles and pools and supports an insect population of stoneflies, caddis and several species of mayfly. Below Kingussie and approaching Loch Insch the river becomes deeper and slow flowing with a peaty bottom. Here the fast water species of insects give way to lake dwelling types more characteristic of the loch itself. This part of the Spey is unique in Scotland as it has the only known population of migratory arctic char, *Salvelinus alpinus*, which come up from Loch Insch to spawn in the tributaries of the Spey at certain times of the year. In addition to the char, Loch Insch is the home of pike and some large brown trout. Permits can be obtained from Invereshie House Hotel, which also keeps a boat on the loch.

Below Loch Insch, the emphasis on salmon fishing increases as one goes downstream. Usually, on the main river, the trout fishing forms part of a combined salmon and sea-trout permit, although the many lochs in this area offer fishing for both brown and rainbow trout.

On this part of the Spey itself the fishing is managed by the two main associations of Strathspey and Abernethy. The Strathspey Angling Association offers permits for seven miles of the Spey from Grantown up to Broomhill Bridge and twelve miles of the River Dulnain. The Abernethy Angling Improvement Association controls a further six miles of the River Spey from Broomhill Bridge up to Boat of Garten. Permits for both stretches of water can be obtained through local shops and hotels. Access to other parts of the river can be obtained from various agencies such as the Osprey Fishing School at Aviemore, and several hotels, farms and estates offices in the area. Apart from the rivers, the lochs in this area provide interesting trout fishing. Loch Alvie can be fished from the three boats of Llynwilg Hotel. Loch Morlich can be fished by permit from the Forestry Commission in Glenmore Forest Park and permits for Loch Vaa and Avielochan can be obtained at Avielochan or from several hotels in the local area. These lochs are stocked with both brown and rainbow trout.

Below Grantown the salmon reigns supreme and there are few formal facilities for trout fishing although permission may sometimes be granted by the local riparian landowners or arranged by the local hotel. Even the associations of the lower river are mainly interested in salmon but permits for trout fishing can be obtained at Aberlour, Rothes and Fochabers. There are still, however, the major tributaries. The Rivers Avon, Fiddich and Livet all carry good trout stocks and permission can be obtained in Tomintoul and Ballindalloch for the Avon, at Dufftown on the Fiddich

and the Glenlivet Angling Association issues permits for the Livet.

Deveron

The River Deveron rises in a high, wild area north west of Huntly in Aberdeenshire, known as the Cabrach, with one hill, the Buck, over 2,200 ft high. The young Deveron flows gently east until it is joined by the Blackwater, at which point its status rises from hill burn to river. The main activities in the area are farming and grouse shooting, each done by different groups of people.

The inbred trout of the hill burn areas are very small; any that are caught are caught on worm but as the river flows downstream to Lesmurdie the fish improve considerably and some good baskets can be had. The river here flows through and over a lot of peat: the result is a lot of sediment in the water – and the trout are dark coloured. In such water Dunkeld, Wickhams's Fancy and Cinamon and Gold are the most popular flies.

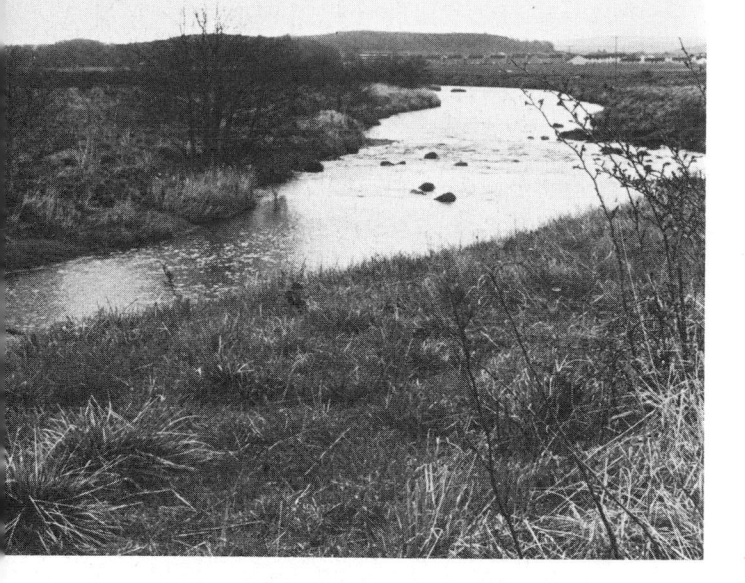

Further downstream, at Huntly, the valleys are more gentle and the ground less peaty. Here the Huntly Angling Association has control of twenty two miles of water (where visitors can obtain tickets). Controversially, clear water worming is allowed during the summer months and there are those who believe that too many of the larger bottom feeding trout which constitute the main breeding stock are caught in this way. UDN decimated the brown trout fishing all the way up the Deveron and it may be that this kind of fishing is holding back its full recovery.

Just below Huntly the river is joined by the Bogie which rises half a mile from the source of the Deveron on the opposite side of the hill – but takes itself through a gentler and more fertile valley, with more sand than peat: although the smaller of the two, it has better feeding and bigger trout. The junction is adjacent to the Huntly golf course beside which the river runs for a spell. The golf balls that make their way down the river bed are supplied by visiting golfers; the locals wade in and rescue their bad shots.

When the water from the two rivers reaches Coniecleugh it seems to have achieved the right mix, for there the trout will be in first class condition with the distinctive yellow colouring and the red spots of the true brown trout. Within the last ten years, it has become noticeable that after the regular noon day rise in April and May, as the water warms up, the trout seem to cease rising. The cause is believed to be fertiliser which has been washed into the river from the farmland and which stimulates the bottom growth thus providing better feeding for freshwater shrimp and other such underwater delicacies.

Downstream again, the Deveron is joined by the Isla, a good sized tributary rising at Loch Park at Drummuir and flowing east through Keith and Grange and meeting the Deveron at Rothiemay. The river now acquires a more stately and serene gait as it flows through Rothiemay and beyond, and here the trout fishing is excellent. As on so many salmon rivers, the main energies go in chasing the salmon and sea-trout while the brown trout are neglected. There are few rivers in Scotland where, when the water is too low, the brown trout provide such a sporting alternative and with the possibility of really heavy fish.

When it reaches the Boat of Turtory and Bridge of Marnoch, the river is ever widening and slowing down but in the faster water between pools the trout fishing is as good as any on the river.

By the time Turriff is reached (where the local angling club has fishing) it is the usual story of either too short a stretch or too many members, and the brown trout have a struggle to get established. And so to Banff, through some of the most sought after salmon and sea-trout fishing, where the river slips quietly into the North Sea, as if over awed by meeting such a volume of water.

Anglers' techniques must change with the trout's altered habits. In March and April, March Browns and Greenwells will still catch fish, but in June (when once the dry fly fishing was excellent) the best method is to fish a nymph or a wet fly cast upstream and allowed, more or less, to bounce down the bottom.

Don

For top rate brown trout sport the River Don has few equals. In fact, on the Grandhome, Parkhill and Fintray beats one can cast a line for 'brownies' only a matter of minutes from Aberdeen city centre. Against a backcloth of paper mills and countless oil related projects, these beats not surprisingly are prone to pollution from time to time. On the whole however – thanks to the efforts of those responsible – the overall situation is quite satisfactory. Grandhome is deep and canal like in parts but has various glides which call for a long cast and infinite patience. During the months of April, May and June here, the brown trout man

Big trout lurk even in the thin waters of the upper Don

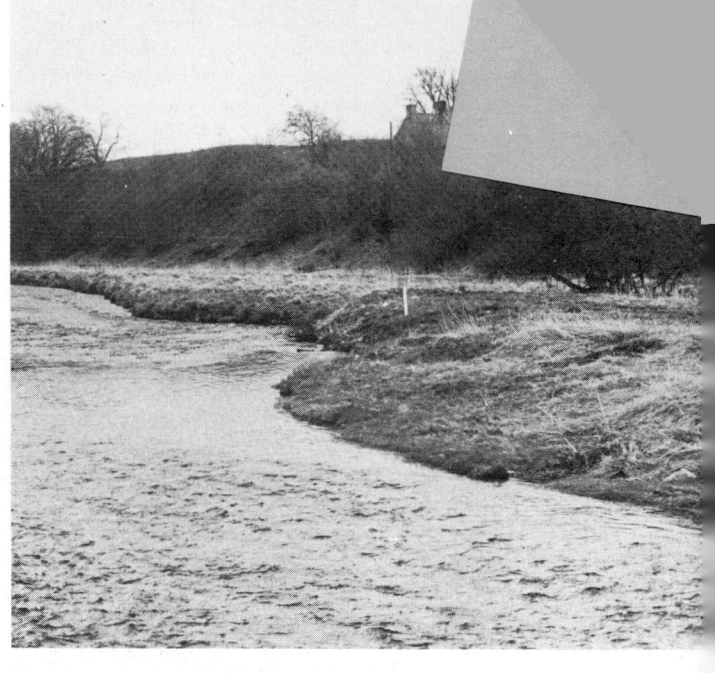

is best served with size fourteen or sixteen doubles and a floating line with a sunk tip. Pools such as Benzies, Snuffies and, upriver, the Mill Stream are ideal for this mode of fishing. The scenery may not be all that beautiful, but the trout belie this background. It is not unusual to latch on to brownies in the one and a half to two pounds category in these areas and they will be 'wild' trout in every sense of the word and fighters all the way. Moving upriver towards Fintray, Thainstone and Kintore one comes across more white faster flowing waters and these call for a change of tactics. A fully floating line with a lengthy leader will often do the trick – particularly if one has something else like a March Brown on the dropper and an ever dependable Greenwell's Glory on the tail. As to sizes I personally wouldn't go above a size twelve single and I would always have a Black Spider or Bloody Butcher on standby. As one moves upstream to the Inverurie and Manar beats the background scene changes. With good, well stocked water to fish one can also feast one's eyes on Donside proper, with its lush agricultural land set in hills and forest. Fishing at Inverurie is an all-methods-permitted set up and consequently the fly only man may be hard pushed at times to find a suitable area; even so, by getting to the top of the beat – somewhere immediately above the Black Pot – he or she may well find their personal Shangrila. The Kypie, Boat Pool and Rowehead stretches are also ideal venues.

A mile up river is Manar. A two mile long beat, it will satisfy even the most ardent brown trout enthusiast. Moving from the Rae Pot downstream to the Sheep Pool, there are at least half a dozen prime areas. Each one can, on its day, yield occasional trout in the two to three pounds class. I personally go for the dry fly fished wet on these waters, particularly if I am using flies with either predominantly yellow or wine hackles in their make up. Sizes? The smaller the better with perhaps a sixteen being the best bet. The lower part of Manar, which includes the Wood Pools and the Chapel Pool, is also productive. Given a rise any angler worth his salt can hope for a bag of half a dozen good trout in the space of an hour or two. Pre-booked day tickets for the Manar fishing are available at Inverurie. On now to Kemnay and the Fetternear fishings, where is found some of

the cream of the river with the Top Hut Pool, the Mill Stream and Gilbert Pot being outstanding. From here on the further one moves up the river, the better the fishing. In this respect the Grant Arms Hotel beats at Monymusk are in a class of their own. Never overfished and situated amid a whole range of hills and beautiful countryside, the waters here range from long drawn out glide like pools to short, fast flowing, white water stretches. I never fish light on these beats. Apart from dealing with large brownies, there is more than a chance of contacting a small salmon or, later in the season, a grilse. With this possibility in mind therefore – unless dry fly fishing – double hooks are recommended.

A few miles up country the whole scene changes yet again. The hills are more pronounced and the river narrows; almost Highland countryside in fact. That is the backcloth to the Brux fishings. From the Brux Pool and down through pools such as the Laidner, Inchdonald, Craig Logie and Upper Forresters' there is fishing to set the pulse racing. Here the use of small, hackle only flies is recommended. Now, as one wanders further up Donside to the Glenkindie, Glenbuchat, Candacraig and Edinglassie beats, one becomes increasingly conscious of yet another change in the immediate surroundings. The hills tower above the river, which runs through a valley that might never have seen the hand of man. Just to fish the Tumbling Bank, Muckle Stone or Bridge Pool at Candacraig is a joy in itself. From a background of industrialisaton on its lowest reaches to awe inspiring beauty on its uppermost beats, the Don is a river which not only provides good sport, but serene and unforgettable beauty.

LOCHS AND LAKES

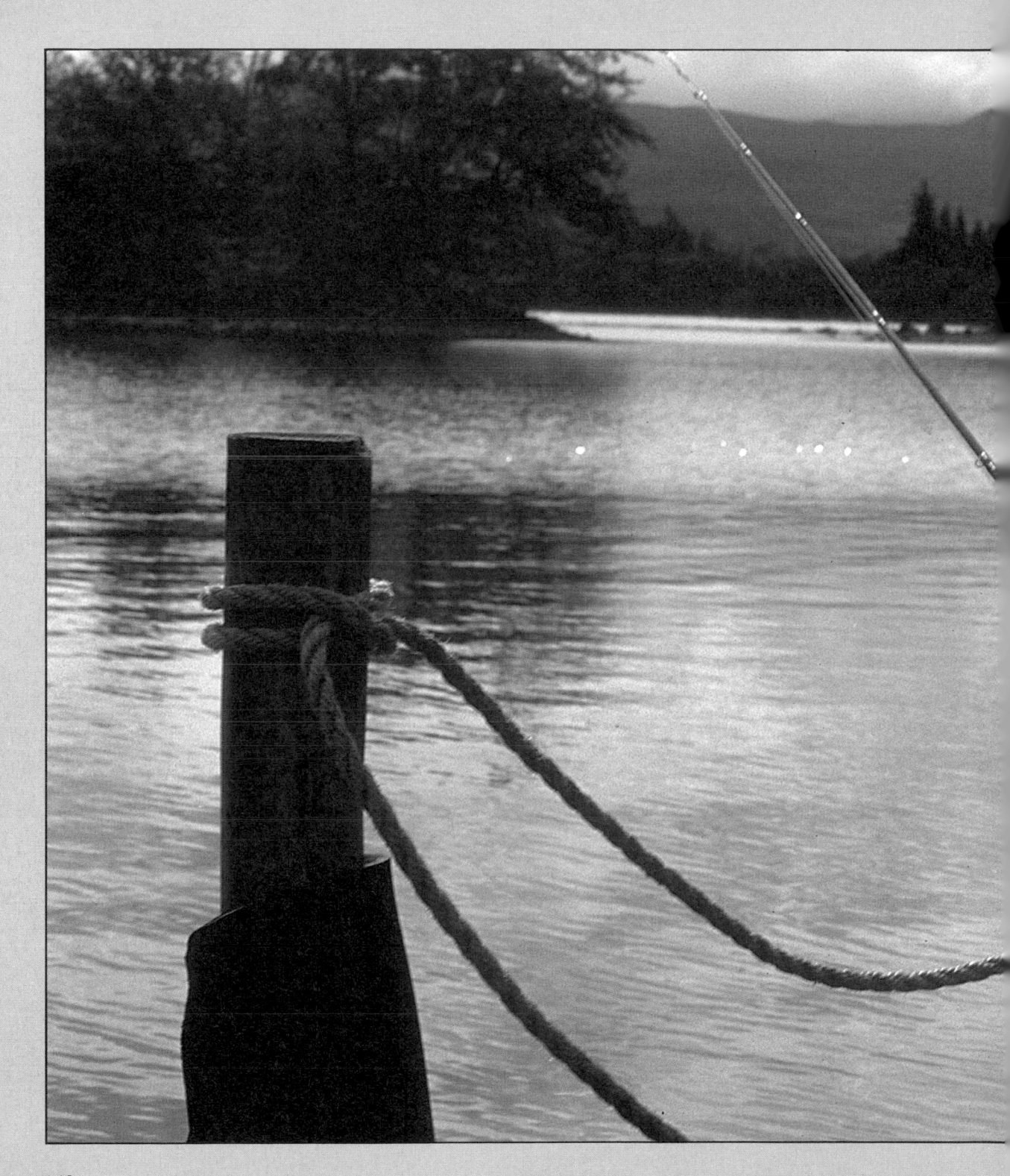

Loch Awe, Argyll

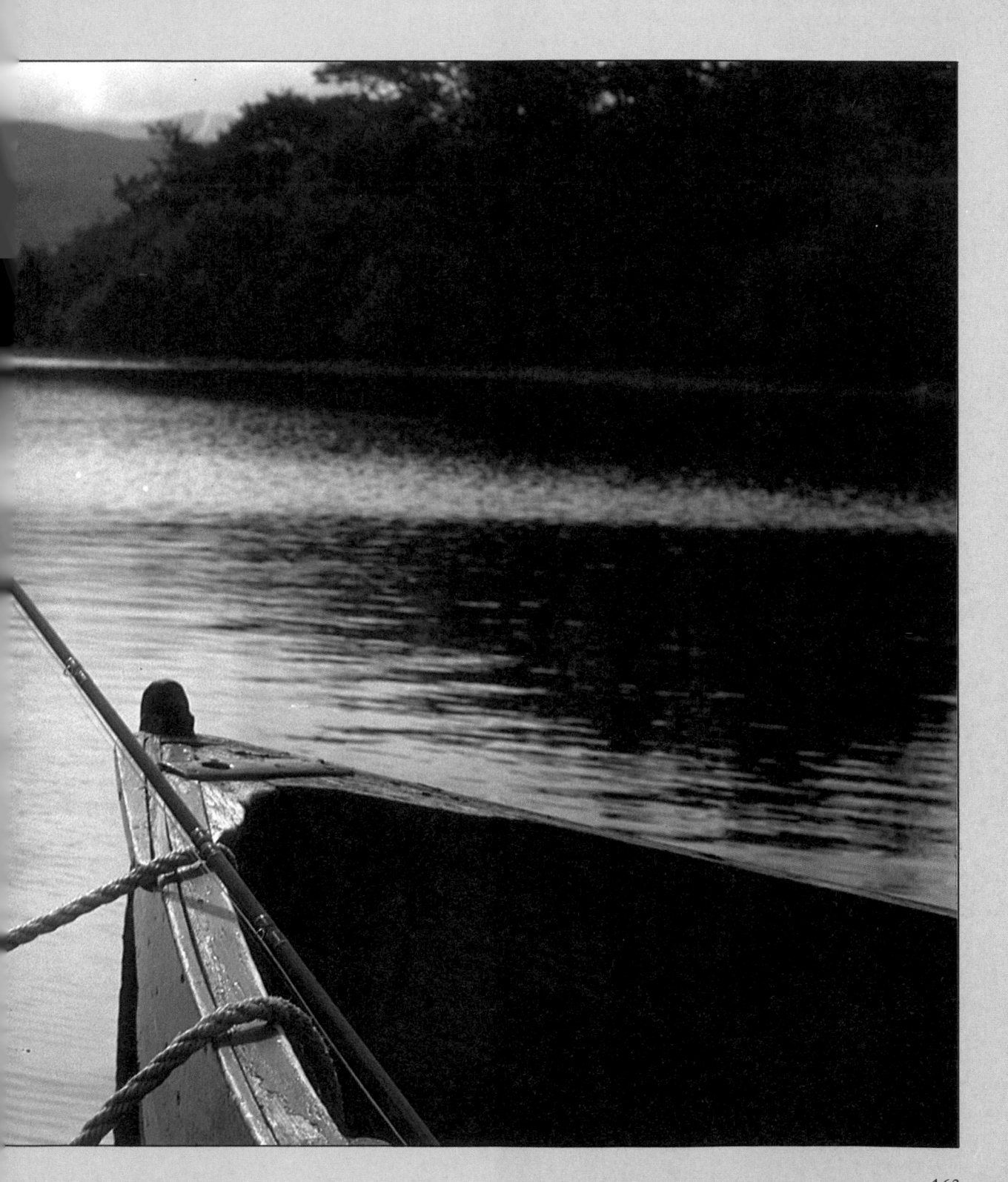

Bottom left: Harray, the largest of Orkney's trout lochs
Top: Awe, home of the ferox

Loch Leven

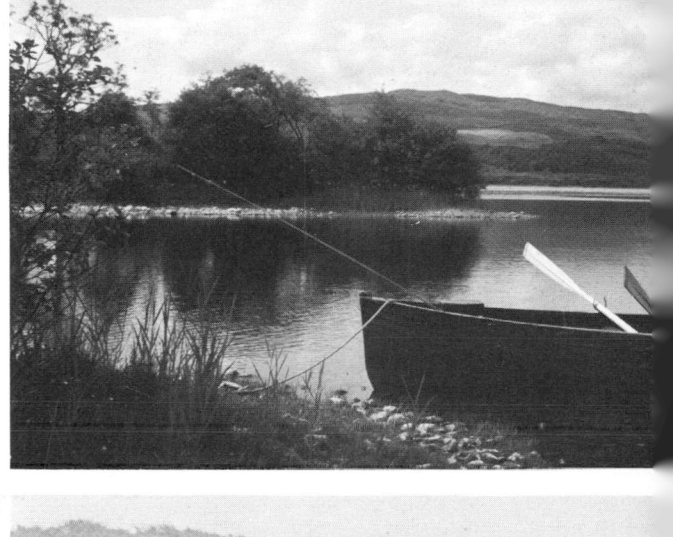

We believe that loch contains more trout for its size than any other loch in Scotland.
W C STEWART 1857

Loch Leven is without doubt the most famous of the Scottish trout lochs. It is a national nature reserve and is the long standing venue for national and international angling competitions. The traditional style of Scottish loch fishing using a team of wet flies from a drifting boat is the usual method of fishing.

Its particular strain of pink fleshed, silver trout with black spots were once thought to be a separate species and the eggs of the *Salmo levenensis* were exported around the world from the Howietoun hatchery in the 1880s.

It is a rich shallow loch averaging only twelve feet in depth and extending to 3405 acres, it is the largest natural eutrophic water body in Britain. This richness has been its greatest problem in recent years. Additions of nitrates from agriculture and phosphates from sewage have caused further enrichment and changes in the algal and insect life. These changes have affected the numbers of fish caught in recent years but fish of excellent quality remain. The record trout of nine pounds thirteen ounces dates from 1912 but fish of between four and six pounds are still caught fairly regularly. However there is no doubt that the quality of fishing has declined in recent years and the owners recently announced their decision to reinstate the

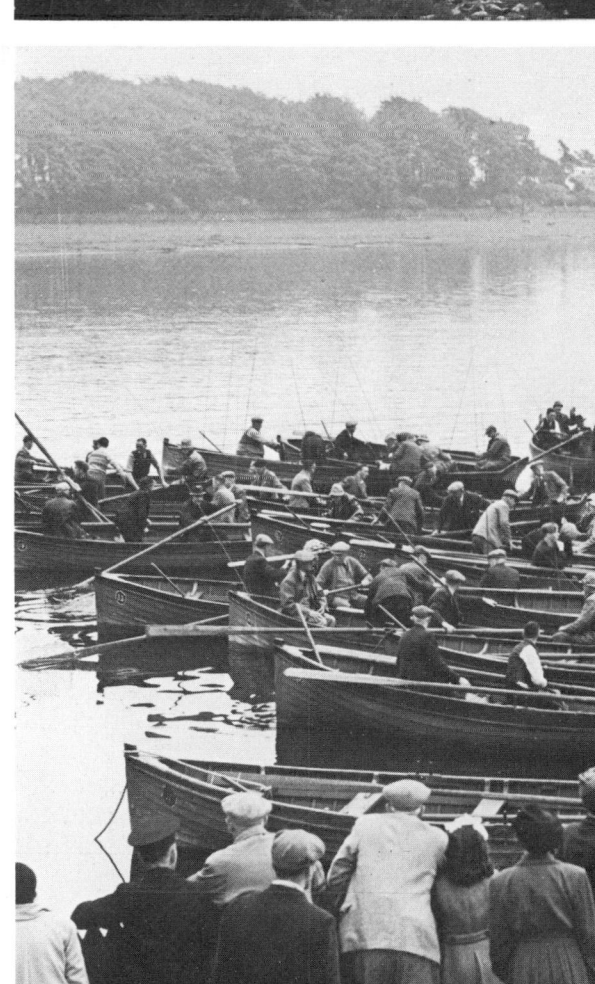

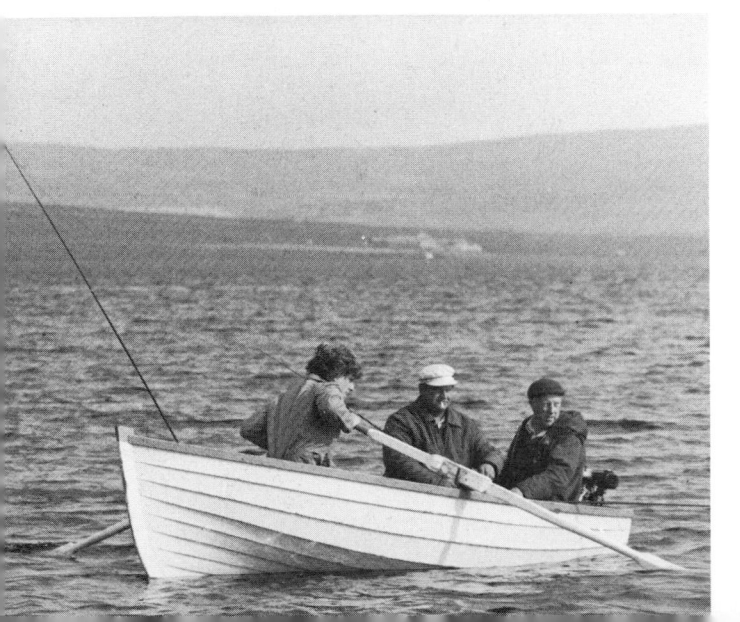

Below centre: Loch Leven in the old days. Scene of international competitions

hatchery and initiate a restocking programme.

Forty boats with outboard motors are available and can be booked through The Pier, Kinross. It is strictly 'fly only' and many of the traditional Scottish loch patterns will take trout under suitable conditions.

Loch Awe

The Oldest Boatman tapped his pipe hard on the flat stone beside him and I started back to awareness of the bright sky and the lapping water.
"That breeze out of the west", said my old friend, "iss too good to be missing".
ALASDAIR CARMICHAEL 1973

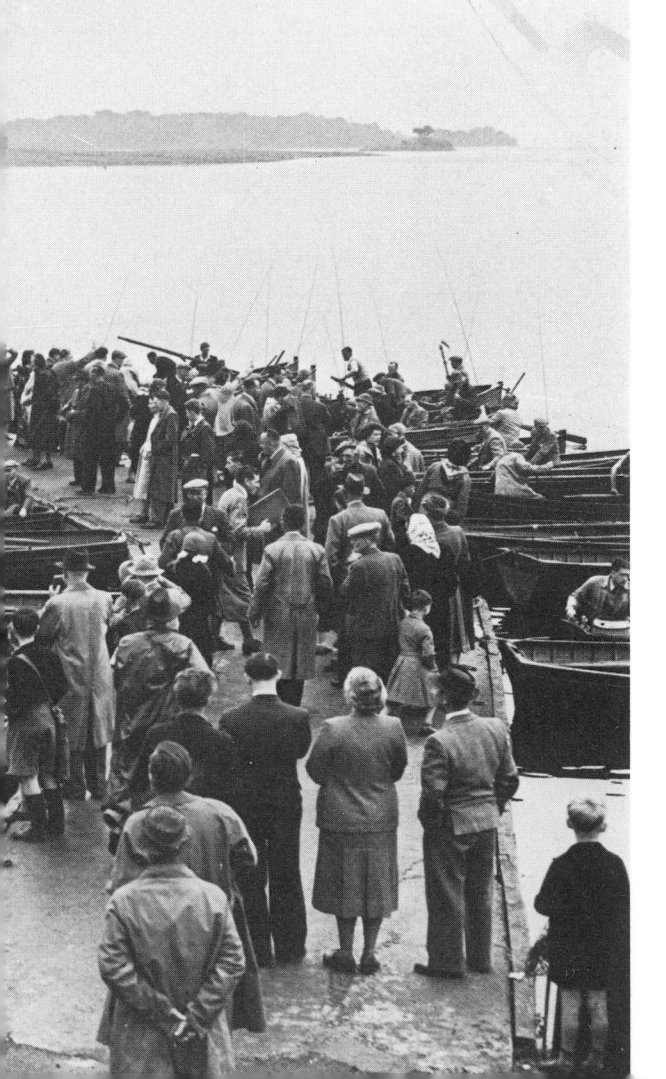

Loch Awe shares with Loch Lomond, the distinction of being the second longest loch in Scotland; it is beaten only by Loch Ness. It is a narrow loch which runs for twenty two miles between forested hills from near the Atlantic coast north eastwards to Ben Cruachan.

Loch Awe is the real 'Long Loch' of the famous *Oldest Boatman* stories of Alasdair Carmichael which have delighted generations of anglers reading the *Scots Magazine* over the years. It is noted for its large populations of wild brown trout ranging between half and one and a half pounds which can be caught throughout the varied drifts over shallows, across bays and among the islands. It is also famous as the home of large 'ferox' trout which used to be caught by trolling and spinning. Loch Awe was credited for many years with holding the record brown trout of thirty nine and a half pounds, caught by Mr Muir in 1866. However this is no longer accepted as a record fish.

Loch Awe has a long tradition of catering for the holiday anglers and there is a wide choice of accommodation from the hotels of Ford, Taychreggan and Portsonachan to the Forestry Commission self catering village of Dalavich.

The fishing season opens on 15 March and Loch Awe is one of the earliest lochs fishing well in March, April and May. No permit is required and all legal methods of fishing may be practised.

Loch Harray

Loch Harray fish are without doubt the prettiest brown trout I have ever seen and their fighting ability puts them completely in a class of their own.
TREVOR HOUSBY 1976

Loch Harray is the largest of Orkney's splendid trout lochs and is separated from its tidal neighbour, Loch Stenness, by the culverts at Brogar Bridge.

Loch Harray covers a windswept 1500 acres surrounded by the neat, dyked hayfields and the rolling moorlands of Orkney Mainland. It is a shallow water with extensive wadeable margins and areas of submerged reefs and shoals separating the deeper parts of the loch. Its clear water supports a rich food supply of caddis and mayfly

Rhododendron time on Loch Awe

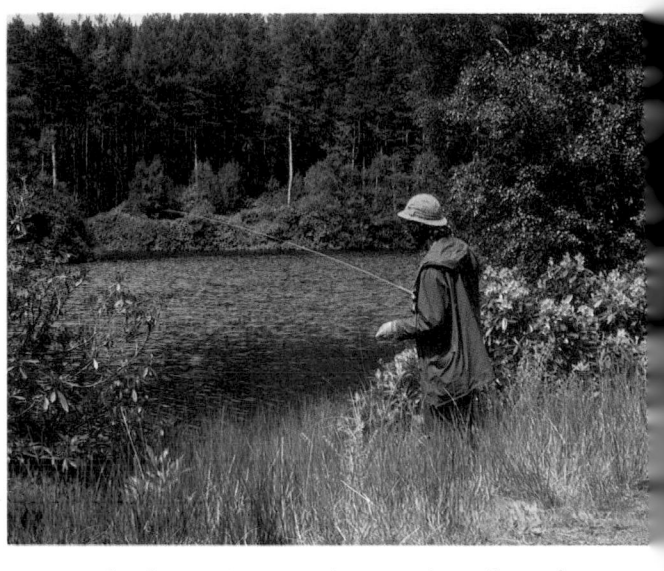

species but, more particularly, large populations of shrimps and snails which give the deep red colour to the flesh of the trout.

The trout themselves are magnificent fish. More like sea-trout than brown trout they are silver in colour with a profuse covering of black markings and a deep red flesh which is excellent eating. The trout average around twelve ounces but fish over three pounds are fairly common while the record stands at seventeen and a half pounds from the 1960's.

Under the ancient Odal law of this Norse part of Scotland, the trout fishing is free of charge and all legal methods of fishing are permitted. Bushy flies in the shape of Zulu, Palmer, Pennel and Ke-He are popular but other loch flies and nymphs can be successful. The Orkney Trout Fishing Association manages Loch Harray and other Orkney waters and a modest temporary membership fee allows the visitor access to their lochside facilities and supports their efforts. Boats can be hired locally and excellent accommodation is available at the Merkister Hotel on the lochside although few parts of Orkney Mainland are too far away from Loch Harray.

Loch Watten

We were fortunate enough to capture among us several dozens of fine trout, some of which were peculiarly marked, and much resembled fresh-run sea trout. . .
THOMAS TOD STODDART 1866

The windswept plain of Caithness is studded with lochs occupying shallow kettle holes in the glacial drift which overlies the old red sandstone flagstones. With an area of 940 acres, Loch Watten is the largest and, arguably, the best of them.

Loch Watten is an exposed, shallow loch with a mean depth of twelve feet which has remained free from enrichment and has retained its clear water. It has a rich feeding of various species of mayfly, stonefly and caddis while good populations of shrimp, snails and stickleback produce a trout which is famed for its pink flesh and silver colouring, similar to Loch Leven trout.

The trout average between three quarters and one pound and fish between three and four pounds

are caught from time to time. It is a fly only fishery and standard loch patterns of Zulu, Pennell, Ke-He and Butcher will produce average baskets of two to three trout per day but catches of up to thirty trout, averaging one pound, have been taken in a week's fishing.

The shallow margin allows safe wading and there are thirty boats available on the loch. Permits can be obtained from the Loch Watten Hotel and from tackle shops in Thurso and Wick.

Loch Sionascaig

. . . it is an awesome loch. . . Awesome, yet beautiful . . . part of a scene that epitomises the last remnants of wilderness in Britain.
RAY COLLIER 1982

Carved by the great ice sheets out of the hard pre-Cambrian rocks, Loch Sionascaig is one of the most interesting waters that stud the desolate landscape of Wester Ross and Sutherland. Situated in the Inverpolly National Nature Reserve and itself designated as a Grade 1 site of special scientific interest, Loch Sionascaig is an excellent example of the trout fishing available in the peaty, more acid, lochs of the north west Highlands.

Loch Sionascaig is an irregularly shaped water whose maximum length of three miles supports

some seventeen miles of shoreline and gives an area of 1500 acres. It is a deep loch, whose underwater contours form an intricate maze ranging from a mean depth of sixty feet down to a maximum depth of 216 ft.

Although the water is low in nutrients, the feeding is sufficient to produce trout whose average size of three quarters of a pound, includes a good number of fish between two and four pounds, while 'ferox' trout up to the loch record of sixteen pounds can be caught by trolling. A good day's fishing could produce a basket of twenty to thirty trout between half and one pound caught on standard pattern loch flies.

Because of the dangerous margins, no bank fishing is allowed but five boats are available on the water. Permits can be obtained from Inverpolly Estates Office, Inverpolly, Ullapool.

St Mary's Loch

The trout of St Mary's Loch, in point of external appearance and edible qualities, vary more than those of any sheet of water I am acquainted with.
THOMAS TOD STODDART 1866

If Loch Leven is considered the 'Mecca' of Scottish trout fishing, then St Mary's Loch must be considered to be its spiritual home. The beauties of the loch and its smaller neighbour, the Loch of the Lowes, have been extolled by Sir Walter Scott, Wordsworth and James Hogg , the 'Ettrick Shepherd'. It was the favoured haunt of Thomas Tod Stoddart and his friends who frequented the 'howff' of Tibbie Sheils Inn during the 1830s and could boast baskets of up to eighty trout including the big, wild 'Yellow Fins o' Yarrow Dale' which scaled up to three and a half pounds.

St Mary's is a rare example of a glacial loch in southern Scotland. Its 635 acres are surrounded by rolling hills and despite depths in excess of 150 ft there are extensive shallows around the edges and where the Megget water flows in. It has good hatches of fly and standard patterns and techniques produce good baskets of trout averaging ten ounces with specimens up to two and a half pounds. Other legal methods of fishing are allowed after 1 May.

The fishing is managed by St Mary's Angling Club which offers boat and bank permits from the bailiff, or from the local hotels. Tibby Shiels Inn and Rodono Hotel also have rights on the loch for residents seeking the 'tap-root' of Scottish trout fishing tradition.

Coldingham Loch

Some of the best trout fishing in Scotland is to be obtained . . . from a comparatively small loch nestling in a pocket of land above the coastal cliffs near Ayton in Berwickshire. This is Coldingham Loch. . .
TOM STEWART 1964

Coldingham Loch is one of the oldest established sport fisheries in Scotland and is the home of very large brown trout.

It is a small, spring fed loch of twenty two acres perched on the 500 ft cliffs at St Abb's Head near Berwick-upon-Tweed. It is also one of the richest stillwaters in Scotland and its high level of nutrients supports dense populations of algae and chironomids which themselves maintain strong populations of snails and sticklebacks. This rich feeding, combined with the constant spring water temperatures provide all year round growth for trout. There is no natural spawning, but stocked brown trout grow rapidly to weights in excess of five pounds and specimens of nine and twelve pounds have been recorded. Although these aldermen of trout do not fall easily to the fly, some are caught throughout the season. The main sport is provided by superb rainbow trout stocked at one to one and a half pounds which quickly develop into red fleshed silver beauties up to seven and a half pounds in weight.

It is strictly a fly fishing water. There are five boats available for hire and a limited number of bank rods are allowed. Although standard loch flies, including the bushy Zulus and Pennels are effective, buzzer patterns and deep sunk lures fished from stationary boats may be necessary to account for many of the rainbows.

Originally developed as a fishery in the 1920s, it is now owned by Dr E Wise, West Loch House, Coldingham, Berwickshire; residential holiday cabins also cater for the holiday angler.

167

The braes of St Mary's

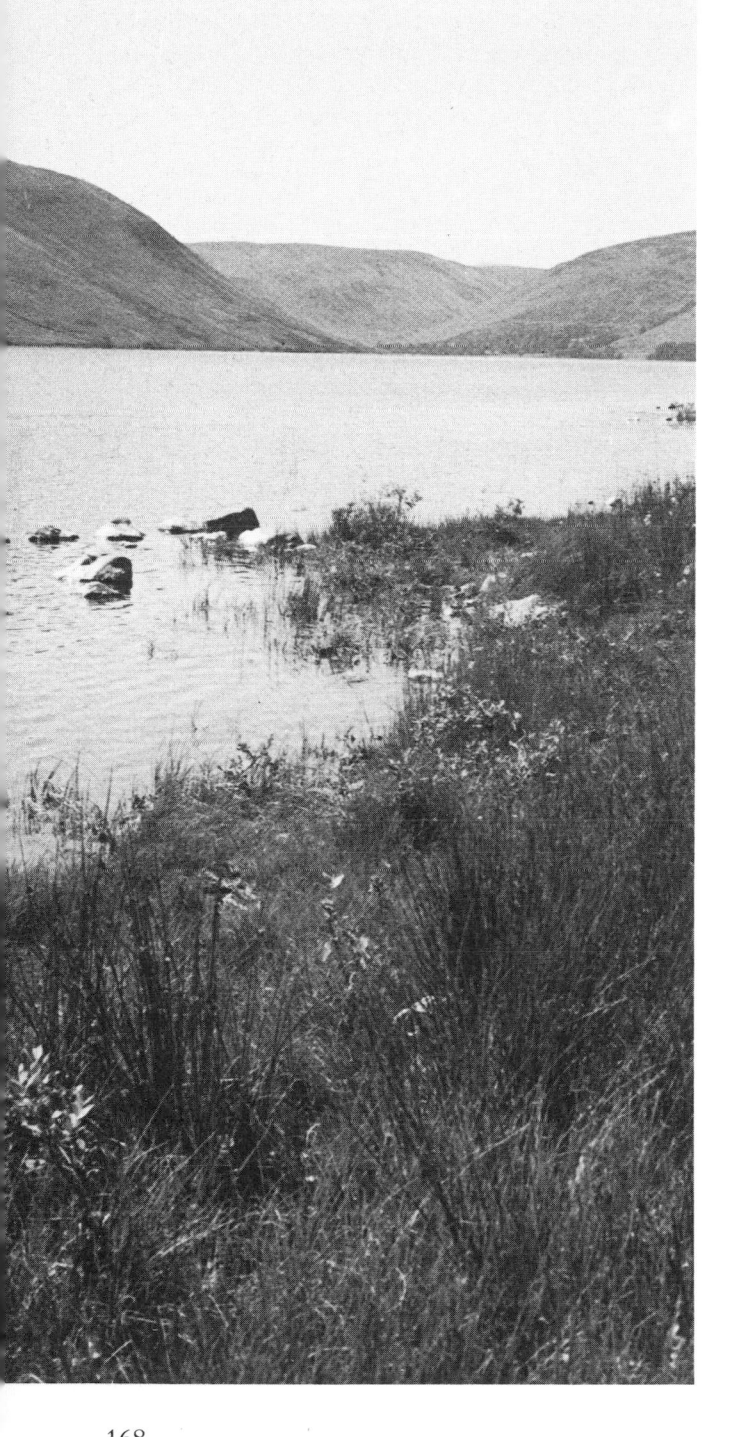

Lake of Menteith

Altogether it is a most luxurious fishery and speaks highly for the enterprise, skill and good taste of the management and their employees.
HENRY LAMOND 1932

The Lake of Menteith, Scotland's only 'lake', enjoys a picturesque position on the northern edge of the Flanders Moss overlooked by the wall of the Menteith Hills leading down from the Trossachs.

The lake covers some 660 acres and is a shallow eutrophic water occupying a kettle hole behind the moraine left by the last ice readvance.

As a fishery it has had its ups and downs since Henry Lamond's glowing tribute in 1932. It subsequently lapsed once more into a pike infested mere and it is only since the 1960s that the present owner, the Lake of Menteith Fishery Company Limited, has developed the lake into one of Scotland's new generation of put-and-take fisheries.

This task involved the systematic clearance of pike with the assistance of the Freshwater Fisheries Laboratory at Pitlochry and subsequent restocking with brown, rainbow and American brook trout.

Twenty boats are available and can be booked from the Lake Hotel, Port of Menteith. It is fly fishing only and while traditional loch patterns and techniques are successful, reservoir tactics of lures on sinking lines or 'buzzer' fishing may be useful for the rainbow and the brook trout.

Gladhouse Reservoir

Gladhouse is well managed, well fished and in many ways is typical of the best local authority controlled fisheries in Scotland.
BILL CURRIE 1980

Gladhouse Reservoir is one of the older water supply reservoirs built in 1874 to satisfy the needs of Edinburgh. It occupies a shallow depression under the ridge of the Moorfoot Hills and with its islands and fringe of woodland it is a very picturesque water.

With an area of 400 acres and an average depth of twelve feet it is a shallow mesotrophic water

Top: Fishing action on Menteith
Bottom: A peaceful scene at Carron Valley Reservoir

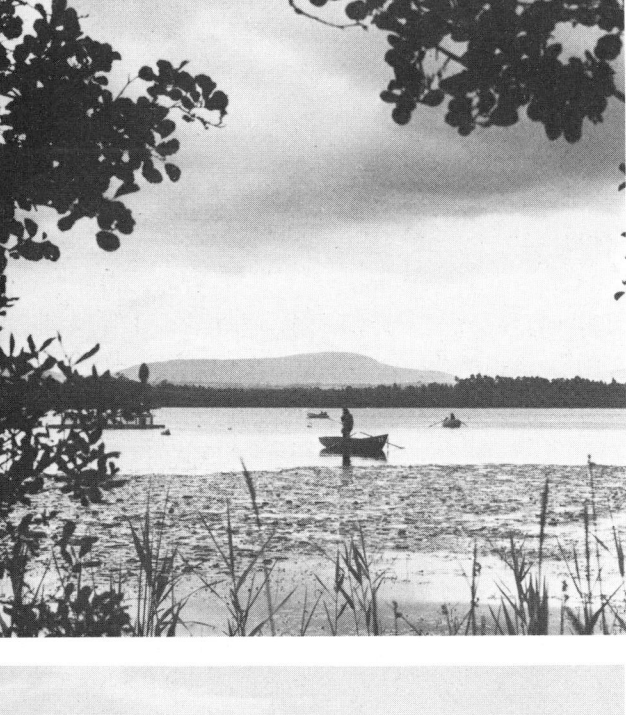

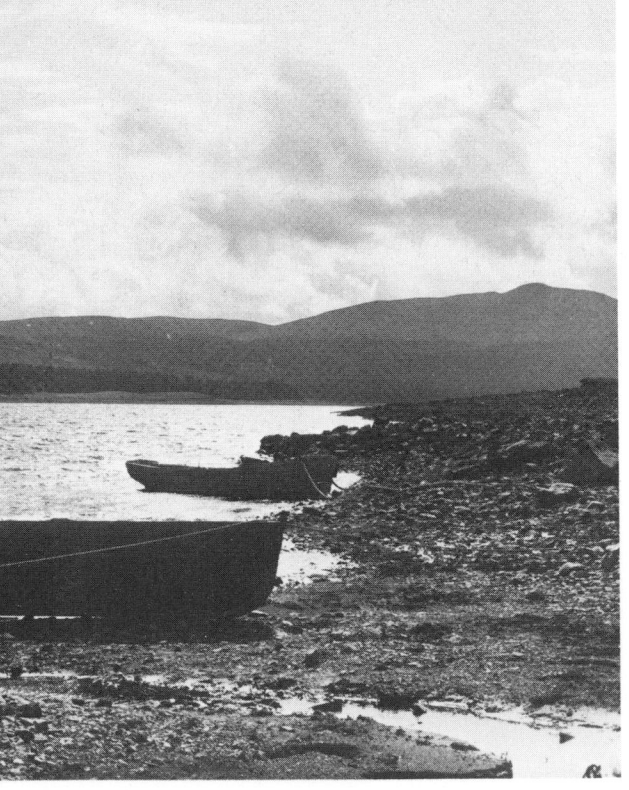

collecting the runoff from the Silurian shales of the Moorfoots. Its excellent spawning and good feeding supports a strong population of wild brown trout averaging eleven ounces. Specimens of three pounds are caught from time to time and the record stands at nine pounds. It is now given a supplementary annual stocking of ten inch brown trout.

It is a fly only water and standard patterns and techniques are effective. Although it can fish well throughout the season it is at its best in the evenings of May, June and July. The fishing is managed by Lothian Regional Council and permits for the boats can be obtained from the Department of Water Supply Services.

It was designated a local nature reserve in 1979 mainly on account of its huge winter population of pinkfoot geese, and these may be seen in the early and late weeks of the season.

Carron Valley Reservoir

The Water Board probably did not realize . . . that they were creating one of the best trouting lochs in Central Scotland, but this is what they certainly did.
TOM STEWART 1964

Carron Valley Reservoir sits high in a forested valley of the Campsie Fells midway between Glasgow and Stirling. Situated so close and accessible to the major urban centres of central Scotland, its 932 acres have been an important brown trout fishery since the reservoir opened in 1940.

Although the reservoir has been stocked from time to time with one year old and two year fish it relies on a natural population of wild brown trout which average between twelve and fourteen ounces. Twelve boats are available with outboard motors and can be booked from Central Regional Council, Director of Finance, Stirling. Early booking is essential.

Carron Valley is fly fishing only and standard patterns and techniques are used. In general small flies and light tackle are recommended and on occasions the dry fly can be successsful. The fishery opens in mid April and closes in mid September with the best months being May, June and September.

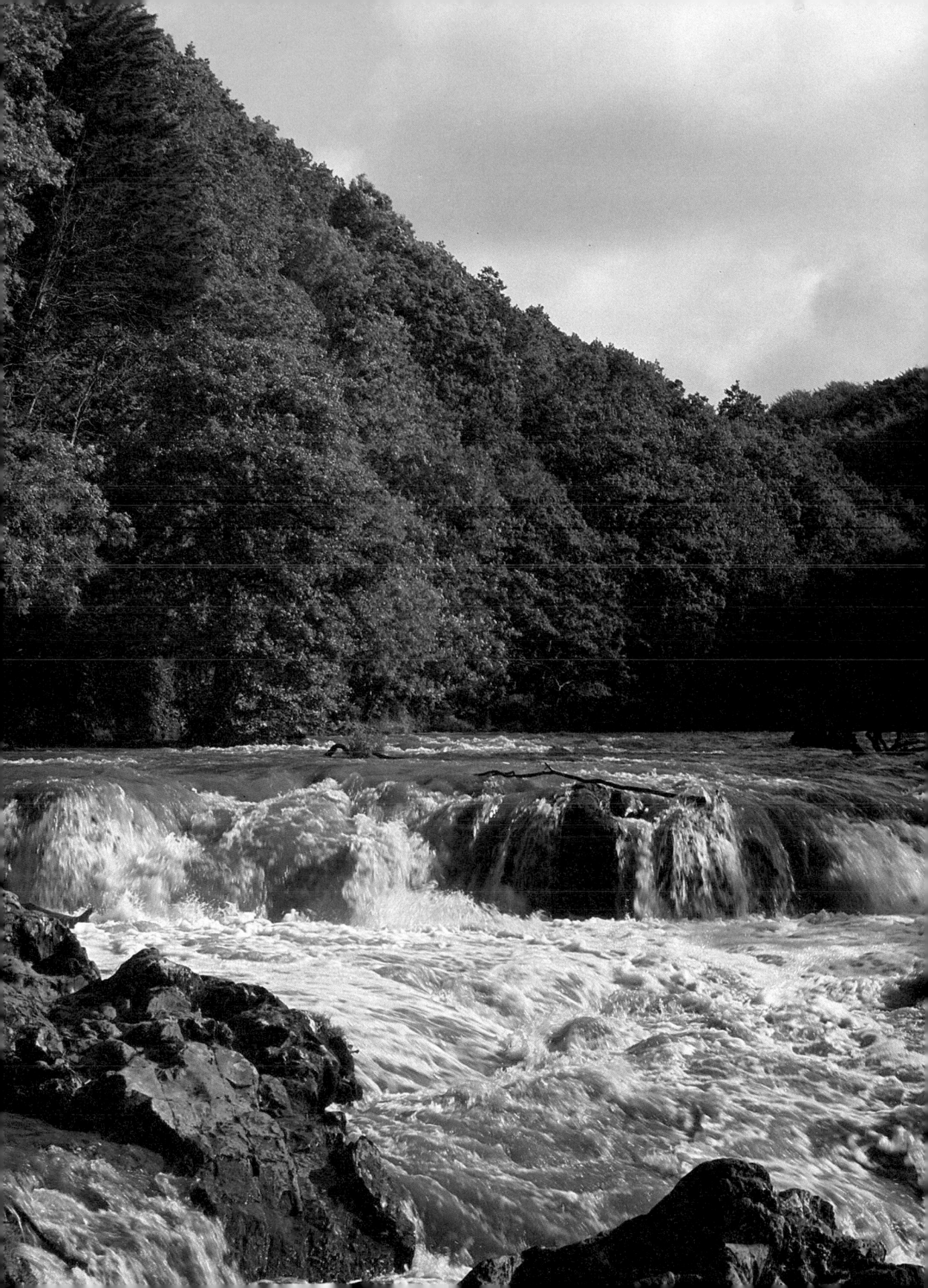

WELSH WATERS

WELSH RIVERS

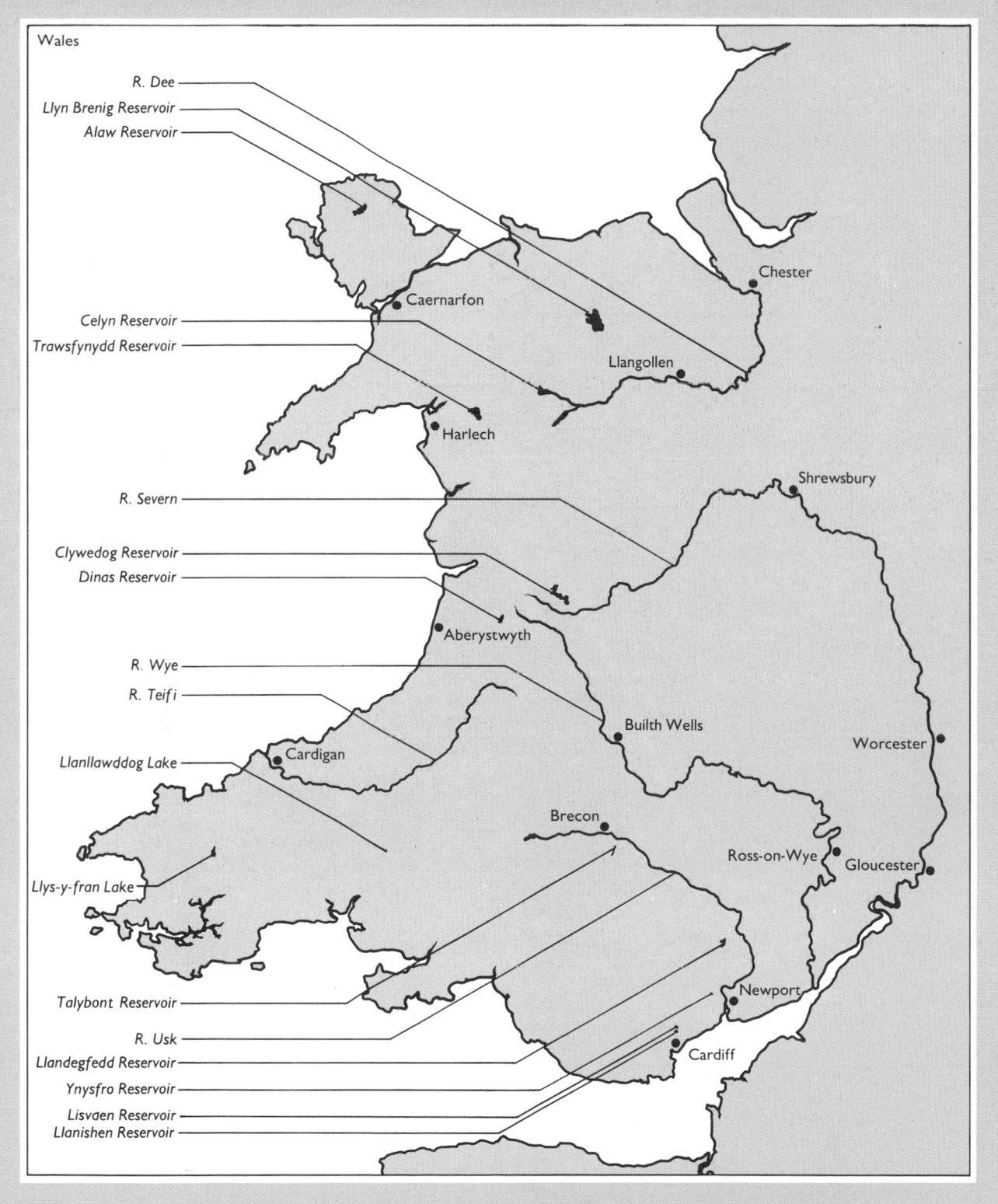

Wales

R. Dee
Llyn Brenig Reservoir
Alaw Reservoir

Chester

Caernarfon

Celyn Reservoir
Trawsfynydd Reservoir

Llangollen

Harlech

Shrewsbury

R. Severn

Clywedog Reservoir
Dinas Reservoir

Aberystwyth

R. Wye
R. Teifi

Builth Wells

Worcester

Llanllawddog Lake

Cardigan

Brecon

Ross-on-Wye

Gloucester

Llys-y-fran Lake

Talybont Reservoir
R. Usk
Llandegfedd Reservoir
Ynysfro Reservoir
Lisvaen Reservoir
Llanishen Reservoir

Newport

Cardiff

Previous page: Cenarth Falls, River Teifi   Unhooking an Usk brown trout

Usk

The River Usk is the finest trout river in the
Pincipality. It flows from the Carmarthen Fan
some 2,500 ft above sea level in a somewhat ir-
regular and erratic path down to Senny Bridge.
The Usk Reservoir in its upper reaches has some
regulating influence although the tributaries of
Crai, Senni and Cilien add to its flow considerably
as it broadens out above Brecon. The tributaries
Honddu, Yscir Fawr and Ysgir Fechan, Nant
Bran and Tarell join the main water course above
Brecon. These tributaries and the main river in
these upper reaches flow over red sandstone which
gives the water its rich red colour in flood times.
In the lower reaches the river flows over limestone, thus giving good water quality from the
point of view of natural feeding for the trout. It
is good food production that gives the Usk trout
their quick rate of growth.

In the middle reaches between the towns of
Brecon and Abergavenny the river is about the
ideal size for the dry fly angler. The runs and
glides offer him the perfect environment to enjoy
his angling. The river is considerably bigger in its
lower reaches and the emphasis is mainly on salmon but the trout fishing is also good. Certain
stretches around the town of Usk hold good
stocks of trout with some like the Usk town water
being stocked annually with twelve inch trout.

The best months for trout fishing are March
and April and most of the trout, especially in the
upper reaches, are taken then by the wet fly. The
Usk river is rich in fly life and in these early
months almost daily around noon a good hatch
both of olives and the March browns put in an
appearance. It is difficult to explain, but the wet
fly, fished downsteam, does really take a lot of
fish in these early days. I've watched anglers fishing just above Brecon even on cold spring days
bring good fish to the net from seemingly a dead
river. This wet fly fishing is practised also after a
flood and when the river is thinning down.

In the Senny Bridge area, where the river tends
to move quicker and the angler has to take fish
from the broken waters behind boulders and in
forceful runs, the use of the wet fly fished upriver
is effective. Some of the locals here use fairly long
rods which enable them to control their lines

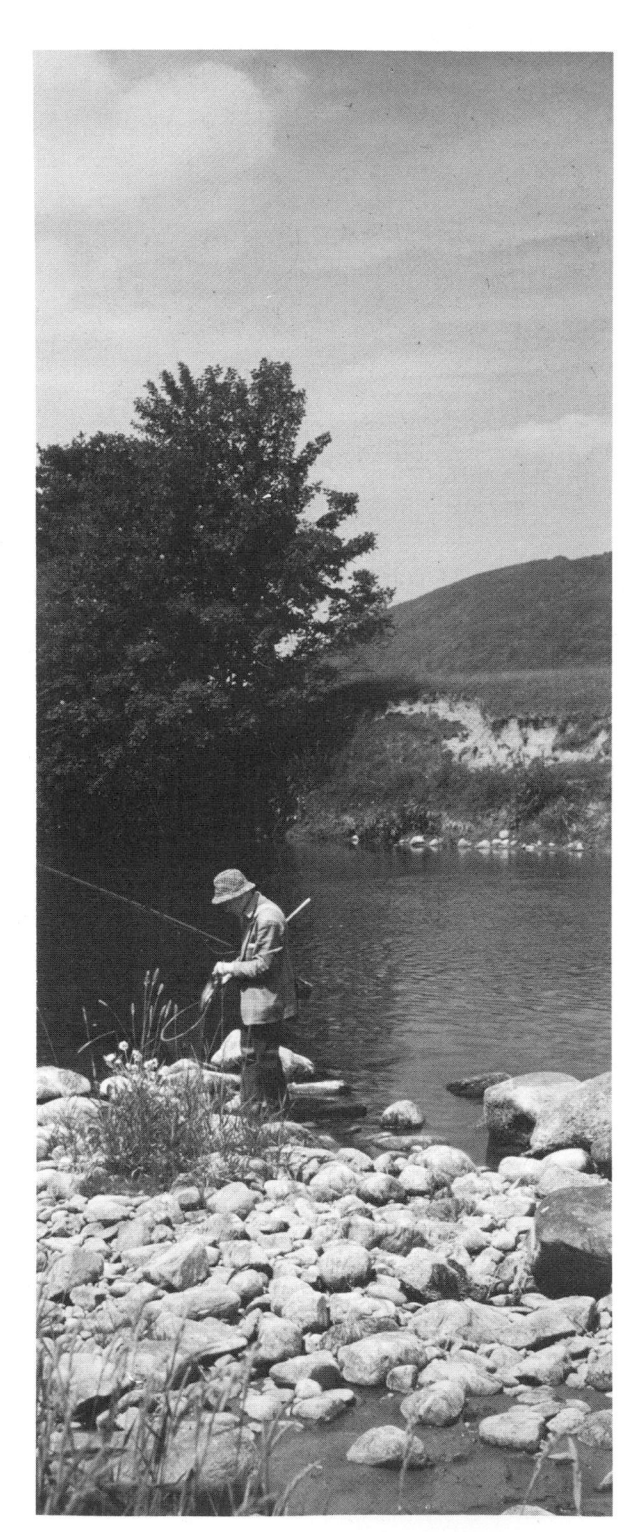

Usk's golden waters

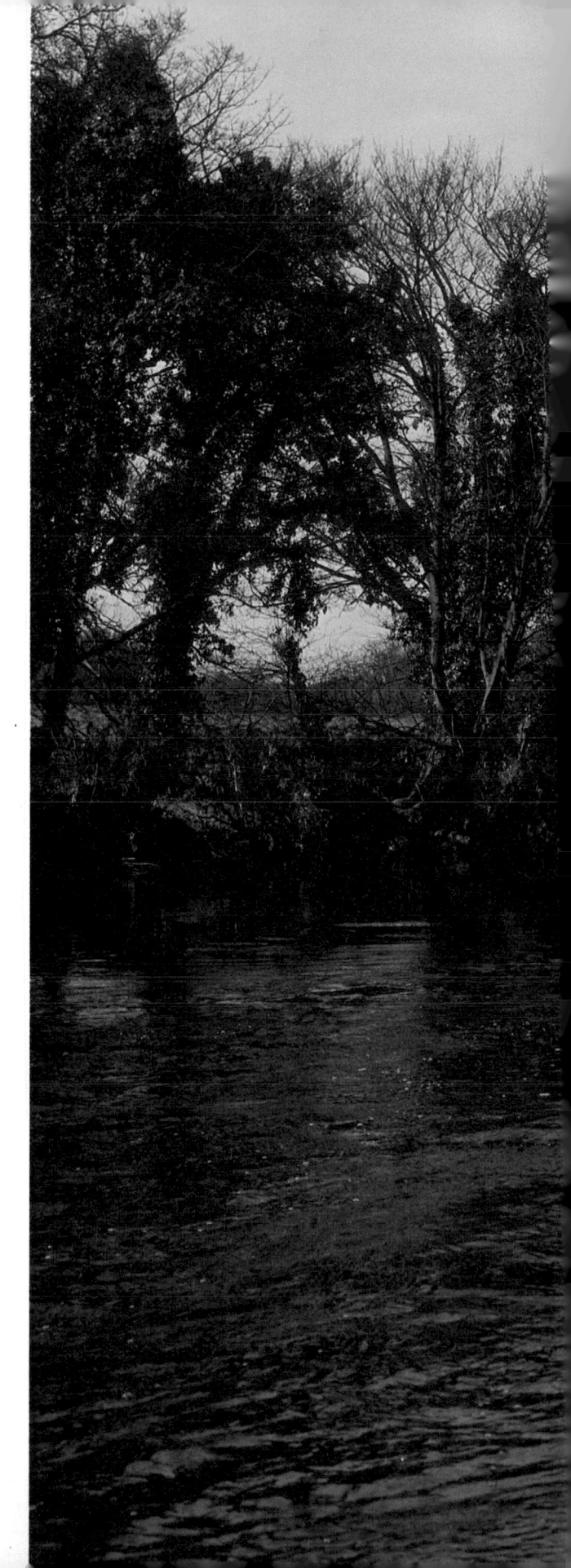

much better. They use the long rods to hold their lines well clear of the current after they have presented their team of two flies into the small holding areas behind the boulders. This is often a far more effective method of fishing this type of broken water than either the dry fly or the normal downstream wet fly.

The upstream nymph fishing can be effective especially on fishing like that managed by the Gliffaes Hotel near Abergavenny. This is superb water, ideal for the classical upstream nymph fishing method. The nymph method is also productive on waters which are fished by a fair number of anglers, such as that of the Abergavenny Town Council which is about one mile on the left and right bank downstream of Llanfoist Bridge.

The River Usk is really a dry fly river and early Welsh publications prove that it has a wealth of history of fishing the dry fly. One of the great Usk fisherman of yesteryear was the barber cum fly dresser Harry Powell of the town of Usk. He was responsible for developing such patterns as the Dogsbody which is such an excellent dry fly even on rivers other than the Usk (where of course it reigns supreme). The story goes that he gave a particular dog a trim while its master had a haircut and tied a fly with the dog's hair which is now known far and wide as Dogsbody. He taught Molly Sweet, the wife of the renowned Lionel Sweet, the salmon fly caster extraordinaire, and she in turn taught Jean Williams who now runs the Sweet Tackle Shop and still produces dry flies in the truly Usk style. No angler visiting the Usk should fail to visit this establishment.

Much of the trout fishing on the river Usk is in private hands but there are considerable stretches for which daily permits may be purchased. Some of these stretches are stocked annually but as this stocking is of a somewhat irregular nature, the would be visitor is well advised to make enquiries prior to his visit. The towns of Abergavenny, Brecon and Usk have ticket water available and at the right time of the season offer capital sport. Some hotels and farms offer excellent fishing such as the Gliffaes Hotel at Crickhowell. Some angling associations also control waters and one can recommend the association at Senny Bridge where the pressure is not too great.

Visitors to the area are well advised to think in terms of fishing the tributaries especially in late

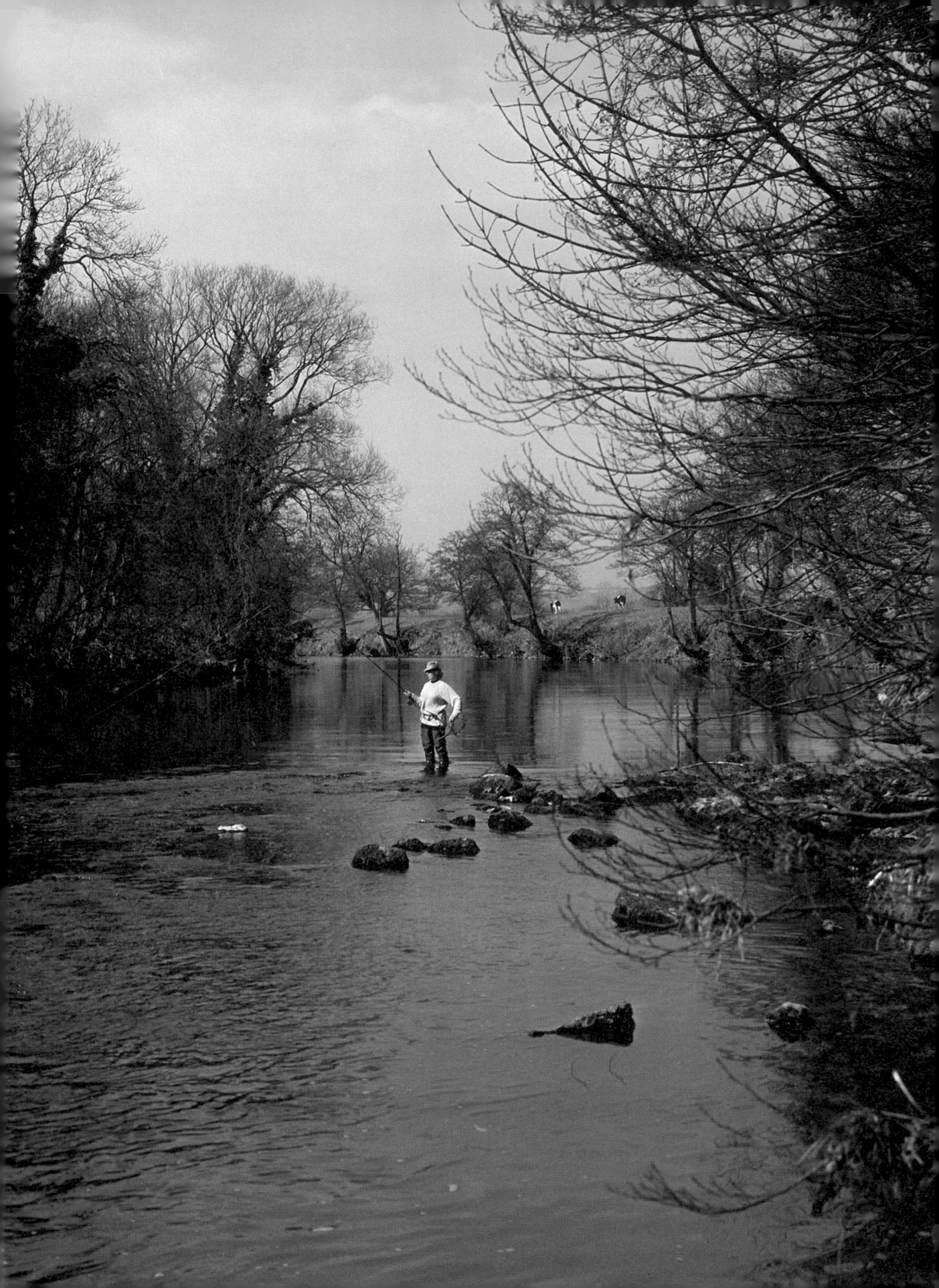

A fisherman fishes Teifi's deep pools

Teifi Pools, source of the Teifi

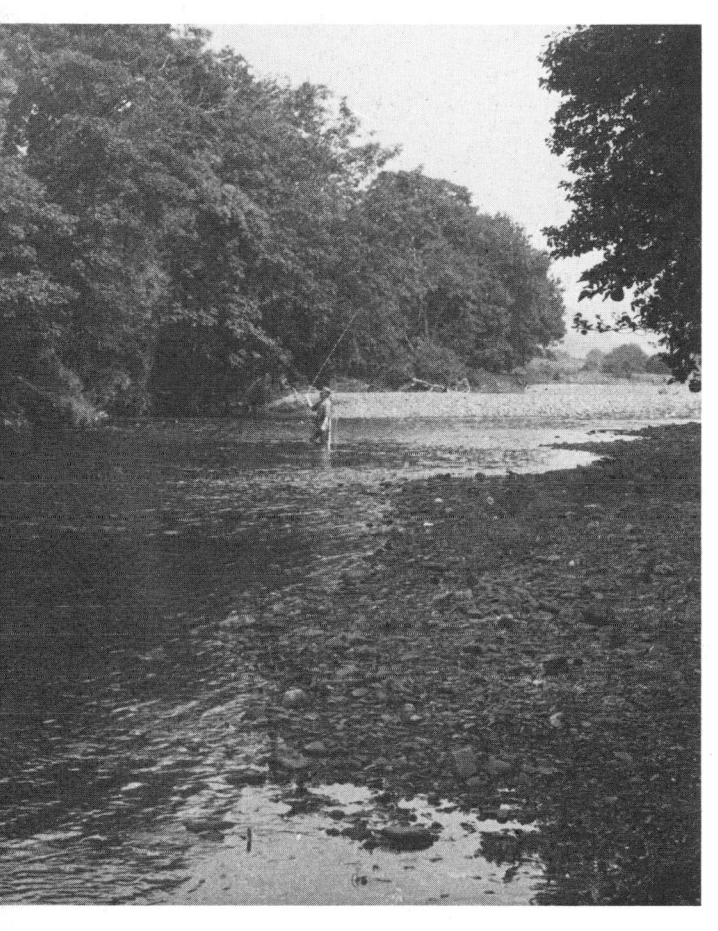

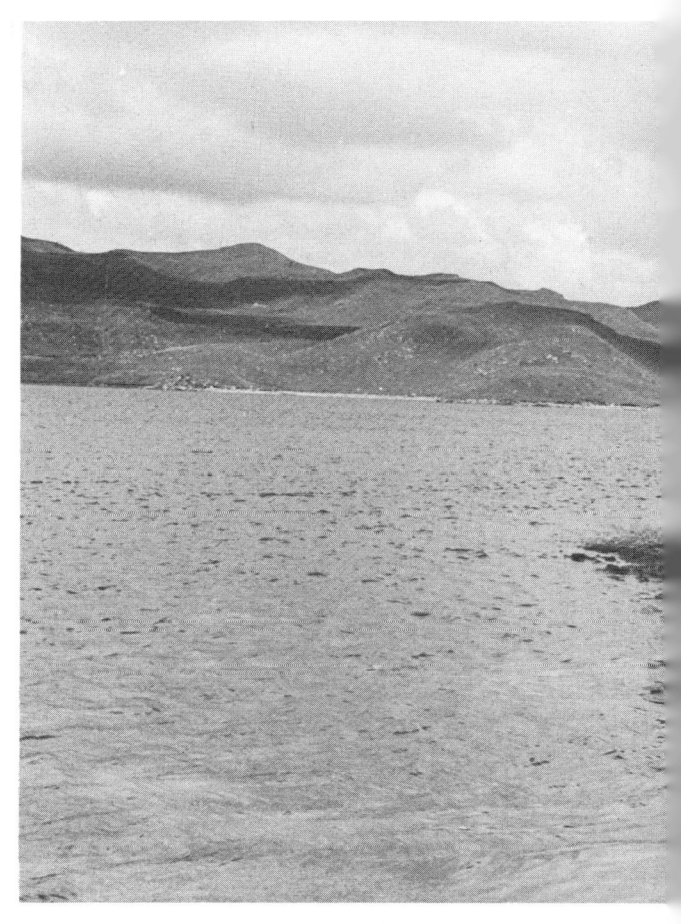

season. Some of these offer good and exciting trout fishing and are very reasonably priced, as is the Aberllech water on the Cilieni river. Some of the tributaries on the lower reaches, especially the Llwyd, although well stocked have been known to be polluted from time to time.

Teifi

The River Teifi has been described in an angling book as 'The Queen of Welsh rivers that wears her title with dignity!' It is that. It hails from the hills of mid Wales, from a cluster of five lakes known as the Teifi Pools, a wild grey country, home of the kite and the curlew, where buzzards hang motionless, suspended in the void as if by invisible threads. Here the river follows the path of the glacier of long ago through bulrushes and briars like an impetuous infant clattering and scurrying in a hurry to complete its journey.

On reaching the valley floor it travels in a lower gear through the village of Pontrhydfendigaid and into the seven mile long Caron Bog, an important nature reserve. It enters the bog as a juvenile and emerges fully mature. From Tregaron down to Lampeter the river, full bosomed, proud and of a more matronly decorum, flows majestically through lush meadowland. The pool, riffle and deep glides nature of the river make it ideal for the dry and wet fly angler. Between the towns of Lampeter and Llanybyther the river still holds good trout and, surprisingly, one pocket of grayling. The sewin are becoming more numerous than they were in this section. The serious trout angler can be advised to ignore the stretches below

The might of a fine Welsh river

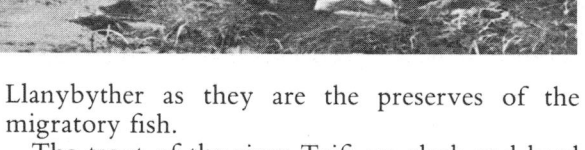

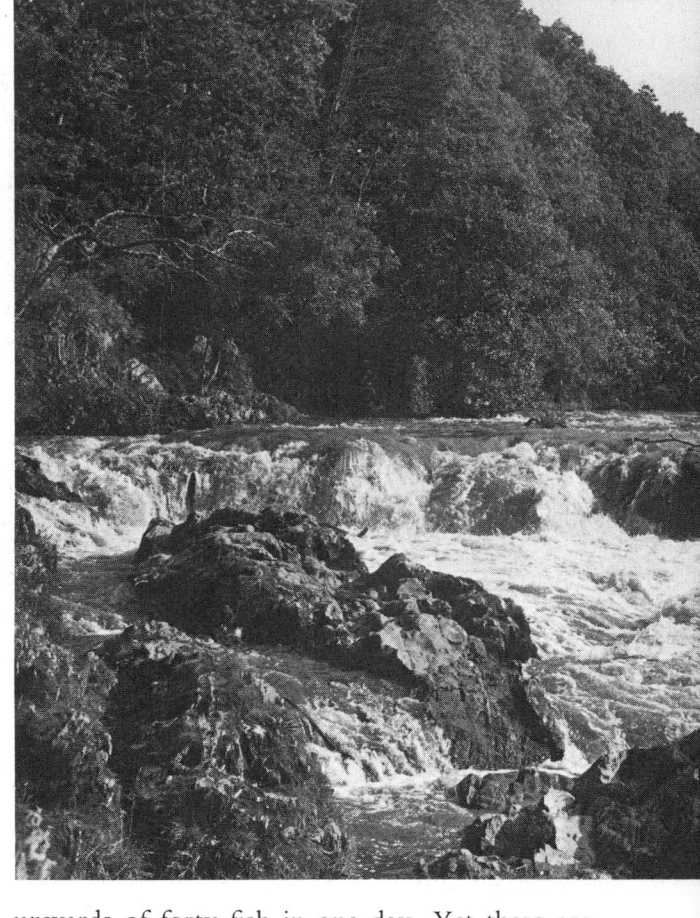

Llanybyther as they are the preserves of the migratory fish.

The trout of the river Teifi are sleek and hard and not of the bulging proportions of trout from rivers with better food supply. The trout are truly wild stock with very little re-stocking taking place. In the upper reaches the trout average about four to six ounces. In the middle reaches around Tregaron the average is up to ten ounces while in the area around Lampeter they can average as much as twelve ounces. The records of fish taken by anglers of yesteryear show that the average size of the trout has deteriorated and the three pound wild brown trout are unusual and not the commonplace as they were in 1832, as recorded in the book written at the time by George Hansard. They are also not as numerous as they were in the early fifties of this century when the late Rev Edward Powell used to visit Tregaron and take

upwards of forty fish in one day. Yet there are sufficient trout available to satisfy most anglers and the quality and quantity are showing slight improvements in the early eighties.

The fishing on the Teifi is of a traditional nature. The season opens on 20 March and from then until mid April the three fly cast fished down and across is still the popular method of taking fish. Even in March it is possible to take trout on the dry fly. For some reason the trout thus taken are of a better quality than those taken on wet fly. The late Ollie Kite used to visit Tregaron for his early season fishing and surprise the locals with his technique. It was at Pontllanion, some three miles downriver of Tregaron that the now famous Imperial dry fly was born. Ollie Kite used it in the spring of 1963 to entice trout, good conditioned trout, from pools which were skirted by twelve week old ice. The locals tend to use the three fly

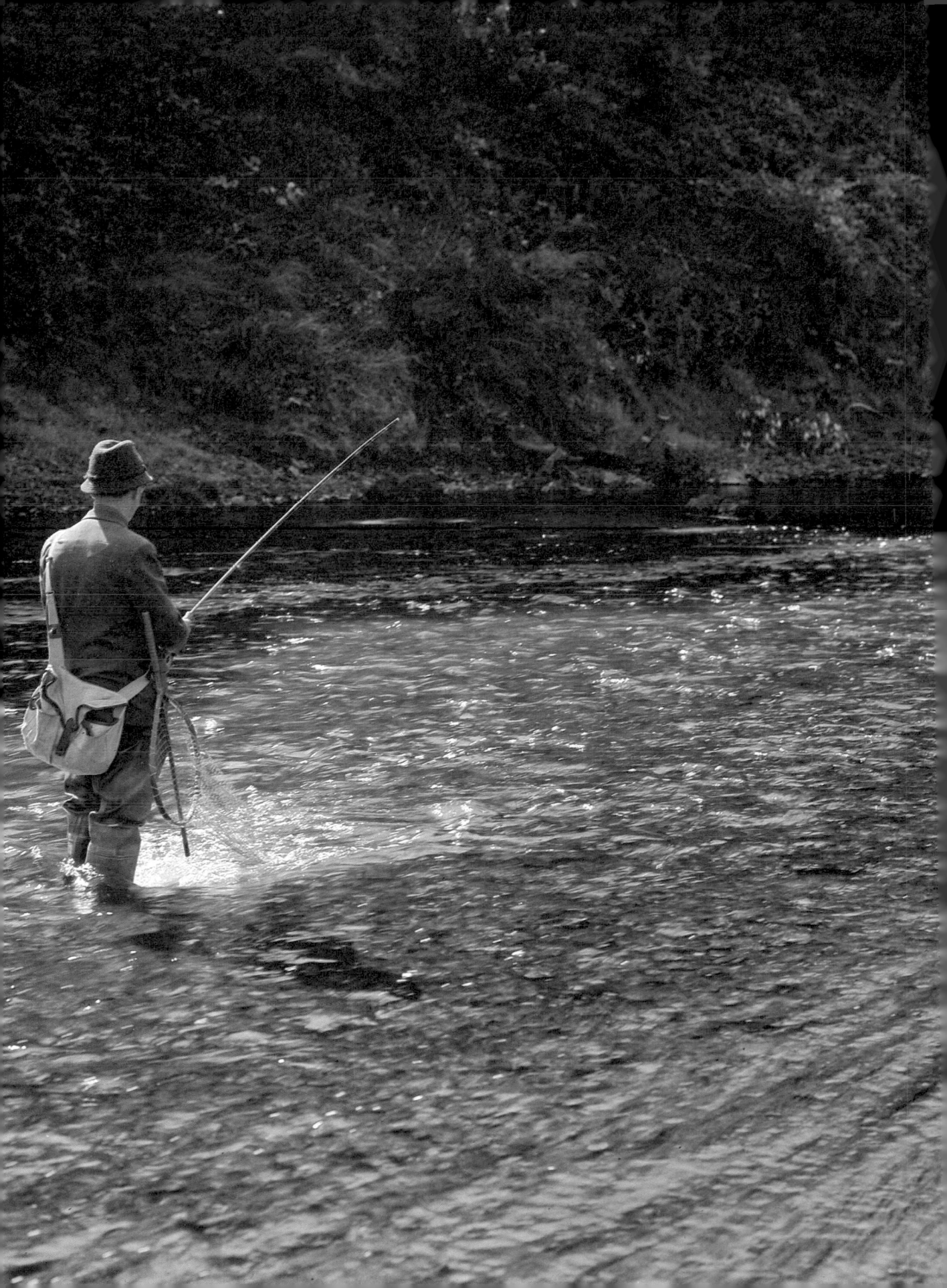

Left: Dry fly on the Teifi
Below: River Edw (Wye tributary) at summer level

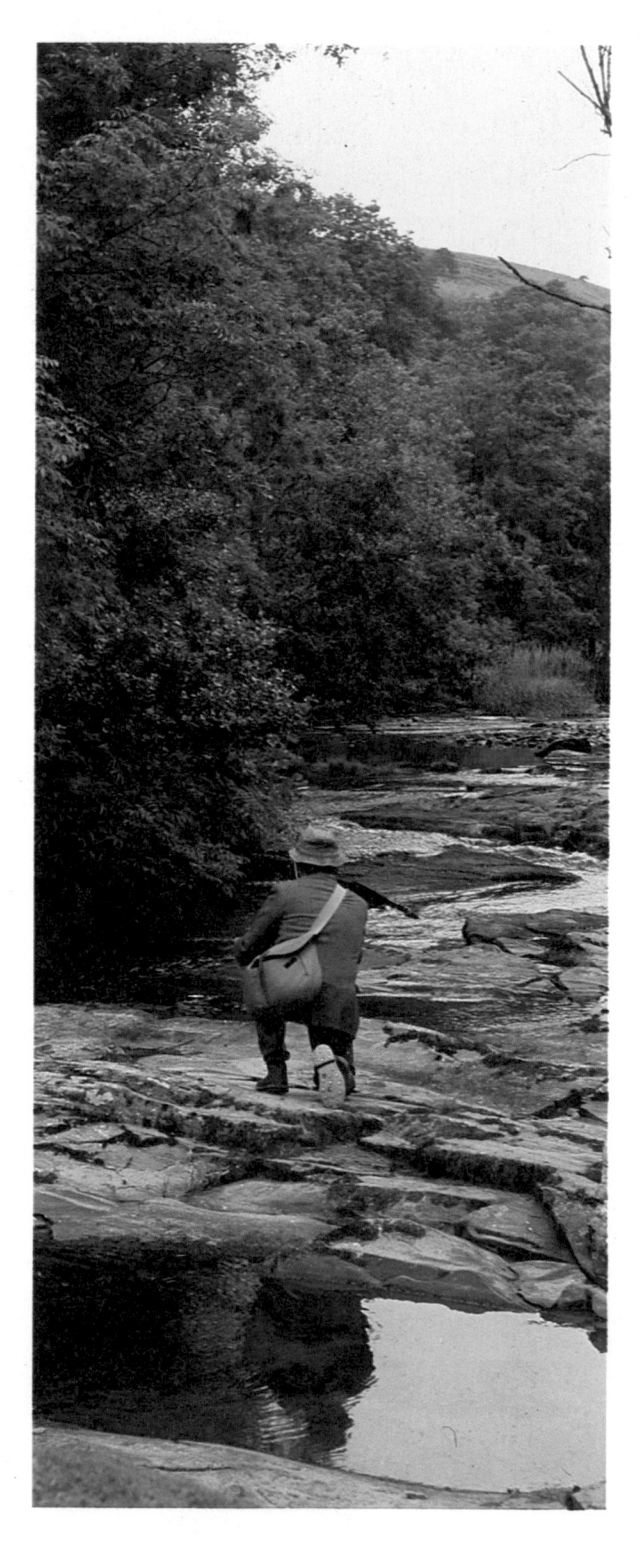

wet cast of Snipe and Purple, Greenwell and a dark Pheasant Tail. These are cast across and retrieved as they swing downwards and across the river. They change to the dry fly after the grannom hatches of mid April.

The dry fly offers the best sport on the river Teifi. There is a tendency to use a big bushy dry fly in the upper and middle reaches. Lightly dressed flies do better around the Lampeter area. The patterns of Vicar Powell, the Baby Sun Fly, the Devonshire Doctor and the Paragon will serve the angler well. Many of the successful dry fly anglers fish the broken water after May and the dry fly has to be an excellent floater. Often trout can be taken from these runs with little more than four inches of water by letting the dry fly float like a ping pong ball down the broken runs. The evening fishing starts in earnest in late May and it is then the best fishing time until September, when the day time fishing becomes more productive again.

There are virtually no restrictions on methods of fishing for trout on any of the stretches of the Teifi. The angler visiting the river does not need any specialised tackle. In the upper reaches around Pontrhydfendigaid where the wet and dry fly do well from early May onwards a nine foot rod or shorter would do well. Here the trout move quickly and the angler's reaction must be the same. Here the angler should take a leaf from the snipe shooter's book, that is to take a light heart and light tackle and be prepared to walk. The fishing in this area is controlled mainly by the Pontrydfendigaid Association but it would seem that it is shortly to be amalgamated with the Tregaron Association which controls much of the water down river as far as Lampeter. From Lampeter downriver the Llandysul and Llanybyther associations control good stretches.

Wye

The River Wye is rightly recognised as the premier salmon river in England and Wales and one of the best coarse fishing rivers in Europe. Its record for trout fishing is not in the same high category but it does nevertheless offer the trout angler good sport. Most of the good trout fishing

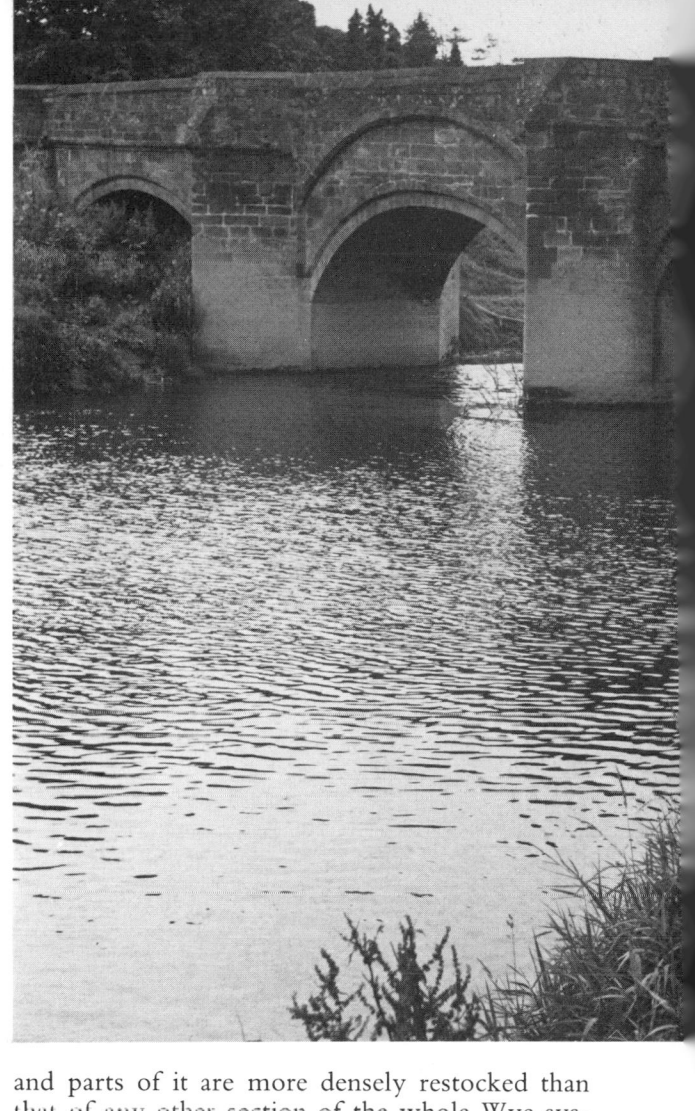

is to be had in the upper reaches of the river and in the tributaries, although there are a few pockets of trout here and there in the course of the main river in the middle and lower reaches.

The River Wye falls off the eastern slopes of Plynlimon mountain in mid Wales and covers some 150 miles before it enters the Severn estuary south of Chepstow. In its infant stages the Wye is a rushing boulder strewn mountain stream which drops some 1000 ft in a short distance. This area is the game angler's preserve. The Wye, joined by the fast flowing Tarenig, matures by the time it reaches Llangurig which is the first major fishing station on the upper river. From Llangurig to Rhayader the fishing for the modestly sized brown trout is very reasonably priced and is really interesting. The Rhayader Angling Association, which controls the Hedre water at Llangurig, and the Clockfaen Estate have ticket waters in these upper reaches. The Elan Valley Hotel, in Elan Village, caters for anglers and in addition to being an ideal centre for an angler visiting the area is conveniently placed near to the Elan Valley Reservoir complex. These reservoirs offer good sport at times but it is advisable to contact local anglers to discover the latest fishing bulletins.

A few miles north of Rhayader, the Wye is joined by the Marteg which like the upper Wye offers its best fishing after the waters have warmed up in May. Two miles below Rhayader the River Elan joins the Wye and it could be described as the first of the major tributaries. The Elan flows from a big reservoir complex and is therefore to some extent a controlled river, running over rock and gravel. Some anglers would say that its cold water released as compensation water adversely affects the fishing downriver.

Two important tributaries join the Wye before it gets to Builth Wells; they are the Ithon and the Irfon. The Ithon runs through a broad based valley and moves slowly below Penybont. It is a super river for the dry fly angler and is fairly heavily fished. Visiting anglers can secure angling on hotel water at the Severn Arms Hotel at Penybont and the Walsh Arms water at Llanddewi. The Llandrindod Angling Association have five miles of water which is open to visiting anglers and is very reasonably priced.

The River Irfon is a popular river which gives excellent fishing with the dry fly. It is well stocked

and parts of it are more densely restocked than that of any other section of the whole Wye system. The Lake Hotel at Llangamarch is a lively centre for the angling visitor. Its waters are stocked annually and in addition to four miles on the Irfon, it has one mile on the Dulas and one mile on the Chwefru.

The Cammarch Hotel (also at Llangammarch) has water on the Irfon itself, the Cammarch and the Dulais. It is gratifying to note that both hotels have fly only stretches. Upriver on the Irfon from Llangammarch the next centre is Llanwrtyd Wells famed as a health spa half a decade ago with its medicinal waters.

Fishing permits are available from the Neuadd Arms and the Dolcoed Hotel and also from the local angling association at Llanwrtyd. From Builth downstream the River Wye becomes a predominantly salmon and a coarse fish river, but it is interesting to note that the trout although far, far fewer in number are of better average size. Yet by the time the river reaches Hereford, trout fishing has virtually died as a sport.

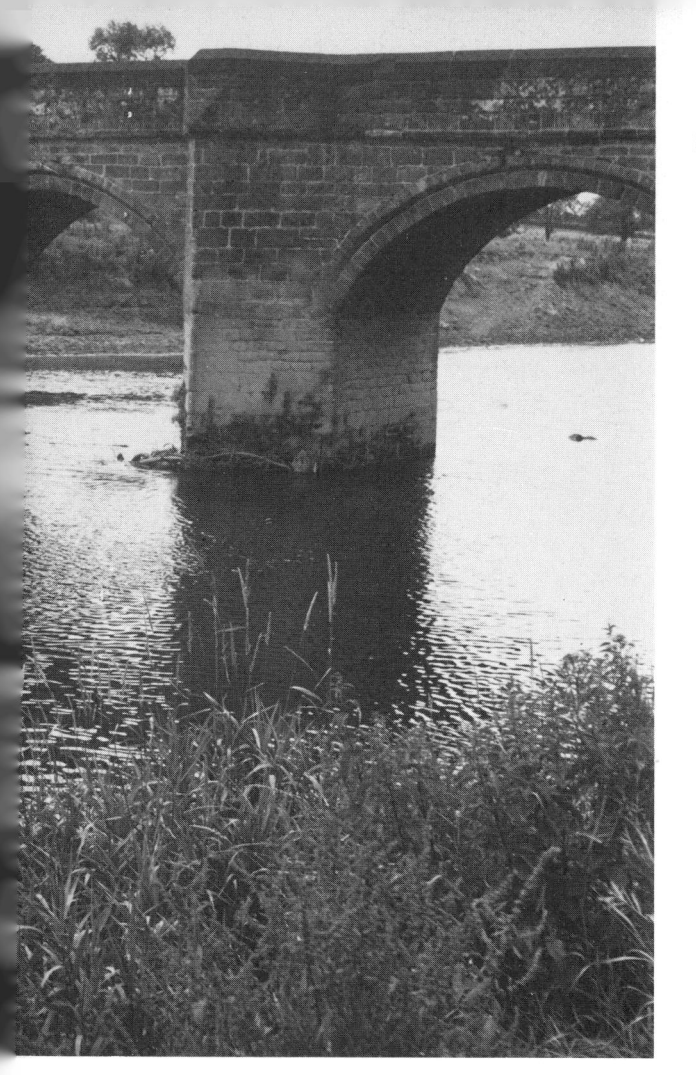

Bridge over the Dee at Farndon

The Monnow, probably the best trout water in the whole of the Wye system joins the Wye just below the town of Monmouth. This lovely little river, forming the boundary between Herefordshire and Gwent, contains numerous trout which rise freely to the floating flies, although some of the old anglers will maintain that this is not with the regularity of yesteryear. The sedges, March browns, mayflies and olives still occur but not in former profusion. Many of the regular dry fly purists are now using the wet fly despite, as one put it, being a bit chancy and slightly unethical.

The dry fly has produced angling giants in this border country and the Grant's Indispensable, Barrett's Professor and Powell's Orange Otter are still thriving despite the demise of their creators.

Dee

The River Dee rises on the Aran mountains in Mawddwy Gwynedd and flows through Bala, Corwen, Llangollen, Overton and Chester. The trout angler's attention should be focussed on the upriver stretch from Llangollen, together with a few of the main tributaries downriver. It is a major salmon river and holds good stocks of dace, roach and bream.

In its upper waters the Dee is a mountain stream, swift flowing and offering interesting fishing to the angler who is prepared to work for his rewards. Stretches on the Dee, Lliw and Twrch are held by the Llanuwchllyn Angling Association whose daily permits are very reasonably priced. Many of the local anglers do well with the worm fished in the running sections. The Dee then enters Bala Lake, the biggest natural lake in Wales which holds thirteen different species of fish including the rare gwyniad. The season opens for trout fishing on this lake on 15 January, certainly a very early kick off for a fishery consisting mainly of wild brown trout.

Below Bala the trout fishing improves and Bala Angling Association issues tickets for the upper Rhiwlas Estate water. It also has good water on the River Treweryn which holds a good stock of fish. This river is the canoeists' playground but the canoeists and anglers in Bala have an excellent relationship. The trout fishing in the Corwen area is really good though somewhat difficult of access for the visitor. Two hotels at Glyndyfrdwy, the Berwyn Hotel and the Royal Hotel, issue day permits for some four miles of fishing just below the Glyndyfrdwy bridge with the former also having nearly two miles of fishing above the bridge for its residents.

The most important station for the trout angler on the River Dee is Llangollen. This town is famed for its International Eisteddfod and the visiting angler would do well to miss the Eisteddfod week (the first week in July) if he needs accommodation in the area. The visitor would do well to call on Neil Elbourne, the secretary of the Llangollen Association at his newsagent shop. He will there be advised on the trout fishing on the six miles that is managed by the association. Much of this water is stocked annually and there is a fly only stretch above the chain bridge. The area fishes best from June onwards.

The River Dee is often undervalued as a trout fishery. Many anglers will claim that it is not as good as it was a decade ago but careful scrutiny

Trout water on the upper Severn

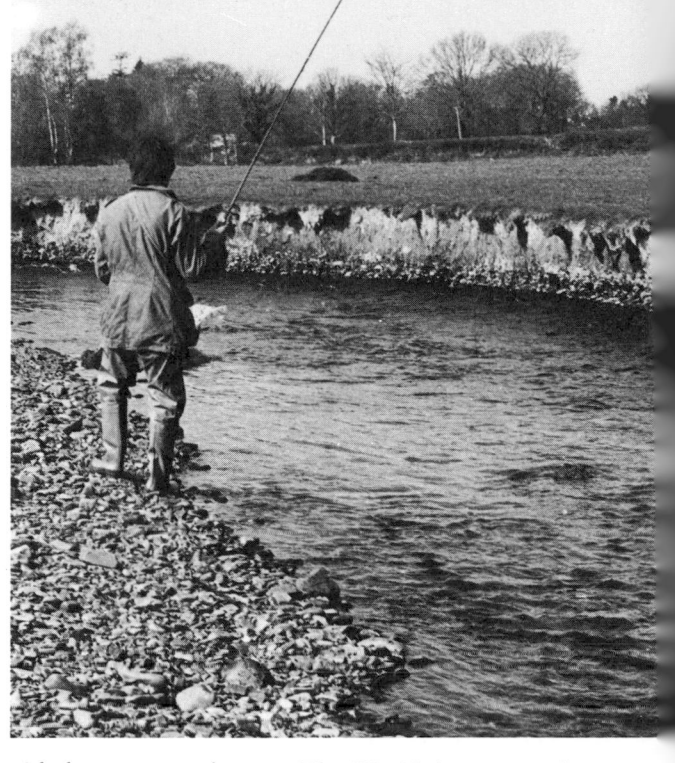

of recorded catches reveals that it still offers interesting fishing. I found that the dry fly took the better trout from some of the more popular stretches and that the stocked fish quickly adapted themselves to provide worthwhile sport. The Llangollen Association in addition to offering good fishing for the fit angler is doing excellent work for the handicapped angler too. It is indeed a lively club and a very good place for the angler to visit.

Down river from Llangollen, near the town of Chirk, the tributary Ceiriog joins the Dee. The Ceiriog has a special attraction for most Welsh anglers in that it gave its name to one of the most popular poets ever to write in Welsh. He wrote a very attractive poem about the mountain river and the very word Ceiriog brings the mind to focus on the small mountain river rushing down the valley. The trout fishing in its lower reaches to the junction with the main River Dee is managed by the Chirk Angling Association and the water is confined to fly fishing only. Further upriver by the Golden Pheasant Hotel at Dolywern the fishing is reserved for hotel residents only. It is an attractive hotel run by an attractive family and well worth a call. The upper reaches at Llanarmon are available to the visiting angler on application to the West Arms Hotel. The river runs through a truly picturesque valley and despite the fact that on each of the last three visits that I have paid there, the heavens have wept and the mountains have been shrouded in pregnant black clouds, I still think the poet was a fortunate man to have been born there.

The Alun tributary is the last major tributary to join the Dee and has considerable trout fishing available for visitors. The Gresford and Rossett Angling Association stocks annually as does the Wrexham and District Angling Association, so the Alun can be described as a pleasant river to fish. A number of the stretches are fly only; wet and dry fly are equally effective.

Severn

Most Welsh children will have learnt the little poem about three important rivers once sleeping on the Plynlimon mountain and of how they de-

cided to race to the sea. The Rheidol went crashing down into Cardigan Bay, the Wye took a longer course to Hereford and the Severn flowed 220 miles to provide anglers with a superb coarse and game river before entering the Bristol Channel. The trout angler must concentrate his efforts on the upper reaches and on the tributaries.

Above Llanidloes the Severn is little more than a narrow, shallow trout stream, with intermittent deep pools and fast runs. The acid nature of the water ensures that the trout are small but give good sport with a fly. The Birmimgham AA stretch is fly only but the Llanidloes stretch is open to all methods.

Downsteam of Llanidloes at Llandinam the Severn and Trent Water Authority control four and a half miles of both banks where fishing is available on day and season permits. This without doubt represents the best trout fishing on the Severn. The stretch is known as the Dinam Estate fishery. The river is an attractive fly water with pools, fords and gravel bottomed glides. Nearly 2000 brown trout of around eleven inches are stocked, some early season and the rest in mid season. The trout there, I found, are not too sophisticated in their tastes and the normal dry fly patterns will suffice. A lightly dressed Hare's Ear does well especially when the olives are hatching. One bonus on this particular stretch is the controlled outflow from the nearby Llyn Clywedog which ensures that the river is in condition when

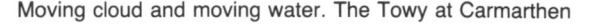

Moving cloud and moving water. The Towy at Carmarthen

the adjoining tributaries are running high and discoloured. It is too often inadvisable to quote the permit price to fish a particular stretch of water as prices vary from season to season and a price quoted can be disastrously wrong before the statement appears in print. Yet this stretch is still very very reasonable for a four quality fish limit fishery.

The river, because of its meandering course, slows between Caersws and Newtown and the trout population thins out considerably. The best grayling in the river Severn are found in this section. The tributaries of Carno and Rhiw contain some trout fishing which is available on a daily permit basis.

The only other trout fishing in the Severn system is that on the Vyrnwy. This river flows out the Vyrnwy Reservoir where a super fishery is promoted. The Vyrnwy Hotel, which is everything that a fishing hotel should be, is responsible for the fishery and stocks annually with predominantly brown trout. Below the dam the River Vyrnwy is also managed by the hotel. The Vyrnwy is joined by the Banwy and the Tanant. The latter is small and shallow yet surprisingly good for trout, flowing through beautiful hill country. There are ample places for the visiting angler to secure a day permit on the three rivers.

Lesser Rivers

There are many rivers in Wales which are designated as migratory fish rivers and very little serious trout fishing is conducted on them. Most of the fishing on such rivers is done with big flies and baits for the salmon or the sewin. In recent years, with the decline in the salmon runs, the sewin runs seem to have become better both in quality and quantity. Some anglers do however fish for trout on these rivers with very encouraging results.

Towy
The Towy in south west Wales is rightly famed for its sewin. The construction of a massive dam in its upper reaches has resulted in a more regular flow and the growth of some weed. In the middle reaches around Llanwrda the trout fishing has

Top: In the upper Dovey valley
Bottom: Relaxing beside the Mawddach

been improving during the early eighties and offers satisfactory sport, especially in the evening to the serious sewin angler as he waits for darkness before commencing his sewin fishing.

Camddwr

In the upper reaches of the Towy above the Brianne Reservoir, the rivers Doethie, Camddwr and Towy have developed into a fair trout fishery. The pick of the three is the Camddwr which has miles of open fishing where the upstream wet fly scores well. The road leading to the little chapel on the mountain called Soar, skirts the Camddwr for most of its length and permission is readily given by farmers; some stretches are covered by associations. This area offers superb chances for a serious young angler to learn the dry fly. These remote fisheries are best reached by travelling on the mountain roads from Llandover or Tregaron.

Tawe

The River Tawe which enters the sea at Swansea is another migratory fish river with an extensive trout fishery. Unlike the previous fishery this one tends to be rather heavily fished but it has an extensive stocking policy. The Tawe and Tributaries Angling Association breeds some seven to eight thousand brown trout in a rearing pond at Craig-y-Nos and these are released into the river during the season. Extensive drainage schemes have denuded the river of much of its holding pools but it still provides, in that area, opportunities to enjoy trout fishing.

Taff

A dramatic change is taking place in the rivers of South Wales and the rivers that have run 'Bible black' with coal dust for the last century are now supporting trout. Big trout are even seen in the middle of Merthyr town the heart of the industrial area. Stocking is conducted in various sections of the River Taff but it will be the latter half of the eighties before it is fully recovered and offers serious game fishing.

Neath

The Neath which rises in the Brecon Becons is also recovering from pollution and is re-stocked annually by the Neath & Dulais Angling Club and

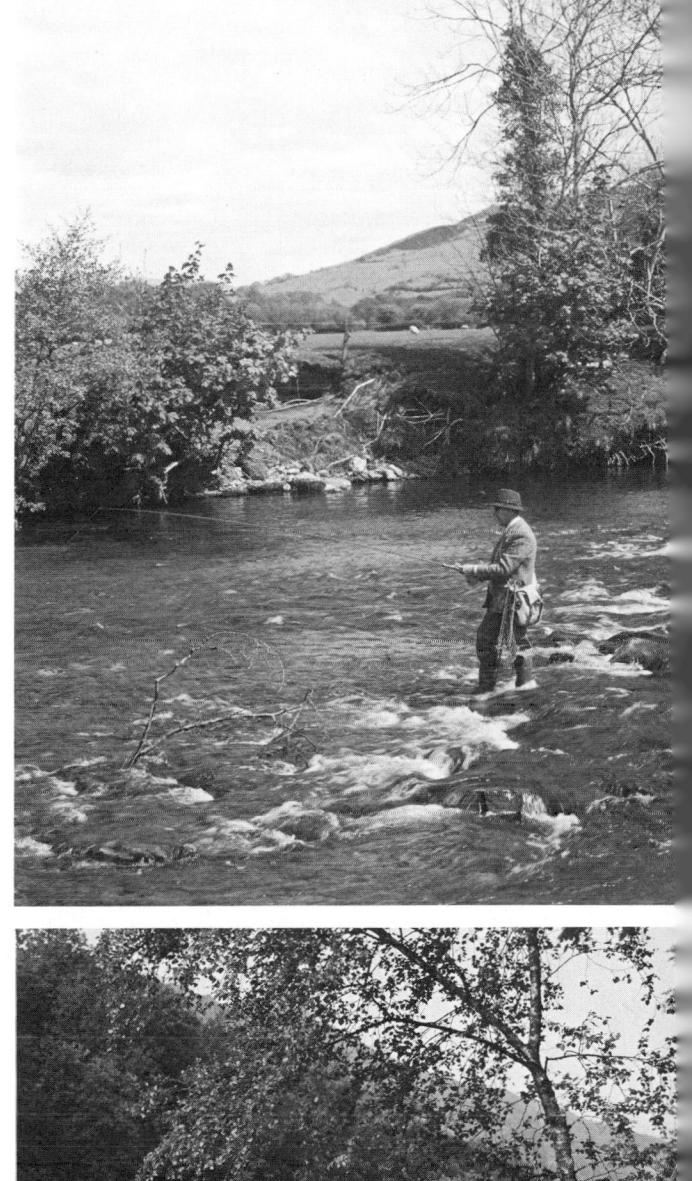

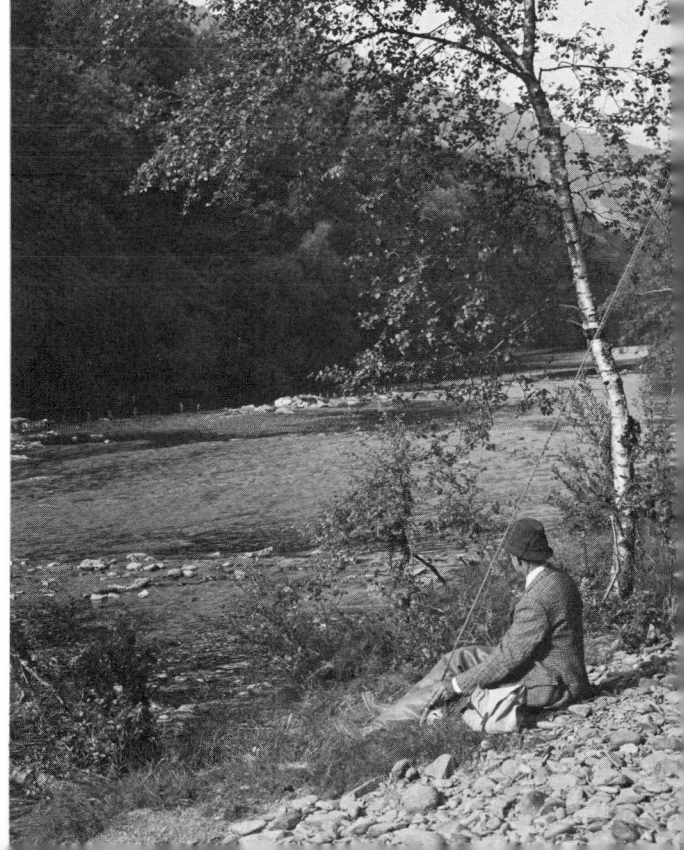

The Ystwyth provides some rugged fishing

the Glynneath Angling Club. The same is true of the Ogmore and the Ewenny at Bridgend.

Aeron, Ystwyth and Rheidol

The rivers of mid Wales, the Aeron, Ystwyth and Rheidol have fair trout angling in the upper reaches only. Permission to fish for the comparatively small trout in these areas is quite easy to obtain from the riparian owners. Upriver of Llangeitho on the Aeron the terrain is difficult but in late summer the trout fishing is interesting.

Dovey

The River Dovey is rightly famous as an outstanding sewin and salmon river but little can be said about its brown trout. There is one tributary, the Twymyn fifteen miles of which is controlled by the Llanbrynmair Angling Club, which has trout fishing of a fair standard and very reasonably priced.

Disynni

One of the most picturesque lakes in Wales is Talyllyn which is just north of Machynlleth. The River Disynni rises on the southern slopes of Cader Idris and flows into the lake. Talyllyn lake is predominantly a trout lake which is fly only and is managed by the Tyn-Y-Cornel Hotel and is mainly reserved for residents. A few day tickets are available to visitors. The Disynni has trout fishing along its whole length; eight miles of this river are managed by Estimaner Angling Association which stocks the river annually. Permits may be obtained from the Sports Shop at Towyn.

Wygyr

Anglesey has no mountains and so no rivers of significance. The River Wygyr falls into the sea at Cemaes Bay and the Wygyr Angling Association stocks it annually. Most of the other small rivers on the island, including the Cefni tend to be managed by farmers who may give permission to anglers. The Lleyn peninsula has become a very popular tourists' playground in the last decade. Tourism and good trout angling do not necessarily go hand in hand. Nevertheless the trout angler finding himself in this country will do quite well if he goes to the rivers Erch and Soch which have ticket water available from the Pwllheli Angling Association, and avoids the tourists.

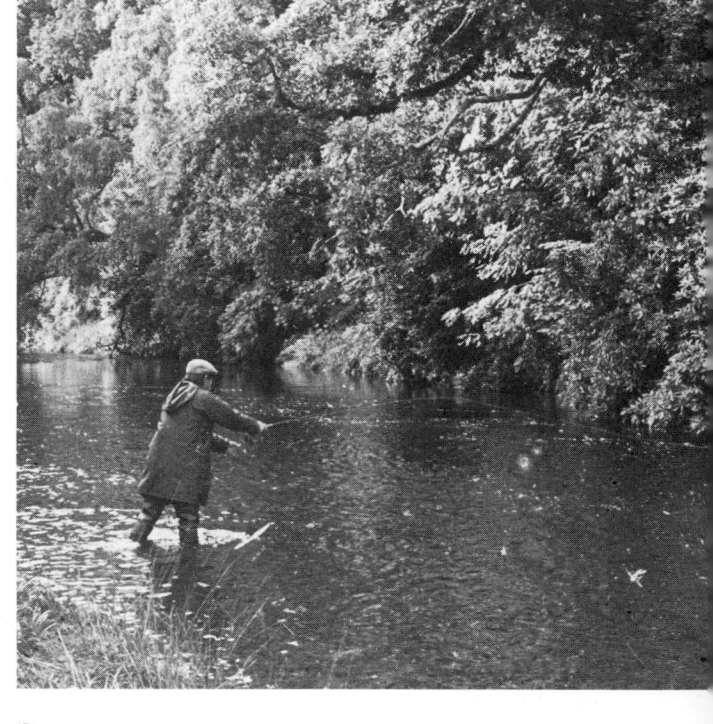

Conway

Another famed sewin river in Wales is the Conway, with such stocks of migratory fish that it is virtually impossible for the river to sustain a good trout fishery. However there is trout fishing available on the upper reaches, where the migratory fish cannot reach. The River Llugwy and its tributary Gwyrd have been stocked from time to time and offer fair trout fishing. The angling association at Betws y Coed provides day tickets. In the Ysbyty Ifan area and on part of the Machno and Glasgwm, the fishing is extremely reasonable and can be rewarding to the angler who is prepared to fill his creel by the sweat of his brow.

Many of these lesser rivers in Wales are set amid simply wonderful scenery and for the countryman the trout catching is often a bonus. The River Ogwen falls into this category. It rises in Ogwen Lake half way between Bethesda and Capel Curig and stretches are leased by the Ogwen Valley Association from the Penrhyn Estate. Some restocking is being carried out and this river is steeped in angling tradition. The first ever Welsh book on fly patterns came from this valley, suggesting that our forefathers really knew how to fish the fly.

STILL WATER FISHERIES

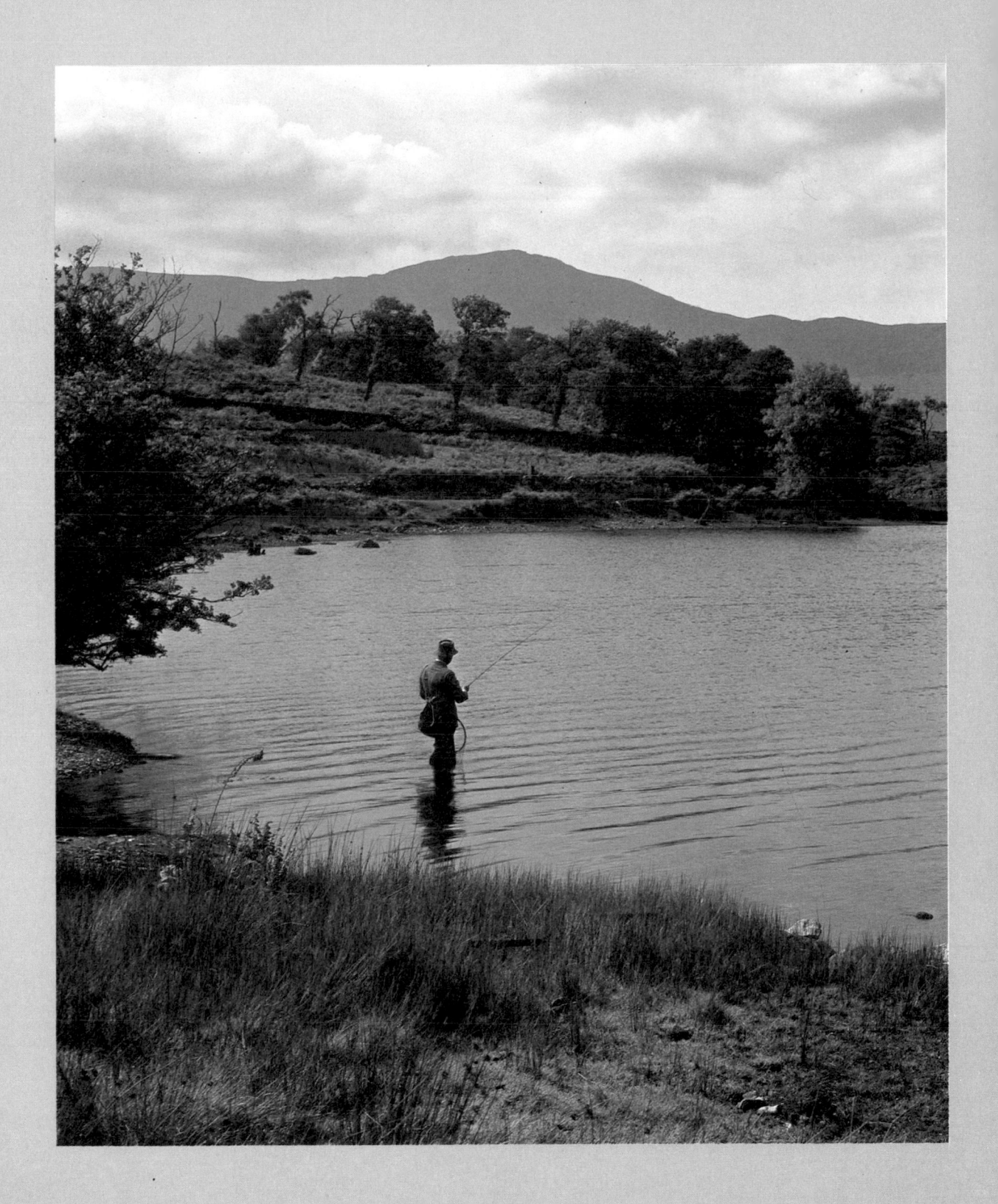

Opposite: Searching for a ripple on Lake Nannau   Below: Dinas Reservoir where the fishing can be bleak

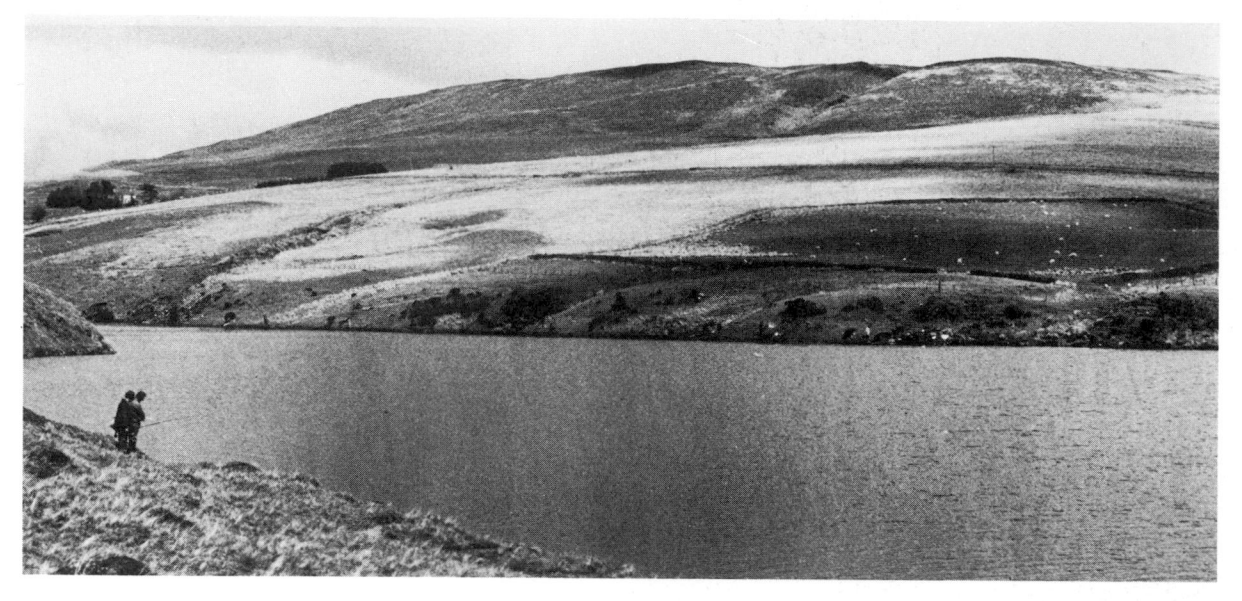

Wales abounds with lakes and reservoirs and great strides have been made in their promotion as first class fisheries in the last decade. Probably the fact that Wales contains so many productive rivers was responsible for the apparent apathy towards the still water fisheries. Few reservoirs in Wales with the possible exceptions of Alaw in Anglesey and Llandegfedd in South Wales have the water quality that will ensure the enhancement of stocked fish. In short, it is often a strict put-and-take, with the taken fish having gained in wisdom and conformation but not in weight.

The Welsh Water Authority manages most of the Welsh reservoirs but in many instances, alas, without profit. This has led to the uneconomic reservoirs being leased out to outside interests. It is the case of the amateurs taking over where the professionals have failed; this may be a paradox but it is as well to remember that the amateurs built the ark and the professionals the Titanic.

South East

Llandegfedd Reservoir (429 acres. 4 April – 14 October) is in the lower Usk valley not far from Pontypool. It has twenty boats all of which are for rowing. The brown and rainbow trout do well there and it fishes well to all modern reservoir methods. The dry Daddy-long-legs is a must from August onwards.

Upper & Lower Ynysyfro (10 and 16 acres. 4 April – 15 October) not far from Newport offers good brown trout fishing.

Talybont Reservoir (318 acres. 4 April – 14 October) A very picturesque reservoir in the upper reaches of the river Usk at Brecon. Fishes well in the evenings during the sedge period.

Llanishen & Lisvaen (59 and 19 acres. 21 March – 30 September) As there are predominantly rainbow fisheries the closing date of the season may be extended until January. These two reservoirs in the capital city of Wales, Cardiff, are only a few hundred yards from Ninian Park the home of the famous Welsh rugby team. They are very well stocked and provide good fishing in a concrete bowl, amid suburban surroundings.

Merthyr Tydfil, once the centre of the industrial revolution is now a centre for six fishing complexes. They are Llwyn-onn, (150 acres); Upper Neuadd (57 acres); Dol-y-gaer (96 acres); Beacons (52 acres); Pontsticill (253 acres); Lower Neuadd (12 acres). The season for all six is 21 March – 30 September, except for one or two that will have the season extended. The Lower Neuadd is promoted as a big trout fishery and therefore costs are twice as high as for the other reservoirs.

187

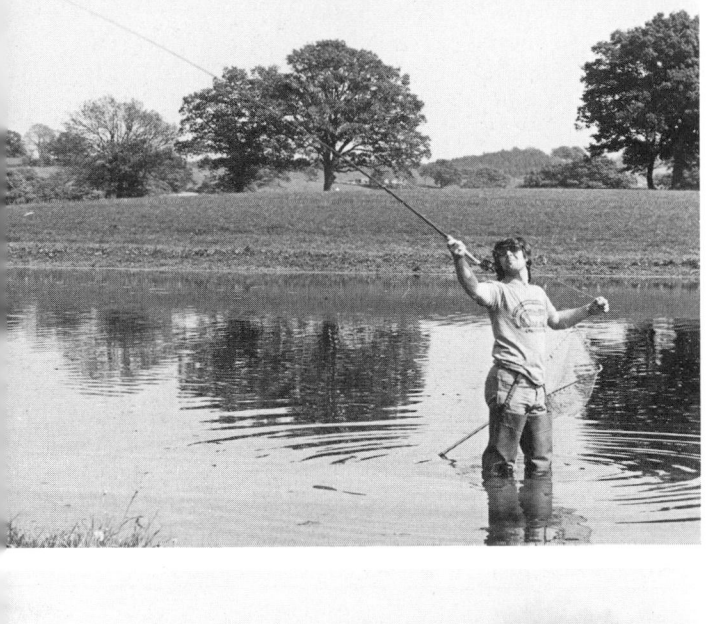

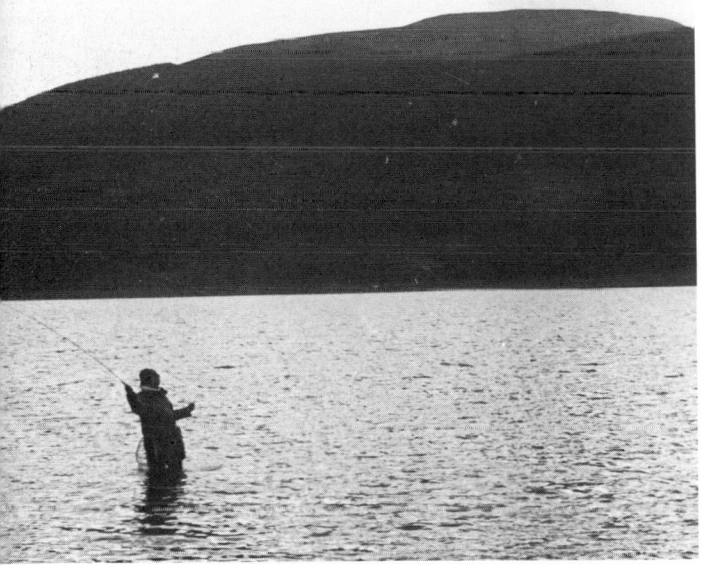

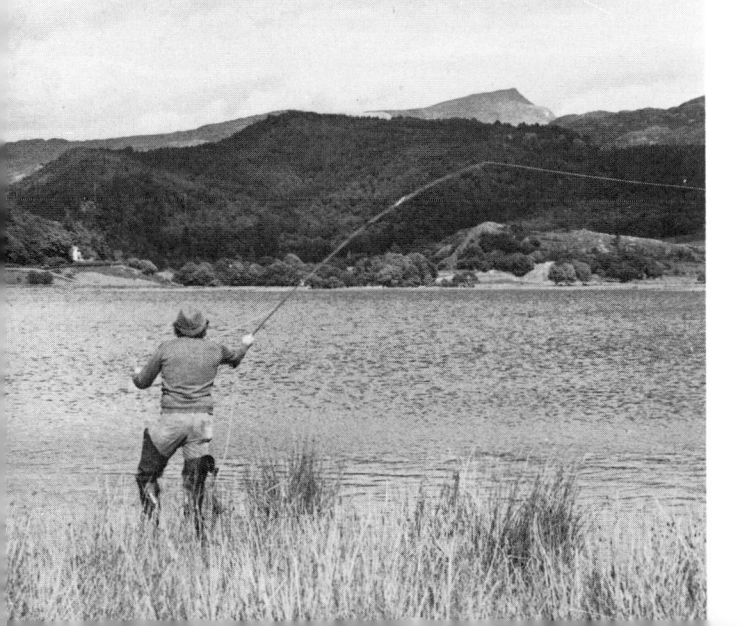

Top: The reservoir technique on Llandegfedd
Centre: Evening at Talybont
Bottom: Llyn Dinas, a lure for anglers

South West

Llysyfran (187 acres. 1 April – 30 September) A delightful fishery, tucked away far from the madding crowds. Well stocked, it fishes well to old traditional methods, from a boat. The bank fishing is not so attractive.

Llanllawddog a small fishery near Carmarthen. It is well managed and gives capital sport on small flies. The evening fishing is very good in the summer months.

Teifi Pools (Llyn Hir, Llyn Egnant, Llyn Teifi, 20 March – 17 October.) These comprise a cluster of small lakes in the heart of the mid Wales mountains. Llyn Teifi is stocked with rainbow trout and is a multimethod fishery; the others are brown trout fisheries, fly only. Excellent value for anglers visiting the upper Teifi valley.

Dinas Reservoir (69 acres. 26 March – 30 September) An intensive multi-method fishery, it is stocked weekly and is very popular.

North West

This area of Wales is peppered with natural lakes most of which are run as fisheries by angling associations. The stocking, where it is done, is of moderate proportions and the best fishing is during the warm evenings in summer. Some are inaccessible by car and are not subjected to much angling pressures.

Trawsfynydd Reservoir: (1200 acres. 1 February – 30 September) The first reservoir to open in Wales on 1 February, it is a very popular fishery during the early months. It has extensive boat facilities and is the national and international venue for competitions. It fishes well to the bob fly and is an early and a late season fishery.

Alaw Reservoir (777 acres. 1 April – 30 September) A multi-method fishery which once enjoyed a reputation for very big brown trout. It has many features to commend it, none less than the wealth of wildlife it boasts. No longer is there boat fishing, which is a pity.

Top: Brenig. A small one for the pot
Centre: Fishing a calm Clweddy lake
Bottom: On the dam at Usk Reservoir

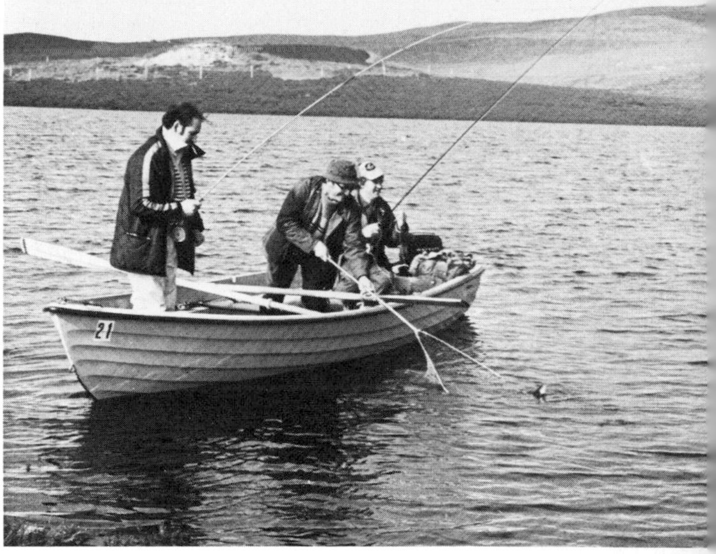

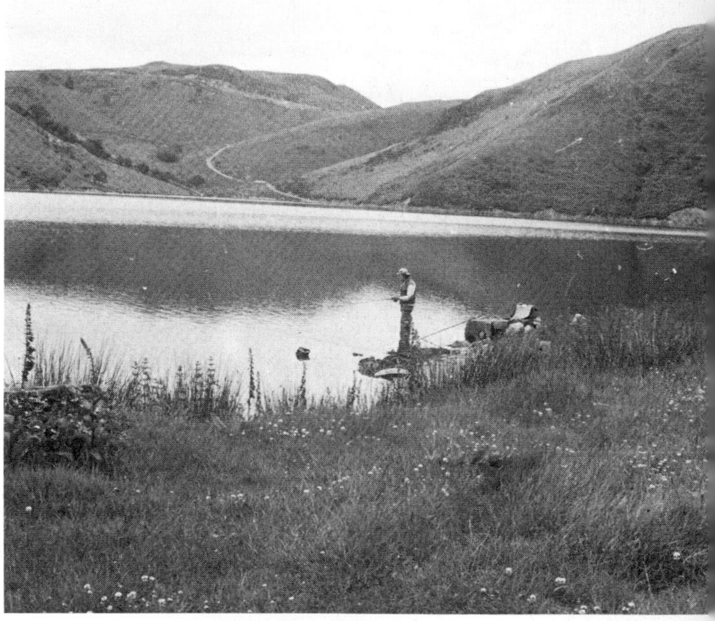

North East

Llyn Brenig (918 acres. 1 April – 15 October) The premier reservoir fishery in Wales and one of four in the Dee valley. It is well stocked with pound plus trout. Twenty five powered boats are available and the best fishing is certainly to be had from the boat. It is used for promotions in connection with disabled anglers and was the venue for the international match for disabled anglers in the Year of the Disabled 1981. Its altitude is 1400 ft and it tends to be rather exposed during windy weather and does not really warm up until late May. It is already producing wild native brown trout of nearly one pound in weight and these add to the stock of rainbows that are injected to the fishery on a monthly basis.

Celyn Reservoir (800 acres. 1 April – 30 September) Near Bala in the Dee valley. May become a great reservoir but has not been developed to its full potential. The Welsh Water Authority has plans to build a big hatchery just below this reservoir and it could then develop into a truly great fishery by the mid eighties.

Clywedog Reservoir (600 acres. March – November) This fishery, although in Wales, requires a Severn and Trent Water Authority licence. It is stocked regularly and is managed by the Llanidloes Angling Club. It offers excellent sport for the dry fly enthusiast especially after the weather warms up in late May. Despite its stocking, this is a very lightly fished fishery and allows the angler to wander along the bank at will, taking fish often within a yard or two from the bank.

There are two other excellent wild brown trout fisheries in Wales namely the Claerwen near Rhayader in the Wye valley and Nantymoch near Aberystwyth. Both are very reasonably priced and offer really challenging fishing for the good angler who likes wild fish. Both are full of empty spaces for the angler to conduct his fishing, amid Welsh mountains in his own company.

Who knows, some day, we as anglers will become sufficiently educated to appreciate the true value of these wild trout fisheries.

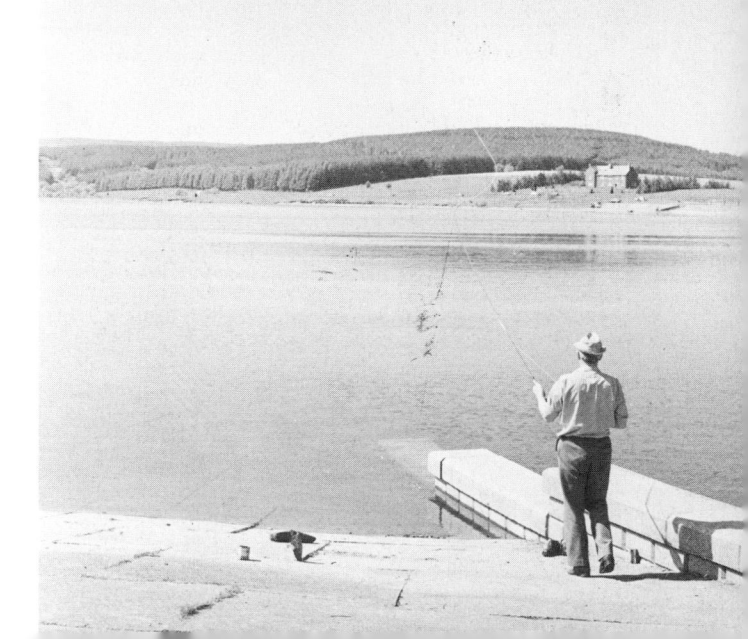

INDEX

Picture Credits